MENTAL HEALTH
in Education

HENRY CLAY LINDGREN
San Francisco State College

HENRY HOLT AND COMPANY · NEW YORK

To
L O R I ,
who has taught me more about
children than I can ever say.

PREFACE

ONE of the reasons many teachers have become attracted to the various concepts loosely represented by the mental-hygiene viewpoint is that the mental hygienist is one who, for the most part, "keeps his eye on the ball," figuratively speaking. He is likely to be a person who remembers that the central purpose of education is that of all child-welfare services —helping children to grow up to be adequate, effective, healthy, and happy adults. Beyond that he recognizes that each of the agencies and institutions responsible for some part of the child's development (this includes the family, the school, the church, youth group activities) have specialized contributions to make and roles to play, contributions and roles that change with the maturing needs of the child. Therefore, although the school is specifically charged with promoting the intellectual growth of the child, it has a basic responsibility to promote his social, emotional, moral, and physical growth as well. This is a responsibility it shares with the other agencies of the community and society. Even if the schools *wanted* to ignore and to abdicate its other responsibilities and to concentrate on the intellectual aspects of learning it could not do so successfully because the child's intellectual adequacy is closely related to his adequacy in other areas of life. Furthermore, even the school that tries to avoid the area of, say, the emotions, teaches children something about emotions. Perhaps it teaches that emotions are not a legitimate part of life, that they are bad, something to be ashamed of.

It seems then that one of the functions of the mental-health worker is to remind us of our responsibilities to the whole child, to the development of his whole personality. If we can listen to him and learn from him, we should be able to see our work in better perspective. Not only will his behavior and the whole educational scheme make better sense to us, but also we should be able to see how and where we can distribute our energies to best advantage in the day-by-day task of helping children to learn.

The chief concern in this book is with the normal child, the normal child who has a few problems (and who has not?), but particularly the normal child who has a healthy need to progress and to develop in ways that are socially and emotionally mature. The behavior of the vast majority of children in our classrooms is within normal limits; if we can do a good job of understanding the emotional needs basic to this behavior, we shall have made much progress toward being ready to give students the help they need in coping with their problems of learning.

Many of the concepts and techniques discussed in this book may be new to readers. Some of them have been a part of professional lore in education for only the last decade or two. If the desirability of using new methodology seems questionable, let it be suggested that we would do well to look at the other sciences and professions that are far more receptive to newer methods than is education. Medicine is an example. Eighty percent of the drugs prescribed today did not exist fifteen years ago. However, the number of innovations to which teachers are asked to accord their tentative acceptance is quite small. The rate of invention proceeds slowly in education, and the rate of acceptance of new techniques and concepts lags far behind even this slow progress. There are many reasons for this, of course, not the least of which is the need to adjust educational philosophies of millions of teachers and laymen to the desirability of using newer methods. An educational technique can receive a fair trial of its effectiveness only if it is used in a favorable emotional climate. It takes time to develop favorable climates. Then, too, educators generally have been slow to develop newer and more effective methods of teaching. In general, those schools that are doing the best jobs of educating students are those that are most sympathetic to the development and trial of experimental techniques and curricula. And, as the reader will discover, students from such school systems are, if anything, better prepared for further education and for life than are graduates of traditional schools.

The introductory chapter in this textbook is concerned with the development of what might be termed a mental-health point of view in education. The nature of this viewpoint is explored and questions are raised regarding the differences in attitudes between mental-hygiene workers and schoolteachers.

The next few chapters are concerned with providing a background for understanding why children (and adults) behave as they do. Chapter 2 is concerned with how a child develops concepts and ideas regarding himself and the people around him. It is also concerned with the social forces that help to direct and shape the formation of these concepts. A portion of this chapter has been paraphrased from the author's article "The Problem of the Adolescent; Its Roots and Origins" (*The Clearing House*, 27:195–202;1952).

Chapter 3 is concerned with motivation—what lies behind actions, attitudes, thoughts, and beliefs. Behavior is considered here as something that is done to satisfy the normal or basic needs of the individual, or as something that the individual does to protect himself from the pain and tension of anxiety. In effect, Chapter 2 tries to explain children's behavior in terms of perception—in terms of the way children see themselves and the world in which they live, whereas Chapter 3 attempts to explain why children develop these perceptions.

The subject of Chapter 4 is the problem of growing up,

becoming emotionally more mature. Special attention is paid
to the role of the school in helping children to mature, as
well as to the contribution that the child's growing emotional
maturity makes to his desire to learn. Emotion also enters
into the discussion presented in Chapter 5, which deals with
problem behavior, some of its common patterns, and some
of its causes. Problems that result when children encounter
difficulties that temporarily or chronically impede their normal growth toward emotional maturity are discussed in
Chapter 5, together with some kinds of behavior which present problems but which represent the influence of cultural
patterns which differ from those of the school. Chapter 6
explores these divergent cultural patterns even further, with
particular emphasis on socioeconomic factors.

Chapters 2 through 5 are concerned principally with the
individual, how he develops, and how he behaves. The next
group of chapters, 7 through 10, are concerned more with
the relationship between the individual and the group and
relationships within the group itself. Chapter 7 discusses
communication—that process or function that makes the existence of groups possible. Chapter 8 deals with the development of relations between the child and the groups with
which he comes in contact, as well as with the problems that
develop as a result of this contact. Chapters 9 and 10 are
concerned with the dynamics and interrelationships within
groups.

With Chapter 11, the emphasis swings to the role of the
school in helping children and adolescents become socially,
emotionally, and intellectually mature. Chapter 11 contrasts
three different philosophies of education and discusses their
implications for emotional health. Chapters 12 and 13 explore the part the teacher plays as a leader in the classroom,
as a builder of classroom groups, and as a person of power
and authority. Chapter 14 investigates some of the relationships between the parent and the school that have an important bearing on the mental health of children.

The next three chapters, 15 through 17, are devoted to some of the ways that the school influences children, recognizing that education, as it exists today, will at times have a disintegrative effect on mental health and at other times a constructive or integrative effect. Chapter 17 is concerned with the ways in which school personnel can work individually and together to provide a more therapeutic and beneficial environment for children.

Chapter 18 deals with problems of evaluation and diagnosis—how tests, measurements, and other evaluative devices are used to improve or deter the development of mental health in the school.

Chapter 19, the final chapter, is devoted to the teacher and his problems of adjustment, in consideration of the fact that the more problems of adjustment he has, the more difficulties he will encounter in helping children learn. This chapter also discusses some of the ways that teachers can maintain and develop their own emotional health.

A word about the case material that appears at various points in this textbook is in order. This material is drawn from many sources, largely from my own experience or from experiences of colleagues, students, and counselees. I have deliberately reworked and fictionalized the characters and incidents in each case so that they cannot be identified by the participants. Although any resemblance to real persons and events is coincidental, I have tried to give these anecdotes a sense of realism so that they might be illustrative of problems actually faced by teachers. I have been particularly concerned about describing the feelings and emotions of the fictional participants because I have wanted to show how feelings arise and interact in the interpersonal relations of children, teachers, administrators, and parents.

It is obviously impossible for me to mention by name the many persons whose ideas and concepts I have borrowed and reworked preliminary to weaving them into the fabric of this book. However, I should like to note my debt to

R. Freeman Butts, who has been kind enough to examine the manuscript critically and to such leaders in the field of mental health as Harry Stack Sullivan, Erich Fromm, Karen Horney, Talcott Parsons, Kurt Lewin, Carl R. Rogers, A. H. Maslow, Theodore S. Newcomb, and Fritz Redl. I would especially like to express my appreciation to Miss Jo Josey of Kingsburg High School, Kingsburg, California, for her help in reading and commenting on portions of the manuscript; to members of my family-life-education seminar who also read chapters of the book; and finally, to my wife, Fredi, who not only prepared the manuscript for the publishers, but who made many suggestions that helped to improve the quality and sense of the text.

H.—C.—L.

San Francisco State College
November 15, 1953

CONTENTS

1

INTRODUCTION

OUR CHANGING ATTITUDES TOWARD CHILDREN

THE last three decades or so have witnessed a minor revolution in what might be called "the official attitude" of the American public toward children. Books and articles written for parents have changed from being concerned with the physical condition of children, or with techniques for direction and control, to concern for their emotional health. It would be difficult at the present moment to determine whether this change in attitude on the part of the "experts" is reflected in any real changes in the behavior of the American parent. If any marked changes have occurred, they may be limited to that minority of parents who read such articles and books. Although it is difficult to say at this time whether or not parental behavior has changed to any great extent, it is quite likely that the general tone of these articles points to the beginning of a broad and pervasive change in the attitudes toward children on the part of everyone—parents and teachers, as well as the general public. It may be many decades before this change has run its course, but the growing number of the child psychologists, psychologically oriented pediatricians, and other mental-hygiene workers, as well as their increasing agreement regarding the problems of child-hood, is convincing evidence that the revolution may already be upon us.

One of the characteristics of our newer attitude toward children is an awareness of the part played by feelings and emotions in growth and development, including learning. Inasmuch as education is concerned largely with learning, one might think that educators would be quick to accept this newer approach to the problems of learning. But, taken as a group, educators are basically conservative, and they were at first slow to employ these more dynamic concepts of learning. Since the end of the 1930s, however, there has been an increasing number of textbooks in education concerned with this approach. Daniel A. Prescott and his group produced *Emotions and the Educative Process* in 1938 [1], the same year that saw W. Carson Ryan's *Mental Health through Education* [2]. Recent years have seen the appearance of such texts as *Helping Teachers Understand Children*, published by the American Council on Education [3], as well as *Fostering Mental Health in Our Schools* and *Growing up in an Anxious Age*, both published by the Association for Supervision and Curriculum Development of the National Education Association [4, 5]. Also worthy of mention are Norman Fenton [6], Fritz Redl and William W. Wattenberg [7], Charlotte Buhler, Faith Smitter, and Sybil Richardson [8], and Hilda Taba [9, 10, 11] who, among many others, endeavor to incorporate "a mental hygiene viewpoint" into the textbooks they have written for teacher education.

MENTAL HYGIENE AND CLASSROOM PRACTICE

SOME of the current readiness of education to accept the teachings of the newer viewpoint springs from some of the disappointments teachers have had with earlier, more mechanistic and more intellectualized theories of learning. Proponents of earlier theories somehow encouraged the belief that teaching was primarily a sequence of techniques—that is, if the teacher did certain things in the classroom, certain learnings would be bound to occur. Unfortunately, the desired outcomes often did not materialize. The educational psychologist had an explanation for this: The child was not psychologically "ready" for the learning. But he was not of much help in telling the teacher how to bring children to the desired point of readiness. The difficulty was, of course, that most of the psychological experiments with learning were concerned with the *process* of learning rather than with the events that preceded it. Children came to the classroom situation from such a variety of backgrounds; in each case the sequence of prior events was quite different. Therefore, the problem of readiness seemed baffling and elusive. What was needed, therefore, was an approach that would help teachers understand some of the forces which influenced the behavior of children, that would explain some of the unexpected and sometimes illogical occurrences of the classroom.

The answers to these problems could not come from the laboratory; workers there were primarily occupied with exploring and testing the laws of learning. The answers could and did come instead from the psychological clinic, from work with seriously disturbed adults and children. At first blush, this appears to be somewhat illogical—how can our knowledge of abnormal psychology help us with the problems of normal childhood? The answer to this question lies in the fact that the symptoms displayed by persons suffering from severe emotional maladjustments are but exaggerations of the problems experienced by people in the normal range of behavior. Hence, by studying the causes and the treatment of symptoms in the clinic, we have been able to develop data, theories, and concepts that are proving most useful in understanding the behavior of persons in the normal range. It is this material that provides the basis for most of our understanding of mental health today. It should be noted that in recent years this knowledge has been further supplemented by the findings of social psychologists working with group processes. The great bulk of the material used in this textbook has been drawn from these two sources.

STUDYING CHILDREN'S BEHAVIOR IN TERMS OF ITS CAUSES

ONE of the problems in helping teachers to use mental hygiene concepts in their dealings with children has been that of getting them to think of behavior in terms of causes rather than in a symptomatic fashion. It is understandable that teachers would tend to use the latter approach, inasmuch as it is the more obvious one—the one we have always used. It is much simpler, and momentarily more satisfying emotionally, to deal directly with behavior instead of stopping to pry beneath the surface into its causes. However, as Ralph H. Ojemann notes, this "surface" approach to behavior produces and aggravates emotional conflicts and strains in both adult and child.

For example, if a child attempted to overcome a feeling of inadequacy by wanting to be first so often that it interfered with class activity, the teacher who approached this behavior as a surface phenomenon would try to stop it by such methods as reprimanding the child, making him go to the end of the line, or sending him out of the room. She may do this without thinking about or inquiring as to the causes of the behavior. Since the feeling of inadequacy remained in spite of the scolding, going to the end of the line, or leaving the room, the child would still be under a strain and would attempt more vigorous action or a different approach. The teacher would soon observe that her attempts to stop the behavior were not successful. She would then intensify her attempts to stop the pupil's interfering behavior and the whole round of strains would rise to a new level [12].

Ojemann noted that teachers were not alone in this approach to problems. Parents, too, tended to use a "surface approach."

When the child was very young, the parent would try to control the child by telling him or commanding him what to do, punishing him, coaxing him, and so on. When this failed after years of trial, some parents would give up. This left children to their own devices for meeting their problems and they often failed in finding satisfying and cooperative solutions. . . . [Other parents] would doggedly persist only to meet with increasing resistance and conflict [12].

It would therefore seem that if adults attained a better understanding of the background, attitudes, feelings, worries, and concerns of the children they supervise, they would be able to work more effectively with them.[1] A study by Wilkinson and Ojemann provides evidence that supports this hypothesis. When teachers came to understand the emotional basis of their pupils' behavior better, the children's attitude toward the school became more favorable, and they made better progress in their school work [14]. Thus it would appear that if teachers develop a good grasp of the fundamentals of mental hygiene, they are able to teach more effectively.

THE IMPORTANCE OF THE PERSONAL AND HUMAN FACTORS IN EDUCATION

THE older and more traditional approaches to education tend to "depersonalize" the classroom situation as well as to deny the importance of emotions and feelings. Such an approach ignores the importance of the interpersonal relations that are such an important part of what goes on in the classroom. It is perhaps not an extreme statement to say that there are some persons, both educators and laymen alike, who appear to look upon the children in the class as a sort of captive audience and the school as merely the building that en-

---

[1] A comparison of the ways in which teachers use the "surface approach" and the "causal approach" may be found in Table 1–1.

TABLE 1–1. THE "SURFACE APPROACH" TO CHILDREN'S
BEHAVIOR CONTRASTED WITH OJEMANN'S "CAUSAL AP-
PROACH" AND VIEWED IN TERMS OF CLASSROOM BE-
HAVIOR OF THE TEACHERS [13].

SURFACE	CAUSAL
1. The teacher responds to the *what* of the situation in an *emotional* way.	1. The teacher responds to the *why* of the situation *objectively*.
2. The teacher does not appear to think of the causes of behavior when he	2. The teacher appears to be thinking of the causes of behavior when he
a) responds to the *action* rather than to the reason for the action,	a) runs over *possible reasons* in his mind for the action,
b) labels behavior as "good," "bad," etc.	b) *seeks the meaning* of the behavior and avoids snap judgments or hasty interpretations.
c) makes *generalizations* to apply to every situation, e.g., "all boys are like that."	c) searches for *specific* and concrete *clues* derived from details of the behavior.
d) responds with a *stock solution* or *rule of thumb* procedure, i.e., lateness is punished by staying in after school.	d) *varies* the method; uses a tentative testing or trying-out approach, e.g., will try other ways of dealing with a situation if one does not work. In seeking for a solution, takes into account motivating forces and particular method used.
3. The teacher does not take account of the multiplicity and complexity of causes.	3. The teacher thinks of *alternative explanations* for the behavior.
	a) The proposition that behavior has many causes may be elaborated as follows:
	(1) The same cause may result in a variety of behaviors.
	(2) A variety of causes may result in similar behavior.

[TABLE 1–1—(CONT.)]

SURFACE	CASUAL
4. The teacher fails to take into account the *later effects* of the technique employed, but assumes the effects.	4. The teacher *checks for the effects* of the method he employs, and considers its effects before using it.
5. The "surface" approach is characterized by a rigidity of techniques—essentially static.	5. The "causal" approach is characterized by a flexibility, a tentativeness, a trying-out technique, which accommodates new information as it is accumulated —essentially dynamic.

closes it [15]. The fact is, of course, that classes do not behave like captive audiences are supposed to behave. They are far more than collections of unrelated individuals; they have an organic life of their own, above and beyond the lives of the individuals who compose them. Schools, too, are composed of networks of interpersonal relations which help give them character and meaning for the individuals who are a part of them. The mental-hygiene worker who strives to understand and explain human behavior knows that he must have a grasp of these matters, and that he must also be aware of the psychological stresses and strains, the hidden symbolic meanings, the mutual expectancies, that are so much a part of the daily classroom drama. Did Miss Kinney make an extra heavy assignment in geography because the class elected the class clown as president instead of the girl she suggested? Why does Jimmy Horton work hard at his reading when Mrs. Herman is at the other end of the room, but always plays when she comes close by? Why does Sylvia always try to answer the questions the teacher asks, even though she seldom knows the answer, while Gregory, who always knows the answer, never volunteers?

These are the types of questions which have been plaguing teachers. They are also the kinds of questions that mental-hygiene workers try to answer. The answers they give do not always work, and sometimes they seem illogical; yet, there is enough in what mental-hygiene workers suggest either to provide teachers with the answer to their problems or, better still, to get teachers to work on their problems from a different approach than they have used before. As Jules Eisenbud says,

> Mental hygiene is not a set of abstract notions, nor is it a set of principles or vague generalizations to be taken out of the ether of platonic ideas and applied on request to a given person or situation in order to produce an expected result. Essentially, it is a frame of mind, a point of view influencing the thinking of an increasing number of people of differing pursuits and professions who have at least the one common goal of promoting the conditions for a more satisfying human life [16].

If we can accept this description of mental hygiene, we can see that mental hygiene is not of itself going to solve any of our problems for us. Its chief contribution is that of giving us a different approach to problems of human relations, an approach that will serve as a starting point for the learning of more effective methods of education. If we are able to accept the implications of the newer viewpoint—for example, the idea that emotions or feelings are basic to all kinds of human behavior—we then are in a position to use some of the concepts and ideas that have been evolved by other workers in the field of mental hygiene.

THE INTELLECTUAL VERSUS THE EMOTIONAL APPROACH

ONE of the chief differences between the traditional approach to education and the newer, or mental-hygiene, approach lies in the stress placed on intelligence, will power, and emotion. The traditional approach assumes that children (and adults) always know why they do what they do and can control their behavior *if they want to*. According to this belief, the child who misbehaves can control or inhibit his misbehavior by exercising will power, or the child who is not popular with other students can become popular by acting in a friendly manner toward others. There is, of course, some truth in these ideas—they seem to work, sometimes. But more often they do not.

On the other hand, the mental-hygiene approach assumes that behavior is complex and that its causes lie deep within the emotions of the person concerned. The plain fact of the matter is that children usually do not know why they behave as they do. Actually, adults are not much better at explaining the *real* causes of their behavior. We *appear* to be better explainers than children because we are more proficient in language, more experienced at giving excuses, and more aware of what kinds of explanations are commonly believed and accepted. But in terms of *knowing* why we actually behave as we do, we are not much better off than children. The reason for this is that our real motives are either hidden from us or operate beyond the limits of our awareness. Our everyday logic cannot adequately explain why we remember some things and forget others, or why we feel uncomfortable when we talk to policemen, or why we feel pleasant some days and irritable on others. In order to understand these things, we have to probe beyond the surface of our everyday lives and look for causes that are emotional rather than intellectual or "logical."

Mrs. Stark, elementary supervisor, lingered a moment when Miss Travers' fourth grade was dismissed for the noon recess. Miss Travers' handling of the class during her half-hour visit had been adequate—though certainly not inspired. Of course, that could be due to having a supervisor in the room. There was nothing unusual about that—many teachers tense up when a supervisor walks in. But there was something about Miss Travers' manner that indicated to Mrs. Stark's experienced eye that she wanted to talk about a problem.

Hence she was not surprised when, in reply to her casual

question as to whether there was anything that needed discussing, a worried frown passed over Miss Travers' face and she said:

"There's a boy—Bruno Richter—that really has me stumped. He just can't get anywhere in arithmetic. I've gone over his arithmetic tests and I can't find any sense or pattern to it. He does well on some difficult problems, but he gets really weird answers on some easy ones. He is pretty good at figuring out 'thought' problems, but falls down on computation. His IQ is 112, so it can't be intelligence. Besides he does satisfactory work in other subjects."

Mrs. Stark picked up her purse and suggested: "Maybe we can talk about him while we have lunch."

As they sat down in a corner of the cafeteria, Mrs. Stark said: "Tell me more about Bruno Richter."

Miss Travers replied: "I've gone into his background but there aren't any clues that I can see. Bruno's father came over from Austria just before the war. He runs a little grocery store. I've never met him, but Bruno's mother came to PTA once. She was very quiet—sat in the back row and never entered into the discussion. When I found out who she was, I went over to talk to her. She seemed very shy and I wasn't able to get much out of her."

Mrs. Stark was thoughtful. "Well," she said, "perhaps I can talk to Bruno for a little while after school. I'm not at all sure, from what you say, that I can help him but I would like to see how he goes about working a problem. Could you have a couple of problems picked out that he has had difficulty doing?"

Miss Travers promised to have some problems ready and then added: "I've talked to Bruno about his difficulty in arithmetic. Sometimes he says that he doesn't understand the problems because he has trouble in reading and sometimes he says that he is not as smart as the other children. But you can see from his other work and from his IQ that this is simply ridiculous. If he weren't such a really well-behaved child I would think that he was trying to get attention."

Later in the day, Mrs. Stark was back in Miss Travers' room and was talking to Bruno, while Miss Travers went to talk to the librarian about a list of supplementary materials. She wanted very much to listen in on their conversation, but she knew that her presence would make it harder for Bruno to talk.

After Mrs. Stark had asked Bruno a few questions about the things he liked to do, she came to the point of their interview.

"I'd like to see you do a few problems in multiplication, Bruno," she said. "Will it bother you if I watch? Don't worry too much about mistakes—just go ahead and do your best."

She handed him an arithmetic book and indicated a problem. Bruno copied the problem down on his paper and then started to multiply. Mrs. Stark stopped him.

"Isn't there something you've forgotten?" she asked.

Bruno trembled violently. "What do you mean, I forgot something?"

Mrs. Stark pointed to the problem in the book. "You left out the '7' when you copied the first number."

Bruno seemed greatly upset. "I didn't see it; I didn't see it," he mumbled.

He very carefully erased the numbers he had written down and began to copy the problem over again. When he came to the "7," he hesitated, then made a "7" with a crossbar, Continental style. He quickly erased it and made another, this time without the crossbar. In working the three problems Mrs. Stark asked him to do, he omitted almost every "7." When Mrs. Stark reminded him of his omissions, he became upset and said that he had not seen them. In copying problems over again he twice tried to make Continental "7's."

In talking to Bruno after he had done the problems, Mrs. Stark discovered that his father insisted on his making Continental "7's" whenever he helped him in the grocery store, and, although Bruno praised his father and was very critical of himself, Mrs. Stark got the impression of a father who was demanding and overcritical, who was never satisfied with his son's performance.

After Bruno left and Miss Travers returned, Mrs. Stark told her that she had a hunch that the boy's arithmetic problem was related to his father's attitude toward him and was focused on the confusion between the American "7" and the Continental

"7." Miss Travers received this information rather skeptically. "After all," she commented, "being able to do arithmetic is strictly a matter of learning a skill, and I can't see how Bruno's father has anything to do with it, unless he is trying to teach the boy to do arithmetic in a way that is different from our methods. Parents do that some times, you know."

Mrs. Stark was dubious. "Well, you may be right. But I think this hunch of mine is worth a try. Why don't you talk to Mr. Richter and explain '7's' to him?"

And so a note was sent home by Bruno, and the next afternoon Mr. Richter appeared in Miss Travers' classroom, accompanied by his son. They talked about "7's" and the problems of adjusting to American ways. Mr. Richter was very respectful, very polite, and seemed willing to cooperate. Miss Travers told herself that Mrs. Stark's hunch was surely wrong. But as she watched Bruno and his father leave the school building and go down the walk, she realized that Bruno was getting a severe scolding, probably for having disgraced the family with a teacher. Even from a distance Miss Travers could sense the scorn and sarcasm that Mr. Richter was heaping on Bruno's defenseless head. It rather frightened her. She hoped that she had done the right thing. She wondered whether Bruno's work would get worse.

But it didn't get worse. It got better. And by the end of the term, Bruno had caught up with the class. Miss Travers still wasn't sure how it had come about, but there was no denying that improvement had taken place.

We have told this story in order to contrast an intellectual approach to a learning problem with an approach that not only takes account of emotional factors, but also assumes that there are likely to be emotional factors in the background. Miss Travers was stumped because she was looking for a "logical" explanation to Bruno's difficulty. Because Mrs. Stark was sensitive in dealing with learning problems that were really emotional problems, she was able to see how a confusion between American and Continental methods of writing "7's" might be related to Bruno's inability to do arithmetic. Such a relationship does not, on the face of it, seem "logical"—in a way it is an insult to our common sense. But Mrs. Stark knew that the "logic of the emotions" frequently seems nonsensical by the standards of everyday common sense. Furthermore, she knew that emotional problems and roadblocks to learning commonly go hand in hand. If she had insisted on using an "intellectualized" approach and had denied the importance of emotional factors, it is unlikely that she would have been of much help to Bruno. True, Bruno might eventually have been able to grow out of his "unreasonable" fear, but only at the expense of much anxiety and the loss of valuable classroom time—not to mention the continued frustration and annoyance of his teacher, who would be more than human if she did not take Bruno's inability to do simple arithmetic rather personally. Teachers are inclined to do this, in spite of their best intentions, when students repeatedly fail to learn for no discernible reason.

It is not easy for teachers to recognize and to accept the idea that the crucial factors in learning and classroom behavior are emotional. This goes against much of what we call common sense, or what might be better called "the folklore of everyday life." Yet, as we shall point out again and again in the pages of this textbook, the deepest and most powerful currents of human motivation are emotional, and it is on his ability to read the emotions of children correctly that the teacher must base his understanding of the behavior of children and the events of the teaching day.

DIFFERENCES IN ATTITUDES BETWEEN MENTAL HYGIENISTS AND TEACHERS

It may be well, at this point, to review some of the viewpoints maintained by mental hygiene workers and to compare and contrast them with viewpoints held by teachers.

One of the best-known attempts to approach this problem systematically is the study conducted by E. W. Wickman in

1928. Wickman asked a group of 511 elementary school teachers to rank a list of 50 school behavior problems in order of their degree of seriousness. He then submitted the same list of problems to 30 clinical psychologists and asked them to rank them from the standpoint of mental hygiene. The ten symptoms believed most serious and the ten believed least serious by these two groups are presented in the first two columns of Table 1–2. A comparison of these two lists reveals that teachers tended to classify sex problems and ag-

TABLE 1–2. THE SERIOUSNESS OF CHILDREN'S BEHAVIOR PROBLEMS, AS RATED BY 511 TEACHERS AND BY 30 CLINICAL PSYCHOLOGISTS IN 1928 (WICKMAN'S STUDY) AND BY 481 TEACHERS AND 70 WORKERS IN CHILD GUIDANCE CLINICS IN 1952 (STOUFFER'S STUDY).

Teachers (1928)	Clinicians (1928)	Teachers (1952)	Clinicians (1952)
UPPER TEN	UPPER TEN	UPPER TEN	UPPER TEN
1. Heterosexual activity	1. Unsocial, withdrawing	1. Stealing	1. Unsocial, withdrawing
2. Stealing	2. Suspiciousness	2. Cruelty, bullying	2. Unhappy, depressed
3. Masturbation	3. Unhappy, depressed	3. Heterosexual activity	3. Fearfulness
4. Obscene notes, talk	4. Resentfulness	4. Truancy	4. Suspiciousness
5. Untruthfulness	5. Fearfulness	5. Unhappy, depressed	5. Cruelty, bullying
6. Truancy	6. Cruelty, bullying	6. Impertinence, defiance	6. Shyness
7. Impertinence, defiance	7. Easily discouraged	7. Destroying school materials	7. Enuresis
8. Cruelty, bullying	8. Suggestible	8. Unreliableness	8. Resentfulness
9. Cheating	9. Overcritical of others	9. Untruthfulness	9. Stealing
10. Destroying school materials	10. Sensitiveness	10. Disobedience	10. Sensitiveness

[TABLE 1–2—(CONT.)]

Teachers (1928)	Clinicians (1928)	Teachers (1952)	Clinicians (1952)
LOWER TEN	LOWER TEN	LOWER TEN	LOWER TEN
41. Dreaminess	41. Masturbation	41. Attracting attention	41. Carelessness
42. Imaginative lying	42. Disobedience	42. Slovenly appearance	42. Masturbation
43. Interrupting	43. Tardiness	43. Restlessness	43. Impudence, rudeness
44. Inquisitiveness	44. Inquisitiveness	44. Tardiness	44. Inquisitiveness
45. Overcritical of others	45. Destroying school materials	45. Thoughtlessness	45. Disorderliness in class
46. Tattling	46. Disorderliness in class	46. Tattling	46. Tardiness
47. Whispering	47. Profanity	47. Inquisitiveness	47. Interrupting
48. Sensitiveness	48. Interrupting	48. Interrupting	48. Profanity
49. Restlessness	49. Smoking	49. Imaginative lying	49. Smoking
50. Shyness	50. Whispering	50. Whispering	50. Whispering

gressive acts of various sorts as most serious and to look upon behavior that might be classified generally under "withdrawal from others" as least serious. Psychologists, on the other hand, felt that "withdrawal behavior" presented far more of a threat to mental health than did the more aggressive forms of behavior [17].

Wickman's study has often been cited by psychologists to show that teachers are not aware of the mental-hygiene implications of classroom behavior, or, at least, that they were not aware of them twenty-five years ago. However, this study has been criticized by Goodwin Watson [18], L. Peck [19], and D. B. Klein [20]. Chief among these criticisms has been that the instructions Wickman gave to the teachers were different from those he gave to mental hygienists. He asked the teachers to rate the behavior according to the degree to which it presented problems in classroom management, whereas the clinical psychologists were asked to rate the behavior on the basis of how serious the problems were for the future of the child in question. Nevertheless, a number of later studies do confirm the general character of his findings —that is, that teachers and mental-hygiene workers vary widely in their appraisal of classroom behavior [21, 22, 23].

A recent attempt to ascertain whether teachers have made any progress in their understanding of mental hygiene in the last twenty-five years is a study made by George A. W. Stouffer, Jr. Stouffer duplicated Wickman's study by administering the questionnaires to 481 elementary school teachers, "chosen as a representative sample of teachers from all parts of the country, teaching pupils of various racial extractions and socio-economic status, in rural and urban schools, with a variety of educational philosophies," as well as to 70 mental hygienists. The latter consisted of psychologists, psychiatrists, and psychiatric social workers on the staffs of 13 child-guidance clinics throughout the country [24]. The ten problems considered most serious and least serious by each group are presented in the last two columns of Table 1–2. Again, the results appear to confirm Wickman's findings because the ten most serious symptoms listed by each group contain only two problems in common—"cruelty, bullying" and "unhappy, depressed."

When Stouffer analyzed the results further, he found that the most marked differences between teachers and mental hygienists were in ratings of the following problems:

Disobedience	Smoking
Impudence, rudeness	Masturbation
Impertinence, defiance	Heterosexual activity
Disorderliness in class	Obscene notes, talk
Profanity	Unsocial, withdrawing

Stouffer comments as follows on these items:

It would appear that these problems, all of which seem to represent an objective form of behavior, might be thought of as problems that outrage the teacher's moral sensitivities and authority, or that frustrate their immediate teaching purposes. According to the rating by the mental hygienists, however, only the "unsocial, withdrawing" behavior could, with reasonable certainty, be considered as representing a serious future to the school child's stability [25].

At this point, Stouffer undertook a different approach to the analysis of his data. By checking teachers' ratings against mental hygienists' ratings according to a statistical formula, he found that both teachers and mental hygienists were essentially in agreement in their ratings of eleven problems:

Resentfulness	Physical coward
Nervousness	Restlessness
Domineering	Imaginative lying
Easily discouraged	Thoughtlessness
Suggestible	Lying
Sullenness	

Furthermore, when Stouffer compared the ratings of his group of teachers with those of Wickman's group, he found that

. . . several of the problems concerned with withdrawing, recessive personality traits—*i.e.*, unhappiness, depression, unsociability, and withdrawing—have moved toward the top of the list as rated by today's teachers. Masturbation has dropped sharply in the teacher's estimation as a serious behavior problem. Interesting changes in position downward as to seriousness are those of smoking and profanity, in which there were striking shifts of position [26].

However, teachers in Stouffer's group still regarded problems relating to honesty, sex, truancy, and classroom order much as teachers did twenty-five years ago. On the other hand, when Stouffer gave the teachers an additional questionnaire bearing the same instructions as those used by the mental hygienists—that is, to rate the behavior in terms of its seriousness for the child's future—an even higher degree of similarity with the ratings of mental hygienists was achieved by teachers, indicating that some of the apparent differences between the two groups were the result of asking one group to think about the behavior in terms of a classroom and the other to consider it from the standpoint of the clinic. Nevertheless, even with the same instructions, there were some marked differences between the ratings.

Stouffer makes this comment on his findings:

> In analyzing the lists of problems, it would seem that the behavior-problem child in school is still, as he was twenty-five years ago, identified chiefly by annoying, disorderly, irresponsible, aggressive, untruthful, and disobedient behavior. Teachers of today, however, are not so oblivious to behavior indicative of social and emotional maladjustment as were those reported in Wickman's study.
>
> All the evidence would seem clearly to indicate that the passage of years has brought changes in teachers' recognition, understanding, and practice in the area of the mental hygiene of the . . . [school] child. The teachers' changed attitudes might be attributed to a change in the total social and, in particular, school situation as it exists today. If we accept the judgment of the psychologists, psychiatrists, and psychiatric social workers as an adequate criterion, we can authoritatively say that teachers have grown in their knowledge of how the school child develops and behaves [27].

In some ways, it is quite understandable how teachers and mental-hygiene workers happen to rate children's behavior differently because, as Stouffer points out, teachers are subjected to pressures to "educate" the child. The mental hygienist, working in the relative seclusion of his clinic, is insulated from this pressure. Furthermore, teachers are far more concerned about community standards of behavior than are clinicians. Stouffer states: "Teachers are undoubtedly aware of the dire consequences for the child, the school, and the teacher if community opinion is outraged by a violation of conventional sexual taboos [28]."

Another question that arises—and it is one that we shall

take up again and again throughout this text—is the extent
to which the classroom produces or aggravates the problems
that the mental hygienists regard as serious. To quote Stouffer again: "It would appear that our tradition-bound school,
with its regimentation and regimented teachers, of necessity
fosters behavior that is pathological from a mental-hygiene
point of view. If this is true, who is to accept the responsibility for the teacher's attitude [28]?"

Stouffer draws the following conclusions as a result of his
findings:

1. There must be continued instruction of the teacher in the
dynamics of child behavior. New knowledge must continuously
be made a part of the teacher's understanding and approach
to the child. Some teachers undoubtedly will need re-education
and eradication of fixed attitudes in regard to the emotional
and experimental factors that produce behavior problems in
children.

2. The public—and parents in particular—must be reoriented, where necessary, as to the role of the school and the
teacher in the education of children, and they must constantly
be given information to assist them in understanding what
could and should be accomplished in the best interests of the
child.

3. Psychologists, psychiatrists, psychiatric social workers,
and teachers need to exchange ideas and experiences in regard
to the behavior problems of children. It would appear that
these professional people have much to offer one another, and
from their mutually increased knowledge would come marked
advances toward the goal of complete understanding of the
child. Continued and cooperative research in the multiple issues of child behavior is important. If education for life is to
become a meaningful concept, we will need to know more
about and constantly to investigate the social and emotional
dynamics of behavior as well as the intellectual development
of the child [29].

Other recent comparisons of teachers and clinicians, also
based on Wickman's study, have been made by Charles A.

Ullman [30], John C. Mitchell [31], and Jack Norman Sparks [32]. Ullman and Mitchell confirm Stouffer's findings that teachers and clinicians are much closer today in their appraisal of children's problems than was true in 1928. Indeed, Ullman interprets his data to mean that much of the existing difference between the ratings asigned by teachers and clinicians is the result of the fact that teachers must function "under pressure [33]." [2] Sparks found that teachers who had received education beyond the bachelor's degree appeared to be closer to the clinicians in their evaluation of children's behavior than were teachers with less education. On the other hand, he found that "teachers with varying amounts of experience differ little in their attitudes toward seriousness of behavior problems to the future adjustment of the child exhibiting the problems."

THE TEACHER AS A MENTAL-HYGIENE WORKER

WHAT is needed therefore, is better communication and cooperation among and between mental-hygiene workers and teachers, if we are to make headway in helping children to grow up emotionally and intellectually and in solving the problems of the classroom. This means that mental-hygiene workers must be drawn more into the educational picture, and that teachers must become more conscious of their roles as mental hygienists. We may infer from Eisenbud's description of mental health, quoted earlier in this chapter, that those people who have the common goal of promoting conditions for a more satisfying human life are, in essence, mental-health workers. Teachers would certainly be included in such a group, inasmuch as the improvement of human welfare, particularly as it relates to children, is a goal to

---

[2] That is, they must so often deal quickly and decisively with the problem behavior they encounter and cannot use the more deliberate methods of the clinician.

which most of them would subscribe. Whether or not the teacher subscribes to this viewpoint, he cannot avoid becoming involved in mental hygiene, for it is inevitable that he would have some effect on the emotional adjustment of the children in his classes. To be sure, he may attempt to ignore or to minimize his role in this regard, but he will, nevertheless, have a negative effect on the lives of some children and a positive effect on the lives of others. He could not play a completely neutral role even if he wanted to— after all, "doing nothing" to children is "doing something." Since the teacher is bound to have some effect on the development of children, it behooves him to gain some understanding of the emotional life of children, so that he can at least become more aware of the effect he has on children, to the end that he reduces the negative influences and augments or increases the positive. Realistically, it is too much to expect that *all* teachers have positive effects *at all times* on *all children*. Even the most effective teacher, the teacher who has a good understanding of the emotional life of the children in his classroom, will occasionally have a negative effect on a child or two, but as he uses his knowledge of children (and of himself) to improve his skill and understanding in human relations, the examples of negative influence should grow fewer in number and smaller in importance.

RESPONSIBILITY FOR MENTAL HEALTH

THE problem of providing for mental-health needs is one that all individuals in the community must accept responsibility for sooner or later. If the responsibility is not accepted earlier, it must be assumed later, because the results of inadequate attention to mental health are crime and delinquency, broken homes, emotional maladjustment, commitments to mental hospitals, alcoholism, and just plain human unhappiness. The last alone would be sufficient cause to be concerned about mental hygiene because it lies at the bottom of most of the other ills we have listed. Furthermore, unhappy people are seldom unhappy by themselves; they usually express their unhappiness through making other people unhappy.

The family and the school are the institutions that bear the heaviest burden of what is done in preventive mental hygiene, for most of the patterns of behavior that lead to adult maladjustment and unhappiness have their bases in the experiences of childhood. This means that, next to the parent, the teacher plays the most crucial role of any adult in determining the mental health of future generations. This means, further, that the teacher and the school have mental-health functions and responsibilities that they are unable to avoid and that must be carried out if the needs of the community are to be met.

It is only in recent years that we have realized that our responsibility for mental health was a community responsibility. An example of this belated recognition is the National Mental Health Act which the Congress passed in 1946. The act provides for the training of mental-health personnel, for research on mental illness, and for the development by state governments of preventive mental-health programs. The purpose of the act is not to take the responsibilities for mental health from states or their communities, but rather to encourage them—to remind them, so to speak, of their responsibilities. More specifically, the responsibilities for developing sound mental-health programs depend on the "men and women who are closely in touch with the resources and needs of their community and who are deeply concerned with bringing optimum mental health to all their neighbors [34]." There is no question but that this definition includes teachers.

The growing realization of the part played by emotional health in the welfare of both children and adults is reflected in President Eisenhower's first presidential proclamation, issued February 20, 1953, setting aside May 1 as Child Health

Day. In the main paragraph of his proclamation, President Eisenhower urged all persons and organizations concerned with the welfare of children "to increase their understanding of the emotional, social, and spiritual growth of children, so as to apply this understanding in their day-to-day relations with the rising generation [35]." [3] The mental hygienist cannot help but note how this proclamation indicates that the emphases of past decades on physical well-being and intellectual attainment have given way to a more rounded approach to the understanding of child development. Indeed, it appears that emotional health is becoming to be accepted as playing a key role in the growth of children into mature and responsible citizens and parents.

The *Pledge to Children* of the Midcentury White House Conference on Children and Youth provides further confirmation of this trend. The first six statements of the pledge provide a sample of how the concern for emotional health influenced the thinking of the delegates to this conference.[4] The members pledged as follows:

From your earliest infancy we give you our love, so that you may grow with trust in yourself and in others.

We will recognize your worth as a person and we will help you to strengthen your sense of belonging.

We will respect your right to be yourself and at the same time help you to understand the rights of others, so that you may experience cooperative living.

We will help you to develop initiative and imagination, so that you may have the opportunity freely to create.

We will encourage your curiosity and your pride in workmanship, so that you may have the satisfaction that comes from achievement.

We will provide the conditions for wholesome play that will add to your learning, to your social experience, and to your happiness [36].

---

[3] The full text of this Proclamation will be found in the Appendix.
[4] The full text of the *Pledge to Children* may be found in the Appendix.

The conference also adopted a 67-point platform concerned principally with furthering the development of a healthy personality.[5] The seventh point in this platform is of special relevance to this chapter. The conference recommended:

> That all professions dealing with children be given, as an integral part of their preparation, a common core of experiences dealing with the fundamental concepts of human behavior, including the need to consider the total person as well as any specific disorder; the interrelationship of physical, mental, social, religious, and cultural forces; the importance of interpersonal relationships; the role of self-understanding; and emphasis on the positive recognition and production of healthy personalities and the treatment of variations; and that lay people be oriented through formal or informal education to an understanding of the importance of the foregoing concepts [37].

The statements that we have cited and quoted above are not the individual expressions of isolated individuals and groups. Instead, they reflect the attitudes and beliefs of persons who are the leaders in the professions that are concerned with the welfare of children. This textbook and the courses for which it was written are also expressions of this same body of opinion and are, indeed, attempts to carry out the spirit and intent of the growing number of lay and professional people who believe that the development of healthy personalities in children requires and demands teachers who have learned the importance of understanding children and of developing relationships with them that are emotionally healthy.

REFERENCES

1. D. A. Prescott, *Emotions and the Educative Process.* Washington: American Council on Education, 1938.
2. W. C. Ryan, *Mental Health Through Education.* New York: Commonwealth Fund, 1938.

---

[5] Portions of this Platform are reproduced in the Appendix.

3. *Helping Teachers to Understand Children*. Washington: American Council on Education, 1945.

4. Association for Supervision and Curriculum Development, *Fostering Mental Health in Our Schools*. Washington: National Education Association, 1950.

5. Association for Supervision and Curriculum Development, *Growing Up in an Anxious Age*. Washington: National Education Association, 1952.

6. N. Fenton, *Mental Hygiene in School Practice*. Stanford: Stanford University Press, 1943.

7. R. Redl and W. W. Wattenberg, *Mental Hygiene in Teaching*. New York: Harcourt, Brace, 1951.

8. C. Buhler, F. Smitter, and S. Richardson, *Childhood Problems and the Teacher*. New York: Holt, 1952.

9. H. Taba and D. Elkins, *With Focus on Human Relations*. Washington: American Council on Education, 1951.

10. H. Taba *et al.*, *Diagnosing Human Relations Needs*. Washington: American Council on Education, 1951.

11. H. Taba *et al.*, *Intergroup Education in Public Schools*. Washington: American Council on Education, 1952.

12. R. H. Ojemann, "How the Integrated Plan for Education in Human Relations and Mental Health Developed." Unpublished, mimeographed paper, State University of Iowa, 1949. (This material appears in rewritten form in: R. H. Ojemann, "An Integrated Plan for Education in Human Relations and Mental Health," *Journal of School Health*. 20:99–106;1950.) Reprinted by permission.

13. R. J. Tasch, "Use of Causal Approach in Daily Relations with Children," in R. H. Ojemann, *Study of the Effect of a Teaching Program in Human Behavior and Emotional Development on Children of Different Age Levels and Backgrounds*. Unpublished, mimeographed paper, State University of Iowa, 1952. Reprinted by permission.

14. F. R. Wilkinson and R. H. Ojemann, "The Effect on Pupil Growth of an Increase in Teachers' Understanding of Pupil Behavior." *Journal of Experimental Education*. 8:143–47;1939.

15. Midcentury White House Conference on Children and Youth, *A Healthy Personality for Every Child*. Raleigh, N. C.: Health Publications Institute, 1951. P. 116.

16. J. Eisenbud, "Mental Hygiene," in S. Lorand, ed., *Psychoanalysis Today*. New York: International Universities Press, 1944. Pp. 135–36.

17. E. W. Wickman, *Children's Behavior and Teachers' Attitudes.* New York: Commonwealth Fund, 1928.
18. G. Watson, "A Critical Note on Two Attitude Studies," *Mental Hygiene.* 17:59–64;1933.
19. L. Peck, "Teachers' Reports of the Problems of Unadjusted Children," *Journal of Educational Psychology.* 26:123–38;1935.
20. D. B. Klein, *Mental Hygiene.* New York: Holt, 1944. P. 498.
21. W. E. McClure, "Characteristics of Problem Children Based on Judgments of Teachers," *Journal of Juvenile Research.* 13:124–40;1929.
22. J. Yourman, "Children Identified by Their Teachers as Problems," *Journal of Educational Sociology.* 5:334–43;1932.
23. S. R. Laycock, "Teachers' Reactions to Maladjustments of School Children," *British Journal of Educational Psychology.* 4:11–29; 1934.
24. G. A. Stouffer, Jr., "Behavior Problems of Children as Viewed by Teachers and Mental Hygienists," *Mental Hygiene.* 36:271–85; 1952.
25. *Ibid.* P. 276. Reprinted by permission.
26. *Ibid.* P. 278. Reprinted by permission.
27. *Ibid.* Pp. 282–83. Reprinted by permission.
28. *Ibid.* P. 284.
29. *Ibid.* P. 285. Reprinted by permission.
30. C. A. Ullman, *Identification of Maladjusted School Children.* Public Health Monograph No. 7. Washington: Federal Security Agency, 1952.
31. J. C. Mitchell, "A Study of Teachers' and of Mental Hygienists' Ratings of Certain Behavior Problems of Children," *Journal of Educational Research.* 39:292–307;1949.
32. J. N. Sparks, "Teachers' Attitudes Toward the Behavior Problems of Children," *Journal of Educational Psychology.* 43:284–91; 1952.
33. Ullman, *op. cit.* P. 39.
34. *The National Mental Health Program.* Mental Health Series No. 4. Washington: Federal Security Agency, Public Health Service, National Institute of Mental Health, June, 1948.
35. D. D. Eisenhower, "Child Health Day, 1953—A Proclamation," *The Child.* 17:138;1953.
36. *Proceedings of the Midcentury White House Conference on Children and Youth.* Raleigh, N. C.: Health Publications Institute, 1951. P. 28. Reprinted by permission.
37. *Ibid.* Pp. 30–31.

SUGGESTED READINGS

H. W. Bernard, *Mental Hygiene for Classroom Teachers.* New York: McGraw-Hill, 1952.

L. Kaplan and D. Baron, *Mental Hygiene and Life.* New York: Harper, 1952.

H. J. Otto, *Principles of Elementary Education.* New York: Rinehart, 1949. Chapter 6, "Educating for Satisfying Human Relations."

G. H. Preston, *The Substance of Mental Health.* New York: Rinehart, 1943.

H. Witmer and R. Kotinsky, eds., *Personality in the Making.* New York: Harper, 1952. A report on the Midcentury White House Conference on Children and Youth.

See also items 1, 2, 3, 4, 5, 6, 7, 8, 9, 10, 11, 20, and 36, listed in the References for this chapter.

SUGGESTED FILMS

Emotional Health. Shows the relationship between childhood experiences and difficulties in late adolescence. Obtainable from McGraw-Hill and New York University.

Learning to Understand Children: Part 1. A Diagnostic Approach, and *Part 2: A Remedial Program.* Steps taken by one teacher to understand the problems of a ninth-grade girl and to help her to make a better adjustment to school.

2

THE DEVELOPMENT OF THE CHILD AS AN INDIVIDUAL

UNDERSTANDING THE CHILD

MANY, if not most of us, will admit that we are perplexed by the behavior of the children and adolescents for whom we are responsible as teachers and group leaders. At times they seem quite rational and "adult"; at other times, overemotional and childish. We have difficulty in predicting what they will do. They reject the well-meant advice of older folk and seem to prefer the foolhardy counsel of their peers and age-mates, even though they seem to have the intelligence and good sense to know better.

Sometimes we try to explain these phenomena to ourselves physiologically—by the need children have to adjust to bodily changes, particularly to the changes of puberty; sometimes we try to relate them to the presence of international tensions and the threat of war; and sometimes we say that society expects too much of children and that, at the same time, it does not expect enough, with the result that children are bound to be confused and frustrated.

Although there is a measure of truth in each of these explanations, there is much that they do not explain. For example, they do not account for the hostility that adolescents in our culture feel, individually and collectively, toward adults as a group. And they do not explain the difficulty experienced by well-meaning adults who attempt to interest children in socially acceptable behavior. Yet, if we as teachers expect to be successful in our work with children, it is important that we acquire a deeper understanding of the emotional factors which underlie the surface behavior of children and which have their roots in infancy and early childhood.

There is much concern in education these days about "understanding children." Most educators accept this task as one of their chief responsibilities. However, what passes for "understanding" in actual practice takes on forms which are so varied that the objective onlooker is hard pressed to find any similarities. Let us look at some common examples of "understanding."

Miss Gard is telling a younger teacher how she gives examinations in biology.

> You have to keep on your toes, because you never know what they'll try to get away with. Why, the other day I caught a boy who had the answers written on his fingernails! The only way to keep up with them is to patrol the aisles, and if you catch them doing anything suspicious just confiscate their papers. It's a good thing I understand boys and girls, or they'd be putting something over on me all the time!

Mrs. Henry, the kindergarten teacher, also feels that she understands children.

> I always try to establish some routines in the first week or so of school because I find that five-year-olds feel more secure if they know what's coming next.

And Mr. McCully, the algebra teacher, feels that *his* understanding of children has been of great help to him.

> I'll have to admit that the first year of junior high teaching was a rough one. The kids made life miserable for me, and I

don't think they learned much algebra either. I spent the summer trying to figure out ways and means of controlling the class and getting them to buckle down to work. Finally, I hit upon the plan which I have used ever since, and, believe me, it really works! I divided the class into teams and worked out a scoring system based on the grades the team members received in the semi-weekly quizzes. Then I posted the scores on the board each Monday. Believe me, I had no idea I could get the kids to work the way they do! I think most problems could be solved if teachers would take the time and trouble to understand their students the way I did.

Each of these teachers feels that he understands children, yet each is talking about something different. Miss Gard wants to be sure that no one cheats in her examinations, and her understanding of children tells her, rightly or wrongly, that all children cheat whenever they have a chance. Mrs. Henry uses her understanding of the psychological development of five-year-olds to provide emotional security for them, whereas Mr. McCully uses his understanding of ninth-graders to get them to work harder.

"Understanding," as we shall use the word in this book, is a very broad concept. It is a blending of skills and attitudes. It is primarily concerned with the welfare of children, rather than with subject matter or the convenience of adults. Probably Mrs. Henry's use of the word, in the examples given above, comes the closest of the three to the meaning we have in mind.

Let us consider the matter of attitudes. A prerequisite to understanding children is a desire to understand them. This is not as simple as it sounds. Miss Gard, in one of the examples given above, *thinks* she wants to understand children, but her very pronounced opinions get in the way of any real understanding. A teacher who really wants to understand children should be prepared to learn things which do not fit in with his preconceptions of them and must be prepared to readjust his opinions from time to time as circumstances require.

A teacher who really wants to understand will make two-way communication a reality. We shall have more to say about communication in the chapter devoted to that subject, so we shall not treat it extensively here. Let us say, however, that in order to understand children, it is important to be receptive to what children have to say. This means, further, that teachers will provide opportunities for children to express themselves and that they will be receptive and attentive. Not all the "messages" which children emit are verbal. Very often, an act is far more significant and expressive than a written or oral statement. Therefore, teachers who sincerely wish to understand children will have to be alert and sensitive to communication of the nonverbal, as well as the verbal, variety.

This of course requires skill. Some teachers develop this skill more quickly than do others. In any case, the use and development of this skill requires sensitivity, patience, and humility.

The teacher who understands children is able to see them and their world from *their* point of view. Many of the things which children do seem quite senseless and irrational to adults, although we would find a certain logic to them if we could see things the way they see them. For instance, parents and teachers are often baffled and annoyed by the tendencies of teen-agers to prefer the opinions and advice of other teen-agers to those of adults, even in cases where adults clearly know what they are talking about. From one point of view, this unwillingness of teen-agers to consider good advice just does not make sense. Yet when we look at adults through the eyes of teen-agers who often have ample reason to be suspicious about the "good" intentions of adults in general, who feel that adults are concerned more about their own convenience and comfort than they are about the rights and feelings of teen-agers, and who sometimes resent the greater power and freedom of the adult, it becomes clearer why it is difficult for teen-agers to be influenced by adults, even when it is for their own good.

The teacher who is aware of the tendencies which are typical of children at various stages in their development is in a better position to understand them. And because of his better understanding, he is able to make adjustments and allowances where he can, to anticipate some of their attitudes and behavior, to avoid certain methods of presentation, and to select others which his understanding tells him would be more effective.

The understanding of children should not, of course, end with a general knowledge of what affects children at various stages and in various situations. It also requires that teachers be prepared to understand children who are different, who do not live up to or conform to the expectations which one might have as a result of expert knowledge. This means that we must be prepared for differences and deviations, and, furthermore, when we find them, we should strive to find out why these differences occur.

Mrs. De Witt teaches the fourth grade in what might be called a slum district. Most of the children in her class are friendly and a little on the "rowdy" side. Mrs. De Witt is a pleasant, good-humored woman, who can also rule with a firm hand when disturbances are too frequent or when they interfere with the business of the class. She is able to use freedom and control when they are most needed and appreciated by her group, and she can do this because she has a sympathetic understanding of the children in her class. However, in almost every one of her classes there have been one or two children who are different from the group. Often they are more withdrawn than the others. Sometimes they are studious and sometimes they are not. Mrs. De Witt always spends extra time in studying these children and what she finds out helps her to handle them more intelligently.

Sometimes what she finds out leads her to urge the child to work more closely with the group; sometimes she permits the child to continue to work by himself and may even give him special assignments. In a few instances, she refers the child to the child-guidance services. In each case, she acts according to her understanding of the situation faced by the child, as well as the forces in his environment that affect his behavior.

HOW CHILDREN DEVELOP CONCEPTS OF THEMSELVES AND OTHERS

THROUGHOUT this book we shall be concerned with the behavior and personality of the child and shall use these two words almost interchangeably. Our use of the word "personality" will thus be somewhat different from the everyday use of the word. In everyday conversation, when we speak of a person having a "nice personality" or an "unpleasant personality," we usually have reference to the outward shell or superficial aspects of his behavior. From the standpoint of the psychologist, personality involves far more than this. As C. M. Harsh and H. G. Schrickel point out, personality involves the individual's temperament (the emotional quality of his behavior), his character (the principles by which he operates, his "inner self"), and his "stimulus value" (the superficial aspects of his behavior we referred to above) [1].

The behavior displayed by the infant is a composite result of the interaction between his basic physical and emotional needs and his physical and emotional environment. He feels the need for food, he cries, he is fed, and expresses satisfaction, or he is not fed and expresses frustration rage or even fear. He cries for his mother and is quieted by her warmth or he expresses frustration because she does not appear. As the infant grows, the picture becomes more complex (or appears to do so—perhaps the infant's world seems less complex because we know less about it). No longer can we speak only of basic physical and emotional needs, we must think of these needs as becoming more mature, more complex, and we must take into account *social* needs, which involve the child's seeking status and acceptance by members of the family group. Furthermore, his environment becomes more complex. Not only is a social component added, but also there is an aspect of *interpretation*. We no longer can think of environment in terms of those forces which can be observed or measured by the onlooker, but in terms of what these forces *mean* to the child. To some babies, the appearance of a man is cause for rejoicing because they have learned to know that this man will fondle them and play with them. To other children, living with an estranged mother, the appearance of a man is cause for fear and anxiety because this man will take them from their mother for a prolonged period. As the child grows and matures, the greater his range of experience, the more meaning his environment has for him.

IMPORTANCE OF UNDERSTANDING CHILDREN'S SELF-CONCEPTS

The way in which a child behaves and develops will be determined to a large degree by such "meanings"—how he sees himself, how he sees the people around him, and how he views the world in general. A child who looks upon himself as essentially a "good" person and who looks upon his peers as potential friends and upon adults as essentially friendly and helpful will have different attitudes and will behave quite differently from the child who feels essentially that he is "bad," who is afraid of his peers, and who does not trust adults. In general, the first child would make an easier adjustment to most school situations than the second child. Most teachers have had experiences with children who feel that they are "dumb" and who cannot therefore make effective attempts to learn the skills and the knowledge set out for them by the curriculum. They have no hope that they ever will be able to learn; hence, they are unable to undertake the problems of learning in an efficient manner. Other children are supremely optimistic about their ability to learn, yet they lack the ability to make the abstractions and discriminations which are so important for success in school. Such children continue to fail, but still "come back for more," unable to profit by their mistakes. Certainly, the ways in which children view themselves and their environment do not contain *all* the answers to the explanation of their behavior, but they nevertheless do contain many of them.

THE ORIGINS OF SELF-CONCEPTS

We can explain the development of these concepts in part by the attitudes possessed by parents. The development of the child's self-concept begins before he is born. To some extent, it has its roots in his parents own self-concepts, for in a very general way he is likely to look upon himself in the way in which his parents see themselves. The child who is self-depreciating very often has a parent who is self-depreciating, and the child who always counts on winning and *must* be the one to win usually has a parent who is also keenly competitive. Children even share their parents' neuroses. In a study of 52 children referred to the guidance center at Arlington, Virginia, E. Lakin Phillips discovered that 71 percent shared at least one of their symptoms with their mothers and 48 percent shared a symptom with their fathers. In many cases symptoms had their roots in the attitudes parents had developed toward themselves and toward life in general, attitudes which were then taken over by children and which appeared to be related to the shared symptom [2].

Yet there is more to the development of a child's self-concept than a rough duplication of parents' attitudes toward themselves. Parents will have some attitudes toward their child-to-be months, and sometimes years, before he is born. They may prefer a girl or they may prefer a boy, or one parent may prefer a girl and the other a boy, or they may not want a child at all. Again, they may be so happy about having a child that they genuinely do not care what sex it will be. Then there are the expectations. What kind of person should this child be? If a boy, should he be vigorous, aggressive, and "masculine"? Or should he be kindly and sympathetic—not "feminine," but not "masculine" either, in the sense of being rough and antisocial. Should he be the kind of person his father wanted to be but could not? Should he be the kind of person his mother wishes his father would be —but is not? These questions cover a fraction of the attitudes which parents develop before the birth of a child. For the most part they are unconscious, but they nevertheless play an important role in the formation of the child's attitudes and self-concept.

These prenatal attitudes and expectations are suddenly crystallized when the child is born. It is a boy, and they wanted a girl. Or they wanted a child, but they were not prepared for the dislocation and readjustment of their lives that a baby brings. Or they had not wanted a child, but cannot help loving this one. Or the father had not realized how much of the mother's time would be taken up in caring for an infant. Sometimes these early attitudes persist indefinitely, as in the case of the parents who always wanted a boy and never quite accepted the girl they got, or the father who decided that his newborn son would grow up to take his place in the family business.

SELF-CONCEPT: EARLY STAGES

Many children are at the height of their acceptance during their first year or two of life. After all, everyone knows how a baby ought to look and behave, and no one expects him to be any more than a baby. But as he grows old enough to walk and talk, then the expectations of his parents and the other members of his family begin to be of major importance. Particularly after the age of two he is drawn deeper and deeper into the tug of war between himself and the significant people in his life—the tug of war which will be so important in deciding the kind of person he is to be. In general, this tug of war is between the child wanting to be himself, doing what *he* wants to do, and his family wanting him to "become someone they can be proud of," to do what *they* want him to do.

In our Western culture, the child usually resists these demands for a while, with major clash of wills occurring during the third year of life, followed by alternating periods of peace and minor skirmishing during the rest of childhood and adolescence. Some children continue to have difficulties over the issue of who controls whom, whereas others are more fortunate.

During this third year of life the child experiences a change in the relationship he has had with his parents. If he grows up in the usual middle-class home, perhaps he feels that things are going reasonably well. If his parents have rejected or punished him at various times, he is unaware of this because his memory is imperfect. Only if he interprets the home *atmosphere* as tense, anxious, or unfriendly, is he upset. However, if he feels that his parents love him and his siblings more or less accept him, he is reasonably satisfied.

But this ideal state does not continue. As he grows more curious, more active, and more destructive in attempting to satisfy his curiosity and his needs for large-muscle activity, it becomes necessary to set limits to his behavior. Regardless of attempts to "clear the decks" so that he might play in a hazard-free area, he seems to have a genius for getting into trouble. And sometimes it is necessary to be firm, perhaps to punish, in order to help the child to learn that certain kinds of actions are harmful, dangerous, disapproved, or otherwise inappropriate.

Most children do not accept these limitations easily and gracefully. In fact, the third year of childhood is recognized by observers as a period marked by temper outbursts, negativism, crying, and ill feelings. In the usual situation, the child eases gradually into more mature behavior and accepts restraint. This does not mean that the child accepts these limitations willingly or pleasantly. Usually it is more or less upsetting for the child to realize that his loving parents can apparently withhold their love from him (for this is his interpretation of punishment).

He would like to feel able to do anything he pleases and at the same time to feel completely secure in his parents' love. Their ability to punish him (withhold love) indicates to him that this cannot be. This is puzzling, upsetting, anxiety-provoking, frightening, and he will respond to the situation with whatever negative behavior is appropriate to his temperament and personality.

Eventually he learns that in exchange for his continued good behavior, he is entitled to remain in his parents' good graces. At first he learns to do this in the parents' presence; later he learns that these parents of his can learn about the perpetration of misdeeds even though they have not witnessed the act. Because of his immature perception he does not understand how they do this. Perhaps he attributes this to their possession of magical powers. What can he do against such people who are so powerful and possess such magic? He resents this and wants to fight it somehow, but there does not seem to be a way.

Gradually, or more likely, spasmodically, he gives up and accepts parental domination. He probably does not see any "reason" for parental ways to be any better than his ways, it is just that they are stronger than he, or perhaps because they are so able to paint frightening pictures of what may happen to him if he breaks the household laws: he may burn his hand if he plays near the stove, he may cut himself if he plays with the knife, etc.

The first stage of the parents' victory is complete when the child is able to abstain from wrongdoing in their absence. At such times it is almost as though he had created for himself a small parental image which he installed in the "back of his mind" and which forbade him to engage in prohibited activities.

Although the kinds of prohibited activities vary from family to family, there are certain types which are common to various cultural patterns. In essence, parents are doing two things when they restrain their child and "limit" his behavior. In the first instance, they are attempting to prevent him from harming himself and others, and in the second place, they are "transmitting the culture" to the child. It can be argued that these are essentially the same. For example, Japanese families are careful to keep their children from sitting or playing in the doorway because they feel that this is the weakest part of the house and that even the weight of a small baby will bring the edifice tumbling down. In our culture, some parents go to great lengths to prevent children from touching their genitals because of the fear that the child may become perverted or even insane if this behavior is permitted.

Of great interest to us is the second category—that behavior which is forbidden or enforced for obviously cultural reasons: insisting that a child keep his person and his clothing clean; insisting that a child eat at specified times and always clean up his plate; prohibition of swearing, relating phantasies, lying, and fighting; forbidding a child to associate with children of different color or religion. Requirements of this type are of particular interest because they are less "rational," i.e., they are less related to the personal welfare of the child, and because most parental decrees or "verbots" usually fall into this category. We insist on these behavior patterns and prohibitions because *this is the way that it is done*—no other way is acceptable.

One wonders whether the child realizes, unconsciously at least, that most of the demands made on him carry this weight of irrational authority, that they are demands which must be obeyed without question, not because they serve some useful purpose, but because deviation will not be tolerated by society in general and his parents in particular, who represent society in their role of transmitters of the culture. Apparently, some children feel that since most demands and prohibitions levied on them are for the benefit of persons in authority rather than themselves, that *all* demands and prohibitions fall into this category. If this is so, it helps to explain the headstrong, rebellious, daredevil conduct which is typical of some children, particularly at later stages of development.

Perhaps we can distinguish among three kinds of demands and prohibitions: (1) those made for the personal comfort and safety of the child; (2) those made for the comfort and safety of others; and (3) those made to insure conformity to a social norm. One is tempted to add a fourth category— demands and prohibitions made to show a child "who is boss"; however, any of the three types of demands and prohibitions may be invoked with this additional purpose in mind.

In any case, those demands and prohibitions made to insure conformity to a social norm and those made even in part for the purpose of demonstrating authority are the ones which tend to cause the most anxieties in children, possibly because of their essentially irrational quality, and even more possibly because these are the areas of conduct which arouse anxieties on the part of adults. After all, nonconformity to a social norm is cause for rejection, loss of status, and ostracism among adults.

Most of us derive reassurance from being able to control the behavior of others, whereas challenges to our authority only serve to remind us of the existence of inadequacies we would like to forget. Thus, when we see children refuse to conform or when they object to our authority, it is little wonder that we become tense and anxious. Dictatorial parents and teachers produce children who are not only tense and anxious, but who will also become dictatorial when the opportunity is provided.

DIFFERENCES IN PERSONALITY PATTERNS

Children differ, of course, in the ways in which they express anxieties and tensions. Some children decide that the world is a very unsafe place, and they withdraw into quiet, solitary activities which enable them to avoid the risk of nonconformist behavior. If they do not venture out into "the world," they will thus reduce the number of occasions adults will have to use them as a means of demonstrating adult authority. Children who adopt this pattern of behavior tend to repress the hostility which is engendered by persons in authority. They become submissive, because they do not want to risk the danger of punishment with its consequent implications of rejection and loss of love. This pattern tends, in our culture, to be more typical of girls than boys, although large numbers of boys are drawn to this solution.

Other children express their resentment of adult authority openly, either against adults themselves or toward their peers, or both. Their aggression may take the form of fighting, swearing, or destructiveness, or it may lead to large-muscle activity of a more or less aggressive nature. In the former case, such children usually receive the label of "problem children," because they constitute such an open threat, such a flagrant violation of our culture's mores and our authority as individual adults.

A third pattern is followed by children who endeavor to find out what the approved forms of behavior in our culture are. These children have a strong drive to like, admire, and respect adults. They would like to be powerful the way adults are, and they can see themselves getting a little adult power by cooperation, submission, and living the roles adults expect of them. Such children, in effect, strike a bargain with adults; they perform according to expectations, and, in exchange, adults approve of them (love them) and permit them limited freedom of activity (power).

Children who adopt this pattern of solution constitute the great middle group, the ones who have worked out the most effective compromise with life. This group, too, tends to repress its anxieties, although, probably because of better relations with adults from the start, they have fewer anxieties to repress, and are better prepared to deal with problems as they occur. There are more girls than boys in this group, probably because early home conditions in our culture (mother at home, father at work) favor the psychological development of girls rather than boys.

It should be noted that most individual children would probably defy absolute classification into any one of the foregoing categories because their behavior tends to present a mixed pattern. However, there is usually an identifiable trend that dominates the behavior of most children.

THE DEVELOPMENT OF THE SELF-IDEAL

As a result of the demands made on the child during his early preschool years, he is very likely to get the idea that the "person he is" is different from the "person he ought to be." In most homes, he is likely to realize that his parents would like him to be different, in some respects, from what he actually is. They wish he would stop wetting the bed at night, or that his table manners were better, or that he would not embarrass them in front of company, etc. Out of his awareness of his parents' disapproval develops what psychologists have variously called the "self-ideal," the "ideal self," the "ego ideal," or the "superego"—in everyday language, the "conscience." (In order to be consistent with our use of the term "self-concept"—the individual as he sees himself—we shall use the term "self-ideal"—the individual as he thinks he ought to be—to refer to this aspect of the child's personality.)

In a large sense, the self-ideal is a disturbing element in

the child's life. On the one hand, it provides the means whereby the child is socialized—learns to be amenable to the requirements of society and considerate of the rights and needs of others. On the other hand, the anxieties that are aroused when a child acts contrary to his self-ideal, or when he is appalled by the great difference between what he is and what he ought to be, make it easy for him to be overcontrolled and overdominated or pushed and pulled about by other children and adults. Often these anxieties drive children into behavior that is the very opposite of the self-ideal. (Some of the symptoms of anxiety-driven behavior will be discussed in succeeding chapters.) An example of this oppositional behavior is the relationship between toilet training and bed-wetting among children being treated at a child-guidance clinic, explored by John Bostock and Marjorie Shackleton. As a result of their study they reported that there was a pronounced tendency for bed-wetting to be associated with rigid toilet training in infancy [3, 4].

Nor is there always an obvious connection between the expectations and demands of parents, on the one hand, and the behavior of children, on the other. For example, W. H. Sewell reports the existence of a relationship between bowel-and-bladder training in infancy and tendencies toward nail-biting in later life. Even though these two aspects of life appear to be unrelated at first glance, Sewell notes that children whose parents did not make severe demands in the way of early bowel-and-bladder training were less likely to become nail-biters [5]. A possible inference here, of course, is that children whose parents were relaxed, were themselves relaxed and hence did not feel the need to engage in behavior symptomatic of tension such as nail-biting.

The self-ideal also has its origins in the expectations and hopes that parents have for children, particularly when children's behavior does not measure up to the hoped-for ideal.

Jimmy is three years old and can already recognize some of the letters of the alphabet. His parents' pleasure at this feat is somewhat clouded by the realization that three-year-old Jane, next door, not only can recognize every letter in the alphabet, but can even read a few common words.

The parents of five-year-old Georgia are concerned because she will not put her toys away and hang up her clothes unless she is reminded many times and sometimes scolded. These expectations are at variance with their own behavior (both parents leave books and magazines strewn about the house) as well as with the behavior of most five-year-olds. Her parents are unaware of these inconsistencies, however, and feel that their expectations are modest and reasonable.

The publication in the popular press, in recent years, of information regarding the effect of premature and rigid toilet training on the personality and development of children has led a few parents to develop a studied permissiveness toward this aspect of child training, but without extending this attitude toward other dimensions of child-parent relations. Bruno Bettelheim tells of a mother who could accept the need of her eighteen-month-old son to establish toilet controls at his own rate, but who was keeping a list of words he was learning. She had calculated that he was learning two new words a day, and it was plain that she was determined that he should maintain this rate or even improve on it. The new words were discussed every day in the home and were the main subject of her letters to her parents and in-laws. Bettelheim says, in part:

The mother could allow herself much greater pressure with respect to her son's intellectual progress, since her leniency about toilet training had established her clearly as permissive, not only in her own mind but before her enlightened friends. Yet, in a way this boy was worse off than if his mother had imposed a too early toilet training. Because the sequence of development was here reversed, the ability to verbalize extensively preceded toilet training instead of coming after it. . . . [In other words, toilet training,] for which he was . . . ready, was delayed, and verbalization, for which he was by no means ready, was pushed.

It is not difficult to assume that this child felt under much greater pressure as things were, and was hence much more tense than he might have been had the mother just settled for an early toilet training [6].

As a result of such inconsistent pressures, some children develop self-ideals that vary markedly from their self-concepts and consequently experience feelings of profound guilt and anxiety at their inability to live up to these ideal standards. On the other hand, many children, as Gardner Murphy says, "simply develop a realistic acceptance of the fact that other people approve certain lines of conduct and disapprove of others, and adjust themselves to the standard of approval and disapproval *without* developing much conscience about it [7]." More exactly, they will take over some of the general ideas, but may distort or minimize certain aspects. Thus, a child who is asked occasionally to "show off" when strangers are present may gain an exaggerated sense of his talents and showmanship. Another child in a similar situation may come to feel that his parents do this to embarrass him and may consequently develop a depreciatory attitude toward his abilities. He may actually do more poorly when others are watching him.

During the preschool years the child will learn whether he is expected to think and act for himself most of the time, or whether he must depend on adults to decide what he is to do or perhaps even to do it for him. He may learn that his parents always expect his requests to be unreasonable, but also that they grant them if he screams loud enough.

There is seldom, if ever, a one-to-one relationship between parents' expectations of their child and what he develops as a self-ideal. Although communication is perhaps one of the greatest of human inventions, it is nonetheless an imperfect instrument. Hence, we can be fairly certain that children will distort and misinterpret what their parents expect of them. Furthermore, because of a strong drive in some children to "be themselves" at all costs, or, rather, *not* to be what others want them to be, some children seem to take a perverse pride in developing self-concepts or self-ideals and engaging in activities that are directly opposed to what their parents expect of them.

ATTITUDES TOWARD OTHERS

The child's concepts of others will also be colored to a great extent by those of his parents. The child who grows up in a home where there is little conversation is likely to grow up expecting that no one should talk much, and that people should keep their thoughts to themselves. If parents are highly critical of relatives and friends and are not given to making kind and generous comments, who can be surprised if children grow up with rejecting and supercilious attitudes? Children learn their strongest prejudices from their parents and siblings.

In a study of informal conversation in families, Bossard, Boll, and Sanger found that a number of types were readily discernible.

For instance, some families talk chiefly about themselves; their experiences, achievements, misfortunes, plans, and problems. Other families, by way of contrast, talk mostly about persons or events outside of the family.

Similarly apparent is the contrast between family patterns of conversation that are analytical or evaluating. The first-named are those which consist chiefly of the analysis, description, and interpretation of persons, objects, or events. The interest is to tell about the subject under discussion. One has something to tell here, and the overtones may be those of humor, mystery, drama, or simply recording. Over against this type is that where the underlying motif is that of passing judgment. Motives are impugned, purposes are evaluated, persons and events are "placed in their proper light." These are the family conversations devoted to "talking about someone." Comments are chiefly critical, depreciatory, belittling. The boss is flayed, a competing neighbor's child is depreciated, the teacher is criticized, a social rival is ridiculed, a relative is castigated, a public official is denounced, the children are nagged, or the food is declared unpalatable.

Somewhat akin to this latter type is the pattern where conversation comes to be a kind of exhibitionism, as showmanship. The emphasis is not so much on expressing a thought as on giving a performance. The aim may be at cleverness, and may achieve that purpose or degenerate into mere smart-aleckiness; or the conversation may take the nature of a sadistic performance, where the purpose of hurting expresses itself in cutting speech; or the objective may be primarily that of holding the floor, so to speak, with a juggling of verbal balls, sometimes of gold but more often of tinsel. In most cases, this type of speech seems designed basically to call attention to the speaker, and may be related to a deep-seated inferiority complex.

Other contrasts in these family patterns of conversation are to be found in their tonal qualities. At one extreme are those conversations which abound with "snarl words," and much of the talk consists of spasmodically throwing verbal bits at one another as one throws sticks at a dog. In contradistinction are those family conversations which suggest a Sunday afternoon symphony concert. Instead of loud noises, wrangling, and constant interruptions, there is a quiet and polite exchange of ideas, even allowing for disagreement in conviction. People are allowed to finish a sentence. Even the children are allowed these courtesies.

One important by-product of this study is the impression one gains of these patterns as unconscious, even if persistent, habits of family living. That is to say, the families studied had no awareness, seemingly, of the extent to which their patterns of conversation conformed to a given type. There was no awareness or thought either to their nature or of their role in the development of the child members or in the relations between the adult family members [8].

Through the medium of casual family conversation, as well as through the general behavior of family members, the child learns how his parents and siblings regard themselves and life in general. The way in which he perceives their attitudes and behavior will govern the attitudes he will develop regarding himself and others. He may learn, for example, that he should be afraid of others and withdraw from close contact, or that he should fear others and hence attack them, if possible. Or perhaps he learns that the safest thing to do is to wait until others make the first move and then act accordingly.

Another factor that operates is the feeling of inadequacy and inferiority which most children have where adults are concerned. Adults are large and strong. They are skillful, crafty, and all-powerful. Children see themselves as powerless to resist adults for very long. Furthermore, adults are very necessary, not only as protectors and as suppliers of food, shelter, and clothing, but also as sources of love and approval. Therefore, the child normally realizes that he must keep on the good side of adults most of the time so as not to cause them to withhold or withdraw their support and love. One of the ways to keep from offending adults is to adopt their ways of thinking, and furthermore perhaps one can become as strong and powerful as an adult by thinking and acting like him. Hence, children usually incorporate some of their parents' values and points of view into their self-ideal.

THE CULTURE AND ITS CONTRIBUTION TO THE SELF-CONCEPT

LET no one think that parents are completely free agents in shaping the concepts and attitudes of their children, any more than they themselves had free rein in forming their own self-concepts when *they* were children. Parents play their roles as shapers of their children's personalities very largely as agents of the culture in which they live. Thus, if the culture specifies that boys should grow up to be aggressive and warlike, as in the case of the Sioux, parents will strive to produce these effects in their children. And if the culture specifies that children should be prepared to take their role in a peaceful and cooperative society, as in the case of the Zuñi, the parents will act accordingly. There are usually a few parents who, for various reasons, lead lives which are at variance with the culture and who attempt to inculcate differing values in their children. Whether their children, too, will deviate from accepted cultural patterns will depend on their relations with their parents and on whether they will yield to or withstand the pressure brought upon them by their peers and adults outside the family. During a recent political campaign the author and his wife strongly favored Candidate "X." Hence, they were somewhat taken aback when their five-year-old daughter loudly declared herself for Candidate "Y." After some questioning it developed that the families of all the other children in her kindergarten group were for Candidate "Y." Even after she was reassured about her right to deviate from the opinion expressed by her classmates, she was still dubious and said that she would probably favor *both* candidates. The point is that even kindergarteners are sensitive to the attitudes expressed by persons outside of their family group, and when there is a difference, it is resolved largely on the basis of the choice which involves the least risk or anxiety.

ARE SEX DIFFERENCES BASICALLY CULTURAL?

For the most part, we are unaware of how our self-concepts, attitudes, and behavior are influenced by our culture, since this influence pervades so much of our daily lives that we accept it unthinkingly. Let us consider one aspect of everyday life which illustrates this—the psychological differences between men and women that we assume exist. We are all aware that women taken as a group are more interested in the care of children, are more concerned with the humanitarian aspects of life, and in general are more law-abiding than are men. Boys create more disturbances in class than do girls. Boys are more athletically inclined; girls are more scholastically inclined; men are inclined to be more aggressive and domineering. We are all aware of these differences and tend to attribute them to the "natural order of things"— males behave this way because they are male, and females behave this way because they are female.

Yet the research of anthropologists like Margaret Mead raises grave questions about the validity of this explanation. Mead has found tribes in Melanesia where men behave in ways which we would consider to be essentially feminine, and women behave in ways which we would consider essentially masculine. Women in these groups tended to be aggressive and to carry on the bread-winning functions, whereas men tended to be passive and to be concerned with the aesthetic side of life. In another tribe there was no sharp differentiation between the attitudes and behavior displayed by men and women, except for the purely physical functions of procreation and childbearing [9].

If we are alert and sensitive to what goes on around us, we can perceive the forces in our own culture which make for masculinity and femininity. Mrs. Baker had been using the family car to take her six-year-old daughter to school seven blocks away, and was complaining how it "broke up her day." Mr. Baker asked why June was not able to walk to school. He had been talking to some of the neighbors and found that there were six-year-old boys on the same block who walked to school. Mrs. Baker replied:

"Well, they're boys! It's too far for a girl."

Mrs. Baker is implying, among other things, that boys are much stronger than girls, although boys and girls are about on a par at six years of age. There are other implications, of course, one being that girls should be privileged to ride, and another being that girls should not walk with boys and probably need the protection of their parents at this age more than boys do.

Now there are no objective, scientific data which support Mrs. Baker's statement, yet her attitudes are similar to those held by many middle-class parents. It is just that we *feel* different about boys and girls. We *expect* girls to need more protection, to be weaker, to be interested in playing with dolls, and we expect boys to be vigorous, aggressive, mischievous, and more interested in sports and games. And boys and girls usually turn out in accordance with these expectations, not because the expectations were "correct," but because the expectations themselves exert such a powerful influence during the formative years. Again we should note that there are always a few children who do not conform to the expected pattern. These children are always under great pressure, applied by adults and children alike, to change their ways. Boys who are interested in playing with dolls are criticized as being "sissies," and girls who prefer to climb trees with boys are called "tomboys," and are, in general, more likely to be rejected by their peers, although there is a greater tendency to reject boys who behave differently, in comparison to girls. According to J. H. S. Bossard, we let boys and girls know what kinds of behavior we expect of them by such statements as, "Little girls don't talk that way," or "A lady never raises her voice," or "He sounds like a boy, all right [10]." Children are quick to sense the meaning of such remarks.

There are other ways in which the culture, operating through parents, teachers, peer groups, churches, and the mass media of communication, exerts powerful influences which shape the self-concept, self-ideal, attitudes, and behavior of a child. We shall have more to say about them in the chapters that follow.

INDIVIDUAL PERSONALITY DETERMINANTS

BOTH within and beyond the immediate experience of each individual there are forces, conditions, and events that help him to be like all other persons, like some other persons, and like no other persons [11]. Clyde Kluckhohn and

H. A. Murray, in writing on the development of personality, call these the "determinants" of personality because they play such an important part in *determining* the kinds of people we are or will become.

Biological or "constitutional" determinants comprise one class of such forces, according to Kluckhohn and Murray [12]. Each child has an inherited pattern of biological characteristics which resembles the patterns of others somewhat, but which is also different from any other. Inherited characteristics will have an effect on his height, weight, body-build, facial contours, muscular and glandular development, and even on his temperament. Being taller than the other boys in the class may be a physical advantage. It will also bring into play certain personality characteristics that might have lain more or less dormant. Being taller than most girls may be considered disadvantageous and may encourage the development of what is popularly known as an "inferiority complex." Boys who are shorter than the rest of the group often turn out to be pugnacious and "scrappy."

However, we must studiously avoid the easy generalization of assuming that children develop certain kinds of personalities solely because of their height. One commonly hears the remark: "I can understand why Brian always has a chip on his shoulder—he's so much shorter than the rest of the boys"—the inference being that Brian is the kind of person he is solely because of his shortness. The truth of the matter is, of course, that Brian's cockiness is the result of a combination of forces. The fact that our culture looks upon tallness as a kind of virtue is undoubtedly a factor. Perhaps Brian has been teased about his height; perhaps his father is short, too, and has covered up his feeling of inferiority by an aggressive and pugnacious manner; perhaps Brian bears a grudge against the world because he feels that other children in his family are favored. There are literally thousands of possible explanations of his attitude toward himself and others, and we must know him much better before we can name those conditions or forces that appear to lie at the basis of his pugnacious behavior. His shortness is only one aspect of his problem, but it is a condition that helps to dramatize how Brian feels about himself and life generally.

In other words, biological determinants are only part of the picture that is the child's personality. For example, Lorraine may have a physiological predisposition to be asthmatic. If her mother is inclined to be overprotective and anxious or overrejecting and preoccupied, it is likely that Lorraine will have much difficulty with asthma [13]. Because of this, Lorraine may have to be very careful what she eats and the kinds of activities she engages in. She may, therefore, develop a very cautious and timid attitude toward life, an attitude that may color her entire personality. On the other hand, if Lorraine's mother is not overprotective or overrejecting, asthma may never get to be a problem, even though she is physiologically vulnerable.

The important thing to remember is that no biological determinant taken by itself is sufficient to have a predictable effect on the self-concept or personality of a given individual. A so-called physical defect, for example, must be considered in the light of such things as: How do others regard his appearance and manner—do they admire and accept him, or do they ridicule him, or do they ignore him? How does he regard himself? Is he anxiously concerned about his appearance, or does he take it for granted? Does he think that his parents would like him better if he were better looking? Does he daydream about being more attractive to the opposite sex? In other words, the important factor is not so much what an individual's physical characteristics are as it is how he regards them and how he thinks that others regard him.

Kluckhohn and Murray also distinguish a class of personality determinants they term "group membership determinants" [14]. By this they mean the characteristics individuals develop by reason of growing up among and belonging to national groups, cultures, subcultures, and communities. For example, Miss Finch is partly the kind of person she is because she is an American, a member of the middle class, and grew up in a small town in the Deep South. Mr. Jones possesses the attitudes and self-concept he has because he has lived and worked most of his life in a small fishing village on the coast of Newfoundland. We tend to draw some of the "flavor" of our personalities and viewpoints, to a greater or lesser extent, from the intimate and long-term association with certain groups.

Kluckhohn and Murray also indicate that the roles that people play influence their personalities to a marked degree [15]. Part of a teacher's personality is shaped by his role as a teacher; the cost accountant is likely to develop certain attitudes and viewpoints because of his professional role; and the ward politician's self-concept is shaped by his role in life. The roles of children are to a large extent in flux, for they pass from one set of roles to another as they proceed through various stages of childhood. Some roles are more permanent: the oldest child is always the oldest child, and the demands that this role makes often have a marked effect on his personality. The sex role, as we noted earlier, results clearly recognizable personality patterns.

The fourth category noted by Kluckhohn and Murray is termed by them "situational determinants." These include "things that happen a thousand times as well as those that happen only once—provided they are not the standard for the whole group [16]." Under this heading would be included divorce or separation of the parents, the existence of a handicap or of unusual talent, having a father whose occupation keeps him away from home most of the time, living in a neighborhood where there are very few children, etc.

All of these forces or determinants exert some influence on the personality of the child, but because of the ways in which they interact and sometimes counteract each other, no trait of personality can be readily ascribed to a single determinant. Furthermore, any given condition involves several determinants simultaneously. Being the oldest son involves a situational determinant, but it also involves a role determinant, in that we have certain expectations of how oldest sons should act. And we would like to mention again, for emphasis, that as important as determinants are in shaping personality, what has the greatest effect on the individual's behavior are his attitudes: How does he regard himself (his self-concept)? What does he think others expect of him? What does he expect of himself (his self-ideal)? How does he regard others? And, finally, how does he regard the world around him?

REFERENCES

1. C. M. Harsh and H. G. Schrickel, *Personality*. New York: Ronald, 1950. Pp. 4–8.
2. E. L. Phillips, "Parent-Child Similarities in Personality Disturbances," *Journal of Clinical Psychology*. 7:188–90;1951.
3. J. Bostock and M. Shackleton, "The Enuresis Dyad," *The Medical Journal of Australia*. 3:357–60;1952.
4. ———, "Enuresis and Toilet Training," *The Medical Journal of Australia*. 2:110;1951.
5. W. H. Sewell, "Infant Training and the Personality of the Child," *American Journal of Sociology*. 58:150–59;1952.
6. Bruno Bettelheim, "Mental Health and Current Mores," *American Journal of Orthopsychiatry*. 22:76–88;1952. Reprinted by permission.
7. Gardner Murphy, *An Introduction to Psychology*. New York: Harper, 1951. P. 429.
8. J. H. S. Bossard, E. S. Boll, and W. P. Sanger, "Some Neglected Areas in Family-Life Study," *Annals of the American Academy of Political and Social Science*. 272:68–76;1950. Reprinted by permission.
9. Margaret Mead, *Sex and Temperament*. New York: Morrow, 1935.
10. J. H. S. Bossard, *The Sociology of Child Development*. New York: Harper, 1948. P. 187.

11. C. Kluckhohn and H. A. Murray, *Personality in Nature, Society, and Culture.* New York: Knopf, 1948. P. 35.
12. *Ibid.* P. 38.
13. I. D. Harris, L. Rapoport, M. A. Rynerson, and M. Samter, "Observations of Asthmatic Children," *American Journal of Orthopsychiatry.* 20:490–525;1950.
14. Kluckhohn and Murray, *op. cit.* P. 39.
15. *Ibid.* P. 42.
16. *Ibid.* P. 43.

SUGGESTED READINGS

The following references should prove helpful in providing background regarding the development of the self, the self-concept, and the self-ideal:

S. E. Asch, *Social Psychology.* New York: Prentice-Hall, 1952. Chapter 10, "The Ego."

Association for Supervision and Curriculum Development, *Growing Up in an Anxious Age.* Washington: National Education Association, 1952. Chapter 7, "How Children Learn Roles and Expectations."

H. Bonner, *Social Psychology.* New York: American Book, 1953. Chapter 5, "The Self and Its Involvements."

H. Cantril, *The "Why" of Man's Experience.* New York: Macmillan, 1950. Chapter 6, "The Nature of the 'Me.'"

A. T. Jersild, *In Search of Self.* New York, Bureau of Publications, Teachers College, Columbia University, 1952.

H. C. Lindgren, *Psychology of Personal and Social Adjustment.* New York: American Book, 1953. Chapter 2, "The Development of Personality: The Self."

G. H. Mead, *Mind, Self, and Society.* Chicago: University of Chicago Press, 1934.

T. M. Newcomb, *Social Psychology.* New York: Dryden, 1950. Chapter 9, "Role Behavior and the Self;" Chapter 11, "The Patterning of Self-Other Attitudes."

D. Snygg and A. W. Combs, *Individual Behavior.* New York: Harper, 1949.

P. M. Symonds, *The Ego and the Self.* New York: Appleton-Century-Crofts, 1952.

The following references are suggested as background reading with regard to determinants of personality:

L. W. Doob, *Social Psychology*. New York: Holt, 1952. Chapter 3, "Socialization and Learning."

C. Kluckhohn, *Mirror for Man*. New York: McGraw-Hill, 1949.

H. C. Lindgren, *The Art of Human Relations*. New York: Hermitage, 1953. Chapter 4, "How We Got to Be Who We Are."

————, *Psychology of Personal and Social Adjustment*. New York: American Book, 1953. Chapter 8, "The Forces That Mold Us: Determinants of Personality."

F. Redl and W. W. Wattenberg, *Mental Hygiene in Teaching*. New York: Harcourt, Brace, 1951. Chapter 5, "Influences That Shape Lives."

See also items 9, 10, and 11, in the References for this chapter.

SUGGESTED FILMS

The Feeling of Rejection. National Film Board of Canada. Available through McGraw-Hill.

Preface to a Life. U. S. Public Health Service. Available through Castle Films, 1445 Park Avenue, New York 29, N. Y.

3

MOTIVATION: NORMAL

NEEDS AND ANXIETY

INTERNAL AND EXTERNAL FORCES

IN THE last chapter we attempted to describe human behavior as the indirect product of external forces—forces that exist *outside* the individual, as it were, that operate to shape his self-concept and self-ideal, and that push and pull him into various attitudes and decisions. Even the self-concept and the self-ideal are in a sense the expression of external forces, because they are composed so largely, as Harry Stack Sullivan implies, of the reflected appraisals of others [1]. In this chapter, we shall examine some of the forces that appear to operate *within* the individual. Actually, of course, we cannot say whether a person performs a given act specifically as a result of either external or internal forces. Usually these forces operate together and are, in fact, often indistinguishable from each other. When ten-year-old Gregory throws a spitball across the room at 2:30 on a hot, sultry afternoon, he is prompted by a combination of forces. He may be trying to compete for the leadership of the "rowdy element" in the class and at the same time attempting to express the feeling of extreme boredom and general irritability that sometimes comes over ten-year-olds toward the end of a long, hot day. Or he may be defying the teacher and at the same time reaching to express feelings of anxiety and guilt which are so strong that he feels he ought to be punished for something.

It may be that all these forces are operating simultaneously and are interrelated. If so, some are probably more potent than others, at least as far as Gregory's day-to-day conduct is concerned. Furthermore, they all have internal and external aspects which blend one into the other. We are introducing a quality of artificiality by making a distinction between internal and external motives or forces. Thereby we can develop some hypotheses and draw some conclusions which may help us to understand children better.

BASIC NEEDS

ONE of the fundamental assumptions which underlie the thinking presented in this book is that all individuals are motivated by both basic needs and anxiety.

Basically, the actions of all organisms, human or otherwise, are the result of a need to maintain and enhance the organism [2]. This basic need, however, is expressed in an endless variety of ways, depending on such conditions as the maturity of the organism and the situation in which it finds itself. For the purposes of the present discussion, a classification of needs similar to that developed by A. H. Maslow appears to have the advantages of being simple enough to be grasped easily and complex enough to serve as a basis for differentiating needs at various levels and stages of development [3, 4].

The system of basic needs as conceived by Maslow and as modified by this writer is as follows:

1. *Bodily needs:* hunger, sex, the need to breathe, to eliminate wastes, and so forth.

2. *Safety:* the avoidance of and defense against external dangers, against forces which might produce injury, pain, impairment, extremes of heat and cold, and so forth.

3. *Love:* the need to be given love, warmth, and affection by someone.

4. *Self-esteem:* a need to feel strong and adequate, to have the respect and the confidence of others.

5. *Self-actualization:* the need for self-fulfillment and self-expression, to use and develop one's talents, to become the most one is capable of becoming.

HOW BASIC NEEDS OPERATE

In general, this set of needs constitutes a developmental series in that individuals are normally able to satisfy needs toward the end of the list more and more adequately as they advance through each stage of development. Infants, for example, are concerned almost exclusively with the first three needs on this list because these are the needs most essential for life and growth. It is obvious that the ability of a child to grow and develop depends upon whether his needs for nourishment and safety are met. However, it is not so obvious that he needs to be loved. Although mothers have suspected for centuries that their children need their love, it has only been recently that we have been able to demonstrate psychologically and experimentally that lack of love seriously impairs the normal development of children.

For example, R. A. Spitz found that children growing up in an orphanage where they received little mothering were retarded in physical and behavioral development, whereas children in another institution, where there was ample mothering, developed normally [5, 6].

Another study, made by E. M. Widdowson of children in two municipal orphanages in Germany, seems to indicate that love is more important than calories. Widdowson's account goes as follows:

Near the industrial town in Germany where our unit had its headquarters in 1948 there were two small municipal orphanages. We may call them for the present purpose "Bienenhaus" and "Vogelnest." Each houses about fifty boys and girls between 4 and 14 years of age; the average age was 8 years and 8 months in both homes. These children had nothing but their official rations to eat, and, although these were considerably better than they had been in 1946 and 1947, they were still barely adequate for the children's requirements. The children were below normal as regards height and weight, those at Bienenhaus being a little worse than those at Vogelnest. We decided to follow the heights and weights of all these children by weighing and measuring them every fortnight for a year, during the first half of which neither one of the homes would receive any additional food, but during the second six months one of the homes, Vogelnest, would be supplied with unlimited amounts of additional bread, so that all children could satisfy their appetites to the full. Extra jam would also be provided to spread on the bread, and concentrated orange juice to serve as a drink. Supplementary bread had already been shown to promote excellent growth at another orphanage . . . . During the second six months the children at Bienenhaus would continue to be weighed and measured as before but would receive no additional food. In this way it was hoped to get a direct comparison of the growth-rate of children with and without the additional bread. . . .

As the first six months went by it became apparent that the children were gaining weight at very different rates in the two homes. A group of boys and girls should gain an average of about 1.4 kg. [approximately three pounds] in six months. . . . At Vogelnest the average gain was almost exactly 1.4 kg.; at Bienenhaus the mean gain was less than 0.5 kg.

During the second six months the position was reversed. In spite of the extra food provided for the children at Vogelnest, their average growth-rate was less than it had been during the first six months when no additional food was supplied. . . . At Bienenhaus, on the other hand, the weight curve immediately began to rise steeply, although these children were getting only their German rations as before. There was clearly some other factor at work which was more than counteracting the beneficial effect of the additional food we supplied.

At the beginning of 1948 Bienenhaus was in charge of Fräulein Schwarz, while Vogelnest was presided over by Fräulein Grün. Just at the time when the additional food was first provided at Vogelnest it so happened that Fräulein Grün left the orphanage. . . . Fräulein Schwarz was thereupon transferred from Bienenhaus to Vogelnest, and a third woman, Fräulein Weiss, came to take charge of Bienenhaus. Fräulein Grün and Fräulein Weiss were very similar in temperament, bright, happy persons, genuinely fond of the children and the children of them. Fräulein Schwarz was quite different. She was older, rather stern and forbidding, and she ruled the home with a rod of iron. Children and staff lived in constant fear of her reprimands and criticisms, which sometimes seemed quite unreasonable. For instance, one day a child was scolded for wearing gloves and getting them wet; the next day the same child was in disgrace for not wearing gloves. Fräulein Schwarz often chose the times when the children were at their meals to administer public rebukes and would single out individual children for special ridicule. The children had to sit in silence while this was going on, with their bowls of soup in front of them. By the time she had finished the soup would be cold; all the children would be in a state of considerable agitation, and several of them might be in tears.

Fräulein Schwarz had her favorites, however, and when she was transferred from one home to the other she persuaded the authorities to allow her to take these eight children with her. These children could do no wrong and they were always assured of praise rather than blame. . . . During the first six months, while they were at Bienenhaus, these children gained more weight than the others in the same home, and from the day they went to Vogelnest and got the additional food they started to put on weight very rapidly, so that in the next six months they gained more than twice the standard amount [7].

These studies of Spitz and Widdowson indicate how the physical development and maturation of the child can be endangered or severely compromised when its love relationship with a parent or a parent substitute is defective or deficient. Nor is childhood the only period of life affected by these experiences. After reviewing the research on the subject of maternal deprivation (i.e., motherlessness) for the World Health Organization, John Bowlby came to the conclusion that the lack of a real or substitute parent during infancy and early childhood constituted a severe handicap to the normal social and emotional development of most individuals in later childhood and adult life. He found that children who had suffered such experiences were more likely to become neurotic, psychotic, or delinquent as adults, and he makes the point that "mother-love in infancy and childhood is as important for mental health as are vitamins and proteins [8]."

We have given this stress to the need for love for a number of reasons. In the first place, although most of us are likely to be aware of the physiological needs and the need for safety, we are less conscious or aware of the need for love. Secondly, because we are less aware of the need for love, we tend to overlook its importance. Thirdly, teachers are continually having to work with children whose problem behavior is related to at least a partial stifling of the need for love. And, fourthly, accepting the existence of a need for love may help us to recognize and to accept the other needs (self-esteem, self-actualization) which are likewise of a less tangible nature.

HIGHER LEVEL NEEDS

The need for self-esteem is largely centered around the group—the family at first, then the other children and adults with whom the child is acquainted. It is through his relations with others that the child learns to earn the respect and appreciation of others. Each stage in his development provides new opportunities to meet this need, and, at the same time, poses new problems. The child entering school, for example, is largely "on his own" when it comes to winning the respect of his peers and acceptance by his teacher. This is a severe trial for some children who hitherto have had little need to *win* the good will of others because good will had been given to them by their family as a matter of course. Similarly, as the child progresses in school, his social relationships become more complex. To win acceptance in the classroom does not automatically win acceptance on the playing field or within the scout troop. To be popular with the girls and boys of one set may make one unpopular with another set. Nor is self-esteem something which can be won once and for all, for it ebbs and flows, depending upon the circumstances, situations, and the effectiveness of social skills.

Self-actualization is more than a basic need—it is also a limitless goal. It is possible for one to say, at times: "I am—for the moment—adequately meeting my needs for biological functioning, safety, love, and self-esteem. I am doing as much as can be done." But one can never say: "I have reached the limit of self-fulfillment." This is a goal which is never really attained. Even when one reaches the limits of one's talents in one field, there are always new and unattained reaches of talent and experience.

PROBLEMS POSED BY THE NEED FOR SELF-ACTUALIZATION

Children and adolescents present special problems with regard to the need for self-actualization because it is difficult to determine what are adequate standards. Should teachers expect ten-year-olds to do independent research in the library? Well, some can and some cannot. Some can do it alone, but not in the company of other children. Some can do it with a minimum of supervision. It is difficult for adults to understand all that is involved here because adults do not have the same kinds of problems in looking up things in the library, particularly when they are already familiar with the subject and are acquainted with library procedure. Our competencies as adults seem constantly to get in the way of our evaluation of the competencies of children. Children feel this much more than we do. They are keenly aware of the gulf which separates them from adults. Sometimes they take their cue from adults who are sarcastic and critical and decide that there is no use trying. They think: "Maybe it takes an adult to find something in the library." Sometimes they react with suspicion to the attempts of adults to encourage them. At such times they might say or feel: "Other fourth-graders don't look up things in the library on their own. Maybe she's telling us to do it just because that's her job. If we try and fail, the other kids will make fun of us. Maybe she *wants* us to look silly."

Ideally, of course, we really want children to live up to standards that are appropriate to their level of development. But we are all somewhat impatient, adults and children alike, to see evidence of progress in learning. The fact is, learning is a process of growth; it proceeds slowly and not at all evenly. As a result, we are often irritated by the seeming unwillingness of children to learn, and they, in turn, are depressed by their inability to live up to our expectations. This situation is a little better than it used to be. We now have a better idea of what we can reasonably expect of children at various ages and we have made some changes in the elementary school curriculum as a result. But these changes are not universal, nor have we as adults uniformly altered our beliefs of what we should expect of children. And, furthermore, the problem of the child whose performance lags far behind the average of the group is still largely unsolved.

THE PRIMACY OF BASIC NEEDS

Returning to the consideration of basic needs, it is worth noting that Maslow feels that it is difficult for individuals to meet needs adequately at the end of the list—needs for self-esteem and self-actualization, for example—if needs at the head of the list are unmet. This is why the child who is undernourished is a poor learner. It is too much to expect that a child should show any real improvement in arithmetic when his concern is principally with food. Similarly, it is too much to expect a child to make much progress in school when his family is in the throes of being split by divorce. He is understandably much more concerned about whether he will still have a mother or father who will love him than he is about learning to read and spell.

On the positive side, the concept of basic needs is potentially a reassuring one to the adult who has to deal, as the teacher does, with human relations and social processes. It is helpful to know, for example, that children basically *want* to learn to express themselves and to develop talents and skills which will make them more adequate as persons. Indeed, the need for self-actualization forms the basis of much of the more permanent learning which results from school experiences.

ANXIETY

ORIGINS OF ANXIETY

Many workers in the field of human relations believe that anxiety appears very early in life. Harry Stack Sullivan describes the infant as experiencing anxiety when it senses that its mother is unhappy, angry, or frightened, and he points out that when babies are fed by mothers who are under some unpleasant emotional tension, feeding problems usually result [9].

Children—even babies and infants—are undoubtedly more alert to the emotional states of their parents than we commonly believe. Whether they pick up this information from the changed tone of voice which parents use, or whether mothers who are tense hold nursing babies more rigidly and awkwardly, or whether parents handle them more roughly, it is hard to say. But the fact is that they do sense disturbances and tensions and are affected accordingly.

The needs for security and love are intimately associated

with the welfare and comfort of the child. If he feels that he is in danger of losing love or if he is discomforted by being held or handled awkwardly, it is quite understandable that he should be upset. It is natural that this should occur even though the emotional tension experienced by his parents is not directed at him. Children (and even adults, to a large extent) relate whatever goes on about them to themselves. The logic of this might read somewhat as follows: "Mother is irritated. She is obviously irritated at me because she is behaving differently toward me." Furthermore, this reaction is very likely accompanied by a feeling of helplessness and terror. The logic of this feeling might read: "Mother doesn't like me, where can I turn for love? There is no place I *can* turn. I am really lost." Thus what may be a burst of indignation or irritation directed by the parent at some person or object outside the home is magnified by the child and distorted into a rejection. Fortunately babies and small children do not brood over these matters, and when the home atmosphere becomes friendly and relaxed again, their moods change accordingly.

THE NATURE OF ANXIETY

As children grow older and can talk and get about, they begin to differentiate between the negative emotions—irritation, rejection, disapproval, and so forth—which are directed at them, personally, and those which are directed at others. They are still made uncomfortable by any kind of dissension (most of us never completely lose this feeling), but their anxieties are raised most sharply when they are the targets.

Now it would be highly inaccurate to say that all children are upset to the same extent by criticism and disapproval. The important consideration is: How does the child *feel* about the criticism? If a child perceives criticism as a potential danger to his feeling of being secure and being loved and accepted, he will experience anxiety; otherwise, he will not. In many families, particularly in slum areas, harsh words and invective are part of everyday talk and they have nothing to do with whether a child is loved or not. Very often, indeed, they are the expression of warm affection. Children in other situations are extremely sensitive, and interpret even innocent and casual comment as a form of rejection. In other words, if a child sees himself as being rejected, he will experience anxiety.

This in itself might not be of much importance to teachers, if it were not that anxiety is one of the most painful of all emotions. It is so painful that we will go to great lengths and do all sorts of apparently illogical things in order to avoid experiencing it. The threat of anxiety raises the possibility of being cut off from others, and the sharpness of its pain is a cue to how important others are to us. Anxiety is painful because others are so important to us. We cannot live without others—not so much because we are dependent on them for food, shelter, and clothing, but because we are dependent on them for love, for self-esteem and status—for our very selves. Without others, we are nothing, and, as Rollo May says, anxiety is to a large extent the fear of being nothing [10].

ANXIETY AND INTERPERSONAL RELATIONS

Anxiety is an emotion that has its roots in a disturbance in the relationship between the individual and others. This is true even in situations where no one is apparently involved other than the individual himself. For example, a three-year-old child may reach out his hand to pick up an ash tray—a forbidden object—and then may suddenly stop and look puzzled, confused, and anxious. There is no other person in the room, hence the question arises: How can this anxiety be considered a function of interpersonal relations?

What has happened here is that the child's behavior is in conflict with his self-ideal, and his self-ideal represents the standards and judgments of his parents. His relationship to his self-ideal resembles his relationship to his parents. Since he would be anxious if his parents expressed disapproval, he is made anxious by the disapproval "voiced" by his self-ideal. Very often, when we are faced by marked differences between our self-concepts (what we *are* doing) and our self-ideal (what we *ought* to be doing), we punish ourselves as a way of avoiding or getting rid of the feeling of anxiety. The child who handles the ash tray may do this in a direct manner, by slapping his own hand or scolding himself. The self-torture of guilt is another way of reacting to this situation. Often the feeling of guilt is not by itself enough to rid us of anxiety, and we are forced to take further measures—blaming others for our predicament, asking for forgiveness, or expressing hostility toward others for making us feel anxious and guilty.

Teachers should be aware that reminding students of the difference between their self-concepts and their self-ideals produces anxiety. Sometimes children need this kind of reminder to aid them in developing or establishing desirable behavior. But this device, like other devices and techniques, can be overworked. If it is used too often, children may become used to it, or the teacher may create a state of chronic anxiety in his group that will lead to increasing difficulties.

THE RELATIONSHIP BETWEEN ANXIETY AND HOSTILITY

It should be clear, then, that any behavior that runs counter to the standards of society, and particularly the accepted standards of the group, will arouse some anxiety. The expression of hostility is a good case in point. Our middle-class culture does not approve, generally, of the free and open expression of hostility regardless of whether this expression be through physical or verbal attack. There are some exceptions and special conditions, of course, but this is the general attitude of our society, particularly as it applies to children. On the other hand, the feeling of hostility is a perfectly normal emotion. It is a natural consequence of being thwarted or frustrated or threatened. In this respect, we are somewhat unrealistic if we expect children never to fight, swear, steal, or hurt each other's feelings. Part of our job as teachers is, of course, to teach them how to express feelings of hostility in other ways, how to "work them out," and how to avoid getting into situations where hostilities will be aroused. If we can do this easily, pleasantly, and firmly, well and good. But the difficulty is that we ourselves are so anxious about our own hostilities (or hostility in general) that we stigmatize as wicked and unpardonable *any* feeling of expression of hostility. As a result, there is a general tendency to make children feel guilty even about *having* hostile feelings, let alone *expressing* such feelings through hostile words or deeds. Some children come to feel so guilty and anxious about their own hostilities that they will not even speak up in their own defense when unjustly or mistakenly accused by a teacher or a fellow student. For them, it is easier to bear censure and punishment for a crime they did not commit than it is to bear the anxiety resulting from standing up for their rights.

ANXIETY AND INSECURITY

Another source of anxiety, one that is indirectly related to relations with others, may be found in experiences that involve frequent change in the lives of children. Children are innately conservative. They tend to "like things the way they are." This holds true even when "the way things are" is not good. For example, a boy may lead a miserable and unhappy existence with a drunken father and immoral and irresponsible mother. An obvious solution to his difficulty is to take him out of such unhealthy surroundings and place him in a foster home. Yet persons who work with children who live under such circumstances are often struck by the tenacity with which children will cling to such inadequate parents. There are usually a variety of factors involved in such situations, of course, but one of them is the desire to hold on to what security and stability and scraps of love one has. The child, in such circumstances, prefers the miserableness of his present existence to the unknown factors of a new and untried experience. Not all children are made anxious by change, of course. Many of the children of migratory workers, for example, appear to show no evidence of anxiety at being constantly on the move. But the child who has come to *expect* some stability and security to his life is upset and anxious and insecure when he is faced by a new and (to him) threatening situation. Most of the children we work with in schools *do* have such expectations, and, consequently, we can expect them to develop symptoms of anxiety and insecurity during times of change—on entering school, when the family is moving to a new house, when there is a new brother or sister, when the family is in the process of breaking up, and so forth.

It is not always easy to see how the anxiety touched off by a major change in a child's life has its roots, as we have said, in the relationship between a child and others. For example, in what way does moving to a new home constitute disturbance in interpersonal relations?

As we study the child's experiences at such a time, we are struck by the fact that the family is preoccupied and concerned with the details and problems arising from the move. They are momentarily unable to give the child the love, personal care, and attention that he is used to receiving. Perhaps he is old enough to understand why this must be. If so, he is less likely to blame the family for ignoring him, but this understanding does not necessarily make him feel better. Whenever a family moves, the interpersonal relations shift and change. They are never quite the same in the new home as they were in the old one. Maybe they are better, but they are not the way they were. Perhaps it takes father longer to get to work, so that he must leave home earlier in the morning and return later in the afternoon. The room arrangements are different; everyone sounds and looks different in the new setting. Even the child himself feels different, and this is vaguely disturbing. But what is probably the most vital factor is the idea that one's world can change and that one can do nothing about it. Perhaps the child thinks, in effect: "Maybe nothing is permanent that I used to think was permanent. I used to think my mother and father were permanent, that they would always be here and always love me. If I can lose the old house that I loved, maybe I will lose my parents that I love."

If this line of thought seems strange or illogical, let us not forget that for many children, particularly young children, *change* means *loss*. They are not concerned so much about the new situation they are entering as they are about losing the old situation. And their fear is that if they lose this part of their world, they may lose all of it. Most children increase their ability to master such irrational fears as they grow older. In fact, the ability to keep irrational fears in check is a measure of emotional maturity, a measure that holds good whether we are talking about children or about adults.

ANXIETY AND THE PERCEPTION OF REALITY

One of the qualities of the emotion we call anxiety is its tendency or ability to blind us to the realities of life on occasion. This is likely to happen whenever admitting or accepting a certain fact would damage our self-concept or would make us aware of a large gap between our self-concept and our self-ideal or would show that some significant person (a parent, a teacher, or a friend) disapproves of us or rejects us. An example of the latter situation is the brief anecdote recounted by Helen Trager:

Halfway through one of her yarns, Dorothy said, "My mother picks up our baby and she says all the time, 'You're the best one of my children. You're the best baby in the world.'" Then Dorothy added as an aside, and without self-consciousness, completely forgetting her role as a story-teller, "I guess she's only kidding [11]."

Another quality that anxiety possesses in common with other emotions is its ability or tendency to be transmitted easily and quickly from one person to another. Thus, the anxieties of the teacher tend to arouse anxieties in the students, and this often happens even when the teacher has gone to great effort to keep his anxieties out of sight.

NORMAL ANXIETY

Psychologists and other mental-health workers usually think of anxiety in terms of something that is to be avoided or reduced, and much psychological literature is concerned with this approach. However, because psychologists are usually concerned professionally with the problems of people who are the victims of too much anxiety, or *neurotic* anxiety, it is understandable why this viewpoint is so prevalent. Nevertheless, if we carry the idea of eliminating anxiety to its logical conclusion, we would find ourselves saying that no one should ever be rejected or censured, no matter what he did.

Actually, anxiety is like fire—it is both useful and dangerous, depending on the amount, the form of expression, and the way in which it is controlled. The positive or "useful" form of anxiety we shall term "normal anxiety," to distinguish it from the anxiety that cripples and distorts, which we shall call "neurotic anxiety."

In the previous chapter, we discussed the controls that small children develop in the third year of life as a result of the disapproval expressed by their parents at certain kinds of behavior. These controls, which become the core of the self-ideal, are reinforced by anxiety and are a very necessary and important mechanism in the child's personality. When he violates or runs counter to these controls, he becomes anxious and guilty. Thus, observing the standards that have been set for him enables him to avoid the experience of anxiety. At first the child refrains from doing those things which will call forth his parents' disapproval. Later, as he becomes motivated by a need to show others his love or friendship, his normal anxiety helps him to be sensitive to their needs and wants.

The child who grows up without normal anxiety, or with anxiety at abnormally low levels, is one who is unconcerned about the rights and feelings of others, who is either unaware or unconcerned about the consequences of his actions. Such a child grows into the adult who exploits others without shame, embarrassment, or guilt. Such persons are the psychopathic personalities who frequently end up in prison.

Children without anxiety, although not unusual, constitute only a small percentage of the school population. Children who misbehave or are delinquent are more likely motivated by an *excess* of anxiety rather than by its absence, although their behavior frequently resembles that of the child who lacks sufficient anxiety.

Although anxiety can be very painful, it is a necessary factor in the development of a healthy personality. Because of the proddings of normal anxiety, we learn to anticipate the consequences of our behavior, to be concerned about the future and about the potentialities of the situations in which we find ourselves. Because of our normal anxiety, we are interested in understanding our social environment; hence, it prompts much of the learning that occurs in school and elsewhere.

BEHAVIOR PROBLEMS AND ANXIETY

Although normal anxiety is usually on the side of law and order, altruism, and positive learning, teachers will find that a student's normal anxiety is no guarantee that he will do what the school expects of him. One of the problems involved here is the student's concern for the opinions of other students. This problem arises when students' values are markedly different from teachers' values. Many groups of boys, particularly in junior high school and high school, are inclined to ridicule the student who gets good grades. The individual student is thus caught in a cross-fire—no matter what he does he will incur disapproval. His concern for the good opinion of his teachers and parents makes him want to cooperate with the school, whereas his concern for the good opinion of his agemates leads him to reject the idea of cooperation. Most students resolve this problem by accepting one standard or the other, deciding that it is better to suffer the criticisms of the teachers or one's schoolmates, as the case may be. Others are less able to make a definite decision as to which way to turn and, consequently, are greatly troubled by this problem. Usually, these are the students who are, psychologically speaking, more vulnerable, who are more troubled by anxiety than others, and who are more inclined to interpret the everyday events of life as disapproval or rejection. As a result, these individuals are plagued with a superabundance of anxiety—neurotic anxiety.

NEUROTIC ANXIETY

Virtually all persons, adults and children alike, are troubled to a greater or lesser degree by neurotic anxiety. When anxiety, or, for that matter, fear of anxiety, rises to the point where we can no longer be objective and completely rational, where we do things which are not in our own best interests, and where our tensions are so strong that they may even affect our health, we are victims of neurotic anxiety. Perhaps an example will help to demonstrate the effects of this troublesome emotion.

Elvira was in most respects a normal fifth-grader. She did average work for her grade, was the middle child in a family of three, and was fairly well liked by the other children in her class. However, after Elvira had been in the grade a few months her appearance began to change. She was the first of the fifth grade girls to enter the puberty cycle. As is usually the case with children who are becoming adolescents, her interests began to change. She became more interested in boys and began to be seen at the soda fountain with some of the members of the eighth-grade basketball team. At the same time she tried to maintain relations with her fifth-grade friends on the same basis as before. Soon it was apparent that a slight feeling of resentment was coloring her relationship with her classmates. Some of them started saying that Elvira was "getting high hat." Hence, it was no surprise that Elvira was not invited to Emily's birthday party. Emily and Elvira were not close friends, but Elvira had been invited during the last two years and had invited Emily in return.

As the date of the birthday party drew closer, it became apparent to Elvira that she was not going to be invited. She became depressed and withdrew from all classroom activities. At home she moped about the house, picked at her food without interest, and had difficulty in getting to sleep. Matters finally came to a head when she refused to serve on a social studies committee. She had always liked committee work before this. At this point, Miss Bates, the teacher, realized that Elvira was deeply disturbed about something and asked Elvira to see her after school. She saw Elvira several times during the following week for brief periods and finally had a talk with some of the more popular girls. Elvira never regained her former status in the group, but somehow everyone felt better after Miss Bates had talked to them.

The behavior displayed by Elvira when she was rejected by her classmates is, of course, motivated and conditioned by anxiety. It was neither rational nor reasonable for her to behave as she did, yet who could seriously condemn her? None of us is likely to behave reasonably when we are disturbed, and few things are more disturbing than to be rejected by our friends.

Another situation which commonly produces much neurotic anxiety is speaking before a group. There appears to be little relationship between the amount of anxiety, or "stage fright," and the existence of any real danger in the situation. The victim of stage fright cannot express himself as easily and as simply as he can to one or two intimate friends, he says things that he does not mean, he forgets important points, and so forth. As in the case of Elvira, his actions cannot be considered to be in keeping with his best interests.

Although neurotic anxiety is commonly produced by a fear of not being accepted by others, it does not, ironically enough, help us to establish better relations. If anything, it works to our disadvantage—it worsens rather than improves our relations. This occurs largely because we are so concerned with our anxiety and with avoiding or reducing the acute psychological tension it produces that we are unable to act quite rationally. The obvious remedy for the feeling of rejection is to become accepted, but it is difficult or even impossible to defend ourselves against others and get them to accept us all at the same time. The two maneuvers are mutually incompatible. Thus the child who is desperately unhappy because the other members of the class do not like him is by very reason of his unhappiness and desperation unable to establish the relationships which would lead to acceptance. The person who is troubled by anxiety often seems bound to sabotage his own efforts through awkwardness or overeagerness. Because he is unable to establish good relations with the group, he feels insecure. The more insecure he feels, the more others appear to reject him; the more others reject him, the greater his insecurity. And so it goes. As the symptom grows, it feeds the very condition that aggravates it.

BEHAVIOR MECHANISMS

One of the reasons why we are not more conscious of the situations and occurrences of our everyday life which are potential producers of anxiety is that we have developed techniques of ignoring or misinterpreting them and thus avoiding the anxiety we would experience if we saw them in their true proportions. Furthermore, when our anxiety *is* aroused we continue using the same techniques so that we shall not feel its full force.

Psychologists have coined or appropriated a long list of terms they use to designate these "avoidance" techniques or methods, called "behavior mechanisms" or "mental mechanisms" or "mechanisms of defense and escape." We shall list and describe a few of them here.

It is important to note that these methods of dealing with anxiety operate unconsciously, or almost entirely so. In other words, when we employ a behavior mechanism, we are not only unaware of the anxiety we are avoiding or disguising, but we are even unaware that we are using a device to avoid it or to disguise it. For example, some persons overeat when they are troubled by anxiety. Often, they are not even conscious of eating more than usual. Even when they are conscious of doing so, they are unaware that it has the psychological purpose of avoiding or disguising anxiety. This quality of unawareness or unconscious motivation is characteristic of most of our experiences with anxiety. This is one of the chief reasons why it is so difficult to change a child's behavior pattern. He is not only unaware why he behaves the way he does, but also he resists any attempts at change, even when the attempts are instituted by himself. Adults experience much the same phenomena when they try to stop smoking.

It should be clear, therefore, that there is nothing unusual or abnormal about the use of behavior mechanisms—we all use them, adults and children alike. As Clara Thompson says,

> . . . Probably no one exists who is so healthy that he can make all the compromises necessary for survival without occasionally resorting to mechanisms of escape, or at least temporary denials of reality [12].

Rationalization. The practice of giving explanations for behavior which is quite reasonable, but which does not re-

veal the more basic and fundamental reasons for the behavior is called rationalization. A student does not show up
for a scheduled appointment with a teacher. When asked
about it later, he apologizes and says that his watch stopped.
His watch *may* have stopped, and he *may* sincerely believe
that this is the reason for the missed appointment, but a
more basic reason may be that he was engaged in an exciting game of baseball and to have walked out of the game
to keep an appointment with a teacher might have incurred
the scorn of his companions. Perhaps an even more basic
reason is that he values his association with his peers more
than his responsibilities to adults. If this is the case, it should
not surprise us because such feelings are very common
among adolescents and preadolescents. It is important to remember, however, that the student is unaware of the existence of the more basic reasons and sincerely believes that
his stopped watch is responsible for the broken appointment.
As long as he can believe so, he is protected from the anxiety
which would result if he admitted to himself that he was
somewhat lacking in dependability when it came to appointments with teachers. He views himself as a responsible person, and it would be inconsistent with this self-concept for
him to admit to himself that he is irresponsible in some ways.
Such an admission would arouse anxiety, which he avoids
(unconsciously, of course) through his "reasonable" explanation.

Repression. The process of unconscious forgetting, termed
repression, figures very largely in most manifestations of
neurotic anxiety. The student who accuses others of poor
sportsmanship is repressing the memories of the occasions
when he acted in an unsportsmanlike manner, whereas the
above-mentioned student who broke the appointment not
only repressed his memory of the appointment, but also the
more basic emotional reasons for breaking the appointment.
Essentially, repression occurs because we are attempting to
avoid experiencing the anxiety which might result if we re-

membered. Psychologists make a sharp distinction between repression and suppression. We have no conscious control over the process of repression. Suppression, on the other hand, consists of the process of consciously putting something out of one's mind. It is repression that causes us the most trouble.

Conformity. Conformity, particularly *neurotic* conformity or *over*conformity, is another common means of reducing or avoiding anxiety. The overconforming person represses all thoughts, attitudes, or ideas which may be considered in the least bit individualistic or in any way different from those of the group he is with because he is afraid that any deviation may earn for him the rejection of the group. Some persons adopt overconformity as a way of life, never daring to have an original thought. Indeed many groups of children, as well as of adults and adolescents, exact overconformity as a price for membership. For example, many preadolescent boys who might be friendly with girls are afraid of doing or saying anything which would reveal their true feelings, because to do so would arouse the scorn of their contemporaries, who cordially hate girls. Similarly, sorority girls on some campuses are subjected to severe censure if they date men who are not members of recognized fraternities. The more tyrannical the group, the greater the pressure for complete conformity.

Daydreaming or *Fantasying.* When one escapes from the anxieties of everyday life into the realm of unreality, he is daydreaming or fantasying. Sometimes daydreaming may have a constructive aim, as for example when an individual lays plans for future action which are both feasible and practical. During the preschool years much of the play and conversation of children is colored by fantasy. Often they have no clear idea of where their fantasy leaves off and reality begins.

On one occasion a child of nursery-school age and I were leafing through a magazine when we came upon an advertise-

ment for a fire insurance company which depicted a family
discovering a fire burning in their living room. We happened
to be in the kitchen at the moment, so she insisted that we investigate to see if a fire were burning in *our* living room. When
we looked and found that there was not, she seemed reassured,
but a few minutes later she asked me if the fire were still burning. Knowing that she meant the fire in the advertisement, I
told her that the people had undoubtedly called the fire department, who then put it out. "No," she said, "the fire's still
burning." And she showed me the picture of the burning living
room to prove her point. Because of her relative inability to
distinguish fact and fiction, the picture of a fire awakened in
her some of the anxiety and fear that would have resulted from
an actual fire.

The anxieties of adults and children alike are easily
aroused by situations and events that have no well-defined
and clear-cut meaning. Adults deal with this anxiety in various ways: they may investigate the puzzling situation and
find out its meaning; they may ask other adults what it
means; they may decide that it is similar to other situations
with which they are already familiar; or they may decide
that the situation is not important, that it does not concern
them personally. In the latter case they may not notice it at
all and thus avoid experiencing the anxiety that would result from puzzling over an ambiguous situation. Children,
on the other hand, do not have the skills for investigation or
the sources of information possessed by adults and they
have not yet learned how to be selective in their perceptions
—that is, they have not learned how to ignore or simply not
to notice situations that do not affect them personally. On
the other hand, they do not perceive other situations that are
vital to their welfare and happiness, situations that they
ought to perceive. Let us say that they do not know enough
to be anxious about the "right" things and are anxious about
the "wrong" things. (We use the words "right" and "wrong"
advisedly, because "rightness" and "wrongness" in this sense
are determined by adult society, and there is much evidence

that adults, too, are very often anxious about the "wrong" things and not anxious enough about the "right" ones. Much of the task of education lies in helping people to become anxious about the things that ought to concern them and allaying anxieties about things that are irrelevant and unimportant.)

Fantasy is an essential part of a young child's life. It is his way of coping with his fears and anxieties, expressing his hopes and wishes, and participating in the world as he sees it. As he moves into middle childhood, his everyday behavior becomes less and less colored by fantasy, and the fantasy that remains becomes less individualistic, more stereotyped, and more in keeping with the norms and standards of the group. For example, a four-year-old might wriggle around the nursery school floor day after day, pretending he is a boa constrictor, while the rest of the children play out individual and unrelated fantasies. But a ten-year-old who attempted such behavior would call for the scorn and ridicule of the group. He would not be permitted the free and open expression of an individually conceived fantasy, unless it happened to fit in with the play of the group. In other words, he might be allowed to act the part of a boa constrictor if the group were pretending that they were explorers in the jungles of the Amazon, but if they were pirates or cowboys and Indians, the boa constrictor role would not be appropriate.

Thus the trend in childhood is for older children not to give their fantasies public utterance but to indulge in them through daydreams. Virtually all school children do some daydreaming and fantasying, but it gets out of control in an occasional child, like Jeannette, whose case is described by Charlotte Buhler:

> Jeannette was six and in first grade. She was considered bright because she talked well. Her parents were proud of her unusual vocabulary which she acquired very early. She would tell weird stories about flowers, animals, and creatures with

strange names to whoever would listen. Yet at the same time she never talked to a person, nor did she do anything with another person. The children called her crazy long before the grownups became aware of the pathology of her inner life. Gradually she became so out of step with everything that happened around her that she could not remain in school [13].

One of the things that makes Jeannette so peculiar and marks her as a mentally ill child is her inability to have normal relations with other children. This fact, coupled with her weird fantasies, indicates a child who needs psychotherapy.

Projection. Another type of mechanism that involves some measure of irreality is projection. It appears in situations where individuals ascribe their own motives or feelings to the acts or statements of others.

Randall is a boy who is chronically quarrelsome. He explains his difficulties by saying everyone is against him or that the other fellow always starts the fight. (Actually, there is likely to be a certain amount of truth in what he says because once a child has established a reputation for being quarrelsome and pugnacious, other children *are* likely to be against him. The more quarrelsome he is, the more other children are against him, and the more they are against him, the more quarrelsome he becomes). Randall "projects" his anxieties in an attempt to handle them by attaching them to some person or group, the general idea being that he can handle people he can see and talk to easier than he can an anxiety that is much less tangible.

One of the qualities of anxiety is that the anxious individual does not know the real source of his anxiety. Since the roots of Randall's anxiety are hidden from view, buried, more than likely, in the earliest experiences of his childhood and infancy, he has no way of getting at its source. All he knows is that he feels uncomfortable, uneasy, and "threatened." It is only natural, when one feels threatened, to look about one to discover the source of threat, rather than to

look into one's own behavior and experience. Thus Randall
feels uneasy and insecure because "someone has it in for
him." By blaming others and by fighting them, on occasion,
he feels that he knows what is bothering him and that he is
doing something about it. As we indicated above, we feel
uncomfortable whenever we are faced by an ambiguous
situation, particularly when it is an experience that arouses
our anxiety. Therefore, Randall actually "feels better" about
projecting his anxiety because to him it "makes sense." The
fact that his methods are both unrealistic and antisocial
means that they will eventually make more trouble for him
than if he had faced his problems more directly. He does not
know how to face his problems, but he *does* know how to
blame others and to fight.

What will happen to Randall depends on many factors—
his experiences with parents, teachers, siblings, and playmates; his personality; and the combination of events that
will occur in his life. He may discover that his rejection by
other children arouses more anxiety than he avoids through
projection, and this discovery may lead him to re-examine
his motives and approach to life. He will probably never discover the original source of his anxieties, for it is buried too
deep beyond the reach of his awareness. With the aid of
sympathetic teachers and age-mates, he may grasp enough
of the essential meaning of his current attitudes to serve as
the basis for reformed behavior. Or he may be so deeply involved in his neurotic anxiety that the sympathetic help of
a counselor or a psychotherapist may be needed.

Projection also occurs when individuals misinterpret or
distort their perceptions of persons, situations, or events.
Randall does this when he interprets an innocent chance remark as an attempt to start an argument. Or, a teacher who
is overly eager to be accepted and liked by all the children
in her class may accept at face value an overtly flattering remark made by a student and, by the same token, inadvert-
ently overlook or ignore occurrences that should clearly in-

dicate that some of the students do not like her. Naturally, we do not consciously distort, misinterpret, or ignore what goes on around us—we do it unconsciously and automatically, as a way of avoiding or reducing the anxiety that would be aroused if we saw things as they are.

The findings of A. L. Edwards are typical of the results obtained in many studies of projection and unconscious distortion of environmental factors. Edwards found that a neutral speech on a controversial political topic was interpreted as favorable by persons already in favor of the issue discussed and as unfavorable by those who had previously indicated they were opposed to the proposal [14].

Regression. Another mechanism frequently employed as a means of coping with anxiety is regression—recourse to behavior patterns that are more typical of earlier levels of maturity. For example, an adolescent who is usually able to make his own decisions and act for himself may, under stress of anxiety, be no more able to think through a problem and take proper action than, say, an eight-year-old. At such times he may become more dependent and seek help and direction. Regression is commonly associated with other mechanisms. Most attempts to deal with neurotic anxiety usually involve immature behavior of some sort. This is what we mean when we say that a grownup who sulks and is petulant is "acting like a child"—his behavior is not mature, according to adult standards. We all regress at times; it is difficult to act in a mature and adult manner when everything seems to be going wrong or when we are under severe emotional stress. Children, too, do not always act in accordance with the behavior patterns appropriate to their level of development.

James L. Hymes feels that children regress because they were deprived of certain needs at earlier stages of development:

> Children have purposes. Children need things out of life at
> every age level. If they do not get them, they come to want

them deeply and badly. The children get older but—reasonable or not, right or not, nice or not—they continue to strive for what they once needed and did not get. They *must* have the satisfactions all humans need in order to be free to grow [15].

According to this theory, a ten-year-old child who regresses say, by thumb-sucking, does so because his need for sucking was frustrated when he was an infant, perhaps through too early weaning. Research findings are inconclusive with regard to the association of thumb-sucking with early weaning. Perhaps a more defensible hypothesis would state that individuals under stress of anxiety are likely to fall back on forms of behavior (such as sucking) that gave them satisfaction at earlier stages in their lives.

Overcompensation. Overcompensation is a device we use to bolster up our feelings of adequacy as a way of avoiding the anxiety that would be incurred in facing or admitting some real or fancied weakness. A common example is that of the student who does not do well in the classroom and who devotes as much of his time and energy as possible to athletics. He may rationalize his behavior by saying that fellows who are interested in schoolwork are "sissies." His counterpart is, of course, the student who does not do well at athletics or is afraid of the rough and tumble of body contact sports and who instead works extra hard at his studies. Both are equally unaware of the fact that they are trying to hide from themselves some real or fancied weakness or shortcoming.

A special form of overcompensation which is of interest to teachers is called *reaction formation.* Children (and adults) who employ this maneuver, develop actions or attitudes which are at opposite extremes from impulses which they fear and which would produce much anxiety if expressed. We can see the operation of reaction formation in the behavior of student councils who sometimes are assigned the job of meting out punishment to those who break the rules of the school. Often such councils are far more punitive and severe than adults would be. They are, in effect, bolstering their own feelings of righteousness, and at the same time denying any antisocial tendencies which they might have. They are unconsciously using the severity of their punishment to frighten themselves into continued good behavior and at the same time reassuring themselves of their correctness.

Another example of reaction formation is the adolescent who takes grave chances with his own life—by reckless driving, for example. Often this is an attempt to assure himself that he has no fear. His logic would go somewhat like this: "I wonder whether I am really a coward. But if I take chances like this, I certainly cannot be considered a coward." That he must take these chances again and again is witness to the fact that his method of treating this form of anxiety is unsuccessful and essentially irrational.

Indeed, it is characteristic of most of our attempts to reduce neurotic anxiety that they are chronically unsuccessful. The price exacted by neurotic anxiety is a sort of emotional blackmail because the victim must pay it again and again. There is no escape, until the anxiety itself has been faced squarely and eliminated. And this is something the individual must do for himself; no one can do it for him. It may be crystal clear to all of Sally's teachers that she is entirely too dependent, that she needs to make some decisions for herself. Yet Sally will continue to seek advice and reassurance until she herself can face the fact that she is old enough and competent enough to make some decisions for herself. It does not help to tell her that she is too dependent because this upsets her and hurts her feelings. She does not see herself this way, for in her eyes she is just a poor, lonely girl, who needs a great deal of sympathy and understanding. After all, if others had been through what she had been through. . . .

Maybe Sally will go through life being overdependent. Maybe she will meet some teacher or counselor who is will-

ing and able to help her talk out her involved personal problem. Maybe she will "snap out of it," as many do when they
leave the more or less sheltered environment of high school
and find that they must wrestle unaided with the more tangible problems of life.

LEARNING: ITS RELATIONSHIP TO BASIC
NEEDS AND TO ANXIETY

ONE way of summarizing the rather complex concepts
which have been presented in this chapter is to relate them
to the problem of learning.

What we have tried to say in this chapter is that the feelings, thoughts, and actions of people stem from two main
sources: basic needs and anxiety. It is not always possible to
separate these two sources of motivation, nor is it always
desirable. Yet the differences are important enough to warrant our attention and consideration.

Learning is a normal process of human growth. In order
for us to meet our basic needs we must learn about ourselves
and our physical and social environment. Thus children
come to school with a great deal of natural motivation to
learn, motivation which stems from the very process of living, growing, and developing. Perhaps the more pleasurable
forms of learning fall into this category—the enjoyment at
developing a new skill, at creating something useful or
beautiful, and at discovering a new world.

But there is also the learning which is prompted by normal anxiety. This kind of learning, which is related to developing concern for the rights of others, to planning for the
future, and to understanding the consequences of one's own
acts, is equally important, if children are to live in peace and
comfort in a world inhabited by others, but it is not likely
to be as enjoyable as the first kind of learning. After all, what
we are asking children to do is to *give up something*—to give
up doing things *their* way, to give up the idea of *always* be-

ing first, to give up the lion's share for an equal share. Giving is easier for adults than it is for children. Some of us even enjoy giving, now and then, particularly if we are teachers or parents and have something to give which is valuable and which is needed by those who need what we have to give. But giving is hard for children. Giving is at the heart of the socialization process. Socialization can be taught as a part of a program which is fun and it can be presented in a way which is less threatening and upsetting than a bald demand that the child yield or give up his way of doing things. Yet, essentially it is painful. Perhaps if we knew this and kept it in mind, we, as adults-in-charge, would be more sympathetic with the struggles of children to resist this aspect of education.

Because schools often try to socialize children too quickly or because some children come emotionally unprepared for any kind of learning, or because classes are so big and teachers are so busy, or because of a variety of other reasons, schools provoke a great deal of neurotic anxiety. Neurotic anxiety results in learning, too. But this kind of learning is not usually beneficial either for the child or for the teacher whose job it is to help him. In order to cope with neurotic anxiety, children develop patterns of behavior and attitudes which are best described by the following phrases:

> Never mind about learning anything. Just do exactly what the teacher says. Avoid saying anything or asking questions, and you'll keep out of trouble.
> The teacher is always against you. Never do what she asks, if you can help it. You can get back at her by stirring up trouble, but the most effective revenge is not to learn anything.
> Don't make friends with other children. They'll hurt you if they get a chance. It's better to stay away from them.
> There's no point in trying. You can never satisfy the teacher or your folks. I just don't have what it takes.

The lives of some children are dominated by thoughts like these, but for most, such feelings wax and wane, depending upon the circumstances. When matters go well, anxieties disappear, only to reappear in the presence of conflicts, tensions, and frustrations. There probably never will be an educational system which will not produce some anxieties, hence part of the learning process should be aimed at helping children to face and to deal with problems and thus avoid or reduce anxiety. Probably we do not do very well with this phase of learning. Although there is some good teaching in this field, most of it occurs in the classes of teachers who have the freedom, the ability, and the time to do something about human relations in their classroom. Only too seldom does this kind of education occur as part of a well-conceived plan of instruction.

REFERENCES

1. H. S. Sullivan, *Conceptions of Modern Psychiatry*. Washington: Wm. Alanson White Psychiatric Foundation. 1947. P. 10.
2. D. Snygg and A. W. Combs, *Individual Behavior*. New York: Harper, 1949. P. 58.
3. A. H. Maslow, "Preface to Motivation Theory," *Psychosomatic Medicine*. 5:85–92;1943.
4. ———, "A Theory of Human Motivation," *Psychological Review*. 50:370–96;1943.   ,
5. R. A. Spitz, "Hospitalism. An Inquiry into the Genesis of Psychiatric Conditions in Early Childhood," *Psychoanalytic Study of the Child*. 1:53–74;1945.
6. ———, "Hospitalism: A Follow-Up Report," *Psychoanalytic Study of the Child*. 2:113–17;1946.
7. E. M. Widdowson, "Mental Contentment and Physical Growth," *The Lancet*. 260:1316–18;1951. Reprinted by permission.
8. J. Bowlby, *Maternal Care and Mental Health*. Geneva: World Health Organization, 1951. P. 158.
9. Sullivan, *op. cit*. P. 7.
10. R. May, *The Meaning of Anxiety*. New York: Ronald, 1950. P. 193.
11. H. Trager, "The Primary Teacher," in *Intercultural Attitudes in the Making;* Ninth Yearbook, John Dewey Society. New York: Harper, 1947. P. 62. Reprinted by permission.

12. C. Thompson, *Psychoanalysis: Evolution and Development*. New York: Hermitage, 1950.
13. C. Buhler, F. Smitter, and S. Richardson, *Childhood Problems and the Teacher*. New York: Holt, 1952. P. 140. Reprinted by permission.
14. A. L. Edwards, "Political Frames of Reference as a Factor Influencing Recognition," *Journal of Abnormal and Social Psychology*. 36:34–50;1941.
15. J. L. Hymes, Jr., *Teacher Listen: The Children Speak*. New York: New York Committee on Mental Health of the State Charities Aid Association, 1949. P. 28.

SUGGESTED READINGS

H. W. Bernard, *Mental Hygiene for Classroom Teachers*. New York: McGraw-Hill, 1952. Chapter 4, "Meeting the Needs of Children."

K. Horney, *The Neurotic Personality of Our Time*. New York: Norton, 1937. Among other things, Horney discusses some of the sources of anxiety in our culture.

W. C. Langer, *Psychology and Human Living*. New York: Appleton-Century-Crofts, 1943. Discusses basic needs, anxiety, mechanisms, and repression from the standpoint of Freudian psychoanalysis, but nevertheless in simple and understandable terms.

H. C. Lindgren, *The Art of Human Relations*. New York: Hermitage, 1953. Chapter 5, "Anxiety: Friend or Foe?"

———, *Psychology of Personal and Social Adjustment*. New York: American Book, 1953. Chapters 3 through 5 deal with unconscious motivation, emotion, anxiety, and behavior mechanisms.

R. May, *The Meaning of Anxiety*. New York: Ronald, 1950. Worthwhile reading for anyone interested in exploring the philosophical and psychological aspects of anxiety.

F. Redl and W. W. Wattenberg, *Mental Hygiene in Teaching*. New York: Harcourt, Brace, 1951. Chapter 5, "Behavior Mechanisms."

L. F. Shaffer, *The Psychology of Adjustment*. Boston: Houghton Mifflin, 1936. Part 2, "Varieties of Adjustive Behavior."

G. E. Swanson, T. M. Newcomb, and E. L. Hartley, eds., *Readings in Social Psychology*, rev. ed. New York: Holt, 1952. Part IA, "Some Forms of Interpersonal Influence."

See also items 2, 8, 12, and 15, in the References.

SUGGESTED FILMS

Meeting Emotional Needs in Childhood: The Groundwork of Democracy. Available through New York University Film Library.

Unconscious Motivation. Available through Association Films and the Psychological Film Register, State College, Penn.

4

EMOTIONAL MATURITY

EMOTIONAL maturity is a relatively new concept in psychology and mental health. It has come into use as an attempt to get away from the unfortunate implications or connotations of such terms as "good adjustment" and "normality." As Fritz Redl and William W. Wattenberg point out, it is possible for a child to be either "well-adjusted" or "normal" and still be someone who needs the special attention of the teacher or even a school psychologist [1]. For example, the child who reacts to the everyday give-and-take of life in a typical school by withdrawing, keeping to himself, and avoiding contact with others has developed a mode of adjustment. He may even find this adjustment satisfying in that he is able to maintain anxiety at a level that is "comfortable" most of the time; yet it is obvious that this is not a healthy kind of existence. And there are other modes of adjustment which are equally unhealthy. Thus we need a term or a concept which fits our criteria of mental health better than "adjustment."

Similarly "normality" covers a number of conditions which do not meet the criteria of mental health. It is "normal" for adolescents to have conflicting feelings and anxieties about

relations with authority and about sexual matters. If we accept "normality" as our standard, then we can dismiss the
troubled adolescent with the statement: "It is normal for
adolescents to have such problems." Yet from the standpoint
of better mental health, these problems should be a matter
for concern because they produce far more than their share
of neurotic anxiety both on the part of adolescents as well as
the adults who have to work with them.

The concept of emotional maturity does not have these
shortcomings, although it does have some disadvantages. In
the first place, it is not a part of our everyday language;
hence, we may have some difficulty in making ourselves
understood if we use it without an explanation. In the second
place, we must remember to use it in reference to stages of
maturity that are appropriate to the age of the children concerned, rather than to some arbitrary standard of maturity
that is more characteristic of what adults expect of children.
In the third place, there is no single standard of maturity.
What is mature behavior for children in one kind of environment is not appropriate for children in another setting. By
way of example, we would expect a five-year-old raised on
a farm to be able to find his way unaided down the lanes and
paths for perhaps several miles around, whereas most five-
year-olds in middle-class residential areas would be lost
more than a block or two away from home.

Part of the job of growing up consists of developing the
feelings, behavior, and controls which are appropriate to
each new stage of development. Infants react to minor frustrations by crying. We consider this behavior normal and
appropriate at this stage of development. But the three-year-
old who reacts to every minor frustration by crying is not
behaving in a way which is emotionally mature for his age.
If the three-year-old eats with his fingers, we are not
alarmed. It is a habit which is very common among children
at this age, and it normally drops out by the time they are
ready for school. But a nine-year-old, growing up with a
middle-class family, who habitually eats from his plate with

his fingers may be considered to be immature in some respects. It would not be considered emotionally immature for a nine-year-old to engage in fist-fights, but an eighteen-year-old who uses this method would be considered to be engaging in behavior inappropriate for his age level, at least by middle-class standards.

EMOTIONAL MATURITY AS A PROCESS OF SOCIALIZATION

GROWTH in emotional maturity may be considered to some degree as stages in socialization. A baby or a small child is concerned with others largely as sources of food, help, attention, and love, for his interests and feelings are self-centered. As he grows older, he begins to realize that what affects others also affects him, and he develops some concern for the welfare of persons who are important to him, particularly members of the same family. His earliest play is self-centered, even when he is with other children, for he engages in what we call "parallel play" rather than "participating play." His first attempts at participating in the play of others are limited to small groups, usually just another child and himself. Later, during the early years in school, he develops friendships with a wider circle of children and learns to work and play with larger groups.

At first the emotional ties of group members are relatively loose, but they become stronger during the prepubertal years. At this time also there tends to be a distaste for the company of the opposite sex, particularly among boys. Members of the opposite sex become more attractive to each other during the years of adolescenthood, while at the same time loyalties to peer groups continue to be strong. As adolescents grow into adulthood, they participate in a widening circle of groups, but in general, this participation is less intense than it is during the prepubertal and adolescent years.

We have described these stages of socialization in the light of the behavior displayed by most individuals who are in these stages of development, but it is important to note that the changes in behavior are produced by the changes in feelings and attitudes which occur during these periods, as well as by the social situations in which these individuals find themselves. These changes occur partly because we are able to expand the scope of our emotional involvement to include more persons, and partly because we expect more socialized attitudes and behavior of each other. To put it somewhat differently, these changes occur because we are able to give more of ourselves emotionally and also because the group demands that we establish certain controls. By way of example, persons in their twenties generally make more adequate marriage partners than persons in their middle teens because they are mature enough to make an emotional investment in each other as well as the marriage itself. Furthermore, they are more able to limit and control the self-centered aspects of their behavior out of consideration for their spouses. The higher rates of divorce and the greater incidence of unhappy marriages among teen-agers probably reflect their general inability to make difficult emotional adjustments. However, it should be noted that a large minority of teen-agers do have successful and happy marriages, whereas a large minority of persons in their twenties contract marriages which fail. This is witness to the fact that stages of emotional maturity do not come at the same time for everyone. Some teen-agers have developed attitudes, feelings, and standards of behavior which are indistinguishable from those of typical adults, whereas some adults seem to be dominated by patterns of emotional behavior which are more typical of adolescents or even preadolescents.

CHARACTERISTICS OF EMOTIONAL MATURITY

As children move through various stages of maturity, changes take place in their "inner life" as well as in their relations with others.

One such change is the increasing awareness of what we call "reality." As we indicated in the last chapter, younger children are likely to confuse the world of reality with the world of their own fantasies. As they become older, they come to recognize more and more what part of their life is fantasy and what is reality. For example, a five-year-old child may have a phobia about dogs, which means that whenever he sees a dog he is seized by a nameless, unreasoning, and unreasonable fear. Such phobias are very common at this age. At ten years of age he may still be timid about dogs, but he is now experienced enough in the realities of life to know that most dogs are not interested in attacking him. Whereas at five he was unable even to stay in the same room with a dog, at ten he can even play with a dog, even though he is somewhat nervous about doing so.

Another characteristic of emotionally immature persons is that there are rather marked differences between their self-concepts and their self-ideals. Children differ in this respect, of course. Some children's ideal standards far exceed the range of their abilities, whereas other children possess more modest expectations for themselves and therefore are less likely to be plagued by guilt and anxiety at their inability to attain unrealistic standards. One of the factors that determines how realistic children's attitudes will be is the expectations of the adults who are significant in the life of the child. A great many children have a sense of incompleteness about themselves and suffer from guilt and anxiety resulting from a pronounced gap between self-concept and self-ideal. This situation is likely to occur because of the tendency of grownups to expect children to live up to adult standards of behavior. To be sure, we have come a long way from the cruel days when six-year-olds were expected to sit in crowded classrooms for long hours without moving. Nevertheless, we have not wholly accepted what we know about child behavior and development as part of our pattern of expectations of children. In other words, we *know* that children are likely to act like children, rather than like adults, but we nevertheless *hope and expect* that they will behave like adults. Inasmuch as children know that the significant adults in their lives are displeased with their behavior, their anxieties are aroused, with the result that they may behave in an even more immature fashion than would otherwise be the case.

As the child grows into adolescenthood and adulthood, he becomes more able to behave according to adult standards. As this occurs, the difference between his self-concept and his self-ideal usually diminishes and he becomes less anxious and at the same time attains a feeling of greater adequacy.

The existence of a large gap between the self-concept and the self-ideal means that the individual does not like himself. He is likely to be self-critical and discouraged about his ability to do the right thing in the right way. We say that he does not "accept" himself. Immature persons are characterized by a low degree of self-acceptance. It invariably follows that individuals who have difficulty in accepting themselves also have difficulty in accepting others [2]. They may not be aware of the fact that acceptance of self and acceptance of others are interrelated; yet the fact remains that the individual who hates himself is bound to express hostility toward others either openly or covertly.

Evan, who is eleven years old and who cannot read, is an example of the relationship between accepting oneself and accepting others. Because Evan's school has a policy of automatic promotion, he has been moved along with his age-mates and is now in the fifth grade. Mrs. Nissen, his teacher, says that he does not present much of a problem in class as long as she does not put pressure on him to do activities involving reading. He is quiet, almost subdued, in class. Apparently he understands most of what goes on in class, because he is able to give sensible answers when called on or asked to participate in discussions. However, when Mrs. Nissen sits down with him and attempts to help him with his reading, he freezes up and refuses to cooperate. "What's the use?" he says at such times, "I'm just dumb. You're just wasting your time. *You* know that I'll never be able to read!"

Mrs. Nissen so far has been unable to talk him out of his belief that he is too stupid ever to learn how to read. She knows that part of Evan's difficulty is the result of a home situation where he is continually criticized and depreciated. Evan's reaction to this criticism is to agree with it. When his parents and siblings tell him that he is stupid, that he cannot do anything right, he believes this as though it were a proven fact.

So far, it is apparent that Evan has deep-seated feelings of inferiority, that he does not accept himself. However, the evidence that his lack of self-acceptance is coupled with an equally low degree of acceptance of others is less clear. If Mrs. Nissen were a psychologist and had the time and the facilities to do extensive diagnostic and therapeutic work with Evan, she could produce much evidence to show that he hates others as much as he despises himself. However, even in the absence of such evidence, her classroom observations reveal some clues. The most important is his unwillingness to read. One of the reasons Evan cannot read is that by not reading he is able to punish the adults in his life who have helped to make him so miserable. To be sure, his teachers are far more accepting than is his family, but he has been so deeply disturbed by his family's rejection of him that he is unable to make a realistic appraisal of the motives of *any* adult. His resentment and hostility, though not apparent on the surface, are so deep and so pervasive that it will interfere with the attempts of *any* teacher, no matter how understanding and kindly, to help him to read. Naturally, it is unreasonable, irrational, and illogical for him to punish a teacher for the offenses of his family, but neurotic anxiety often makes us act in unreasonable, irrational, and neurotic ways.

Another clue to Evan's basic hostility that Mrs. Nissen has noticed is the fact that he has no close friends and makes no attempt to establish friendly relations with any of his classmates. This symptom, taken by itself, means little, but in context with the other data she has accumulated on Evan, it seems to indicate that here is a child who is not only unable to accept himself, but is unable to accept others.

EMOTIONAL MATURITY THROUGH DEVELOPMENTAL TASKS

By way of summarizing the foregoing discussion we might say that an emotionally mature person is one who is able to live in relative harmony with himself and with his social environment within the limits imposed by the skills and abilities appropriate to his age level. People who are unable to attain this harmonious relationship because their emotional and social development has lagged may be considered emotionally immature.

The idea that emotionally mature persons are those whose competencies have kept in step with their chronological development appears to be related to a concept developed by Robert J. Havighurst and his associates at the University of Chicago. Havighurst describes growth toward maturity as the satisfactory accomplishment of "developmental tasks" —problems that are crucial at various stages of human development and that must be solved more or less successfully if an individual is to develop a satisfactory mode of life during the years that follow. Specifically, he describes a developmental task as "a task which arises at or about a certain period in the life of an individual, successful achievement of which leads to his happiness and to success with later tasks, while failure leads to unhappiness in the individual, disapproval by society, and difficulty with later tasks [3]." For example, the nine basic tasks that must or should be taken up during adolescence are as follows:

1. Accepting One's Physique and Accepting a Masculine or Feminine Role.
Nature of the Task. The goals: to become proud, or at least tolerant, of one's body; to accept a socially approved masculine or feminine role.
2. New Relations with Age-Mates of Both Sexes.

Nature of the Task. The goal: to learn to look upon girls as women, and boys as men; to become an adult among adults; to learn to work with others for a common purpose, disregarding personal feelings; to learn to lead without dominating.

3. Emotional Independence of Parents and Other Adults.

Nature of the Task. The goal: to become free from childish dependence on parents; to develop affection for parents without dependence upon them; to develop respect for older adults without dependence upon them.

4. Achieving Assurance of Economic Independence.

Nature of the Task. The goal: to feel able to make a living, if necessary. This is primarily a task for boys, in our society, but it is of increasing importance for girls.

5. Selecting and Preparing for an Occupation.

Nature of the Task. The goal: to choose an occupation for which one has the necessary ability; to prepare for this occupation.

6. Developing Intellectual Skills and Concepts Necessary for Civic Competence.

Nature of the Task. The goal: to develop concepts of law, government, economics, politics, geography, human nature, and social institutions which fit the modern world; to develop language skills and reasoning ability necessary for dealing effectively with the problems of a modern democracy.

7. Desiring and Achieving Socially Responsible Behavior.

Nature of the Task. The goal: to participate as a responsible adult in the life of the community, region and nation; to take account of the values of society in one's personal behavior.

8. Preparing for Marriage and Family Life.

Nature of the Task. The goal: to develop a positive attitude toward family life and having children; and (mainly for girls) to get the knowledge necessary for home management and child-rearing.

9. Building Conscious Values in Harmony with an Adequate Scientific World-Picture.

Nature of the Task. The goal: to form a set of values which are possible of realization; to develop a conscious purpose of realizing these values; to define man's place in the physical world and in relation to other human beings; to keep one's world-picture and one's values in harmony with each other. Definition: a value is an object or state of affairs which is desired [4].

These are the tasks, says Havighurst, in effect, that adolescents must learn or master if they are to become reasonably happy and successful adults. These are the problems that will concern a large measure of his time and attention during adolescenthood. They must be solved more or less satisfactorily if the individual is to be successful at solving the tasks and problems of adulthood. And, conversely, the adolescent who has not learned the tasks of preadolescence adequately will have difficulty in coping with the tasks for adolescents that we have listed.

There are, of course, no hard and fast standards for the learning and accomplishment of these developmental tasks. Some individuals will do better at some than at others. Some individuals will delay the completion of certain tasks until later years. Still others will never satisfactorily accomplish some tasks and will remain immature in those respects all their lives. An example of this is the middle-aged man who still lives with his parents and who has never been able to establish a home of his own. He may be financially independent, but he has been unable to resolve this problem adequately; his ability to surmount other tasks is impaired, for he was not able, during adolescenthood or later, to establish "new relations with age-mates of both sexes," nor has he done much about "preparing for marriage and family life."

Another example is that of the man who works at one job for a year or two and then goes on to another, whereupon he repeats the same performance. He always starts each new job with enthusiasm, but is "completely fed-up" in a few months. After a dozen years of this, he still has not "found himself." In his case, it is fairly obvious that he has not been equal to the developmental task of "selecting and preparing for an occupation." But there is probably more to his difficulties than meet the eye. There is some likelihood that he has not adequately accomplished the developmental task of "desiring and achieving socially responsible behavior," or it may be possible that he has not achieved "emotional independence of parents and other adults," for one of his problems may be his inability to cooperate with persons in authority, and this, in turn, would go back to his lack of success as an adolescent in dissolving his emotional ties to his parents. It may be that he, as well as the middle-aged person who lives with his parents, was unable to accomplish these crucial tasks of adolescence because of some unusual pressures or combination of circumstances. Or it may be that the personalities or self-concepts these two individuals developed as a result of childhood experiences rendered them particularly vulnerable to even the normal pressures of adolescence. In any case, their failure to accomplish these tasks while adolescents was to a great extent both the cause and the result of their emotional immaturity.

Using the accomplishment of the developmental tasks of adolescenthood as a base, Schoeppe, Haggard, and Havighurst evaluated the maturity of thirty boys and girls as part of the Midwest Community Research Project, "an elaborate interdisciplinary research program carried on since 1942 by the staff of the Committee on Human Development of the University of Chicago for the purpose of investigating character and personality development during later childhood and adolescence in a typical Midwestern community [5]." As part of their findings, they describe some of the adolescents who had high and low rankings according to their criteria. Their description of a highly socialized boy and girl follows:

> Herbert Bond has much less need to conform than does Ann Harper. Both were fortunate enough to grow up in homes where they were accepted and where they were made to feel they counted as individuals. The family relationships were tightly knit, and both were able to see themselves as having secure places in the family. The fact that this was even more so for Herb reappears in his having even more desirable rela-

tions with age-mates than Ann does. Interaction of family members is harmonious, with the result that these children learned to maintain harmony in other social relations. They have been taught the meaning and value of work and internalized the need for working. Controls were exercised when necessary, but the parents attempted to help the child understand the rationality of them. The parents were well-adjusted and not unduly striving to maintain or change their status in society. Thus, since they were acceptant of their own mode of life, the identifying child likewise accepted his. On this foundation the youngsters began school, and because they were well-socialized, the school eagerly accepted them and worked to further their socialization. Each new successful accomplishment made the next one easier for Ann and Herb [6].

The description of two poorly socialized adolescents is in marked contrast to the above character sketch:

Both Martha Gates and Ned Foster are narcissistic and starved for affection. They exert all their energies toward seeking the love of which they have been deprived, but they do so in very different ways, each the result of the unique combination of biological, personality, and social factors. Their lot in early life was not good; neither had a sound home base from which to operate nor exemplary parents with whom to identify.

Martha is an example of a child deprived in the physical, cultural, and intellectual areas. She has responded psychologically by passive submission and strives to make herself invisible in order to avoid any condemnation. Her low intellectual facility, coupled with her lack of any keen powers of observation and insight, has caused her to be nonplussed and overwhelmed by her environment. This behavior may also be more appropriate to the outer world which has been more disinterested and ignoring of her than actively rejecting. Mrs. Gates in particular has shown a desire not to be bothered by Martha, and a lack of interest in her rather than any active antagonism. In her school also she has been more ignored than scapegoated. Consequently, in the home and in the school, there was actually little for Martha to fight back at except a nebulous rejection. Since she is not gifted with capacities for coping with her environment in a retaliative manner, she has simply succumbed —but has not been happy to do this. She is in a perpetual state of inner conflict, and thus uses energy that might otherwise be put to more constructive ends to cope with it. Her rejection, poor family relations, and concept of herself as being worthless have made her feel it futile to try to succeed as her peers do. She has adopted the fatalistic attitude that it is the world that causes her to lose; and since the whole world is against her, it is too much to try to remedy her situation. This attitude, coupled with her very limited abilities, has killed any zest for working on the common tasks for one her age. Martha has adopted an attitude of resignation and despair.

Ned Foster, possibly because of his greater intellectual ability and keener insight, takes steps to be retaliative to his poor lot in life. Moreover, Ned's mother actively and openly rejects him; so he feels a greater need to retaliate and also has greater capacities and imagination to devise means, both conscious and unconscious, to do so. Much of his energy is directed compulsively to expressing hostility toward his parents, particularly his mother. Because he gives vent to his hostile feelings in such negative ways, he continually handicaps himself—he does not win the affection he craves either from her or his age-mates. His failure to win affection makes him even more antagonistic, and the vicious circle widens. Thus it has been for Ned throughout his school history, and his peer relations have become constantly worse. This, in turn, has made him more bitter and negative in his approach to all developmental tasks. In fact, he expends his energy aggressively, fighting the world by means which are self-defeating; then he paranoically withdraws to his only real friends—animals and an older woman to whom he is attached—or he seeks solace in reading. Because of his superior ability, he achieves comparatively well academically in spite of these disturbing forces.

Different constellations of factors account for Martha's and Ned's poor achievement on the developmental tasks. However, their failures have made them more discouraged and more ready to strike out at the world, but each does it in the way his uniqueness prompts [7].

When we examine these four cases closely, it is apparent that the success or the ability to accomplish developmental tasks is cumulative—that is, the four young people who served as the subjects for these thumbnail case histories approached the developmental tasks of adolescence with a history of successes or failures that either helped to carry them through or helped to defeat them. To a large degree, their successes and failures in coping with the developmental tasks of adolescence were based on successes and failures experienced in infancy and early childhood. The emotional maturity of an adolescent is very much related to how well he gets along with his peers, but this ability is, in turn, at least partly conditioned by earlier relationships with his parents. It is this relationship with parents and other significant adults that occupies our attention in the next facet of emotional maturity we shall consider.

THE NEED TO BE INDEPENDENT AND SELF-DIRECTING

THE various stages of emotional maturity may also be viewed as episodes in the individual's struggle to become independent and self-directing. This is actually a dual struggle, having an aspect which is irrational, immature, or neurotic and an aspect which is related to the meeting of basic needs and the achievement of emotional maturity. Let us consider the irrational form of dependency first.

Sandor Ferenczi, the Hungarian psychoanalyst, says that the infant's first feelings about his dependent state of existence are similar to feelings of omnipotence [8]. From the infant's viewpoint, his needs are met merely by *wishing*. He is hungry, and lo—he is fed. His bowels feel congested, and presto—he is relieved. Since he is too immature to organize the data of his senses into any kind of sense-making framework, he is unable to form any realistic sort of picture of what actually happens. He is not able to remember that sometimes when he wishes to be fed, food is not forthcoming, and that sometimes when he is uncomfortable, nothing occurs to relieve him. Nor is he aware that when he is hungry or uncomfortable, he expresses his feelings through lusty cries.

As the infant grows and develops, he begins to realize that wishing alone does not always bring satisfaction, and that sometimes wishes are more effective if supported by cries and gestures. He does not abandon the concept of omnipotence, for he still sees himself as the center of the universe around which his entire world revolves.[1] Parents appear to him as beings who have no choice but to obey him; their only reason for existence is to care for him. He cannot grasp the situation when his wants are ignored; his paroxysms of rage are clues to his inability to accept the fact that his wishes cannot always be satisfied.

When he has developed a large enough vocabulary to understand some of the realities of life, the illusion of his omnipotence comes into rude and dramatic collision with reality. Usually, this occurs during the third year of life and contributes to the turbulence of this stage of development. If the child is successfully disillusioned, he will begin to understand that he is actually weak and relatively helpless and that he is dependent almost for his very existence on the good will and love of his parents. But the illusion of omipotence dies hard for most children; the temper tantrums, stubbornness, or sulkiness of some children are clues to their reluctance to accept their weakness and fallibility.

OMNIPOTENCE AND OVERDEPENDENCY

Even as adolescents and adults we cherish the memories of our lost omnipotence. We daydream about having our problems solved for us; we wish we could press a button and

---

[1] The idea that one is the center of the universe is an idea that persists in childhood and is not uncommon with adults. We are continually struck by how the world changes and tend to ignore or be unaware of changes in ourselves. A child of nursery-school age once expressed this feeling to me by exclaiming, when she tried on a pair of shoes that had been too large for her six months previously: "Look! My shoes are growing into my feet!"

have some magical power do our household chores or mow the lawn; and we are delighted when some chance occurrence eliminates a problem that we were worried about solving. Many of us put much time and effort into amassing enough money "so I don't have to worry," and we envy the rich and powerful who have dozens of servants at their beck and call—who have only to wish that something be done, and it *is* done.

The state of omnipotence is, of course, the mirror image of complete dependency. The infant who feels so "omnipotent" is entirely dependent on his parents. Even the person of wealth and power is similarly dependent on others to carry out his wishes. Indeed, the more power an individual possesses, the more he is dependent on others. Therefore, much of our struggle to become wealthy and powerful and to put ourselves in a position where all our wishes will be granted without our making any noticeable effort, is, in effect, an attempt to return to the state of our lost omnipotence, to the time when we had no worries. To the extent that our efforts are motivated by this dream, they are unrealistic and irrational, for we never can and never will attain such a state of being. An additional neurotic element is introduced by the fact that we seek these goals under the assumption that we are attempting to become independent, whereas actually what we are doing is trying to maneuver ourselves into positions where we can be successfully dependent.

Much of this process is set in motion by our fear of anxiety, both normal and neurotic. In our everyday life we are faced with situations which, for various reasons, are potential producers of neurotic anxiety. Furthermore, the demands made on us by society to be concerned about the feelings, rights, and welfare of others, about the consequences of our own acts, and about our own future produce normal anxiety. It is no wonder that a return to an infantile state of omnipotence and security (actually complete dependency) appears attractive, for if we could make that dream a reality, we could at one stroke rid ourselves of the necessity of ever feeling anxious again! It is quite understandable, therefore, that most of us entertain occasional wistful daydreams about this illusion, and that a few of us seem dedicated to a lifelong attempt to make the dream a reality. Most of the time, however, we are resigned to the necessity of facing our problems and coping with our anxieties, both normal and neurotic, as best we can, without recourse to a former state of magical omnipotence.

DISPELLING THE MYTH OF OMNIPOTENCE

It is one of the important tasks of childhood to prove the unreality of this dream and to recognize that the normal and healthy way of dealing with life is through increased ability to think and act for oneself. By the time children are ready for school, most of them have a fairly good grasp of reality in terms of what they can expect from the world. They are ready to make some decisions and take some actions on their own behalf in certain areas of life and to give themselves over to adult guidance on other areas. There is usually an area of doubt, in which children (and sometimes adults) are not quite sure who should take the initiative and direction. Furthermore, the area of children's competence is quite variable in that it differs with the general maturity of the child, and may differ according to the amount of emotional stress to which the child is subjected. Adults also vary in the amount of guidance and direction which they supply.

However, there are a few children who have not come through the stage of disillusionment successfully. Usually, parents help children to realize and accept the fact that they are not omnipotent by exposing them to small but increasing "doses of reality." Some parents seem unable to bring themselves to do this, but instead they help to perpetuate the myth by overindulgence, by refusing to set reasonable limits to the child's behavior. Sometimes parents are unable to be

firm because they have an exaggerated fear of losing their
child's love, sometimes because it is the course of least resistance, and sometimes because they are reluctant to deny
the gratification of their own wishes or to set limits to their
own behavior. For whatever reason, the child who persists in
the myth of his omnipotence, and who sincerely believes
himself the center of the universe poses many a problem for
teachers and other adults who are responsible for him. Some
of these children are "shocked into reality" by the frustrations generated by the school. Others persist in their self-
centered way and continue to be problems to themselves
and to others throughout their lives.

NORMAL NEEDS FOR INDEPENDENCE

What we have discussed thus far is what might be called a
neurotic or irrational need for independence which is actually a mask for exaggerated dependency needs. However,
there is another kind of need for independence which is
characteristic of the emotionally healthy child. It is normal
and natural for children to develop the ability to think and
act for themselves. The younger they are, the more guidance
and direction they are likely to need, but as responsibilities
and opportunities for choice increase, there is a greater need
for children to make decisions on their own. The right to
make decisions implies the right to make mistakes and to
learn from them. Unfortunately, the making of mistakes
carries the stigma of failure in our middle-class society;
therefore, we probably do not give children sufficient opportunities to do things "on their own," taking full responsibility for laying plans and carrying them out—for failures as
well as successes. Instead, we are inclined to minimize their
ability for independent action and to provide more direction
and guidance than is actually needed. If we expect children
to grow up to be adults who are able to make decisions and
carry them out, as well as to take responsibility for their own
beliefs and actions, we must provide children with oppor-

tunities to have experiences of this type. Children do not learn how to direct themselves unless they can have experiences in which they direct themselves.

When children are faced by situations in which much direction and control are provided, far more than is required either by the situation or by their level of maturity, they are likely to react to it by submission, apathy, or rebellion, depending on their individual approaches to life, the nature of the situation, and so forth. In the majority of such situations (and they are very common in school) most children either submit or are apathetic. The submissive ones are those whose anxieties are raised by the teacher's orders or directions, and their way of controlling their anxiety and warding off the teacher's disapproval is to obey to the best of their ability. The apathetic ones are basically rebellious, but they dare not show their hostility openly. Their anxieties would be raised if they tried to identify themselves with the teacher because they would be running counter to their own self-ideals, or, if they defied him openly, they would evoke the teacher's disapproval. Therefore, they decide that the safest approach is to do as little as possible. The rebellious individuals cannot compromise by submitting to or identifying with the teacher, nor can they compromise with their own self-concepts by doing nothing. They feel almost compelled to make their protests openly.

It should be noted that the teacher who attempts to put his classes on a self-directive basis also has his difficulties. Since most students are used to adults who overdirect and overcontrol, they are suspicious of any teacher who attempts to change the pattern. Indeed, if such a teacher is unable to convince his class of his sincerity or of the reason for assignments which require self-direction, he will have unusual difficulty. On the other hand, if he *is* successful, he will have his greatest success with those who are rebellious or apathetic primarily because they have been denied opportunities for self-direction. Students who are excessively dependent and who are used to submitting to the direction and control of the teacher are made confused and anxious when they are required to think and act for themselves.

EDUCATION FOR SELF-DIRECTION AND RESPONSIBILITY

The problem of helping children to take responsibility for their own behavior is both complex and difficult. One cannot *force* children to be self-directive because such an approach would defeat its own purposes. On the other hand, self-direction and responsibility do not come into being merely by turning children loose to work out their own problems. What is required here is the sensitive, sure hand of the artist in human relations, expressing itself through well-timed devices and techniques.

In an analysis of ways to encourage pupil responsibility for behavior, Jack G. Rockwell makes the following suggestions to elementary teachers. Some of his suggestions are equally appropriate to secondary teachers:

1. *Do you permit the children to arrange the seating in the classroom?* If desks or chairs are not movable, Rockwell suggests that other things in the room be arranged by them to help them get the feeling of "our room."

2. *Do you plan each day's program (in the light of the over-all objectives of the school) each morning with your pupils?* This may involve a review of the previous day's activities, followed by a carefully guided discussion of what should be learned today. Decisions should be made on a careful consideration of the values involved in various choices and not merely on the basis of children liking or not liking certain activities.

3. *Do you review with your class its activities at the end of the day to see how near you came to accomplishing your aims?* For younger children, who have shorter attention spans, this type of evaluation should be held earlier in the day rather than at the end.

4. *Do you plan with your pupils a program that meets their needs?* Rockwell points out that children need opportunities to talk about matters that bother and perplex them. One device he suggests is that of having children write unsigned lists of things they would like to understand more clearly.

5. *Do you permit pupils to set up their own evaluation scales?* Sometimes children can do this by keeping charts or graphs of their own.

6. *Are the child-set standards of your group high enough?* In most classes there is a standard of work consciously or unconsciously evolved by the children themselves that has a greater effect on their performance than the standards set by the teacher. Rockwell suggests that it is the responsibility of the teacher to help pupils set standards on a scale that demands progressively more of each child with each advancement in his total growth and development. He emphasizes that the standards thus evolved must be accepted by children as their own, otherwise they will lose their effectiveness.

7. *Do you provide a place of acceptance for each child in the classroom?* Many discipline problems occur when children feel that they are not a part of the group because they are unable to contribute to the group activities. This means that group projects must be set up in such a way that the skills of all class members can be utilized.

8. *Is your classroom a laboratory for learning that permits each child to succeed and at the same time to assume the responsibility when he does not?* In posing this question, Rockwell is making a special plea to give children the opportunity to learn from their failures. This is important, because we learn to do things the right way by studying our failures. However, children cannot learn from failures if they feel that the doors to success are closed. They will only keep trying in spite of failure as long as they feel that they have a chance to succeed.

9. *Does your classroom have "personality" (individuality)?* Are pupils proud to say that this is their room?

10. *Do you realize the importance of your behavior as a teacher in developing self-control in the pupils in your classroom?* Rockwell is concerned here about how the teacher plays his role and what kinds of attitudes toward children he pos-

sesses. The relationship that grows up between teacher and pupils is the key to the development of responsible behavior among school children [9].

THE TASK OF THE SCHOOL IN PROMOTING EMOTIONAL MATURITY

MOST classroom activities in the schools today are concerned principally with the mastery of subject matter. The heavy emphasis on this phase of education is evident whenever we take a close look at the kinds of tests teachers use as well as their bases for assigning final marks. Thus, if everyday classroom practice may be considered as evidence, we can assume that emotional maturity does not have much status or acceptance as an educational goal. On the other hand, it is very common to find emotional health mentioned as an "end goal" in many curricula—sometimes directly and sometimes indirectly. "Cooperation," "good citizenship," and "social ease" are common examples. There are a number of reasons why we have this discrepancy between practice and ideals—the difficulty of developing teaching techniques appropriate to the teaching of mental hygiene, the problem of developing ways of measuring or evaluating emotional maturity, the conditions and social pressures that force us to emphasize subject matter rather than emotional health, to name a few. These are problems that will be discussed further in the succeeding pages of this book.

We should note, in passing, that one of the most crucial problems is that of curriculum building. What often happens is that a curriculum committee gets to the point of having stated the goals or outcomes it expects to result from the curriculum they are about to construct. Let us say that good citizenship is one of their goals. They may even have been able to agree on some examples of good citizenship. Their problem now is how to translate these concepts into a sequence of classroom events or situations that will produce the desired result, not only for the teachers on the curriculum committee, but also for every teacher who uses the curriculum. Perhaps this is one of the points at which the battle for emotional maturity as an outcome of education is lost. The units of work that begin to appear on paper as a result of the committee's work do not produce gains in emotional maturity when tried out in all classrooms. Perhaps this is because no one really knows what curricular materials will promote emotional maturity; perhaps it is the teacher and his methods, rather than the curriculum, that provide the ingredient that makes or breaks mental health in the classroom; perhaps the gains that are made in emotional maturity depend principally upon the emotional climate that prevails in the school. Committees what work on curricula know, or at least sense, most of these factors. Furthermore, they want their curricula to be accepted by the other teachers in the school. If their curricula depart too far from traditional curricula, they may not be accepted. Hence there is a strong tendency for curriculum committees to "play it safe" and to produce curricula that are traditional and conventional, curricula that emphasize subject-matter competence.[2]

To a large extent, what we have been saying is that schools are really more concerned with the measurable and more "tangible" results of intellectual growth than they are with the more intangible evidences of emotional growth, perhaps on the assumption that emotional maturity follows as a natural consequence of intellectual attainment.[3] How-

---

[2] In general, this analysis holds truer for secondary schools than it does for elementary schools, although there are many exceptions on both levels. However, the tendency is for the primary grades today to be more concerned about self-expression, cooperation, and other attributes of emotional maturity than is the case with other levels of education. As one goes "up the educational ladder," grade by grade, the more teachers are likely to be concerned about subject matter and the less they are likely to be concerned with mental health or emotional maturity.

[3] I have noticed that many college students believe that persons who have a college education have fewer emotional troubles than other people. They often defend this belief by saying: "Educated people think more clearly."

ever, experience indicates that emotional maturity does not come as a result of an increase in intellectual powers, nor can we count on the concurrent development of these two phases of life. Indeed, it is not unusual for persons of high intellectual attainment to need psychological help in dealing with their emotional problems. Some individuals use their intellectual attainment as a defense against the development of emotional maturity.

At this point, the question might reasonably be raised: "Assuming that teachers, as a group, are not actively concerned with the development of emotional maturity in children and adolescents, is there any reason why they *should* be?"

The answer to that question lies in the relationship between emotional maturity and learning, as well as in the results which the public expects from education.

EMOTIONAL MATURITY AND LEARNING

Let us first consider the relationship between emotional maturity and learning. Although it is possible for some individuals to develop intellectual abilities of a high caliber and still remain emotionally immature to a very great degree, the question might also be raised as to whether intellectual attainment is synonymous with intellectual maturity. The answer is that although they have much in common, intellectual maturity presupposes a certain degree of emotional maturity. Without emotional maturity there is a lack of a balanced approach to the problems of life. Emotions may get out of hand to the point of beclouding problems better solved intellectually, or, equally as bad, emotions may be repressed or denied when they most need expression, and the individual may seek intellectual (and usually unworkable) solutions to his problems because his emotions arouse too much anxiety.

However, the usual fate of the emotionally immature individual is not that his intellectual attainment outraces the other phases of his development, but rather that his intellectual attainment lags. The person who is emotionally immature is less likely to be prompted by normal anxiety. Hence, he is less concerned about others and about his future and thus does not possess as much incentive to learn as does the person who *is* affected by these concerns. Furthermore, the emotionally immature person is more interested in maintaining the current state of affairs, emotionally speaking, than he is in learning. Learning always involves changes of some sort. The very thought of change arouses neurotic anxiety in most emotionally immature persons, and this, in turn, leads to exaggerated and pronounced forms of the kind of defensive, neurotic behavior we discussed in the previous chapter.

It should be noted that when we speak of "the emotionally immature person," we have in mind a rather extreme (but not unusual) person, who has more than the usual amount of difficulties. Actually, virtually all children (and adults) are emotionally immature in some respects, which accounts for a good proportion of learning difficulties which all of us experience at times.

However, since most children are in reasonably good emotional health most of the time, much of what they do will be characterized by growth in the direction of maturity, maturity in all phases of life—physical, social, intellectual, and emotional. Growth toward maturity presupposes that learning will take place; there cannot be healthy growth without learning. Therefore, children have a normal desire to learn, to become more competent intellectually, physically, and socially. Emotional competence, in the sense of establishing controls and establishing new relationships, is not always attractive to children, but it must be achieved as the price of intellectual and social development.

Children receive much of their motivation from their eagerness to accomplish the developmental tasks which are appropriate to their age, and it is their willingness to accept the challenges of these tasks that provides the motivation to the positive learning which takes place in school. It is *this* kind of learning—the learning which occurs when the child *learns for himself*—which remains when school days are over. The learning which results from being forced to go through the motions is what is quickly forgotten. This is a rootless kind of learning which is accomplished merely to satisfy the teacher. We as teachers need to be actively concerned about motivation. This means that we ought to be sensitive to children's need for growth and give them opportunities to respond, through learning, to the motivation which springs from their need for growth.

EMOTIONAL MATURITY AND THE EXPECTATIONS OF THE PUBLIC

The second question was concerned with the public's expectations of education. The issue is not whether the public expects subject matter competence or emotional maturity, because the public probably wants both.

The factors that make for success or for failure in life are basically emotional or attitudinal. Most people who are fired lose their jobs because they could not get along with their fellow workers or their supervisors, or because they were irresponsible or careless. Only a minority are fired because they lacked the necessary knowledge or basic skills. An example of the stress placed on attitudes by employers may be found in a booklet published by the National Association of Manufacturers for circulation among young people who are thinking about entering an occupation. In a chapter entitled "How to Progress in Your Vocation," the Association stresses such matters as: making a favorable impression, cultivating a real interest in work, demonstrating initiative and dependability, being courteous, assuming responsibility, and getting along with others. In fact, the latter trait receives extra emphasis: *"Getting along with people is one of the most important requirements for those who want to get ahead on the job—or off* [10]." To be sure, the handbook contains some advice regarding gaining competence in certain skills, but the great stress is on developing certain of the characteristics that pertain to emotional maturity.

Emotional maturity is also the crucial factor in other undertakings of life. Most marriages that end in divorce fail because of the emotional immaturity of one or both partners, rather than from lack of information or skill. And most teachers who fail do so because they were emotionally unprepared or unable to establish sound working relationships with children, fellow teachers, and/or administrators, rather than because of any lack of competence in the subject matter they taught. It is emotional maturity that is characteristic of the good citizen, the good employee, the good spouse, the good parent, and the good teacher.

Subject-matter competence, therefore, plays an important but distinctly secondary role in the *real* education of an individual. The public realizes this fact, although the public often neglects to put it into words. This is what the public means when it says that young people these days are not responsible, or hard-working, or law-abiding, or careful with their money, or whatever. Yet when the public makes these criticisms, it is at least somewhat aware that these qualities are difficult ones to impart. How *do* you teach a child to be responsible? The public does not know, and it is afraid that the schools do not know, either. And much the same situation exists with the other attributes of emotional maturity. Most of the public undoubtedly feels that raising the level of emotional maturity among school graduates is an ideal much to be desired but that probably no one, including the schools, can do much about it.

To the experimentally minded educator this situation presents a challenge that should not be overlooked. There are programs and approaches in a few schools that show much promise with regard to education for emotional maturity. We shall discuss some of them in the chapters that follow.

For the most part, these approaches are experimental and untried. Perhaps what we need to say to the public is something like this:

"Don't be discouraged—yet. There is a strong likelihood that education can produce the kind of graduate you hope for. If you will give us freedom to experiment with the curriculum and with the training and supervision of teachers and will withhold judgment until we have given our ideas a fair trial, we may be able to come out with the kind of educational product that will satisfy your best expectations. In the meantime, we shall guarantee that the qualifications of graduates will be no poorer than they are at present." [4]

The chances of an offer like this being made and accepted are rather slender because the public (who, after all, controls education) is reluctant to permit experimentation either in curricula or methodology, and educators (who must maintain the support of the public if they are to keep their jobs and preserve the progress that has been made to date) are inclined to go along with the public, at least most of the way. Nevertheless, the possibility of giving the public what it really wants from education and at the same time developing a form of education that makes more substantial contributions to the emotional maturity of children is an intriguing one, one that will serve as the subject for discussion and debate for many years to come.

Although school graduates are more likely to fail because of deficiencies in emotional health, the most vocal criticisms of the school are concerned with subject-matter competence. One common complaint is that young people do not write and spell accurately; another is that they are ignorant of American history. It may be that those employers who make such complaints are actually more disturbed by other shortcomings but complain about such specific matters as spelling and knowledge of history because the latter are easier to dis-

---

[4] The success of the Eight-Year Study of the Progressive Education Association lends substance to the latter claim [11].

cuss than vaguer and less tangible matters like dependability and integrity. Research so far indicates that, in general, school children today are more competent than school children were in previous generations [12, 13, 14, 15]. It is also very likely that the average high school graduate today writes and spells better than the average middle-aged adult.[5] Thus the specific complaints that we hear about the preparation of students serve the public as a sort of emotional outlet for a general, vague complaint that might be phrased: "We wish that the graduate of the schools were a better person in every way."

We in education wish this too, and it is incumbent on us to help people to see that: (1) they are really looking for greater emotional maturity as well as greater subject-matter competence in school graduates; (2) it is possible to develop the types of schools that will fill this need; (3) schools presently are doing a better job on subject-matter competencies than they did previously; (4) the greatest area of potential improvement in the schools is in the field of emotional health; and (5) since both the public and the educational profession have common basic goals, there is a need for mutual support and collaboration. Both the educational profession and the general public are, in the final analysis, interested in the education of the whole person rather than in training in some specific competency, and this common interest might form the starting point for closer collaboration.

Emotional maturity is, then, the psychological cement which provides the basis for the more essential and perma-

---

[5] By way of example, J. W. Stansfield, Superintendent of Schools, Coulee Dam, Washington, reports on a number of contests between teams of students from local schools and officers and directors of community organizations. The tenth grade beat the P.T.A. 10–12 at a spelling bee, the seventh grade beat the Rotary Club 14–13 in a geography quiz, and a high school class in social studies beat the American Legion 17–13 in a current affairs quiz. Stansfield says, "Contests were all conducted in good-natured rivalry and simply reminded adults that schools today do teach fundamentals, even though spelling may be called part of language arts and geography and history are parts of the social studies program [16]."

nent kinds of learning. If schools choose to close their eyes to this aspect of development, they run the dual risk of using forms of motivation that are artificial and time wasting and of producing graduates who are unable or unwilling to carry their share of the burdens of life. The successful school is the one which aids students in becoming emotionally more mature and which cues its teachings to the motivation generated by the child's natural desires to become more mature. The less successful school is the one which fails to harness the energy and motivation resulting from increasing maturity or, even worse, attempts to block or frustrate the child's attempts to attain greater maturity.

REFERENCES

1. F. Redl and W. W. Wattenberg, *Mental Hygiene in Teaching.* New York: Harcourt, Brace, 1951. Chapter 7.
2. E. T. Sheerer, "An Analysis of the Relationships between Acceptance of and Respect for Self and Acceptance of and Respect for Others in Ten Counseling Cases," *Journal of Consulting Psychology.* 13:169–75;1949.
3. R. J. Havighurst, *Developmental Tasks and Education.* New York: Longmans, Green, 1950. P. 6.
4. *Ibid.*, Chapter 5, portions reprinted by permission. This material is also treated at greater length in: R. J. Havighurst, *Human Development and Education.* New York: Longmans, Green, 1953. Chapter 9, "The Adolescent Peer Group."
5. A. Schoeppe, E. A. Haggard, and R. J. Havighurst, "Some Factors Affecting Sixteen-Year-Olds' Success in Five Developmental Tasks," *Journal of Abnormal and Social Psychology.* 48:42–52; 1953.
6. *Ibid.* P. 50. Reprinted by permission.
7. *Ibid.* Pp. 50–51. Reprinted by permission.
8. S. Ferenczi, "Stages in the Development of the Sense of Reality," in E. Jones, tr., *Sex in Psychoanalysis.* Boston: Badger, 1916. Chapter 8.
9. J. G. Rockwell, "Pupil Responsibility for Behavior," *The Elementary School Journal.* 51:266–70;1951.

10. *Your Future Is What You Make It,* "You and Industry" Series. New York: National Association of Manufacturers, 1947. P. 24.
11. W. M. Aikin, *The Story of the Eight-Year Study.* New York: Harper, 1942.
12. F. H. Finch, "Are High Schools of the Present Day Inferior to Those of an Earlier Period?" *School Review.* 52:84–91; 1944.
13. ———— and V. W. Gillenwater, "Reading Achievement Now and Then," *Elementary School Journal.* 49:446–54;1949.
14. L. J. Fish, *Examinations Seventy-Five Years Ago and Today.* Yonkers: World Book, 1930.
15. A. A. Haberly, "How Are We Doing? Modern versus Traditional Education," *Curriculum Bulletin* No. 82. Eugene: School of Education, University of Oregon, July 15, 1950.
16. J. W. Stansfield, "We Fling Down the Gauntlet," *NEA Journal.* 42:204;1953.

SUGGESTED READINGS

Association for Supervision and Curriculum Development, *Fostering Mental Health in Our Schools.* Washington: National Education Association, 1950. Chapters 6 and 7 deal with developmental tasks.

R. J. Havighurst, *Developmental Tasks and Education.* New York: Longmans, Green, 1950.

K. Horney, *Neurosis and Human Growth.* New York: Norton, 1950. An account of the neurotic disturbances of everyday life that thwart and frustrate growth in the direction of emotional maturity.

H. C. Lindgren, *The Art of Human Relations.* New York: Hermitage, 1953. Chapter 6, "The Struggle to Attain Emotional Maturity."

H. A. Overstreet, *The Mature Mind.* New York: Norton, 1949. A popular but nonetheless psychologically sound treatment of the development of emotional maturity.

F. Redl and W. W. Wattenberg, *Mental Hygiene in Teaching.* New York: Harcourt, Brace, 1951. Chapter 7, "Adjustment, Maturity, and Normality."

L. J. Saul, *Emotional Maturity.* Philadelphia: Lippincott, 1947. A review of various aspects of normal and neurotic behavior from the standpoint of the psychiatrist.

J. Warters, *Achieving Maturity.* New York: McGraw-Hill, 1949. A textbook for high school students to be used in courses that have mental hygiene content and emphases. Suggested here largely as an example of a well-written book for adolescents about their problems.

SUGGESTED FILMS

Overdependency. National Film Board of Canada. Available through McGraw-Hill.

Shyness. National Film Board of Canada. Available through McGraw-Hill.

5

BEHAVIOR PROBLEMS

THE PROBLEM CHILD

MOST teachers regard the behavior problems of children as an unjust burden which must be borne. Disciplining unruly children is not directly related to the mechanics of teaching; yet it is something that must be done if the teaching is to succeed. No one knows how many teachers seek other forms of employment or go into early retirement because of the nerve-shattering effects of dealing with children whose behavior is disturbing and disruptive, but their number must be large. The problem of "what to do with children who disturb the class," or, as it is commonly phrased, "What shall we do about discipline?" is one most frequently mentioned when teachers are asked what subjects they would like to take up at workshops, discussion groups, and in-service seminars. It is probably no exaggeration to say that the so-called "problem child" is considered by many teachers to be the greatest hazard to their own mental health. Although this problem is widespread, it is not universal. Some schools are more inclined to attract or develop problem children than are others, and some teachers appear to have more difficulty with them than others. Furthermore, there is a tendency for bored and unruly children to be more of a problem in classes devoted to academic subjects than in classes which are more concerned with creativity (like art and music), large-muscle activity (like physical education), or vocational training (like home economics and manual arts). Even so, even nonacademic classes are at times disturbed by children with problem behavior.

The last two generations have seen some marked changes in our attitudes toward problem children. Two generations ago, the tendency was to view the child who chronically misbehaved as a "bad child"—one who was inherently and basically bad. It was felt that it was necessary to "break his will" in much the same way that one might curb a wild horse. Punishments of all sorts, physical and otherwise, were used in an attempt to bring about the desired change, and school and home complemented and supplemented each other both as to philosophy and method. The method "worked"—to the extent that most children were obedient and submissive, at least as long as they were under the direct supervision of adults. Nevertheless, there were always some children who were not converted to good behavior, and there were other children who "behaved," but who also developed emotional problems that interfered with their success and happiness.

CAUSES OF BEHAVIOR PROBLEMS

PARENTAL ATTITUDES

During the 1920's we began to use diagnostic methods in our schools to a much greater degree than we had previously. One of the things we discovered was that there is a relationship between parental attitudes and behavior and the attitudes and behavior of children. We found, for example, that parents who are delinquent tend to rear children who are delinquent. The research into the relationship between parental attitudes and patterns of behavior and the behavior problems of children continues to produce data that confirm these findings.

One study that gives dramatic emphasis to the importance of parental attitudes is the research conducted by J. C. Mark, who analyzed the attitudes of the mothers of adult male schizophrenics [1] toward child behavior. Mark discovered that certain attitudes found greater acceptance among such mothers than among mothers of other, non-psychiatric hospital patients. A review of these attitudes, some of which are listed in Table 5–1, appears to indicate that mothers of this group of mental patients favor close supervision, control, and restriction of children's behavior. Furthermore, the warmth of their relationship to their children was colored by attitudes of both excessive devotion and cool detachment [1].

[1] Schizophrenia is a severe mental disorder or psychosis. Most of the patients in mental institutions are suffering from some form of schizophrenia.

TABLE 5–1. ATTITUDES MORE CHARACTERISTIC OF MOTHERS OF SCHIZOPHRENIC PATIENTS (AFTER MARK [1])

QUESTIONNAIRE ITEMS ASSOCIATED WITH RESTRICTION, CONTROL, AND CLOSE SUPERVISION OF CHILDREN'S BEHAVIOR

Children should be taken to and from school until the age of eight just to make sure that there are no accidents.
A mother should make it her business to know everything her children are thinking.
If children are quiet for a little while, a mother should immediately find out what they are thinking about.
A child should not plan to enter any occupation his parents do not approve of.
A good mother should shelter her child from life's little difficulties.
A mother should never be separated from her child.
It is better for children to play at home than to visit other children.
A young child should be protected from hearing about sex.
A child's friends usually do more harm than good.
Children who always obey grow up to be the best adults.
Too much freedom will make a child wild.
A watchful mother can keep her child out of all accidents.

[TABLE 5–1—(CONT.)]

Children who take part in sex play become sex criminals when
they grow up.
A child should never keep a secret from his parents.
Children seven years of age are really too young to spend summers
away from home in a camp.
If children are to grow up and get somewhere in life, they must be
continuously kept after.
Children should do nothing without the consent of their parents.

QUESTIONNAIRE   ITEMS   ASSOCIATED   WITH
EXCESSIVE   DEVOTION

A devoted mother has no time for social life.
Parents should sacrifice everything for their children.
When the father punishes a child for no good reason, the mother
should take the child's side.
A good way to get children to obey is by giving them presents or
promising them treats.
Parents ought to close their eyes to their children's faults.
One reason that it is sad to see children grow up is because they
need you more when they are babies.
A mother should shower her child with praise at all times.

QUESTIONNAIRE   ITEMS   ASSOCIATED   WITH
DETACHED   COOLNESS   OR   REJECTION

Children should not annoy parents with their unimportant prob-
lems.
Playing too much with a child will spoil him.
A mother has to suffer much and say little.
Too much affection will make a child a "softie."
Spanking a child does more good than harm.
There is little thanks or pleasure in raising children.
It is not the duty of the parent to teach the child about sex.
Some children are just naturally bad.
Mothers should have vacations away from their children.
Children need some of the natural meanness taken out of them.
A child will develop a better character if he works after school
instead of playing.
A child should be weaned away from the bottle or breast as soon
as possible.
Children should always be punished for being bad.

The fact that Table 5–1 contains so many ideas that are
commonly heard on the lips of parents indicates that there is
much more to rearing one's child to be a schizophrenic, so to

speak, than merely voicing certain specific attitudes. Items in Table 5–1 thus indicate that mothers of schizophrenics differ from other mothers more in degree rather than in kind. Nevertheless, Mark's study does raise some interesting questions that are worth further discussion and exploration.

Another piece of research that shows the relation of parental attitudes and home background to children's behavior in later life may be found in the report made to the governor of New York on the background of 102 sex offenders in Sing Sing Prison. A portion of this report is as follows:

> Almost all these 102 men had histories of unusually unfavorable childhoods with severe emotional deprivation. Psychiatric and psychological studies disclosed that basically they all felt they had suffered from neglect or rejection. Their parents, or whoever brought them up, were usually dominating, often brutal or often over-indulgent. . . . A child who has a prolonged continuation of a severely unhappy emotional experience, or who has never acquired a feeling of independence, becomes fearful and insecure. These reactions are often the basis upon which abnormal and delinquent behavior is developed [2].

The relationship between delinquency and emotional deprivation is further confirmed by John Bowlby, who states that he finds two factors that are especially common in the history of persistent delinquents and that differentiate them from children suffering from other forms of emotional and social maladjustment. The first factor is the prolonged separation of the child from his mother (or his established foster mother) during his first five years. The second factor is the child's being more or less unwanted by parents who are themselves emotionally unstable and whose attitudes to their children are hostile, critical, and punishing. Bowlby attributes these unfavorable parental attitudes to the parents' own unhappy childhood, an experience that has made them resentful and hostile toward others. Unfortunately, says Bowlby, the parents of delinquents are usually unaware of the way in which their hostile attitudes affect their treatment of their own children, and the abuse and criticism that society heaps on the heads of these parents is thus not only unprofitable, but worsens their attitudes. What both parents and children need is skilled help and understanding [3].

Edna Brower speaks from her experience as a visiting teacher when she says:

> The rejection of a child in the home leads to poor adjustment at school, with its kindred problems—unsatisfactory work, quarrels with other children on the playground, noise and confusion in the classroom, no regard for authority, apparent suspicion of everyone, resentment toward life in general. The child finds reading and the other tool subjects very difficult to master. He is not a success at home or at school; in his own mind at least, he is a failure and he must live accordingly [4].

We have given this much space to the discussion of the effect parental attitudes and home have on the personality and the behavior of children not because we want teachers to become unduly alarmed at the dangerous potentials that appear to lurk in the background of children's lives, so to speak, but to emphasize the importance of these factors and forces in the personality development of children. In attempting to understand the motivation of children, it is essential to have some idea of parental attitudes and the psychological atmosphere of the home. The studies we have cited show how crucial these matters are. On the other hand, we should not place the blame for the misbehavior of children squarely on parents. As we learn more about the relationship of parents to the behavior problems of children, we are also coming to realize that parents, as well as children, are ofttimes the helpless pawns of the environment and culture in which they find themselves. We are also beginning to see that the school itself may aggravate or worsen the behavior difficulties of children.

AMBIVALENCE ABOUT AUTOCRATIC METHODS

Another factor that must be considered in studying behavior problems is our changing attitude toward the use of autocratic or authoritarian methods in dealing with children. In an analysis of why this is "the age anxiety," Rudolph Dreikurs points out that we are living in a period in which there is a slow turning away from autocratic to democratic methods. In a situation characterized by the autocratic approach the relationship is always between persons of unequal rights, whereas in a democratic situation individuals have equal rights, regardless of whether they are adults or children. One of the ways in which the trend toward democratic relationships expresses itself is in the lessening emphasis on methods that involve force, coercion, reward, and punishment and in an increasing emphasis on permissiveness, respect, and love. Dreikurs says that we have not fully turned away from autocratic or authoritarian modes nor have we completely accepted the democratic approach. Much of the anxiety we experience at the present moment in history comes about because we are inclined to *talk* democracy but to *use* autocratic methods, although we do not apply the latter as drastically as we did, say, fifty years ago [5]. One might say that our anxiety is the natural result of too large a gap between our self-concept (what we *see* ourselves doing) and our self-ideal (what we *should* be doing).

Our conflicting attitudes with respect to the best methods for dealing with children are thus the producers of anxiety and feelings of guilt. No matter how we deal with a problem situation, we are likely to wonder whether we handled it correctly. Children sense our feelings of insecurity and indecision. Sometimes they take advantage of us because they realize that we are vulnerable and they see the opportunity to get revenge for real or fancied wrongs. At other times, however, they misbehave because they, too, are made anxious by our indecisiveness. An obvious solution would be to rid ourselves of indecisiveness, anxieties, and feelings of guilt at one stroke by accepting either an autocratic or a completely permissive approach to problems of discipline. But this is a case where the obvious solution is not necessarily the best solution, inasmuch as a strict adherence to either approach is likely to create even greater difficulties.

UNWILLING STUDENTS

There is an additional reason why the teacher of today is more likely to have difficulty with problem children than was the teacher of fifty years ago. Compulsory attendance laws are more strictly applied than formerly, and they encompass a greater age span. As a result, there are proportionately more children who are in school against their will. Many of these children come from families, particularly in lower socioeconomic groups, whose general attitude to education is unfriendly. Some of these children accept school as a necessary evil, and hence their resistance, if any, is largely passive. Being forced to go to school leads others to express their hostility more openly—through truancy, destructiveness, fighting, or creating disturbances in class. The relation of socioeconomic factors to the behavior and attitudes of children will be discussed more fully in Chapter 6.

THE NEED FOR UNDERSTANDING AND OBJECTIVITY

ALTHOUGH the number of students displaying problem behavior has increased in the last half century, teachers today are in a better position to cope with this difficulty. Because we have better bases nowadays for understanding children's behavior, we can also deal with it more effectively. Because we can understand it better, we can also be more objective. And objectivity can be of great help in dealing with children. Children often develop amazing capacities to

provoke and irritate both teachers and their fellow classmates, and the teacher who loses his objectivity and strikes
out in blind and angry retaliation is likely to worsen the
situation.

Admittedly, understanding children and maintaining an
attitude of objectivity are exceedingly complex skills, and
even the most successful teachers often wish they had more
of these two abilities. We shall have more to say in later
chapters about why we find it so difficult to develop understanding and objectivity; hence, for the purpose of the immediate discussion we shall focus on the causes of problem
behavior itself.

Our understanding of problem behavior is usually helped
if we can get an idea of how the student in question sees himself and his environment, for it is this view that will help
determine how he will behave. Indeed, it is more likely that
his *concept* of his environment will determine his behavior
than the environment itself. This explains, in part, why two
children from the same family can behave so differently—
it is not that the objective facts of their life are so different,
but rather that their views of it differ.

DO CHILDREN IN THE SAME FAMILY HAVE THE SAME ENVIRONMENT?

Let us take the case of James and John Valentine, fraternal
(that is, "unlike") twins. They attend the ninth grade of a
suburban junior high school and live in one of the "better
districts" in town. Neither James nor John is a particularly
good student, although their intelligence, as measured by
tests, is "high average."

James is a quiet boy, who never gets into trouble. He is
neither liked nor disliked by other students—he is tolerated.
He prefers to keep to himself, although he will participate in
group activity with other students when invited. He appears to
try hard at his school work, but he does not seem to know how

to take hold and organize his work. He is getting average grades in English and social studies, is failing in algebra and general science, but is getting good grades in music and typing. James' counselor says that she has tried to talk to him a number of times about his work, but without success. He gives noncommittal replies to all her questions and seems very reluctant to discuss the reasons for his difficulties.

John is always in some kind of trouble. It is never anything serious—using disrespectful language to a teacher, smoking in the lavatory, cutting an occasional class, playing rough practical jokes. He has a wide circle of friends of both sexes. He works at his school assignments sporadically and most of the time appears not to be interested. He does well enough to get passing grades in his final examinations, and so far has not received a failing grade, although he has come close in some subjects. His counselor saw him briefly at the start of the semester, when she helped him make out his program, but has not seen him since, although she strongly urged him to see her from time to time during his study period or after school. Doubtless John will be seen by someone very shortly, because there have been increasing complaints about his disruptive behavior in class. His teachers say that he is always repentant when they speak to him about his behavior outside of class, but that no improvement results from such conferences.

James and John differ from each other in many respects. They both present problems to the school, but of the two, John's behavior is more of a threat to the everyday operations of the school. Furthermore, John's activities have a negative effect on the morale of his teachers in that they are distracted from their main job of teaching. They report that classes are difficult to control when John is in them because he always has a circle of admirers who are inclined to cooperate with him in his pranks and to aid and abet him in his defiance of authority.

The usual and direct ways of dealing with problems do not seem to work with James and John. They do not respond to appeals, reprimands, low grades, and so forth. It is evident that something else must be done if they are to benefit from school. Whatever that "something" is, it will have a better chance to be effective if it is based on an understanding of the factors which underlie their problems.

We have said that children behave differently partly because the concepts of themselves and their environment were different. Let us look further into the background of the Valentine twins to see what conditions and factors may be related to their present behavior.

Mr. Valentine, the father of the twins, came to this country from Central Europe with his parents when he was four years old. He left school when he was twelve and went to work as a delivery boy in a grocery store. By the time he was twenty-one he owned the store. When he was thirty-five, he was the president and general manager of a chain of supermarkets.

Mr. Valentine prides himself on his ability to speak English without a trace of accent. He is a member of the local Chamber of Commerce, has held important positions in service organizations, and has been active in politics. Mrs. Valentine was born in the same region as her husband and has lived here the same number of years. She is reluctant to turn her back on the Old World and to embrace the new way of life as her husband has done. She speaks English with a heavy accent and does not mingle readily with her neighbors. Her best friends are the people she grew up with and who still live, as she once did, in the poorer section of a neighboring city.

During the first dozen years of their marriage, the Valentines quarreled frequently. Mr. Valentine did not like to see his wife maintaining relationships with her old friends: he wanted her to participate more in the social life which is a part of being a successful businessman. Mrs. Valentine resented the continual pressure to change her ways. She was happier with things as they were and could not understand her husband's changing behavior. He no longer attended church as regularly as he did when they were first married, he was away from home most of the time, and he used family funds in ways which appeared extravagant to her. Most of all she did not like his new friends, and when he brought them into the home, she would not join in their conversation, but would remain in the background.

In recent years the Valentines have quarreled less often. Mr.

Valentine goes his way and Mrs. Valentine goes hers. The occasional family gatherings are marked with coolness. Only the least controversial topics are discussed.

James had been closer to his mother. She is inclined to "baby" and overprotect him, taking his part when disagreements develop between him and his father or his brother. There is little love lost between James and his father. Mr. Valentine usually uses a sarcastic tone in speaking to him, and even at best his attitude is patronizing. He feels that James' record at school is about what you would expect of a "Mama's boy." Mrs. Valentine is quite concerned about James' grades and frequently urges him to work harder. Sometimes she tries to help him with his homework, but her own educational level is too low to be of much assistance. However, she continues to be a source of comfort and solace to him when he meets with disappointment and failure at school.

John's relations with his mother have never been very friendly or affectionate. Indeed, in recent years, quarrels have increased in frequency. She accuses him of being disrespectful and insulting, and he accuses her of never being satisfied with whatever he does and of favoring James. His rebelliousness extends even into little things. For instance, both John and his brother learned their parents' native language from their mother when they were small children. James and his mother hold long conversations in it, but when she uses it in speaking to John, he always answers in English. Sometimes, in a burst of exasperation, he will say: "Aw, Ma, talk United States!" Mr. Valentine will speak only English at home. On the surface there do not appear to be any strong ties of affection between John and his father; they get into an occasional argument, but there appears to be a sort of mutual respect or understanding between them. Mr. Valentine would like to see John get better grades at school, but he does not make an important point of it. He is pleased that John has made so many friends and he encourages John's social activities by being generous with financial assistance.

There is little affection between the two boys. Although they are of equal height and weight, James is always complaining about being "picked on" by John. They used to get into fights almost every day, but they now have separate sleeping quarters and this seems to have solved this problem by reducing their contact with each other.

This is a picture of a family that is divided against itself. The two boys who are growing up in this family live in what amounts to different psychological worlds. James' concept of himself is one of someone who needs help, reassurance, and love of others. He has a low opinion of his ability. He would like to please his mother and his teachers by getting better grades, but he feels that he cannot. His father's biting criticism only serves to reinforce this opinion. James sees the world as a place which poses difficult problems, but he is confident that if he waits long enough and struggles along as best he can, someone will either help him or will arrange that he does not have to solve them.

John feels confident that he can do anything that he sets his mind to. He expects people to like him and he reciprocates by being charming and friendly. However, he resents being told what to do and reacts to this by revenging himself on those who issue orders. In some ways, the school appears to him like his mother, and he rebels against the necessity of conforming to its requirements. Other things in life appear to him as more important than school work, and he derides his brother and his mother for taking school so seriously.

FAMILY PATTERNS AND PROBLEM BEHAVIOR

In this anecdotal description of James and John Valentine, we have tried to show how family patterns affect children and their behavior. The important factors here are the basic conflict between mother and father and the identification of each child with one of the parents. The attitudes of the parents toward their children have had great effect on the shaping of their self-concepts and their attitudes toward their environment. There are, of course, an endless variety of family problems that are likely to produce problem behavior in children.

For example, having an alcoholic parent may have a disruptive effect, although this does not necessarily follow. But the presence of an alcoholic parent assumes crucial importance when it affects a child's self-concept. Consider the case of a child who loves his alcoholic and shiftless father more than he loves his hard-working, sharp-tongued mother. He wants to continue liking his father, but since his father is so obviously a burden on the family, he is not sure whether it is right to love him. When his mother says those cruel things to his father, she is probably right. Maybe he (the child) ought to love his mother more because she is right, because she is "better" for him. Yet he still loves his father more. Perhaps there is something wrong with him, just as there is something wrong with his father. With such unresolved tensions preventing him from bringing his self-concept and self-ideal into focus, as it were, it is understandable why such a child might express some of his confusion and anxiety at school in the form of behavior problems.

Family troubles often produce disturbed behavior because children have difficulty in adjusting their self-concepts and their perceptions of their environment. And, if for any reason they become discouraged in their attempts to "make sense" out of life, there is trouble ahead of some sort. The child who is discouraged about his hopes and possibilities for success and happiness in life will adopt some sort of protective behavior. He may become aggressive and hostile, attacking other children, disturbing classes, talking back to teachers, refusing to do assigned tasks, or acting in destructive ways. He may become retiring, withdrawing from contact with others, lacking interest in trying, doing only what is required of him. He may become overdependent, constantly seeking reassurance and help, believing himself unable to perform assigned tasks. These are a few characteristic approaches used by children who have become or are becoming discouraged.

The broken home is blamed for many behavior problems in school. Usually, there are accompanying factors which operate together with the loss of a parent to produce disturbance. A boy lives with his divorced mother. She is a demanding, critical woman. He finds that he is happier with a gang of boys who live in the neighborhood. They become involved in a series of petty crimes. Now, what is the chief factor here? Is it the broken home? The demanding mother? The gang? It could be argued that if the father had been present, this sequence would not have occurred. The chances are that all these factors are important and thus contribute to the behavior problem. In an article written primarily for lawyers and law-enforcement officers, David Abrahamsen, a psychiatrist, has this to say on the subject:

> There has been much written lately to the effect that children must have more and better recreation if there would be less crime. This is all very well, and I am certainly for healthy activity for youngsters. But the core of the crime is within the atmosphere of the home. If we overlook this fact and go on to other things, we are neglecting the real issue and simply missing the fundamental one, for all else is superficial. It is within the home that patterns are formed, and tough gangs notwithstanding, there would be no need of such gangs if relations at home were sufficient and proper guidance were provided.
>
> The insidious factor insofar as tough gangs are concerned is that if there are many homes which provide no emotional security, the boys of the neighborhood will flock together, form a gang, and assume a toughness which will act as a shield for them. This then may grow to such an extent that other children who have a half-way decent situation within the home may join up even reluctantly for fear of otherwise being considered [weaklings] [6]. . . .

A large number of children in most schools come from homes that have been broken by divorce, desertion, or death.[2] Most of them do not develop behavior problems severe enough to warrant the special attention of the teacher or outside experts. However, the child who comes from a broken home, or a home that has a chronic problem, like alcoholism or marked bitterness between parents, is more inclined to be vulnerable than is the child who comes from a more stable environment. In any case, the deciding factors are the child's self-concept, his self-ideal, and his concept of his environment.

CULTURE CONFLICT

ANOTHER fertile source of behavior problems is what sociologists term "culture conflict." We see a double example of culture conflict in the story of the Valentines. Part of the tension in the family results from the reluctance of the mother to abandon the ways of the Old World and from the eagerness of the father to become absorbed in the New World. In many families of first- and second-generation American parents try to rear their children in accordance with Old World values which are often in sharp conflict with the ways of the New. This conflict is further aggravated by the desire of children not to appear different from their schoolmates. Such tensions often find their way into the classroom.

Another sort of culture conflict in the Valentine family is the change which has taken place in their way of life. During the last fifteen years they have moved rapidly up the socioeconomic scale. The way of life in a suburban community is quite different from life in a poorer district in a large city. Furthermore, Mr. Valentine is very seldom at home because his work and his social activities make so many demands on him. This shift in status may not be as important

---

[2] Paul H. Jacobson, statistician for the Metropolitan Life Insurance Company, reports that divorce has in recent years increased more rapidly among families with children than among childless couples. Hence, he believes that the number of children affected by divorce will increase [7].

a factor in the problems of the Valentine children as are the other conditions we have described, but it does contribute to the tensions and conflicts within the family, which in turn produce the problem behavior of the two boys.

The commonest form of culture conflict encountered in schools is that which occurs when the needs of children from lower-class environments collide with the middle-class demands of the school. Behavior standards and values of lower-class groups differ considerably from those of the middle and upper classes, and this difference accounts, in part, for some of the problems teachers (who are largely members of the middle class) experience in dealing with these children. This is a subject we shall explore more extensively and intensively in the next chapter.

PROBLEMS OF CHILDREN IN A CHANGING ENVIRONMENT

Generally speaking, children appear to be more sensitive or vulnerable to rapid and drastic changes in their environment as compared with adults. This is because they have fewer social skills and less valid information that can be used to cope with changing situations. Children are less free to deal with the problems of life independently and hence must depend upon adults for help and emotional support. The sense of bewilderment, loss, and general unhappiness that results when a family moves from one locality to another (thus separating children from their friends) or when a member of the family goes into military service or when a parent is killed, hospitalized, or placed in an institution, very often produces problem behavior of some sort. Such crises are difficult enough for adults; for children, they are often catastrophic. Children who are caught in these circumstances are likely to develop a sense of discouragement that often persists over a long period of time, unless something occurs to alleviate the situation.

The tensions, irregularities, and dislocations that accompany war and mobilization are often cited as causes of emotional disturbances in children. Lois Meek Stolz has the following to say on this score:

> Frustrations can be endless to a little child when war has upset his world. Young children need time, much time to do things; they need freedom for activity, food when they are hungry, sleep when they are sleepy; they cannot wait. They need warm, loving parents who have time to talk and listen and "watch me do this" and tell a story and "fix this for me." When children do not get these satisfactions, they cry and throw things, kick, and bite. They hate and love, but they hate most at that moment. . . .
>
> The two threats that war can bring to the development of a wholesome personality in early childhood are feelings of anxiety and feelings of aggression. These are emotions that basically interfere with relations to people and are the foundations for fear and strife in later years [8].

On the other hand, M. Ralph Kaufman, a psychiatrist writing in *Child Study*, raises the question of whether the crises and tensions of our times are not too easy an explanation of the emotional difficulties that people develop. He asks, how stable was the environment during the Hundred Years' War, the Black Death, or the Crusades [9]? Of course, Kaufman is writing largely about adults, and Stolz is writing about preschool children; and this accounts for the apparent contradiction. Nevertheless, we can make use of both ideas. We must be alert and sensitive to behavior problems that stem from social dislocation, but, on the other hand, we must avoid the trap of explaining all the behavioral difficulties of children as products of a current or recent crises. Some teachers, incidentally, tend to project their own crisis-born anxieties, in analyzing the behavior of children—that is, a teacher who is made anxious and upset by air-raid drills may attribute discipline problems in his class to the anxieties aroused by the drills, whereas it would be more realistic to say that the discipline problems were more the result of the teacher's anxieties than anything else. The point is that our own worries not only may interfere with our ability to analyze children's behavior, but may also aggravate or encourage the development of behavior problems.

RECOGNIZING PROBLEM BEHAVIOR

IT IS often difficult for teachers to become aware of the existence of emotional crises in children's lives, particularly when their attention is occupied with upwards of twenty-five or thirty-five children at any given time. Nevertheless, there are clues that are likely to be symptoms of emotional difficulties. There is the child whose work suddenly falls off, or the child who has been interested in school work and now becomes listless and lackadaisical. There is the child whose level of accomplishment drops far below the expectancy based on his intelligence test scores. And there are the poor readers. Experienced teachers, glancing over a class of second-graders have little difficulty in spotting the poor readers. They are the wigglers. Barbara Biber and her associates, in their study of thirty-five seven- and eight-year olds, found that the poorest readers exhibited the most restless body behavior, changing positions and shifting books ceaselessly, sitting in strange, uncomfortable-looking postures [10].

Thanks to the research and the clinical work with poor readers and with non-readers that has been conducted since 1930, more teachers are coming to see that the emotional problems that are associated with reading retardation far outweigh the technical problems of instruction. In other words, teachers are beginning to understand that the problem of helping a retarded reader is more than merely teaching him to read. Inasmuch as reading difficulties are likely to be symptomatic of emotional disturbances, it is not surprising that efforts to help them can be more effective when directed at alleviating their emotional difficulties than at working with their reading problems. Virginia M. Axline reported marked improvement in the reading ability of a group of retarded readers and non-readers as a result of their participation in a situation which employed principles of group psychotherapy [11].

Another symptom of emotional disturbance is the tendency to have frequent accidents. Vita Krall compared the backgrounds of thirty-two children between the ages of three and eight, who had three or more accidents (as listed in hospital records) during a four-year period, with the backgrounds of an equal number of children who had been free from accidents. She found that accident repeaters were more likely to come from broken homes, to have transferred schools more frequently, and to have come to the attention of guidance workers more frequently [12].

A little earlier we implied that experienced teachers frequently are better able to spot behavior difficulties than is the case of teachers with limited experience. One of the reasons why experience is helpful is that the signs indicating the existence of a problem are not always obvious. Fritz Redl lists some of the "hiding places" for problems:

> If Tom is afraid and wants to hide his problem, he may act especially tough, fresh, provocatively independent.
> If May really dislikes her teacher and is afraid it may show, she may develop an unnaturally extreme form of submissiveness and politeness toward her.
> If Johnny falls in love with Milly before he is ready to admit it even to himself, he may act especially crude and mean to her or any other girls in this group.
> If Bob is becoming increasingly afraid of asking even the most harmless questions about sex, he may start using vile language. For everybody is so used to considering vile language a sign of great sophistication that Bob thinks is the safest cover-up for modesty and innocence [13].

Naturally, the extent to which a teacher can investigate what appears to be the symptom of problem behavior is limited by the amount of time he has available for interviews with students and their parents, as well as by his training and experience in conducting and interpreting such interviews. The task of diagnosis and therapy is largely that of the guidance worker and will be discussed in a later chapter; what we are concerned with here is the need for teachers to be sensitive to marked changes in student behavior, large gaps between reasonable expectation and accomplishment, and other symptoms of problems that may provide clues to situations that are affecting the learning of children. And as we indicated earlier, the better the understanding of the teacher, the better he can guide the learning that takes place in his classroom.

VARIABILITY IN BEHAVIOR

WE HAVE been concerned in this chapter, for the most part, with the external pressures that affect a child's behavior, particularly those forces that threaten his security, arouse anxieties, and lead him to engage in problem behavior of various sorts. However, we should not leave this portion of our discussion without uttering some cautions. One is that not all children react to similar circumstances in the same way and they do not always react as adults expect them to—they react according to their perceptions of the circumstances. By way of an example, a child may be extremely upset because a friend has moved away, but may be quite unaffected by the death of a brother or sister. Nor are all children upset by family crises. However, since children *are* very likely to be affected adversely by the events and circumstances we have mentioned in this chapter, it is well for teachers to be alert to some of the common causes of behavior problems. On the other hand, teachers should avoid the trap of *expecting* children to develop problems merely because they come from divorced homes or deprived surroundings, and so forth.

Nor are all the traditional clues reliable indices of maladjustment. When James C. Coleman and Jean Elizabeth McCalley investigated the incidence of nail-biting, they found that it was commoner than most of us would imagine—25 percent among school children and 20 percent among naval recruits and selectees. As a result of their research, they decided that nail-biting could not be considered an adequate basis for the diagnosis of maladjustment [14].

Obstinacy or stubbornness is sometimes seized upon as a clue of emotional disturbance. But Katharine M. Banham believes that it is a normal reaction in many children and is both caused and aggravated by a conflict between the needs for dependent conformity and independent initiative. Conflicts of this sort are, for example, very likely to be present in adolescents [15].

Another caution is that a study of a child's environment provides only a partial explanation of his behavior. Sometimes it may appear to provide no clues at all. Very often, a child's problem is related to an internal conflict of some sort which must be understood before it is possible to see what it is in his environment that is bothering him. By way of example, a child may become discouraged, and on that account he makes no progress in learning and even develops behavior which disrupts the class, all because he cannot seem to live up to the demands of his self-ideal. He feels guilty and inadequate because he has let himself down.

If we observe these cautions, we shall be less likely to rely on the so-called "easy solutions"—"John will be better behaved if we transfer him out of Miss Murdock's class into Mrs. Kyne's," or "Jill will 'come out of her shell' if we seat her next to Rudolph—he's so friendly." To be sure, such moves sometimes succeed because we have accidentally provided the antidote for a child's difficulties, but more usually the difficulty persists or even worsens because we have not understood the nature of the problem.

REFERENCES

1. J. C. Mark, "Attitudes of the Mothers of Male Schizophrenics toward Child Behavior," *Journal of Abnormal and Social Psychology.* 48:185–99;1953. Portions reprinted by permission.
2. *Report on Study of 102 Sex Offenders at Sing Sing Prison as Submitted to Governor Thomas E. Dewey.* Utica, N. Y.: State Hospitals Press, 1950. P. 14.
3. J. Bowlby, "Research into the Origins of Delinquent Behavior," *British Medical Journal.* 1:570–73;1950.
4. E. Brower, "The Visiting Teacher Looks at the Rejected Child," *Mental Hygiene.* 33:432–35;1949.
5. R. Dreikurs, *Character Education and Spiritual Values in an Anxious Age.* Boston: Beacon Press, 1952. Pp. 3–4.
6. D. Abrahamsen, "Family Tension, Basic Cause of Criminal Behavior," *Journal of Criminal Law and Criminology.* 40:330–43; 1949. Reprinted by permission of the *Journal of Criminal Law and Criminology* (Northwestern University School of Law).
7. P. H. Jacobson, "Differentials in Divorce by Duration of Marriage and Size of Family," *American Sociological Review.* 15:235–44; 1950.
8. L. M. Stolz, "The Effect of Mobilization and War on Children," *Social Casework.* 32:143–49;1951. Reprinted by permission.
9. M. R. Kaufman, "The Two Worlds We Live In," *Child Study.* 29 (3):13–14, 32–34;1952.
10. B. Biber, L. B. Murphy, L. P. Woodcock, I. S. Black, *Life and Ways of the Seven-to-Eight Year Old.* New York: Basic Books, 1952. P. 62.
11. V. M. Axline, "Nondirective Therapy for Poor Readers," *Journal of Consulting Psychology.* 11:61–69; 1947.
12. V. Krall, "Personality Characteristics of Accident-Repeating Children," *Journal of Abnormal and Social Psychology.* 48:99–107; 1953.
13. F. Redl, *Understanding Children's Behavior.* New York: Bureau of Publications, Teachers College, Columbia University, 1949. P. 17. Reprinted by permission.
14. J. C. Coleman and J. E. McCalley, "Nail-Biting and Mental Health: A Survey of the Literature," *Mental Hygiene.* 32:428–54; 1948.
15. K. M. Banham, "Obstinate Children are Adaptable," *Mental Hygiene.* 36:84–89;1952.

SUGGESTED READINGS

R. G. Barker, J. S. Kounin, and H. F. Wright, eds., *Child Behavior and Development*. New York: McGraw-Hill, 1943. See especially chapters by Macfarlane, Jersild, Escalona, Wright, Levy, Keister, and the chapter by Barker, Dembo, and Lewin.

C. Buhler, F. Smitter, and S. Richardson, *Childhood Problems and the Teacher*. New York: Holt, 1952. A warm, sympathetic, and practical approach to the understanding of problem behavior.

W. Dennis, *Readings in Child Psychology*. New York: Prentice-Hall, 1951. Section 8, "Personality."

O. S. English and G. H. J. Pearson, *Emotional Problems of Living*. Analyzes problems and stages of personality development from the standpoint of the Freudian psychoanalyst.

N. B. Henry, ed., *Juvenile Delinquency and the Schools*, 47th Yearbook, Part I. Chicago: National Society for the Study of Education, 1948.

C. M. Louttit, *Clinical Psychology of Children's Behavior Problems*. rev. ed. New York: Harper, 1947. A conservative approach, at opposite extreme to viewpoints expressed in books by English and Pearson.

B. Overstreet, *Understanding Fear in Ourselves and Others*. New York: Harper, 1951.

G. H. J. Pearson, *Emotional Disorders of Children*. New York: Norton, 1949. Diagnostic approach to the problems of disturbed children. Readers should be prepared for a heavy Freudian emphasis.

F. Redl and D. Wineman, *Children Who Hate*. Glencoe, Ill.: Free Press, 1951.

C. R. Rogers, *The Clinical Treatment of the Problem Child*. Boston: Houghton Mifflin, 1939. A middle-of-the-road approach, as compared to Louttit and English and Pearson. Although written ten years ago, this book contains much that is useful.

H. L. Witmer and R. Kotinsky, eds., *Personality in the Making*. New York: Harper, 1952. The fact-finding report of the Midcentury White House Conference on Children and Youth. Chapter 4 discusses the importance of parent-child relations.

See also items 10 and 13, listed in the References for this Chapter.

SUGGESTED FILMS

Feelings of Depression. National Film Board of Canada. Available through McGraw-Hill.

Problem Children. Ohio State Division of Mental Health and Ohio State University. Available through Psychological Cinema Register, State College, Penna.

This Is Robert. Vassar College. Available from New York University Film Library.

6

SOCIOECONOMIC FACTORS UNDERLYING CHILDREN'S BEHAVIOR

"WALTER," Miss Endicott said, kindly but firmly, "I asked you to see me after school because there is an important matter I wanted to discuss with you."

"Yes, Miss Endicott," said Walter, dutifully.

"Walter," she continued, "I am very much concerned about you. Here you are, ten years old, almost through the third grade, and unable to read. I have given you extra help, provided special books, and tried to find out what your interests are, but without any results, as far as I can see. You did not even try to do the reading test I gave you yesterday—all you did was to draw airplanes on the margins."

"Yes, Miss Endicott." Walter hung his head. He liked Miss Endicott. He was sorry he had disappointed her.

"I honestly don't know what to do about you, Walter. I talked with Mr. Graham about you this morning. We think that children should be promoted to the next grade, but in your case, we can't see what good it would do for you to go on to the fourth grade unless you can read. So we're going to keep you here in the third grade at least for a semester to see if we can't make another try at your reading. What do you have to say about that, Walter?"

Walter looked up at Miss Endicott, and his eyes were shining.

"I'll try, Miss Endicott. I really will. Can I go now, Miss Endicott, please?"

"Yes, Walter, I suppose so. I hope you will try. I hope you are not too disappointed at not going on to the fourth grade with the other children. . . ."

Miss Endicott never finished what she had to say, because Walter had scurried out of the room while she was in mid-sentence, his departure undoubtedly speeded by cries of "Where's that Walter?" outside the window. Evidently the sand-lot baseball crowd was becoming impatient.

Later, when she talked to Mr. Graham about her conversation with Walter she said:

"What I can't understand is how easily he took it. He wasn't upset in the slightest. You'd think that he *wanted* to stay in the third grade. Honestly, sometimes I think that I'll *never* understand what makes children act as they do."

SOCIAL-CLASS MEMBERSHIP AS A FACTOR IN MOTIVATION

WHAT Miss Endicott is saying to Mr. Graham is that Walter did not react to the news of being held back in the third grade the way other children would have reacted. She is genuinely puzzled by his indifference, or, as she says, by his apparent pleasure. His pleasure is easy to explain: he likes Miss Endicott, and staying with her another semester holds no terrors for him. But his indifference to being held back has a more complex explanation. In essence, anyone should be upset if denied the right or privilege of progressing with his group. Education, personal progress, and reading all rate high in our system of values, and they rate equally high with most of the children Miss Endicott has in her classes. But they do not rate very high with Walter. One of the very important reasons for this difference is that Miss Endicott and the majority of her pupils are members of the great American middle class, the class that values education, progress, and ambition. Walter's father is a tenant farmer. His parents both left school when they were in the sixth grade. None of Walter's five older brothers or sisters completed the ninth grade. The family is not poor—it provides adequately for itself—but education does not rank very high on its scale of values. Walter's parents do not object to his going to school, but as far as they are concerned, it is a waste of time. Other things in life, to them, are more worth while. A boy can make more money farming or have more fun fishing than he can going to school.

Basing their analysis on these factors, as well as other data they would gather about Walter's family, sociologists would classify them as members of the upper-lower class in their community. In doing so, they would be using a system of social classification developed by W. Lloyd Warner and others [1] which includes the following categories:

Upper-upper Class:[1] Persons with high social prestige and hereditary wealth, the socially elite, the "400."

Lower-upper Class: Persons of wealth, but without the prestige of the upper-upper class; business executives and proprietors of large corporations; wealthier doctors and lawyers.

Upper-middle Class: Members of the professions; white-collar folk in fairly comfortable circumstances; persons with some college education.

Lower-middle Class: White-collar folk; salaried person-

---

[1] A class may be thought of as the largest group of people, in a given community whose members have intimate access to each other—that is, who eat and drink together, freely visit each other's families, talk intimately in social cliques, intermarry—in short, who enjoy the privileges of social equality with each other [2, 3].

nel; some foremen and highly skilled craftsmen; small businessmen; persons with high school education.

Upper-lower Class: Most skilled and semiskilled craftsmen; laborers with steady jobs; persons with grade school education.

Lower-lower Class: Most unskilled workers; migrant workers; persons of little or no education.

If Miss Endicott is like most of us, she is unaware that there is a class structure in her community, a class structure whose value patterns are reflected in the behavior of the children in her classroom. As products of a middle-class way of life, most of us are unaware of how the values of other cultural groups influence their members. Consequently, we are continually puzzled and frustrated when certain children in our classes do not react or behave as we think they should. Our systems of rewards and punishments do not work with them; often they are the children who provide us with behavior problems that seem to defy solution.

Actually, there are two sets of factors that encourage behavior problems among children who grow up in lower-class environments. One set of factors has to do with family friction and what might be called "social dislocation." The members of lower-class society are more likely to lead lives marked by divorce and separation, insanity, and delinquency. Since we have already discussed the effect of these factors on the emotional development of children in previous chapters, we shall not give them intensive scrutiny here. The point is that children from lower-class environments exhibit a higher proportion of behavior problems than is true generally of middle-class children, partly because they are more likely to experience the negative factors we have mentioned.

The other set of factors that causes the behavior of these children to differ from that of middle-class children is that the values that dominate the lower-class way of life are often in direct conflict with middle-class values. Lower-class children behave as they do because this is the behavior they have learned from their families. For them it is the "right" way, the "only" way, just as the way that teachers behave is the "right" way and the "only" way according to the standards and values of *their* culture.

DIFFICULTY OF UNDERSTANDING SOCIAL-CLASS PATTERNS OF CONDUCT

It is hard for us to discuss objectively and freely matters related to social class and social status. For one thing, it is difficult to accept the idea that social classes do exist, even though the evidence is all around us. Indeed, it is part of our middle-class outlook on life to deny the existence of class differences; or to say that if they do exist, they are based on money; or to say that if they do exist, they do not really matter. One of the reasons we have difficulty in thinking objectively about class differences is that we believe that people are basically equal. But we have trouble in disassociating the value of the individual from his behavior. In other words, a person who does not behave "properly" (i.e., according to our standards) is not as "good" as a person who *does* behave properly. Thus, we are put in the position of saying that some people (i.e., middle-class people) *are* better than others because they behave properly, and this statement conflicts with our belief that no one is really any better (worth more as an individual) than anyone else. Such contradictions in our thinking create anxiety, and one of the ways we can avoid such anxiety is to avoid recognizing that class differences do exist.

However, we can view the problem more objectively and thus make good use of the data that have been gathered for us by sociologists and psychologists in understanding children, if we can, temporarily at least, put aside the idea that middle-class patterns of behavior are inherently "better" than are other patterns of behavior. For as long as we insist on categorizing all behavior that is different as "bad" and people who display such behavior as "bad," we shall cripple and severely limit our capacity to understand human behavior.

Hilda Taba describes the difficulty experienced by one teacher in dealing with the children of her first grade located in a lower-class neighborhood.

> Her children had had practically no training in doing anything in groups, such as sitting down to an orderly dinner table. Hence, forming a story circle and sitting quietly and listening was an experience for which they had no precedent. When the teacher asked them to sit down they obeyed but soon each got up and went on his merry way. It seemed to the teacher that the children fought all the time. But when she approached them and told them to stop fighting, they became insulted. They had not been fighting at all. On closer observation it appeared that they communicated a variety of feelings through behaviors that looked like fighting. When they wanted to say "I like you," they would shove the object of their affections. When they wanted attention, they'd put out their foot and trip the fellow whose attention they wanted. Words were scarcely used, and they were shy about expressing themselves in words. These were their skills of communication, but all these skills represented a deviation from what is usually expected in school, and could have been considered a misbehavior by the teacher, had she not been led to explore the situation and the meaning of it [4].

In a survey of the importance of the concept of social class for teachers, Walter I. Murray points up the following implications:

> 1. Teachers should understand that our complex American society consists of individuals who are members of different social-class levels. Each of the levels has its particular culture, learning opportunities, and systems of reward and punishment. Teachers who understand only middle-class behavior are found

all too commonly in our schools. They are much concerned with maintaining the standards of middle-class culture and with securing the "proper" conduct with respect to this culture. A typical example is offered by the elementary teacher who, for instance, does not understand that some lower-class children have seen their parents fight with knives, use vulgar language, and indulge in open promiscuity. . . . Middle-class children are rewarded by their parents for receiving high grades in their school work. Often lower-class children show contempt toward such accomplishments and exert much effort toward not working for high grades.

2. Teachers should know that there are individuals in each of the social-class levels who possess competences necessary for technical and civic efficiency. The "intelligence" of individuals in these groups must be judged in terms of the problem-solving opportunities found in the particular social-class environment. The performance of some individuals in classroom situations may be unsuccessful because their experiences have been either too limited or too different. . . . Greater use of the experiences of lower-class children should be made in developing powers with higher mental processes. Through the use of pupil-teacher planning techniques the teacher can discover what experiences lower-class children have had . . . . Children's games might be studied and devised so as to utilize intellectual skills which the child of lower-class culture considers important to him. . . .

3. Teachers should assume as their responsibility the provision of curriculum experiences which have elements in common to all social-class groups. . . . These experiences must represent a common ground. As such, they will have motivational appeal to a larger segment of our public school population [5].

Jean Grambs, in a discussion of the cultural group membership of children, points out the importance of knowing and understanding what she calls the "group belonging" of children in the classroom. Groups that the teacher should know about are: racial groups, ethnic groups, religious groups, social-class groups, and occupational groups. She suggests that the teacher ask himself:

> Johnny's parents are second-generation Italian, Catholic, and Mr. Rossi works at the Jones Plant as a welder; he is a strong union man. In this town, are these kinds of group identifications thought of as good? How does Johnny feel about being an Italian, Catholic, a child of a father who works in a factory [6]?

The teacher asks himself these questions because he wants to understand Johnny better and because he wants to understand how Johnny's classmates may regard him. Note that the teacher does not ask himself whether *he* thinks these things are "good" about Johnny. But he does want to know what the *community's* attitude is because Johnny's attitudes about himself, his attitudes toward others, and his consequent behavior will be influenced to some degree by the way in which the community evaluates the groups to which Johnny belongs.

The teacher will also ask himself these questions because they will help him to understand the value systems under which Johnny operates. This may mean that the teacher will have to become better acquainted with some of the people who constitute the major subcultural groups in the community because he should not depend upon stereotyped attitudes, hearsay evidence, prejudice, or gossip for his data. Time spent in getting to know community groups better is sound professional investment.

SOCIAL-CLASS DIFFERENCES IN CHILDREN'S BEHAVIOR AND UPBRINGING

As THE teacher circulates in the community, gathering first-hand data on the value systems of various cultural subgroups, he may find confirmation of conclusions reached by sociologists and educators like James H. S. Bossard, Allison Davis, and Robert J. Havighurst.

According to Bossard, the attitudes of upper-class families toward their children are characterized by possessive pride and hope. Children are expected to carry on the family name and to maintain and conserve the family fortune and enterprises. They receive a great deal of care and attention and are granted a great measure of equality and freedom at an early age. There is much concern about social prestige (the reputation of the family), and this increases as children become older. On the other hand, there is relatively less concern about the moral aspects of behavior.

Attitudes toward children in the lower classes present a marked contrast. Bossard states that lower-class parents,

> while not lacking in love and affection for their children, tend to regard them as a sort of inevitable price which fate exacts for sex relations. This is acceptable up to a certain point, when the chief concern comes to center upon their number. With incomes and housing facilities sharply limited, each additional child, after a given point is reached and it is reached early in the family's life, takes on elements of a crisis [7].

Among lower-class groups there is much less family pride, and the family structure is less stable than is the case in the upper class. There is more divorce and desertion and many more temporary, illegal unions. This results in what Bossard calls the "mother-centered" child. In the lower-class family the child is reared largely by the mother, even though he may be punished chiefly by the father. The tendency is for children to go with the mother when the family breaks up, or the mother remarries, or whatever happens.

Child-rearing among lower classes places its emphasis on the child not being a nuisance or an annoyance. Living space is crowded and adults have too many problems to be bothered with children's problems or interests. Great stress is placed on obedience and promptness, and conformity is enforced by physical punishment. Children are expected to devote their energies to helping the family, through financial support, if possible. As a result, lower-class families sometimes come into conflict with laws requiring compulsory school attendance and forbidding child labor.

The middle-class child, according to Bossard, represents to its parents the possibility of fulfillment of hopes. These hopes encompass maintaining middle-class status, moving upward in status if possible, and avoiding any behavior that would be characteristic of lower-class persons. There is much emphasis on "appearances," "what people will say" and "how things will look," whereas the emphasis in the upper classes is on "what would your Grandmother Wickham say?" As a result, the behavioral standards for middle-class children are much more rigid and formal than they are for the other two classes.

Attitudes toward education, too, differ according to class. In the upper class, the importance of education and college is taken for granted. There is a tendency to prefer private schools.

The public school is essentially a middle-class institution, according to Bossard. Its teachers are largely drawn from the middle class, it emphasizes middle-class values, and the persons who control it are mostly middle-class. Middle-class students and teachers speak the same language. Middle-class parents value education highly because it provides the means to rise in the world socially, professionally, and economically.

Children from lower-class families find that their progress in school is severely impeded. They have to learn new words and new grammar with which to express themselves. They are highly critical of the demands that the school makes upon them, because they are unable to see any immediate advantage to themselves. Absences due to work, retardation, and early drop-out are characteristic of a large number of children in this group [8].

In a study of intellectual and personality factors among

children of junior high school age, E. L. Phillips found that certain attitudes and beliefs were typical of children in various social classes. Lower-class children were likely to feel that: it is more fun doing things if a cop is after you; boys and girls who stay in school after the age of sixteen are probably trying to avoid going to work; schools teach many things that just do not work out on the job; and girls and women should take a "back seat" to men and boys in most things. Middle-class children were more likely to endorse these ideas: children who do not do their best in school probably would not amount to much when they grow up; children who do not do things the way other children do are not popular in school; good citizens should support community projects and public activities; and that you can better yourself if you have the ambition. Beliefs that were characteristic of upper-class children included the following: a person should not earn his living by physical labor if he can avoid it; everyone should try to make as much money as possible; it is important not to be seen reading certain magazines that are below one's social level; and it does not pay to try to mix people from different social classes [9].

Allison Davis and Robert J. Havighurst conducted a study of child-rearing practices among middle-class and lower-class white and Negro parents in Chicago that point up a number of differences between the classes, some of which are reported in Table 6–1. In general, Davis and Havighurst found that middle-class families are much stricter than lower-class families in the way children are fed, weaned, and toilet trained. Middle-class families tend to be less permissive and more inclined to stress responsibility and individual achievement. Differences in child-rearing practices were much more marked between the classes than they were between whites and Negroes. In view of the important effect of childhood training on the personality and behavior of children, it appears that the social class into which a child

TABLE 6–1. SOME CLASS DIFFERENCES IN CHILD-REAR-
ING (AFTER DAVIS AND HAVIGHURST [10])

FEEDING AND WEANING

More lower-class children are breast-fed only.

More lower-class children are fed at will (according to their own demand; not on a schedule).

Weaning takes place earlier (on the average) among middle-class children (white only).

TOILET TRAINING

Bowel-and-bladder training is begun earlier (on the average) with middle-class children.

More middle-class parents begin bowel training at 6 months or earlier.

FATHER-CHILD RELATIONS

Middle-class fathers spend more time with children.

Middle-class fathers spend more time in educational activities with children (teaching, reading, and taking them for walks).

EDUCATIONAL AND OCCUPATIONAL EXPECTATIONS

Middle-class parents expect higher occupational status for children.

More middle-class children expected to go to college.

AGE OF ASSUMING RESPONSIBILITY

Middle-class children are expected to help at home earlier.

Middle-class children are expected to go downtown alone earlier.

Middle-class girls are expected to help with younger children earlier.

Lower-class children are expected to quit school and go to work earlier.

STRICTNESS OF REGIME

Middle-class children take naps in daytime more frequently.

Lower-class boys and girls are allowed at movies alone earlier.

Middle-class boys and girls are in the house at night earlier.

is born will have greater effect on his personality than the color of his skin [10].

The personality pattern of a lower-class child is likely to

bring him into sharp conflict with the standards and expectations of the school. Davis points out that certain kinds of
behavior which are considered quite normal and natural by
persons in lower classes meet with the strong disapproval of
members of the middle class [11]. Examples of such behavior are swearing, fighting, wife-beating, sexual promiscuity, and stealing. Children from lower-class environments are
more inclined to settle playground disagreements by violent
means than are middle-class children. They are more likely
to use language which would be considered profane or ob-
scene by middle-class standards. Their parents tend to look
with disfavor on the efforts of the school to inculcate middle-
class standards of behavior. As Davis says, many individuals
from lower classes look with suspicion on children who cooperate with teachers; if a lower-class child gets good grades,
he conceals the fact for fear of giving his comrades the idea
that the teacher is "playing him for a sucker."

There are two significant factors which emerge from this
picture: (1) the behavior and attitudes of children from
lower-class environments are markedly different from those
of middle-class children; and (2) the lower-class child is
likely to be more hostile to schools and what the schools
represent.

According to Davis, teachers and school administrators do
not generally grasp the implications of this situation. Instead of changing the curriculum or teaching methods to
accommodate the differing attitudes and behavior of this
group of children and thus meet them halfway, so to speak,
they usually react by increasing the pressure to make them
conform to existing curricula and the patterns of behavior
traditionally prescribed for the schools. The more or less
latent hostile attitudes of children from this social class are
thus intensified and reinforced. Sometimes they are confused
because teachers stress one kind of behavior and parents another. It is no wonder that most of them become discouraged
and drop out of school as soon as the law allows—sooner, if

possible. The high truancy rate in this group also indicates a desire to avoid the pressures of school.

Since a very high proportion of the children in this group are chronically discouraged about their chances for success and happiness in school, they are likely to develop behavior problems—inability or unwillingness to learn; insubordination; thievery; assault with sticks, stones, or knives; and so forth. Much of this misbehavior is the natural consequence of a major conflict between the middle-class modes of the school and the attitudes and behavior of children from lower classes.

In interpreting this and other research he and his associates have conducted into emotional and intellectual patterns characteristic of middle- and lower-class persons, Allison Davis has come to the conclusion that the public school of today has very little to offer the lower-class child. Children from lower classes are likely to feel discouraged and rejected by their experiences in school. Much of the language and general behavior which is acceptable at home meets with disapproval at school. The occasional lower-class child who does accept the pattern of behavior set for him by the school usually finds that this change in his behavior helps to drive a psychological wedge between him and his family. Bossard describes the reaction of a lower-class father whose son had used the word "preference." He swore at his son and then exclaimed: "Preference, Preference, I'll Preference you. You with fancy words. You can't highhat me as long as I pay the bills [12]." Inasmuch as lower-class homes are so often lacking in security, most children are reluctant to jeopardize existing emotional bonds with their parents by using the behavior and the speech which are prescribed by the school at home.

Davis' research convinces him that children from lower-class environments have potentials of intellectual ability that are untapped because the curricula and methods used in schools today are not attuned to their needs due to the bias of existing intelligence tests in favor of middle- and upper-class children. If we are to provide a real education for the children in these groups, says Davis, we need to revise our curricula, modify our attitudes toward children from lower classes, and construct tests that possess less cultural bias [11].

SCHOOL-LEAVERS

CASUALTIES OF CULTURAL CONFLICT

One of the results of the conflict between the lower-class culture of some students and the middle-class standards of the school is the marked tendency for students from lower classes to drop out of school as early as possible.

In his study of the adolescents of a small midwestern town, A. B. Hollingshead found that some 70 percent of the children he had identified as being in the two lowest social classes left school before they were sixteen, even though the law required that they continue till that age [13]. However, Hollingshead did not attribute this phenomenon to cultural conflict so much as to the differential treatment lower-class children received at school. He found evidence to show that school authorities tended to administer discipline harshly and sometimes unfairly when dealing with lower-class children and were lenient with children from upper-class homes. Furthermore, lower-class children were not accepted on an equal basis by children from homes higher up the social scale. Hollingshead reports:

> The Class V [2] adolescent's family background and prestige are such that he is made to feel unwanted in the classroom, on the playground, or in the clubs and extracurricular activities that are an integral part of the school situation. This same isolating process operates in the churches and youth groups. Within the confines of the adolescent world, intangible barriers are erected against the Class V boy or girl by boys and girls who belong to the acceptable segments of the social struc-

---

[2] Class V is the lowest of the five classes identified by Hollingshead.

ture which channelize the social relations of the Class V young-
ster to his class equals [14].

The picture of the lower-class adolescent barred from
equal participation in the social activities of the school is confirmed, to some extent, by the research of Harold C. Hand,
who found, in a survey of Illinois high schools, that children
from higher income groups tended to participate more fully
in such activities. Furthermore, the greater the income of the
family, the greater the importance of the leadership role carried on by students in extracurricular affairs [15].

Differences in social status also appear in the elementary
grades. Bernice L. Neugarten found that children from upper-class and upper-middle-class homes were rated high by
all other children in such characteristics as good looks, liking for school, leadership, friendship, and other favorable
personal traits; lower-class children were ranked low on the
same scale and were said to be bad looking, dirty, and "people you would not want for friends [16]."

James West shows how parents of middle- and upper-
class children in a small town condition their children to observe class differences:

> Discriminations against inferior people are usually incul-
> cated in terms of family names or at most, the phrase "people
> like that," a phrase which can be used either pejoratively or ap-
> provingly. The child is told, "*You* don't want to play with
> Johnny *Jones! He* (his family, people like *that*) don't know
> how to *act* (talk, play, play right, play nice, play *your* kind of
> games). . . . Why don't you walk home from school with the
> *Smith* children? You'd like to be *seen* with people like that.
> . . . The *Joneses* keep hounds . . . are dirty . . . have bed-
> bugs . . . won't work . . . live back in the timber . . . have
> nothing . . . don't go to church . . . are rough . . . are not
> *our* kind. People would *laugh* if they saw you at the JONESES
> . . . The Smiths are nice (or 'nice average') people like us
> . . . They *live* right and know how to *treat* people right." It
> doesn't take much talk of this kind to teach Junior and his sister

who the Smiths and the Joneses are, but they hear enough to drive the lesson firmly home against the contradictory axiom that "ever'body here is equal" [17].

Still another study of the same general tenor is that of Emil Heintz, who surveyed the social status and emotional adjustment of 222 eighth-grade pupils in Rochester Junior High School, Rochester, Minn. His findings were as follows:

1. Lower-class boys had strong desires to leave school and go to work. They were ill at ease in the presence of the principal. They also felt that teachers overemphasized good order and discipline, did not praise them when they did good work, and did not permit them to express themselves fully.

2. Lower-class girls felt that they were not welcome in school clubs and that teachers permitted a few students to monopolize the attention of the class.

3. Middle-class children of both sexes were more satisfied with rules and regulations, and did not feel that good order and conduct were overstressed, or that teachers were too strict, or that they tended to embarrass students.

4. Upper-class students felt that teachers failed to accept them as friends (especially boys), that school activities were poorly run, and that teachers preached too much (especially girls).

In analyzing his findings, Heintz came to the conclusion that lower-class children do not make good adjustments in situations where they feel they do not belong, while upper-class students made a generally good adjustment, but were confused or exasperated when their normal feelings of superiority were not gratified. Middle-class children were at ease in situations calling for conformity and control [18].

SCHOOL-LEAVERS AND THE TRADITIONAL CURRICULUM

The psychological isolation of lower-class youngsters by fellow students and the staff is not entirely responsible for the high rate of drop-outs experienced with this group. Part of the blame must be shared by curricula that are not keyed to the needs of everyday living and that are, in the eyes of all too many students, intellectual busy-work.

In a pamphlet written for the United States Office of Education, Frances V. Rummel pointed out that more than half of the children who start public school continue through high school graduation. Rummel considers boredom and frustration to be the chief factors behind the drop-outs. It is her feeling that many a child who leaves school would stay if schools could give him help with the problems he currently faces: getting started as a worker, getting along with the opposite sex, obtaining the approval of the group, understanding a maturing body, and settling on a philosophy of life. Other areas of life that provide promising leads for curriculum revision are indicated by the fact that every student is a potential consumer, taxpayer, voter, worker, and family man (or mother). Most schools have not begun to exploit the motivation for learning that lies latent in these present and future needs of youth [19].

WHAT TEACHERS CAN DO ABOUT SOCIAL CLASS

IN A way, this subheading is misleading because there is not likely to be very much that teachers can do about eliminating the factors in American life that produce the social stratification we call social classes. Social stratification develops whenever people work and live together. Perhaps it is produced by fears and anxieties that are older than the human race itself; perhaps it is one of the ways that groups of people naturally develop as a means of working together more effectively. Regardless of which hypothesis we accept, our goal as educators should be to make the system work as democratically as possible. After all, one of the differences between autocratic and democratic countries is that the status system is fixed and inflexible in the former—position is inherited or assigned by the ruling hierarchy. In democratic countries, one may obtain status through one's own efforts— through education and industry, for example.

It is the thesis of W. Lloyd Warner, Robert J. Havighurst, and Martin B. Loeb, who collaborated on a discussion of the relationship between education and social status, entitled *Who Shall Be Educated?*, that in the United States, education constitutes the highway to higher levels of social status. It is the means whereby the child of the slums may become a respected professional, or the daughter of a coal miner may go to college and marry an architect. Even in democratic countries the system does not work perfectly, however. It is easier for the children of upper-middle-class parents to acquire the kind of education that enables them to maintain their status and even to move up. The farther one goes down the status ladder, the more difficult it is for children to avail themselves of the opportunities for education. And the failure to advance leads to frustration and disappointment. Warner, Havighurst, and Loeb have this to say:

> Of the 580 boys and girls in a thousand who reach the third year of high school, about half are taking a course that leads to college. One hundred and fifty enter college, and seventy graduate. These are average figures for the country as a whole. With variations in various parts of the country, an average of some two hundred out of every thousand young people fail to achieve the goal which they started in high school. Thwarted ambition and frustrated hope result. Doubtless many accept the reality easily enough and settle into a niche in life without bitter feelings. But certainly many others develop resentful feelings toward society in general and toward their more fortunate fellows in particular. If they fail to rise in some other ways than through education, they become centers of disaffection, and society loses some of its necessary solidarity [20].

> All these facts tend to show that . . . the school system has severe limitations as a social elevator. Its capacity is limited, and it is not free.

Nevertheless, the American school and college system is the

greatest agency we have for equalizing opportunity and for promoting the rise of able young people. Through it we maintain a degree of social mobility probably greater than that to be found in any other country.

The educational system promotes social solidarity or social cohesion, partly through its provisions for social mobility. A society has social solidarity when its members believe that they have a substantial common ground of interest—that they gain more than they lose by sticking together and maintaining intact their political and social institutions. A certain amount of social mobility seems necessary to maintain social cohesion in our class-structured society. The possibility of rising in the social scale in order to secure a larger share of the privileges of the society makes people willing to "stick together" and "play the game" as long as they believe that it gives them a fair deal [21].

Because of the special function that education provides in our status system, the teacher is called upon to perform a role that he probably is unaware of—the role of helping to decide which children are destined to move up in status and who will not. If the practices reported by Hollingshead and mentioned earlier in this chapter are at all typical, teachers tend to select children who are already in an advantageous position merely by being born into middle- and upper-class families. On the other hand, there are very few teachers who do not provide some encouragement to children from lower-class families who aspire to higher status. Perhaps we do not do enough of this; perhaps our educational practices are so structured that it is easier to discourage people than it is to encourage them.

However, the chief purpose of free public education is not selective—selection is a by-product, so to speak, of the educative process. Its chief purpose is to help young people become the kinds of individuals we would like to be, or, rather, wish we had become—enlightened citizens whose physical, mental, and emotional health is better than our own. If we are to make progress toward that goal, we cannot do so by discouraging, frustrating, and disappointing a third or more of the children who enter the doors of our schools. This is, in effect, what we are doing at present by not providing for the emotional, social, and intellectual needs of children from lower-class homes. This is a problem that requires much understanding, sympathy, and patience. Before we can make much progress in reform, we need to know something about the life and the environment of the child who comes from a lower-class culture. And we need to understand our own reactions to him as well as how the middle-class children in our classes feel toward him. Some schools have used the prejudice that they have found in teachers and students as a starting point for a new kind of education, an education directed against prejudice and toward the need for improved relationships among cultural groups—Intergroup Education [3] [22]

The following statement by Celia Burns Stendler questions practices currently followed in education, practices that ought to be examined carefully and seriously:

> Teachers need to ask whether their expectations are reasonable in terms of what the child has been expected to be by his parents or whether all children, regardless of background, are expected to measure up to middle-class standards. Teachers need to ask whether their expectations are appropriate to the maturity level of children or whether children are being criticized for not assuming adult responsibilities earlier. Finally, teachers need to ask whether their expectations are appropriate for living in a democracy, or whether the school emphasizes superficial behaviors in place of more fundamental ones. When schools attach less importance to neatness, punctuality and nice language, and expect, instead, moral courage, respect for human personality, and a rational approach to the solution of problems, then such a climate will have a positive impact upon children [23].

As teachers improve their understanding of the cultural background of the children in their classes, they will find

---

[3] See discussion in Chapter 10.

themselves interpreting behavior—yes, even problem behavior—differently. Often they will be able to forestall the development of behavior difficulties. Perhaps the curriculum will not change much at first under the impact of this new understanding, but as it does begin to change, there will be more emphasis on content that is of interest and value to children from a wider range of cultures than is true at present. As the attitudes of teachers and school children change and as the curriculum is modified, it will be easier to bring parents of various cultural groups into closer communication with the school. If they can be helped to lose some of the fear and anxiety they now feel toward the school, their defensiveness and hostility will diminish, and it should then be easier for both them and their children to accept the concept of education.

Such an era of better feeling will not be attained easily, yet it should be a goal that must be approached if the school is to fulfill its obligation to the children of the community. Taking the first steps of this process is the responsibility of the teachers and administrators, for they are the only ones who can start such a move. It is they who must decide whether they are ready to change some of their concepts of the educational potential of a good third of the children in our schools.

REFERENCES

1. W. L. Warner, M. Meeker, and K. Eells, *Social Class in America.* Chicago: Science Research, 1949.
2. A. Davis, B. B. Gardner, and M. R. Gardner, *Deep South.* Chicago: University of Chicago Press, 1941. P. 50.
3. A. Davis and J. Dollard, *Children of Bondage.* Washington: American Council on Education, 1940. P. 261.
4. H. Taba, "Human Relations in the Classroom," in *Workshop in Counseling and Guidance,* San Francisco State College, summer, 1951. P. 96. Reprinted by permission.

5. W. I. Murray, "The Concept of Social Class and Its Implications for Teachers," *The Journal of Negro Education*. 20:16–21; 1951. Reprinted by permission.

6. J. Grambs, *Group Processes in Intergroup Education*. New York: National Conference of Christians and Jews, 1952. Pp. 12–13. Reprinted by permission.

7. J. H. S. Bossard, *The Sociology of Child Development*. New York: Harper, 1948. P. 297. Reprinted by permission.

8. *Ibid*. Pp. 296–306.

9. E. L. Phillips, "Intellectual and Personality Factors Associated with Social Class Attitudes among Junior High School Children," *Journal of Genetic Psychology*. 77:61–72;1950.

10. A. Davis and R. J. Havighurst, "Social Class and Color Differences in Child-Rearing," *American Sociological Review*. 11:698–710; 1946. Reprinted by permission.

11. A. Davis, *Social-Class Influences upon Learning*. Cambridge: Harvard University Press, 1948.

12. Bossard, *op. cit*. P. 184.

13. A. B. Hollingshead, *Elmtown's Youth*. New York: Wiley, 1949. P. 331.

14. *Ibid*. P. 358.

15. H. C. Hand, *Principal Findings of the 1947–48 Basic Studies of the Illinois Secondary School Curriculum Program*. Springfield: Superintendent of Public Instruction, 1949.

16. B. L. Neugarten, "Social Class and Friendship among School Children," *American Journal of Sociology*. 51:305–13;1946.

17. J. West, *Plainville, U. S. A*. New York: Columbia University Press, 1945. P. 197. Reprinted by permission.

18. E. Heintz, "Adjustment Problems of Class Status," *Phi Delta Kappan*. 30:290–93;1949.

19. F. V. Rummel, *High School: What's In It For Me?* Chicago: American Technical Society.

20. W. L. Warner, R. J. Havighurst, and M. B. Loeb, *Who Shall Be Educated?* New York: Harper, 1944. P. 156. Reprinted by permission.

21. *Ibid*. P. 157. Reprinted by permission.

22. H. Taba, E. H. Brady, J. T. Robinson, *Intergroup Education in Public Schools*. Washington: American Council on Education, 1952.

23. C. B. Stendler, ed., "How Children Learn Roles and Expectations," in Association for Supervision and Curriculum Development, *Growing Up in an Anxious Age*. Washington: National Education Association, 1952. P. 119. Reprinted by permission.

SUGGESTED READINGS

J. H. S. Bossard, *The Sociology of Child Development*. New York: Harper, 1948. Part 4, "Status and Class Differentials."

L. E. Cole and W. F. Bruce, *Educational Psychology*. Yonkers-on-Hudson: World Book, 1950. Chapter 8, "Growth and Development in the American Culture."

A. Davis, "Child Training and Social Class," in R. G. Barker, J. S. Kounin, and H. F. Wright, eds., *Child Behavior and Development*. New York: McGraw-Hill, 1943.

K. Davis, "Mental Hygiene and the Class Structure," in P. Mullahy, ed., *A Study of Interpersonal Relations*. New York: Hermitage, 1949.

B. Fine, *Democratic Education*. New York: Crowell, 1945.

H. C. Lindgren, *Psychology of Personal and Social Adjustment*. New York: American Book, 1953. Chapter 9, "The Forces that Mold Us: Social Class and Status."

G. E. Swanson, T. M. Newcomb and E. L. Hartley, eds. *Readings in Social Psychology*. rev. ed. New York: Holt, 1952. Part IIIc, "Stratified Role Structure."

See also items 1, 2, 3, 11, 13, 17, 20, and 21 listed in the References for this chapter.

SUGGESTED FILMS

The Quiet One. Athena Films, 165 West 46th St., New York 19, N. Y. The story of an unwanted Negro boy, growing up in a slum environment, who receives therapeutic care in a home for emotionally disturbed children.

Palmour Street. Depicts the development of warm and affectionate family relationships amid difficult economic circumstances. Available through Southern Educational Film Production Service, University of Georgia, Athens, Ga.

7

COMMUNICATION: A SOCIAL PROCESS

THE DEVELOPMENT OF THE SELF
THROUGH COMMUNICATION

DURING the earlier stages of childhood, the child must cope with the developmental task of evolving a self or a personality that expresses his individuality. At first he works at this task through his senses—he finds out what is himself and not himself by touching, feeling, seeing, and so forth. And he expresses himself through such crude means as grasping, crying, sucking, and kicking. Then he graduates into the use of gestures and sounds and finally into the complexities of language and other forms of symbolic behavior.

We cannot interact with others without communication; it is the very basis of such interaction. By communication or interaction with others we find out "who we are." Through communication, the small child finds out who (what family or group) he belongs to and who or what belongs to him. As he discovers these facts, the world takes on more meaning, and his concept of "who he is" becomes sharper, more precise—in better focus, as it were. This process of finding out "who we are" continues most of our lives, although it ordinarily does not dominate our later lives as it did when we were children.

Children, particularly small children, are eternally prying into the meaning of things—partly in an attempt to bring some order into the apparent confusion of their environment; partly in trying to find out the relationship of persons, things, and events to themselves; partly to reassure themselves, to maintain a feeling of security; and partly because the drive to master one's environment is a normal and natural part of maturing, of growing up. It is this need to search out the meaning of things that makes children so eager to learn, and it is the repeated frustration of this need that reduces or destroys this enthusiasm for learning.

Through communicating and interacting with others we learn of their evaluations and expectations of us, and this learning helps to form our self-concept and self-ideal. Thus a middle-class child who is making above-average but not high marks in school learns that he is doing "pretty well" but "could do better." As these ideas and concepts are communicated to him, he develops a self-ideal that is characterized by high scholarship. His self-concept is revealed by his analysis of his situation: "I suppose I'm able to do better, but I guess I'm sort of lazy—I really ought to try harder."

As the individual matures, he learns to appraise himself and his environment more realistically.

Ten-year-old Lawrence heard his father complain about the stupidity of the county board of supervisors. Lawrence could not understand why this should be a problem; after all, the solution was simple: all his father had to do would be to get on the board of supervisors and straighten them out. So he asked his father why he didn't put his name up for election. His father answered that he didn't think he would make a particularly good supervisor, and that he probably couldn't get elected anyway. Lawrence was genuinely shocked. Could this be his father? His father who could do anything?

Many children have exaggerated and distorted ideas about the world around them, and part of learning, part of growing up, is being shocked into reality. Some children cling tenaciously to the idea that there is a Santa Claus. Eventually, the messages and impressions they get from the world around them become too persistent, too much at variance with their fantasy, to be ignored, and they, too, are shocked into reality.

However, it is usually when children have clung to irrealities and fantasies overlong that they must suffer shocks of this sort. Most of the time, reality communicates itself in small doses, doses that occasionally prove uncomfortable, but which ordinarily stimulate the child's interest in becoming more aware of life's realities.

RELATING ONESELF TO THE GROUP

Most of our basic needs (see Chapter 3) are intimately involved with other people. This is particularly true of our needs for love, status, and self-expression. It is also true, to some degree, of our biological needs and our needs for security and bodily safety.

Let us see how this works in the case of a boy whom we shall call William Davies. William was called "Bill" by his family, and this was the name he learned to respond to. When his mother called him "Bill" and smiled at him, he was aware that she was recognizing him and him only and that she was communicating a pleasant emotion. When she called him "Bill!" in a sharp tone, he again knew he was being recognized, but that the feeling was an unpleasant one, one of rejection. Later, he learned that there were other children who also had names. Their names were different, which helped prove that they were different, but the fact that they all had names, just as he had a name, helped prove that they were like him in some ways.

One day he met another child who name was "Bill," also. This was quite confusing and upsetting, particularly when he heard his mother call the other child "Bill." About this time he learned that his full name was Bill Davies and that everybody in his family was Somebody Davies. He took to calling his toys and stuffed animals names like "Big Bear Davies" and "Little Bear Davies." This helped to show that they belonged to him and that they all belonged to a group of Davieses.

Shortly thereafter he found that children who wore blue playclothes and had shorter hair had names that were called "boys' names," and other children who had longer hair and who wore pink, yellow, or red playclothes had other names that were called "girl's names." Evidently he was different from the children with girls' names but had something in common with the children who had boys' names.

So far, Bill's knowledge of "who he is" includes being Bill, being a Davies, and being a boy. Being all these things carried certain responsibilities, responsibilities that were communicated to him by such statements as, "Boys don't act that way," "You don't talk like the Bill Davies I said good-bye to this morning," and "Now don't you try any of those sneaky little tricks of John Hancock's on me, Bill Davies!"

When Bill went to the first grade, the best thing he liked was playing with the other children, especially the boys. Some days, when they were out on the playground, he was the Lone Ranger, sometimes he was a bandit or a deputy sheriff. Sometimes he went so far as to round up a small herd of cattle (who always turned out to be little girls). There were times when the other boys accepted him in these roles and there were times when they said: "Aw, let's play marbles." There were other times when everybody wanted to chase each other, yelling, "Fishface" or "Pumpkinhead," or something equally suitable. But whatever they felt like doing, Bill was quickly caught up in the midst of it. He was very much a part of the first-grade group and he felt very superior to any "kindergarten baby, born in the gravy."

One day his father told him how Grandfather and Grandmother Davies had come over from Wales many years ago. He described the rugged mountains and green valleys of Wales, a country he had visited during the war, and told him of the battles between the British and the Welsh in olden days. As Bill thought about the things his father told him, it seemed to him, for the moment, that he was quite different from children with names like Ricciardi, Smith, and O'Brien, and was more like the people who lived in Wales, and he felt somewhat proud of this difference.

Establishing relations with groups is a process of finding out what one has in common with others in the way of interests, behavior, and values. As we are attracted to a group and seek to be accepted into their membership, we modify our behavior to conform to the norms or patterns they prescribe for their members. By conforming, we communicate our acceptance of the group, while they, by prescribing certain behaviors, communicate the terms on which they will accept members. When Bill was in the first grade, he communicated his fantasies by enacting the role of the Lone Ranger. Sometimes his group accepted him in this role, and communicated their acceptance by adopting role behaviors appropriate to the Lone Ranger legend. At other times they rejected him in this role and proposed another activity. Bill could have withdrawn from the group and played Lone Ranger by himself but he chose, instead, to remain with the group and communicated his willingness by engaging in the play they proposed.

COMMUNICATION AS A MEANS OF PROMOTING DIFFERENCES BETWEEN GROUPS

In developing their concepts of group membership and, at the same time, emphasizing differences between themselves and others, groups often develop forms of language that help to symbolize their solidarity. Thus, teen-agers develop a "jive jargon" that for them distinguishes those that are "hep" from those who are "square."

More often, differences in the use of language are not developed consciously, but nevertheless serve to differentiate between members of a certain group and outsiders. A teacher will occasionally be startled to find that his interpretation of a word differs widely from that of the children in his class.

Hilda Taba tells of the experience of a teacher who read her class a story about Sally, who was lost, for the purpose of developing a lesson on what happens when one is lost.

> Sally was questioned by a policeman and would not reveal her name. The teacher thought that this was a good example of how people even forget their names when they are upset, but when she asked the class why Sally did not give her name, they answered: "Because he would take her to jail."
>
> These children were from a social group to whom "policeman" meant "jail." They always ran whenever they saw a policeman, and, of course, it would not do to give one your name. There was definitely a difference between the teacher's and the children's concept of policemen. Such a discrepancy of meanings behind words is a problem in places where the teacher's social background and the children's social background are different [1].

Differences in language are most pronounced when the teacher works with children from lower-class environments. Ruth Cunningham reports one teacher as saying:

> My youngsters can as easily call each other "bastard" and "son of a bitch" as you or I would say "mischievous child" or "naughty boy." I know they hear these phrases at home. I know they'll get into trouble when they use this vocabulary outside their immediate circle; yet I hate to seem prudish to them [2].

Margaret Heaton reports the following example:

> . . . Teachers may be perplexed when children fight on the playground when their "mothers" are mentioned. The mere mention of the word "mother" seems to start a fracas. The implication of the expression "Oh your Mother" to some children of a lower socioeconomic group is that the mother has a disgraceful reputation. Any child who has grown up with this interpretation is supposed to defend her and to fight. In effect, the very reference to mother is a taunt and a fighting word intended to arouse feelings of anger [3].

MEETING THE NEED FOR
SELF-EXPRESSION

It is through communication that we tell the world, in effect, "who we are." It is through communication that we express our feelings, impress our fellow man, and reveal our expectations of ourselves, others, and life in general.

> Miss Hart had just told Mr. Constant that she didn't think that there was anything wrong with Nadine—it was just that she seemed to be going through a "boy-crazy" stage—when Nadine herself rounded the corner at the end of the hall. She apparently did not notice the teachers, standing partly in an alcove, for she seemed concerned primarily with herself. She stopped, looked at herself in a pocket mirror, touched up her lips, smoothed down her eyebrows, tucked in a stray curl, and walked off. There was something familiar about her walk. It seemed to Mr. Constant that he had seen some stage or television star do an exit like that. And then he wondered whether Nadine had seen them after all, perhaps, out of the corner of her eye.

What Nadine has been doing comes under the heading of "nonverbal communication," a subject we treat later in this chapter. What is significant here is that her every gesture, her walk, her concern with make-up, and even her possible snubbing of the teachers tells us much about her self-concept. They are part of her way of communicating to the world "who she is" or, rather, "who she thinks she is."

> Mr. Burger told Clyde to stop throwing his ball against the wall of the building because it disturbed the class inside. Clyde stopped, but not before he had thrown the ball once more, with a hard, vicious snap to his wrist which said plainer than words that he resented having been told to stop. Most boys in Clyde's class would have stopped as soon as Mr. Burger had spoken to them. By taking one more bounce, Clyde is telling Mr. Burger—and anyone else who wants to know—that he is

different from the others. He is saying that the regulations of the school do not apply to him in quite the same way. To be sure, taking an extra bounce means other things. For example, it is an attempt to see how much defiance Mr. Burger will take. But it is also Clyde's way of telling Mr. Burger how he views himself—the tough character, the one who eventually sur-renders to adult authority, but only begrudgingly.

In the course of the day's events we normally generate feelings regarding ourselves, others, the environment, and life in general. These feelings struggle for expression. We thus feel impelled to communicate them in some way, in that others, too, may know how we feel and perhaps share our feelings.

In this sense, communication is a safety valve for our feel-ings. By finding some way to communicate our feelings, we not only "blow off steam," but we are enabled to clarify, ex-amine, understand, and perhaps accept them. A child who has strong feelings of fear, anxiety, or hostility, and who is prevented from expressing them in some natural or healthy way, is liable to express them neurotically or to build up neurotic defenses against them or to stifle all feeling in order to avoid the ones that make him feel anxious. The days are full of frustrations for children—the requirement to sit still and be quiet when one wants to run around, the requirement to work and listen when one is bored, the requirement to do so many things one does not want to do—it is no wonder that children develop problem behavior. We are much more humane in our approach to these frustrations than we were in bygone years. In most schools we give children opportuni-ties to work off some of their frustrations through games and physical education, singing, folk dancing, arts and crafts, and drama. Some of these activities succeed because they give children opportunities to work off pent-up energy, others are satisfying because they provide the means whereby children can have the thrill of creativity—a basic need.

EDUCATION AS COMMUNICATION

THE problems of education with regard to communication are severalfold. The basic problem is to help children use the skills of communication in working at and completing the developmental tasks of emotional, social, and intellectual maturity. This means helping children to use communication to find out "who they are," to develop satisfactory relations with others, to meet basic needs for self-expression and creativity, and to master skills that they can use now and will need in later life.

COMMUNICATION IN THE CLASSROOM

It is obvious that education is itself a process of communication. Teachers talk, listen, and write; students talk, listen, and write. Most of us would agree, however, that education is communication much more than in the merely technical sense. It is communication in the sense that teachers attempt to communicate to children the values of our society and the lore of the culture. For most of us in education, our awareness of communication ends at this point; that is, we are aware of the speaking and writing that goes on in classrooms and of the fact that we are trying to communicate something to students. But the role of communication in education is much broader and deeper. Indeed some of our failures as educators are due to the fact that we have not recognized the importance of communication, nor have we been aware of what we must do to improve communication in the classroom.

One of the reasons why we as adults have difficulty educating children is that we overlook the dual nature of communication. We are primarily concerned with seeing that our messages are received by students—that is, we are concerned principally with such things as "making ourselves clear," "making sure they understand us," and "explaining what we mean." We are much less concerned with giving children opportunities to express themselves to us. Even when we are attentive to what they are trying to communicate, we are unlikely to spend much time trying to figure out what they mean, if their meaning is at all obscure.

WHY CAN WE NOT COMMUNICATE EFFECTIVELY?

There are a number of reasons why we are more concerned about our own needs for self-expression than we are about the needs of the children we supervise. One important reason is that the many demands made upon teachers by administrators, parents, fellow teachers, and by the children themselves tend to produce anxieties and self-concern. Faced by these demands, teachers feel "on the spot," and are thus likely to direct a great deal of attention to what they say and do. And the more they concentrate on what they are saying and doing, the less likely they are to be sensitive to what children are trying to communicate.

Another reason why adults have difficulty in communicating with children is that we have inherited a tradition that says, in effect, that what children have to say is not very important or significant. Conversely, we believe that what adults have to say *is* important and significant. This philosophy is tersely but amply expressed in the saying: "Children should be seen but not heard."

However, we are beginning to discover that in order to help children to learn, we must understand them, and in order to understand them, we must we able to interpret what they are trying to tell us about themselves.[1] However, we have grown up in the tradition of adult superiority and child inferiority. It is very much a part of our way of thinking and feeling. It is not easy to say: "The tradition is all wrong. I must start accepting children on a more equal basis so I can

---

[1] One pamphlet that capitalizes on this idea is James L. Hymes, Jr., *Teacher Listen: The Children Speak*. New York: New York Committee on Mental Health of the State Charities Aid Association (105 E. 22nd St., New York 10, N. Y.), 1949.

understand what they are trying to tell me." Even if we can accept the need for humility as a way of helping ourselves to understand children better, it is still difficult for us to make any real changes in our behavior, particularly if the people we know and work with still conform to more traditional attitudes and behavior.

WHY WE SHOULD IMPROVE CLASSROOM COMMUNICATION

There are two basic reasons why we should be concerned with seeing that communication in the classroom be maintained on a two-way basis. One is a technical reason, in that it has to do with the mechanics of learning; the other is related to the mental hygiene of the situation.

A teacher can do a better job of instruction if he is aware of the progress which children are making in solving the tasks of learning. This means that he must know what skills they are using successfully and what skills they are using improperly or have failed to learn. He must know how they perceive the concepts and values which are the immediate or long-range goals of the curriculum. As he helps them over the rougher parts of the curriculum, it helps immeasurably if he is able to follow the thought processes of his students. In other words, if the teacher is to do an adequate job of evaluation, he must provide opportunities for children to communicate their progress and difficulties and must be able to understand and interpret their attempts to communicate.

COMMUNICATION AND MENTAL HYGIENE IN THE CLASSROOM

The second basic reason for the establishment of two-way communication is the need for children to express themselves about the problems which trouble them. Dorothy Baruch tells of a poignant case—the story of a little nine-year-old girl named Tina, who drew a picture of a girl cutting up her mother's best hat with a kitchen knife. Her teacher was duly shocked, said it was not a nice picture, and suggested that she draw a nicer one.

Into the wastebasket fell Tina's picture and with it her attempt to share what was wrong inside her heart. This was Monday and last Saturday her mother had walked out on her father, taking Tina along. Saturday and Sunday nights she had cried herself to sleep. She didn't understand the whole business. All she knew was she wasn't going to be with her beloved daddy any more and that there was a hard ache inside her and a feeling of bitter blame against her mother who, she felt vaguely, had made the whole thing happen.

Obediently now she drew another picture—a house with smoke coming out of the chimney in the age-old accepted curlicue pattern and a road leading up to the house in conventional coming-to-a-point perspective. Then the recess bell rang.

On her slow walk across the playground, Tina chewed her handkerchief and twisted it into a hard damp coil. George Washington Carver Thompson walked beside her, his dark face wonderingly intent on the lengthening twist of wet cloth.

And then all at once for no immediate reason, Tina turned on him and cried, "You go away, George Washington, 'cause I don't want any dirty nigger following me around [4]."

Tina's case is not very unusual. There are many children in the schools who come from divided homes. Furthermore, most children are troubled from time to time by hurt feelings, frustrations, and problems which seem, for the moment, more than they can bear. Perhaps it is too much to expect that busy teachers would have time to help all children who have such problems, although such a condition would certainly be ideal. Nevertheless, the mental health of the classroom is better when children are able to express their feelings when the world seems against them.

Perhaps another example would help to demonstrate the importance of maintaining two-way communication.

When Mr. Morgan met his biology class Friday morning, he should have known something was wrong. Students usually walked in quietly or engaged in casual conversation. Today, however, they were all involved in heated and angry discussion. They were so wrapped up in their subject that they did not hear him start his daily lecture, and he had to rap for order rather loudly.

Mr. Morgan always spent the first ten or fifteen minutes of the period explaining the basic principles involved in the work assigned for the day. Students usually listened obediently; those who did not pay attention became the target for sarcastic comment. But today it was different. The class was quiet as Mr. Morgan began his daily lecture, but within a couple of minutes whispering started in the back of the room.

Mr. Morgan glared.

"Apparently I am to have some competition today. May I ask, Lou and Harry, what you have to say that is more important than the laws of heredity?"

Lou and Harry muttered something under their breath and slumped down in their seats. Mr. Morgan continued, only to break off after a minute.

"Francis," he snapped. "I would guess that Lorna doesn't want to listen to you. I would guess that she wants to listen to me. Is that right, Lorna?"

Lorna blushed, and Francis gave intense attention to his biology notebook. Mr. Morgan paused, then continued his talk. Finally, he stopped in exasperation.

"I wish someone would tell me," he complained, "what's going on this morning. I have been trying to give you the essentials of the Mendelian law—a concept which is basic to the work we will be doing during the next month. But I can't seem to get your attention for more than a minute. What should I do to keep your attention—do card tricks?"

Jasper leaned over and whispered in Mavis' ear: "It wouldn't be a bad idea at that!" Mavis giggled.

Mr. Morgan glowered at him.

"Jasper," he snarled, "would you mind sharing your ideas with the class? If Mavis found it interesting, maybe we would too."

Jasper looked embarrassed and mumbled: "It wasn't anything especial, Mr. Morgan."

But Mr. Morgan was not accepting such evasion.

"I demand to know," he rasped, "what has gotten into this class today. If you don't make some effort to enlighten me, Jasper, I shall have to ask you to remain after class."

It was Mavis who spoke up. She was an "A" student, popular with students and well-liked by teachers. Perhaps she felt she had less to lose than some of the other students in the class.

"Mr. Morgan," she said, "apparently you do not know that the whole school is upset by the news that Johnny Pierce has just been suspended from the basketball team because of the fight at the skating rink last night. A lot of us think that it was unfair. I think that is what the kids were talking about."

Mr. Morgan looked at her coldly. "If I had wanted your opinion, Mavis, I would have asked for it. But since you have answered my question, let me say that this is just one more example of how sports interfere with education. I ask you: How can a class concentrate on biology, when their minds are full of basketball?"

He continued: "I want you all to turn to page 436, where you will find a list of ten questions on the laws of heredity. I want you to spend the rest of the period writing out the answers. Your grade for today will be the mark you get on this quiz." He paused, then added, drily: "Perhaps this will help you to keep your mind on biology and off basketball."

Very likely little learning of a positive nature took place in Mr. Morgan's class that morning, although one must concede the situation could have been worse. At least Mr. Morgan knows one of the reasons why the class was not in a mood to receive his communications that morning. However, *he* is not in a mood to receive communications from the class because he is principally interested in what he has to say, rather than in what they have to say. Furthermore, he punishes the class for not being receptive to his communication—first, by making sarcastic comments, and, second, by assigning an unscheduled test. Tests can be the means for communication under some circumstances, but in this instance, where they are used as a penalty by a teacher intent on retaliation, it is doubtful whether much communication will occur.

It is perhaps an oversimplification to say that little learning took place in Mr. Morgan's class on the morning of the above-mentioned incident because there was a lack of communication. Mr. Morgan's attitudes toward students, his preoccupation with his subject, and his lack of interest in extracurricular affairs are certainly factors which limit his effectiveness as a teacher. Yet, there is no denying that one of his basic problems is his inability to understand teaching as a problem in communication—communication which must be two-way if it is to work. Although he is aware that his students' anxious concern about the suspension of a star basketball player makes them inattentive, he does not know how to cope with this situation. Instead of taking steps to improve the communication between him and his students, thus clearing the atmosphere so that the class could then go about the business of learning biology, Mr. Morgan worsens the situation by arousing anxiety and hostility.

Mr. Morgan is not alone in his difficulty to communicate with students. To a greater or lesser degree similar problems exist in other schools and classrooms. David H. Jenkins and Ronald Lippitt studied the interpersonal perceptions of teachers, students, and parents involved in a junior high school in Newton, Massachusetts. Questionnaires concerning interpersonal relations were completed by teachers and students. The study indicated that the teachers tended to see themselves as persons who talked to students in a friendly manner, showed an interest in and encouraged extracurricular activities, helped students with personal problems, praised and encouraged students, were interested in students as individuals, treated students as adults and attempted to understand them, and participated in activities with students. From 30 to 50 percent of the teachers responded to items on the questionnaire covering these activities; yet the same items were mentioned by less than 4 percent of the students. This means that although the teachers in this group saw themselves as concerned with personal, friendly relations with students, students were not even aware of this interest. Perhaps the teachers were not doing these things as much as they thought they were, or perhaps students were so used to receiving these services that they failed to notice them, or perhaps students had a fixed idea of what teachers were like and hence were unable to perceive the evidence of friendly interest [5]. Whatever the explanation, the point is that the teachers in this study, like Mr. Morgan, are out of touch, so to speak, with their students, at least as far as this one area is concerned.

THE IMPORTANCE OF NONVERBAL COMMUNICATION

One of the reasons why we have difficulty in communicating with children is that we assume that communication has to be verbal, whereas a very important part of communication never finds its way into words: it is on a nonverbal or subverbal level. There is the sigh that runs through the class when a particularly heavy assignment is announced. There is the rustle of amusement when someone makes a particularly stupid remark. There is the buzz of activity which results when students are hard at work on interesting problems. There is the lift of an eyebrow and the smirk that says more than mere words. Experienced supervisors can get the "feel" of a class by watching a class at work for five minutes, and I have heard one child psychologist say that he can learn a great deal about the kind of school he is visiting by watching students go in and out of class. These are a few of the nonverbal ways in which students reveal their attitudes, feelings, and morale.

Then there is the kind of listening which is more than mere attention to the *content* of what a person is saying. In doing this kind of listening, we ask ourselves such questions as: "What does he mean that he isn't saying?" or "What she is saying is so, but I wonder if she doesn't mean something over and above that?" or "That was a peculiar thing to say. I wonder why he said it?"

EMPATHY

We all do this kind of listening, although most of the time we are not aware of it. As we talk with people, we are likely to be sensitive to their mannerisms, their tone of voice, the expression on their faces, and the positions of their bodies because these are clues to how they feel about us, and our normal anxiety prompts our concern about others' opinions of us. This awareness of another's feelings is called "empathy" and it is an important dimension of communication. Nathaniel Cantor expresses the idea of empathy in the following description of communication with children:

> What impresses the child is not so much the statements made, the words used, as the feeling-tones and emotional tensions with which they are loaded. The language the parent [or teacher] uses means very little. What the child really responds to are feelings of warmth, security, love, affection, prohibition, deprivation, rejection, fear, resentment, hostility, and so on. The words, quite beyond his understanding, do not carry for the child the ideas they are supposed to represent. The calmness or harshness of voice, the smile or frown on the face, the hug or push, of those in authority determines the child's reaction [6].

Like other forms of communication, empathy can be inhibited or blocked by neurotic anxiety. For example, the individual who is overly concerned about the impression that *he* is making and who is concerned with expressing *his* opinions, is less able to empathize with the people with whom he is trying to communicate. Therefore, he is not as aware as he should be of the reaction which others have to what he is saying; he is so involved in trying to express himself that he does not even know whether they understand him.

Empathy and understanding supplement each other. As teachers become more aware of the feelings and attitudes of their students, they come to understand them better; and as they learn more about the kinds of feelings which children are likely to have, they are enabled to empathize more effectively. The teacher who can empathize effectively is keenly aware that what children say and do should be interpreted with due regard to the concepts they have of themselves, of others, and of their environment. Furthermore, the things children say and do are often clues to these concepts.

UNDERSTANDING CHILDREN'S CONCEPTS OF THEMSELVES AND OF OTHERS

For example, the child who sits in the corner, who does not participate in the class activities is communicating something by his behavior. In order to understand this something, it is necessary to get some idea of how he views himself and the world. But his behavior itself may provide clues. Does he look as though he would like to participate, yet lacks the courage? Or is he scornful of others? Does he appear to fear failure? Or does he occasionally glance at the teacher to see whether he is approving of him? Over a period of time, an empathic person can usually accumulate enough clues to develop some hunches regarding the concepts which the child has developed regarding himself and the world. What the teacher can do with this information varies greatly both as to the individuals, the situations, and the possibilities. The point is, such observations, made empathically and interpreted empathically, are likely to be very useful in understanding children and in improving communication.

Applying these ideas on a broader scale, we can see that teachers who desire to improve their communication with their classes need to be aware of any concepts of self, adults, and the world in general which children in their classes are likely to have. As children communicate with each other, they tend to develop concepts that are similar. Here are some examples. It is common for children in the prepubertal period to regard the opposite sex with some hostility. This is accompanied with some anxiety, particularly on the part of boys, who are quite concerned lest someone think they are "sissies." Children in kindergarten and the primary grades are likely to be more trusting of adults than are children in the upper grades. Adolescents commonly feel that adults do not understand them.

THE NEED FOR CHILDREN TO LEARN TO EMPATHIZE WITH TEACHERS

We should not leave the subject of empathy without noting that the student's effectiveness in communication also depends on his ability to empathize with the teacher. One study of this problem, made by Thomas S. Cohn, seems to indicate that empathy is at least as important as intellectual capacity as far as success in college courses is concerned [7]. This can further be demonstrated by the reaction of students to examination questions. The author has often found that students who receive low marks on examinations are likely to misinterpret or misread examination questions. Probably in most cases there is no deliberate intent, since the student has nothing to gain in replying to a question which simply does not appear on the examination sheet. Evidently what occurs at such times is that the student's ability to interpret (communicate) effectively is warped by neurotic anxiety. Even at best, language is a rather imperfect instrument of communication and needs to be helped out by empathy to make it more effective. The student who *can* empathize with the instructor is more able than his unempathic classmate to determine what the instructor meant by the question. Because he is empathic, he is sensitive to the instructor's attitudes, feelings, and concepts, and therefore is able to make the interpretation of the question that the instructor expected.

This is another reason why it is unwise for teachers to arouse the neurotic anxieties of their classes needlessly. Anxiety interferes with communication, both on a verbal or intellectual level as well as on the nonverbal, emotional, or empathic level. And anything which seriously blocks or impairs communication is likely to interfere with classroom learning.

But children cannot always be held responsible for not understanding teachers. A teacher who is skilled in communicating with children is able to sense as he goes along whether he is being understood. All too often, teachers attempt to communicate, but children misinterpret or do not understand because the teacher is using an adult frame of reference and does not realize its inappropriateness for children.

INTERPERSONAL RELATIONS AND COMMUNICATION

Communication is a many-sided, complex problem, but a problem we must continue to work at if we are to succeed as teachers. Some of the difficulties of communication are described by David H. Jenkins and Ronald Lippitt:

> It is really surprising how little people feel free to communicate with others. To a large extent, . . . we try to do what we think others expect us to do. But if each individual or group has an incorrect perception of what the other individual or group expects of him, his action, no matter how well performed, will not be the right action. Poor communication is at the heart of many human relations problems [8].

Hilda Taba explains how the psychological relations among individuals in the group have an important bearing on the communication that takes place:

> The lines of communication among individuals are determined by psychological reactions of individuals to each other in the group. You find some who are being rejected; you all have seen situations where there was response to ideas that are

not so good, and rejection of others that were very good. You
have seen such things in teachers' meetings. The reaction to
ideas is combined with reactions to individuals. So, if you want
good communication, you must assess what psychological reactions exist among individuals because they do have some
effect on how smoothly communication runs. There are people
with a lot of self-expectation. They expect to come out well
ahead of everyone else. People like this ruin themselves with
others; they block the learning of others. They are not usually
well-liked and very often they are bright people. Then there
are others who do not expect what they say to count. So, often
they do not even attempt to express themselves [1].

COMMUNICATION AND CLASSROOM MANAGEMENT

What Hilda Taba says makes it clear that the teacher who
understands his students will use this understanding in promoting classroom arrangements that will provide for the
maximum in communication. Even seating arrangements are
helpful—children sitting in circles or in horseshoe-shaped arrangements are more likely to interact and to participate in
class discussion. But participation involves much more than
changing the seating arrangements. Taba comments further
on other kinds of changes and arrangements:

> Communication cannot take place in a silent classroom
> where everybody has to be quiet all the time. Communication
> is at a minimum in such an atmosphere. If there is any com-
> munication at all, it will be from the teacher to the child. . . .
> If there are forty people in a room and each communicates
> only to the teacher, the total amount of learning is reduced
> markedly, just as the total amount of participation is reduced
> if the ball always has to come back to the teacher. The teacher
> is a bottleneck, because everything runs through her. . . .
> Some comfortable social space is needed if you want com-
> munication to take place from everyone to everyone. It comes
> to the matter of participation. People need to feel that there is
> a place for what they have to say, and that their ideas are

wanted and invited. To have this social space is a matter of classroom atmosphere and of the way we set up our teaching and curriculum patterns. For example, connectedness and continuity are important. In one class where the teacher was an exponent of progressive education, the children were given assignments—research assignments on which they reported to the class. One child spoke about rabbits, the next one about boats, and the next one about railroads. Even if the psychological conditions are right, it is impossible to communicate when there is no connection between the topics discussed. This kind of curriculum or assignment does not give a good base for communication. Assignments may be diverse, but a common point must be maintained so there is a road or a bridge from one task to another. For instance, if we are all talking about family relationships, but I have read or know about this kind of problem of relationship, you that kind, and someone else another kind—each addition is an exciting addition and has point. Communication lines are more open because we are all looking at relationships, but have different things to point out [1].

It is important for mental-health reasons to keep lines of communication open in the classroom. We noted earlier that the need to express oneself is present in all of us; if this need is continually and chronically frustrated in a classroom, learning itself is likely to be thwarted and frustrated. Much of the communication that could take place in a classroom is blocked by a kind of mutual hostility or resentment. This is particularly true in junior high and high schools. It is as though student and teacher each expected the other to frustrate and misunderstand him. Such conditions are not favorable to learning. On the other hand, teachers can do much to help bring about better learning conditions by making it possible for students to express themselves freely. John W. Thibaut and John Coules found that when two groups of students were deliberately made hostile in an experimental situation, and one group was permitted to communicate back to the instigator of the hostility immediately following the instigation, the students who were permitted this communication felt less hostile and more accepting, whereas the hostility of the other group continued unabated [9]. This experiment points up the need for freedom of expression through channels of communication that are kept open.

THE TEACHER'S ROLE IN COMMUNICATION

Both learning and its chief tool, communication, are outgoing processes, processes whereby the individual absorbs some of the environment and is, in turn, partly absorbed by it. The teacher's role is very largely one of stimulating the absorption and counterabsorption and removing obstacles which impede these processes. Unfortunately, we find ourselves so often in the position of blocking or restricting the communication of children in an attempt to promote the kinds of communication which *we* want. The inevitable result is that many children are unable to communicate naturally in a classroom situation. The antidote to this situation is *not* a lifting of all restrictions and controls, as this would in many cases lead to chaos and disorganization. Rather the need is for a greater sensitivity and awareness with regard to the communicative needs of children. We need to find out what kinds and conditions of communication facilitate and promote learning and what kinds and conditions prevent or inhibit it. And the chances are that when we make this study we shall find that an individual who ignores the needs of his group in an attempt to meet his own needs for self-expression is an individual who hinders the easy and efficient operation of activities which produce learning. This principle certainly applies to a disorganized class, where everyone is talking at once without concern for the needs of the group, but it also applies to the teacher who insists that children remain mouse-still, speak only when called on, and phrase their replies according to rigidly prescribed patterns. He, too, is less concerned with the needs of the group and more concerned with his own needs. The result is highly detrimental to two-way communication.

REFERENCES

1. H. Taba, "Communication," an unpublished lecture delivered at San Francisco State College, June 20, 1951. Reprinted by permission.
2. R. Cunningham *et al.*, *Understanding Group Behavior of Boys and Girls.* New York: Bureau of Publications, Teachers College, Columbia University, 1951. P. 51. Reprinted by permission.
3. M. Heaton, *Feelings are Facts.* New York: National Conference of Christians and Jews, 1952. P. 17. Reprinted by permission.
4. D. W. Baruch, *The Glass House of Prejudice.* New York: Morrow, 1946. Pp. 93–94. Reprinted by permission.
5. D. H. Jenkins and R. Lippitt, *Interpersonal Perceptions of Teachers, Students and Parents.* Washington: Division of Adult Education Service, National Education Association, 1951. Pp. 61–65.
6. N. Cantor, *Dynamics of Learning.* Buffalo: Foster and Stewart, 1946. P. 17. Reprinted by permission.
7. T. S. Cohn, "A Study of Nonintellective Factors in Grade-Getting," unpublished paper read before the Western Psychological Association, San Jose, California, April 27, 1951.
8. Jenkins and Lippitt, *op. cit.* P. 14.
9. J. W. Thibaut and J. Coules, "The Role of Communication in the Reduction of Interpersonal Hostility," *Journal of Abnormal and Social Psychology.* 47:770–77;1952.

SUGGESTED READINGS

H. Bonner, *Social Psychology.* New York: American Book, 1953. Chapter 3, "Language and Behavior."

J. H. S. Bossard, *The Sociology of Child Development.* New York: Harper, 1948. Chapter 8, "Family Table Talk;" Chapter 9, "Family Modes of Expression;" and Chapter 10, "The Bilingual Child."

L. W. Doob, *Social Psychology.* New York: Holt, 1952. Chapter 5, "Language."

E. L. Hartley and R. E. Hartley, *Fundamentals of Social Psychology.* New York: Knopf, 1952. The first third of this textbook is concerned with communication.

S. I. Hayakawa, *Language in Action*. New York: Harcourt, Brace, 1939.

———, *Language in Thought and Action*. New York: Harcourt, Brace, 1949. How people use words and words use people.

W. Johnson, *People in Quandries*. New York: Harper, 1946. Discusses the role of language and communication in personality maladjustment.

I. J. Lee, *Language Habits in Human Affairs*. New York: Harper, 1941.

H. C. Lindgren, *The Art of Human Relations*. New York: Hermitage, 1953. Chapters 6 and 7 are concerned with communication, emotional maturity, and emotional immaturity.

———, *Psychology of Personal and Social Adjustment*. American Book, 1953. Chapter 11, "Communication: The Process of Social Interaction."

D. McCarthy, "Language Development in Children," in L. Carmichael, ed., *Manual of Child Psychology*. New York: Wiley, 1946.

G. E. Swanson, T. M. Newcomb, and E. L. Hartley, eds., *Readings in Social Psychology*, rev. ed. New York: Holt, 1952. Part IB, "Signs, Symbols, and Language in Interpersonal Communication," as well as other selections dealing with communication.

S. S. Sargent, *Social Psychology*. New York: Ronald, 1950. Chapter 9, "Communicating and Symbolizing."

K. Young, *Personality and Problems of Adjustment*, Second edition, New York: Appleton-Century-Crofts, 1952. Chapter 6, "The Development of Language in the Individual."

SUGGESTED FILMS

Finger Painting. How children express their individuality in paint. Available from New York University Film Library.

Understanding Children's Play. Play is also a means of communication. Available from Educational Institute for Learning and Research, 65 East 96th Street, New York.

8

THE CHILD AND THE GROUP

THE subject matter of this chapter is concerned with a process and a dilemma. In it are described the ways in which children develop from self-centered, self-concerned individuals to individuals who merge some of their identity with groups of their peers. In this chapter we also examine some of the ambivalence and anxiety that results when we are torn between expressing our individuality and conforming to the demands of the group and of society. This latter problem is one which must be faced by adults and children alike. However, adults have an advantage in that they have had to resolve this question many times before and have developed their ways of dealing with it. Their methods may not always be satisfactory, but they accomplish the desired results often enough and besides they have a certain familiarity. Children, on the other hand, have less control over their own destiny and consequently have greater difficulties with this problem. The situation is made even more complex by the fact that they must cope with continual change. Decisions and solutions which work in the third grade do not work in the fourth, and the problems which must be solved in junior high are different from those of high school. The adult's problem is somewhat simpler in that he is largely concerned about the adjustments he must make to a society composed of other adults, whereas the child must consider the differing standards of adults on the one hand and his agemates on the other.

Sometimes, when we feel that others are making too many demands on us, we feel like turning our backs on the world and becoming entirely self-centered. Or perhaps we feel like expressing our resentment openly and freely, regardless of the consequences. Yet we seldom, if ever, give free rein to these impulses because we are afraid of losing the good will, the emotional support, and the approval of others. In the final analysis, other people are too important to us.

RELATIONS WITH OTHERS DURING INFANCY AND PRESCHOOL YEARS

OUR LIVES ARE CONDITIONED BY THE FEELINGS OF OTHERS

As we have indicated in the chapter on anxiety, the first glimmerings of this concern about our relations with others begin in infancy, when our emotional life is tied to the moods and feelings of our mothers by a sort of empathic linkage. As our psychological universe expands to include both parents and other members of the family, our relationships with others grow more complex. Our feelings are still empathically related to the moods of others, but some new elements are introduced. For example, we may develop different attitudes toward the feelings of other children as compared with those of our parents. Perhaps initially we are annoyed, but not particularly upset, by the unfriendly feelings of other children—after all, they are not as important to us as our parents are. In effect, we are saying that the attitudes of other children do not matter as long as we have the love and acceptance of our parents. Or, to put it differently, at this age we have enough to worry about in keeping on the good side of our parents without becoming too concerned with the feelings of other children. Furthermore, if our feelings become too ruffled by our encounters with our peers, we can always find solace and comfort in the arms of our parents.

THE CHILD IN THE PLAY GROUP

Most children of preschool age enjoy playing in the company of other children, even though they may be uninterested in playing directly *with* others. At first, the child's activities in the group may be characterized as "parallel play." If we watch two- and three-year-olds in a sandpile, we note that they are busy digging, filling and emptying pails, and filling up holes largely on their own, without much concern for what their neighbors are doing. There is very little cooperative effort, and such cooperation as does exist does not last very long.

With four- and five-year-olds, there is an increase in cooperative play. Children of this age are more likely to form small groups and engage in some joint undertaking. Their attention span is longer, their play more complex and adult-like, and the number involved in the group is larger. However, both the composition and the structure of the group are rather loose, and the membership may change from day to day or even from hour to hour. Furthermore, some members may participate in cooperative play for a while and then revert to parallel play without leaving the neighborhood of the group.

The behavior of children at this age is relatively little affected by the standards of his peers and age-mates. This is partly because the group lacks the cohesiveness and solidarity needed to develop and enforce standards, but principally because children this age feel no need to develop standards of their own. After all, they have their hands full trying to conform to the standards that adults have set for them. However, they do communicate and at times attempt to enforce the standards that adults have taught them. But their power is weak, for groups at this age level do not have the close-knit, cohesive, and persuasive qualities possessed by older groups of children. The preschool child tends to deal directly and individually with his peers and age-mates. This is both an advantage and a disadvantage for adults charged with the responsibility of supervising children of this age group. On the one hand, children of this age are suggestible and are cooperative within the limits of their maturity, but on the other hand, their attention spans are short and they are highly distractible, particularly in groups. Often, when children get together in groups and something occurs to stimulate them, they will interact on each other and produce a chaotic situation that temporarily defies the efforts of adults to restore equilibrium and quiet. Nevertheless, there are compensations: adults in charge of preschool groups do not have to be concerned much about group feeling and morale, and they do not have to deal with the problem frequently faced by leaders of adolescents and preadolescents of "the group being against them [1]."

Toward the end of the preschool years, the attitudes of other children become increasingly important. There is much variation in the rate with which this change occurs, for it depends on a wide variety of factors. Some children are very close to their parents and do not feel the need for the companionship of other children as soon as do others. Hence, they are less likely to attach the same importance to the attitudes of other children than, say, the child who is thrown on his own resources, so to speak, at an earlier age. As a result of this variation in development children enter school at differing stages of maturity with regard to their awareness of the attitudes and feelings of other children.

THE PLAYMATE RELATIONSHIP

About the time of entering school—earlier for some children and later for others—the child is likely to develop a close relationship with one or two other children. These groups seldom are very large; it is as though the child cannot give his attention (or his love, if you like) to several children at once. You can observe this when two children are playing together happily. A third child comes up and wants to enter into their play. They vehemently object to this. If an adult is successful in getting them to admit the third child, the arrangement may succeed, or it may not, depending, among other things, on the social maturity of all three children. In general, however, these "close playmate" arrangements are "closed corporations" as far as the child on the outside is concerned. What frequently happens is that the outsider finds another child who is not a member of a closed group and together they form a two-member group of their own. Sometimes the less mature child needs adult help at this stage—that is, the adult must locate the other child and bring them together with the suggestion that they might like to play together.

Children in nursery school often have a hierachy of preferences in their playmates. For example, June and Mary may be inseparable pals all day long. When Mary is home with a cold, June may prefer to play with George. A few days later, Mary comes back. George tries to continue his relationship with June. June prefers Mary, but she has enjoyed playing with George, so she does not object including him in the group. But Mary regards her relationship with June as her exclusive property and, in four-year fashion, she expresses her resentment at his intrusion in a stream of "bathroom language." George's reactions to this treatment will depend on his personality pattern and his level of maturity. He may run crying to the nearest adult, he may try to hit or push Mary, he may reply with some bathroom language of his own, or he may wander off and look for something else to do. The social structure of a nursery school is composed of a number of such "pal relationships," some of which last for a few weeks and some of which continue for months and years. Some children in this stage of social development participate actively and intensively in such arrangements, others involve

themselves less intensively and spend part of the time playing alone, whereas still others never participate in a group
activity except when supervised by adults. The "parallel
play" of this age is really individual play in the company of
other children. This may be a sort of compromise between
playing alone and participating with others. For example, a
child may be mature enough to want other children about,
but not mature enough to want to involve himself in any
kind of group activity.

HOSTILITY, AGGRESSION, AND NEGATIVENESS

The first social interchanges of children (under eighteen
months) tend to be negative, the results of getting into each
other's way or taking toys from each other. As they begin to
enjoy each other's company in parallel or in cooperative
play, positive expressions increase. Children of this age are
likely to express their frustration and hostility directly, by
pushing or hitting each other. Toward the end of the preschool period, verbal aggression gradually takes preference
over physical aggression.

The question often comes up among adults who work with
children of this age as to whether adults can make any real
contribution to promoting cooperativeness and eliminating
combativeness. M. H. Appel observed a number of nursery
school groups in which the policies differed with regard to
the fights and quarrels of children. In one of the schools
there was more frequent interference in quarrels by teachers
than in another group. During the first year of observation
the children who were subject to more interference had
fewer quarrels than the children who had more freedom.
However, the following year, when the groups moved on
each to a different kindergarten, the children who had done
little fighting doubled the frequency of their quarrels,
whereas the other group actually engaged in less fighting
than they had during the preceding year [2]. A comment

made by Arthur T. Jersild, in reviewing this research, is particularly pertinent:

A finding such as this does not mean that a child of three or four has within him a certain amount of fight which he must get out of his system; rather it suggests that children must practice and have experience in order to work out their techniques of dealing with one another [3].

Children's relations with adults are marked by resistance and negative feeling during the third year of life, as we have noted elsewhere, but as children develop normal anxiety and accept some of the demands and requirements of society, much of this negativism diminishes. After reaching a peak at the end of the third year, it subsides for a while, only to increase again during the fifth year, whereupon it drops off again during the sixth year. However, the general trend is in the direction of less negativism. Probably the child's growing abilities to express himself and to understand what is required of him are factors here.

THE EARLY SCHOOL YEARS

MAKING THE ADJUSTMENT TO THE CLASSROOM GROUP

Entering school is the beginning of an important stage in the emotional life of the child. It is a crucial point in the process of development which will eventually prepare him for life independent of the control and support of his parents. Some children find this change from the intimate relationships of the family to the more impersonal atmosphere of the school upsetting and alarming. Sometimes this happens because they do not know how to establish relationships with other children. Very often their uneasiness in this new situation is aggravated by the attitude of one or both of their parents, who are afraid that their children are not ready to cope with dangers of life away from home. First-grade teachers ordi-

narily realize that they are likely to encounter problems of
this sort among their pupils and are consequently prepared
to play the temporary role of the substitute mother when the
need arises.

Although virtually all children run into some difficulties in
adjusting to life at school, most of them are able to work out
their problems successfully, thanks to their own natural
tendencies toward good emotional health, as well as to the
aid of understanding parents and teachers. Those children
whose social development is retarded at the point of entering school frequently catch up with their contemporaries
within a few months. A few children are unable to make an
adequate adjustment to the demands of the new situation,
and thus become "problems" which remain unsolved, often
year after year.

THE PLAYMATE RELATIONSHIP IN EARLY SCHOOL YEARS

By the time children start school, most of them are enjoying
the company of other children and feel lonely and rejected
when they are excluded from the play of others. Play groups
are small at first, and there is a tendency for the playmate or
"best pal" relationships to occupy the attention of children
this age. Play groups tend to be small because children are
not yet ready to share their affections and to involve themselves very deeply in the lives of others. According to Helen
Hall Jennings,

> At this stage of their development children are apparently
> not very conscious of the impression they are making on one
> another and are relatively self-centered. Shared experience and
> reciprocated affection do not seem as yet to have the great im-
> portance for the individual which they are to have a little later.
> Difficulties between little children arise largely out of this con-
> text of knowing little about each other's feelings. The task of
> adjusting to other people is one of the big problems in their
> world [4].

According to Jennings, the number of paired friendships increases sharply in the second grade, and again at the fourth, sixth, and eighth grades, as well as in high school, although during the middle elementary years, such associations are almost entirely between members of the same sex. About the fifth or sixth grade the social pattern of the classroom becomes more complex. Children belong less exclusively to one small group of friends, but often become members of "chains" of friends. For example, Helen and Josette may be close friends, but Helen is also a good friend of Wilma, who is a good friend of Donna, who is also a close friend of both Jean and Clara. There is also a tendency for closely knit groups or cliques to appear. Jennings believes that this latter phenomenon is due to the fact that children of this age have become thoroughly aware of adult society as well as of their own need to declare themselves independent of it. By banding together in small groups they satisfy their need for mutual support [5].

THE PLAY GROUP DURING THE EARLY SCHOOL YEARS

To the outsider, the person who has not worked much with children, the concern and interest displayed by psychologists and educators in the play of children is perhaps puzzling. After all, since play is a form of amusement and hence not a serious matter, why take it so seriously?

One of the answers to this question is that play is a *very* serious matter to children. At times, it is the main focus of their life. It constitutes the means whereby they express themselves, try out behavior, and learn about their physical and social environment. Another answer is that we can learn so much about children through watching their play, in spite of the fact that our cultural biases lead us to minimize its importance. Clara Lambert says:

> The play life of a child between the ages of six and eight is a mirror reflecting his inner life. At play he exposes the work-

ings of his personal life, tackles problems of relationships, and tries to solve them. . . .

Children who cannot or do not play find it more difficult to make adjustments to their friends, to their families, to school, and to the world. . . . When one parent was told about the power of play, be it messy, disjointed, or destructive, she replied, "It can't be too good for them. They enjoy it too much [6]."

The degree of social consciousness of the child in this age bracket is revealed by the games he prefers. He is more interested in individual-competitive games like tag and hide-and-go-seek than he is in team sports, like basketball and volleyball. He enjoys competition, but he lacks the social skills to cooperate smoothly. When he plays, he still prefers small groups, and the leaders that arise at this age are leaders of small groups. However, the spontaneous groups that are formed at this age are larger than they are with pre-schoolers. Furthermore, they stay together for longer periods and accomplish more.

As children become more important to each other, they gain the power to create happiness through acceptance and anxiety and sorrow through rejection. On occasion, they are warm and enthusiastic, but also, on occasion, they can be cruel and heartless. Thus the child who enters the third grade several weeks after the start of school, when play groups are already formed, may experience difficulty and distress before being included in the playground activities. And children who are looked upon as "different"—because of ethnic background, religion, or social class—may never experience the feeling of being completely accepted. One cannot help noting that in many ways children of this age are like adults in their patterns of acceptance and rejection except that they are much more open and direct. Martha May Reynolds makes this sage observation regarding the social relationships of children of this age group:

The study of social development should teach us more than how five-, six-, and seven-year-olds behave in groups. It should help us understand the give-and-take of group work, of committee management on the adult level. Through it we should develop a willingness to question our own behavior [7].

RELATIONS WITH OTHERS

During this period of development children continue to show an increase in their ability to communicate verbally, particularly as they pick up new vocabulary in and out of the classroom at school. However, the use of a common activity as a means of communicating belongingness and acceptance has great appeal. Hilda Taba gives the example of six children sitting around a table. If one starts to paint a boat, the others may paint boats too [8]. By imitating him and by all working at a similar task, a feeling of relatedness is built up among them. After a day or so of boat painting, they are ready to go on to ideas of their own. They feel free to do so because they have had the experience of achieving a measure of mutuality, of shared experience. Teachers can often help children build confidence and allay their anxieties about being in a new group by providing manual activity that they can do in small groups. Even older children and adults often benefit by being handled in similar fashion. An example of the latter is the weiner roast attended by people who do not know each other very well. The hostess may help people become acquainted by giving them jobs to do as small groups.

Children in the early school years do not communicate all of their feelings directly, although some of the clues they give are quite obvious. Children of this age group tend to be quite self-critical—they are keenly aware of the gulf that lies between what they can do and what older children and adults can do, and to display what they consider to be their puny efforts often embarrasses them. They may express this embarrassment in one of two ways: by shyness or by boastfulness. In either case, the basic cause is likely to be the same—feelings of inadequacy. Sometimes direct reassurance will help, but more often a child can be given temporary help by being assigned some task that is well within his scope of ability. However, like so many problems that involve anxiety, there are no easy solutions. Many a child in this period will never really drop his feelings of inadequacy until he can actually do well what he has set his heart on or until he passes on into another stage of development where differences in accomplishment appear to matter less.

There is less combativeness during this period than there is among preschoolers. Children are beginning to find out how to disguise or conceal their hostilities and how to avoid some people and seek out others. Frustrations probably evoke just as much hostility in the primary grades as they do in the preschool years; it is just that older children are learning to handle their hostility more skillfully (more in keeping with cultural norms and standards).

PREADOLESCENCE

BEHAVIOR PATTERNS OF PREADOLESCENTS

There has been much research on adolescents and children in the earlier school years, but relatively little on preadolescents. Some one has suggested that this is because a preadolescent will not stand still long enough to be observed. Fritz Redl characterizes them as follows:

> Outwardly, the most striking thing about them is their extreme physical restlessness. They can hardly stand still, running is more natural to them than walking, the word sitting is a euphemism if applied to what they do with a table and a chair. Their hands seem to need constant occupational therapy —they will turn up the edges of any book they handle, will have to manipulate pencils, any objects near them, or any one of the dozen-odd things they carry in their pockets, or even

parts of their own body. . . . The return to other infantile habits is surprisingly intensive in many areas: even otherwise well-drilled and very house-broken youngsters may again show symptoms like bed-wetting, soiling, nail-biting, or its substitutes, like skin-chewing, finger-drumming, etc. Funny gestures and antics seem to turn up overnight with little or no reason —such things as facial tics, odd gestures and jerky movements, long-outgrown speech disorders, and the like [9].

No period of childhood development is characterized by such marked contrasts. On the one hand is a strong desire for privacy and secrecy, and on the other is a marked tendency to act in a silly, almost exhibitionistic manner. On the one hand may be an attempt to show off one's sexual knowledge by telling smutty jokes, and on the other may be a shame of undressing and bathing before one's own parents.

There is a "war between the sexes," in which boys and girls vie with each other in taunts. Girls egg boys into teasing them or playing tricks and then get boys into trouble by "telling." For their part, boys appear to collaborate enthusiastically in this process. One principal once became so concerned about the girls' complaints of being teased by boys on the way home from school, that he let the girls out a half hour early. When the boys came out, the girls were waiting for them [10].

Although both boys and girls complain about their treatment by the opposite sex and are immediately alert to point out any real or fancied favoritism accorded the opposite sex, their rivalry apparently fills a psychological need of the moment. The preadolescent enjoys situations where he has an "enemy," and the "warfare" between the sexes provides him with someone who is against him and who he can be against.

THE GANG

Gangs fit into this picture very well, because gangs are groups that flourish on conflict. Inasmuch as the preadolescent is a conflict-seeking and conflict-creating person, the

gang is much more suited to his purposes than the more
loosely structured play groups of earlier stages of development. The gang demands and gets the fierce loyalty of its
members. Wherever possible, its members will adhere to its
standards in defiance of the requirements that adults attempt
to enforce.

The gang does three things for the preadolescent: it permits him to escape, at least part of the time, from the domination of adults; it gives him a code or standard of behavior
to replace the standards of society he is rejecting; and it gives
him reassurance and support in his rebellion against adult
control. Fritz Redl describes the urge to form gangs as follows:

> In no other age do youngsters show such a deep need for
> . . . . *gang formation* among themselves as in this one. From
> the adult angle this is usually met with much suspicion. Of
> course, it is true that youngsters will tend to choose their com-
> panions from among those who are rejected, rather than ap-
> proved of, by their parents. Perhaps we can understand why
> the more unacceptable a youngster is on the basis of our adult
> behavior code, the more highly acceptable he will be in the
> society of his own peers. . . .
>
> . . . . Now he enters the magical ring of peer-codes. And
> the code of his friends differs essentially from that of adult
> society. In some items the two are diametrically opposed . . .
>
> The change from adult-code to peer-code is not an easy
> process for a youngster but full of conflict and often painful.
> For, while he would like to be admired by his pals on a peer-
> code basis, he still loves his parents personally and hates to see
> them misunderstand him or have them get unhappy about
> what he does. And, while he would love to please his family
> and be again accepted by them and have them proud of him,
> he simply couldn't face being called a sissy or be suspected of
> being a coward or a teacher's pet by his friends. . . . Thus
> you find youngsters so scared of being thought bad by their
> parents that they don't dare mix happily with children of their
> own age; and you find others so keen to achieve peer status

with friends of their own age that they begin to reject all parental advice, every finer feeling of loyalty to the home, and
accept all and any lure of gang prestige even if it involves delinquent and criminal activity [9].

Not all preadolescents engage in gangs or ganglike activities. These tendencies, at least in part, depend upon the need
of the children to rebel and consequently to court the acceptance of their peers. Some preadolescents find that their
needs are best met by continued association in loosely structured play groups, and they may meet their needs for defiance against adult society by participating in secret and exclusive but short-lived clubs, an activity that calls for much
less emotional involvement than does participation in gangs.
This pattern is more typical of girls, who are much less gang-
minded than boys, and whose conduct is generally less disorganized and antisocial during the preadolescent period.

Obviously, working with preadolescents places a strain on
the patience and forbearance of adults. However, some of
our difficulties in working with this age group are the product of our own unrealistic expectations. Martha May Reynolds suggests that we are bothered by the behavior of preadolescents because it is obvious that we mean so very little
to them; the comings and goings of adults have no interest
to them [11]. Redl and Wattenberg say that we must develop objective attitudes and not let the low status that preadolescents accord us "get under our skin:"

> Grownups must be able to detach their own hurt feelings
> from the real significance of events. On the one hand, they
> must be willing to sacrifice temporary popularity with the
> children when it is necessary to enforce clear limits on be-
> havior. On the other hand, they must have the courage to allow
> a wide enough margin for even uncomfortable transitional
> conduct, so that personality growth can take place un-
> squashed [12].

The above advice provides a sound basis for dealing with
the behavior of children and adolescents in any context and

at any age, but it is particularly applicable to relations with the preadolescent because of the jarring effect he has on our adult sensibilities.

One further word of advice from the pen of Fritz Redl may be in order:

> Let's not forget that preadolescents are much more expert in handling us than we ever can be in handling them. Their skill in sizing us up and using our emotions and weaknesses for their own ends has reached a peak at this age. . . . This means that if they [try to show] . . . how emancipated they are, they will choose exactly the trick that will irritate us most. . . . Thus, some of them will smoke, curse, talk about sex, or stay out late. Some will stop being interested in their grades, get kicked out of school, or threaten to become the kind of person who will never be acceptable in good society. . . .
>
> But whatever surface behavior they display—don't fall for it. Don't fight the behavior. Interpret the cause of it first, then judge how much and in what way you should interfere. Thus Johnny's smoking may mean he is sore that his father never takes him to a football match, or it may mean he thinks you don't appreciate how adult he already is, or it may mean that he has become dependent on the class clown. . . .
>
> In any case, all these things are not so hard to figure out. Instead of getting excited and disapproving of the strange behavior, just open your eyes for a while and keep them open without blinking [9].

ADOLESCENCE

VARIABILITY IN DEVELOPMENT

Children in any unselected group, like a school grade or class, are at various stages of development at any given time. Thus there will be some children in a typical third-grade class who will behave like preadolescents, and some will be a little babyish, while most of them will conform to the behavior pattern we described as characteristic of children in the early school years. As children become older, these gaps and differences in their maturity become more pronounced and act as a force that often hinders or threatens the development of solidarity and group feeling in the classroom. The disintegrative effects of these forces reach their peak, more or less, in the seventh grade. Alice V. Keliher points out that at thirteen and a half years of age, 60 percent of boys have not reached puberty, 33 percent are in the puberty cycle, and 7 percent have reached physical maturity, whereas only 15 percent of girls have not reached puberty, 35 percent are in the puberty cycle, and 50 percent have reached physical maturity [13]. These differences in physical development also mean that the typical seventh grade is made up of individuals with widely varying interests, attitudes, perceptions, and needs. It is more difficult for seventh graders to work together cooperatively and to arrive at viewpoints in their discussions that are congenial to all members of the class. When one adds to this the tendencies of preadolescents in the class to engage in aggressive and irresponsible behavior, the difficulties experienced by many seventh-grade teachers become understandable.

In adolescence, the hostility that was characteristic of the preadolescent becomes more crystalized, more sharply defined, and less generalized. The preadolescent resents adults, but it is more of a diffuse resentment—he is not really sure why he is resentful, although he is ready to come up with enough reasons on a moment's notice. However, the resentment of the adolescent has a more consistent basis. Specifically, he resents being treated as a child, and not being given a share in the decisions that affect him.

Even so, there are inconsistencies in his resentment. Lois H. Meek and others, writing about adolescent personality, note that adolescents

. . . will often speak with envy of the great freedom enjoyed by older brothers or sisters and at the same time bitterly resent the affectionate care lavished by parents on younger members of the family [14].

Adolescents not only show hostility toward parents, but also toward teachers (because they are parent substitutes), out-groups (members of lower-class and minority groups), and themselves [15]. P. M. Symonds made a study of the fantasy of life of adolescents through the use of a picture-story test and found that aggression was the commonest of the psychological themes appearing in the stories told by his subjects [16].

Another personality trait characteristic of adolescence is insecurity. Although adolescents may try to look, talk, and act like adults, they are chronically unsure of themselves. Much of their rebellious nonconformity and attention-seeking behavior is an attempt to "compensate" for their feelings of inferiority.

However, adolescence is, in general a more "enlightened" age than is the preceding period. Caroline Tryon investigated personality traits admired by some 320 boys and girls when they were eleven and twelve years old and then compared her findings with a similar investigation conducted three years later. At the earlier point in their development, boys valued competence in group games, leadership ability, fearlessness, and willingness to take a chance. They also thought more favorably of being boisterous, aggressive and untidy than they did of being quiet, submissive, and too clean. Three years later, the same boys placed more emphasis on social skills, poise, neatness in dress, and the qualities that go with what is commonly termed "a pleasing personality [17]."

Mary C. Jones followed the interests of 142 boys and girls year by year from the sixth through the twelfth grade, using a questionnaire approach. She found that the number of children checking the item "secret clubhouse" decreased during the period, indicating a drop in "gang" interest. Interest in news magazines gained during this period. Tenth-grade boys and girls favored the item "detective story magazine" over "a magazine with articles about the government and world affairs," but when they were in the twelfth grade, the world affairs magazine received about half the votes of the boys and about two thirds the votes of the girls. In general, there was a decline in interest in reading about romantic and glamorous characters and an increase in preference for factual, realistic reading matter. Although these trends are encouraging, one should not overlook the other findings reported by Jones, namely, that a very high proportion of adolescents of both sexes still preferred reading detective story, motion picture, radio, and western story magazines to reading material dealing with world affairs [18].

GROUP LIFE OF ADOLESCENTS

The social group that becomes prominent during this stage is the clique. William E. Martin and Celia Burns Stendler define a clique as a group of relatively few individuals, sometimes of both sexes, and characterized largely by exclusiveness and stability. It usually does not appear on the scene until adolescence and consists of a subgroup in a larger group. Martin and Stendler distinguish between a clique and a crowd by saying that a crowd is more likely to include both boys and girls. The latter is a larger group, less well organized than a clique, and its membership is less stable [19].

James H. S. Bossard notes that a clique consists of children from the same social status. There is a bond of intimacy, loyalty, and solidarity that unites the members. Membership in a clique involves strong feelings of friendship and mutual responsibility to help each other, a common behavior pattern, and a loyalty to the clique in preference to other groups, even including the families of its members [20]. The clique is primarily a device that operates as a result of school associations and is more characteristic of middle and upper classes.

The insistence on conformity exacted by the peer groups of preadolescence are, if anything, intensified in adolescence.

Few things worry an adolescent more than being different. Unfortunately, the great variability characteristic of this age group makes anxiety inevitable for many. To quote Arthur T. Jersild,

> If the child is fat, he is miserable; if he is skinny, he is sad. If he is tall for his years, he staggers under the responsibilities that fall upon him; if he is short, life is a bitter pill. The woe that goes with a big bosom is equaled only by the misery that comes with a flat chest. And so on [21].

EMOTIONAL CONFLICTS DURING ADOLESCENCE

For many adolescents, the existence of two sources of authority, adults and the peer group, is a source of anxiety and conflict.[1] Most of them resolve it by maintaining peer-group standards wherever and whenever possible and by yielding to adult standards only under pressure or threat of punishment. Most of them recognize that society is adult-dominated and that it is futile to struggle as long as the pressure is maintained. But they delight in using the strength of the group to outwit authorities, as many a principal has found when he tried to discover who broke the cafeteria window.

At the present moment of writing, the newspapers are carrying a story about the setting off of firecrackers by the residents of a dormitory at the University of Delaware. Unable to abate this nuisance, the administration of the university threatened to close the dormitory. The firing of firecrackers continued, and the dormitory was closed. It has now been closed a week, and the culprits have not been apprehended.

Situations like these will appear whenever students feel the need to express their resentment of adult authority through openly aggressive behavior. The fact that group life

---

[1] This and the following eight paragraphs are taken for the most part from H. C. Lindgren, "The Problem of the Adolescent: Its Roots and Origins," *The Clearing House,* 27:195–202;1952. Reprinted by permission.

offers opportunities for communication means that members can learn of the resentful feelings held by others, can plan for revenge, carry through hostile acts, and can use the group as a means of protection against retaliation.

In the adolescent period the peer group reaches new heights of power. Part of this power is derived from the essential nature of the adolescent conflict in our culture. The adolescent is approaching the adult in size, strength, and intelligence; yet he feels insecure and inadequate. He would like to think and act for himself; yet he feels the need to depend on more experienced people for advice and direction. On the other hand, he frequently resents offers of help and attempts to supply direction. He would like to be self-sufficient; yet there are many attractions in having adults nourish and care for him. In his more bitter moments he rejects adult standards as phony, inconsistent, and unreasonable; yet he cannot operate without them and frequently is overly conscientious and hypercritical of his deviations from prescribed norms.

Adults further complicate the adolescent's problems in that they have not come to any clear conclusions about their expectations of adolescents. We tend to prolong the childhood of adolescents far beyond the point where they can think and act for themselves. We wish they would take more responsibility, while at the same time we give them little opportunity to learn and to practice the skills of responsibility. Parents encourage them in their dependency, for they are reluctant to have them leave home, yet they feel that adolescents are capable of contributing to their own support. And when, as young adults, they do leave the home, parents sometimes try to bind them with chains of gratitude —by gifts and grants of money.

It is no wonder that the adolescent is confused. In addition to his interpersonal difficulties, the adolescent has other problems; rapid and irregular growth, the development of sexual functions and drives, plus a variety of health problems. The adolescent's dilemma is neatly phrased in this statement by Gertrude Wilson and Gladys Ryland:

> It is easy to see why adolescents need nine or more hours of sleep and equally easy to see why, in the light of their emotional and intellectual needs, they oppose any such requirement [22].

The development of the adolescent personality has particular importance for those who work with groups of students of this age. The adolescent in school finds himself caught in the cross fire of two cultures—the adult culture whose demands and prohibitions are levied by teachers and parents and the peer culture of which he is a more or less active member.

Each of these cultures brings powerful forces to play on the adolescent; each tries to capture him from the other; each levels the same penalty for nonconformity—rejection. Again and again the adolescent must decide whose rejection he must risk—that of the adults or that of the group. This decision is usually made with difficulty and occasionally with real anguish.

It is at this point that the adolescent who as a child identified himself with the adult culture has some real difficulties because he is torn between loyalty to his friends and retaining their companionship on the one hand and the assimilation of adult standards of behavior and loneliness on the other, for the adolescent who thinks and acts in adult ways must lead a life apart, unless he can find other adolescents who think and feel as he does. Thus, most adolescents remain with their groups rather than suffer ostracism. They recognize that adults are unable to give them the acceptance based on equality that they can get from their group.

THE SOCIAL MATURITY OF ADOLESCENTS

The adolescent we have described in the preceding pages has moved several stages beyond the preschool child. He is less self-centered than the child of five and is able to "give" more of himself. The groups to which he owes his allegiance not only provide him with the means for sharing friendship and love, but they also provide him with the means of coping with the demands of the adult world.

There are some adolescents, of course, who have not reached this level of social and emotional maturity. A few seem to be at the prekindergarten level of social development, in that they cannot involve themselves emotionally in the life of even one other person. Others appear to be at the first-grade level, so to speak, because their friendships are the exclusive, paired relationships typical of these early years. Still other adolescents seem at the preadolescent stage in that they have been unable to make friendships with the members of the opposite sex. These less mature forms of behavior usually signify the presence of conditions or forces that have prevented or are preventing them from developing behavior more appropriate to their age level.

When a child or adolescent is subjected to situations involving unusual stress and anxiety, he is likely to "lose" the more mature behavior which he displays under normal circumstances. In other words, there is a tendency for him to become more worried about his own welfare and less concerned about the welfare of his group. Even this tendency is lessened, however, with maturity because the more mature individual is more likely to demonstrate group loyalty—a realization that the group welfare is also *his* welfare. He is part of the group and the group is part of him, and if he betrays his group in the face of stress and acts in a self-centered manner, he is, in effect, denying this identity.

THE CONFLICT BETWEEN INDIVIDUALITY
AND CONFORMITY

THE PROBLEM OF DIVIDED LOYALTIES

This brings us to the problem we mentioned at the start of this chapter—the ambivalence of children's attitudes regarding their relations with their groups. Again and again children (and adults, too, to a lesser degree) are faced by the necessity of deciding whether they owe allegiance primarily to themselves or to others. To rephrase this more simply, the child or adolescent must decide at these times whether he is going to do what *he* wants to do or what *others* want him to do. Initially, this decision involves mainly his parents—should he follow his own inclinations or his parents' desires? The small child usually works out some kind of compromise whereby he follows his parents' wishes in most respects, and preserves as much of his individuality as possible. To a large extent, he takes over the ideas and attitudes of his parents as his own. If he is able to do this, then they become *his* ideas and attitudes and he feels more relaxed about following them, for his rights as an individual are not challenged. However, in essence, he has given up some of his individuality and conformed to the standards and requirements of his parents in exchange for their continued acceptance. In this way he avoids anxiety or reduces it to the minimum. If he is unsuccessful in bringing about such a state of affairs, he runs the risk of incurring anxiety, which, in turn, leads to emotional disturbances of various sorts.

Much the same problem arises in the middle years of childhood when the child becomes a member of children's groups which have a certain amount of "group feeling," whose members, shall we say, have a consciousness of being identified with a recognizable group. Gangs, cliques, and clubs are groups of this sort. These groups have a certain self-consciousness in that they see themselves as being different from other groups and individuals in the society which surrounds them. They may heighten this feeling of being different by adopting a name, like the "Park School Frank Sinatra Club," or the "Red Destroyers." They may adopt a ritual or a secret password or a secret code. Any of these devices help to sharpen the differences between group members and outsiders and to promote the solidarity and feeling of closeness which are such important rewards of group membership.

GROUPS MAKE DEMANDS ON THEIR MEMBERS

In payment for the satisfactions provided its members, the group exacts a price in return. It requires that its members adhere to certain standards of behavior and belief. For example, in order to belong to some gangs of eleven-year-old boys, one must hate girls. Not to hate girls, or to state openly that one does not hate girls, is to raise a question about one's fitness for membership. A group of fifth-grade girls may be united by the common bond of loving their teacher. To them, she can do no wrong, and no member of the group in good standing would think of criticizing her.

All well-knit groups, whether they are composed of children or adults, have such standards of conduct and belief for their members: they are an integral part of being a member. These standards are not necessarily related to the chief or avowed purpose of the group; often they are incidental— merely a way whereby the group exercises its uniting influence. Thus, the group of eleven-year-old boys we mentioned in the above paragraph may have sand-lot baseball as their chief interest; hating girls is merely something which is expected of each member. And the group of fifth-grade girls does not exist for the purpose of admiring their teacher; its apparent purpose is to provide a means for the girls to have fun together—to go to the movies, watch television, or go swimming. Their admiration of the teacher is one of the several bonds which unites them.

The world of the child in school consists of several sorts of social relationships, each of which provides some rewards and satisfactions and makes some demands. There is a family group, which helps to meet some of his more basic needs. The school also provides satisfactions, although these are of a variable nature—that is, some children find school more enjoyable than others, and some schools are more likely to meet the needs of children than are others. In any case, children have no choice about going to school; hence, by going to school they avoid the disapproval and punishment which would result if they chose not to attend. Going to school is, therefore, a way of avoiding anxiety. Then there are the small informal groups of children we have described in the above paragraphs. They minister to the needs for love, acceptance, and status that otherwise might go unfilled. To participate in the classroom groups and activities of the school also provides satisfactions and social contact which the child needs.

There is also the social group which we call "the adult world," represented largely by teachers and parents. Teachers and parents play dual roles—one being the "helpful" role, the role of personal, emotional support, which is usually on a person-to-person basis. The other role is that of "the representative of the adult world," in which the parent or teacher interprets the outside world and says, in effect, "This is how things are done; these are the things you ought to think about because you will have to work with them later;" and, inevitably, "These are the things that you cannot do, and you must stop doing them." In the first role, the parent or teacher acts the part of a giver, and in the second role, he acts the part of the group member who makes demands on another group member on behalf of the larger group. In effect, he says: "If you wish to maintain your membership, if you wish to have us continue accepting and supporting you, you must conform in these details."

In essence, all the groups we have mentioned make some demands on their members. They exact some measure of conformity as a price for membership. Conformity has a symbolic function in that it symbolizes the acceptance by the individual of membership in the group. By conforming he gives up some of his right to determine his actions for himself. And to some extent, he gives up some of his individuality.

THE NONCONFORMIST

There are, of course, individuals in many groups who do not conform easily. Often this difficulty is related to the fact that they have not really made up their minds whether they want to give up their individuality for the sake of group acceptance. The inability or refusal of an individual to conform to group standards usually makes the other members of the group anxious. They may express this anxiety by talking to the deviating member, "putting pressure" on him in order to get him to change his behavior. If he continues to deviate, they may take measures to punish him—to let him know, in some way, that they disapprove of his deviation. If membership is on a voluntary basis, they may force him out of the group.

Translated into everyday terms, this means that the eleven-year-old boys referred to above will attempt to ridicule or play practical jokes on one of their members if, for example, he should walk home with a girl or do one a favor. A common practice is to place the offending member "in Coventry," if his deviation is considered serious—that is, no one speaks to him for a stated period of time. This is a severe form of rejection because one of the values resulting from contacts with others is the ability to communicate with others. To be rejected by one's companions and to be unable to communicate with them is cruel punishment indeed.

When membership in a group is involuntary, as it is in the case of the family, the school, and society at large, the deviation of a member from the accepted standards for conduct also results in increased anxieties. In the case of children, rejection and disapproval are usually expressed by persons in charge—that is, by parents or teachers. Whether the other children in the group also express disapproval depends on whether they accept the standards which are being enforced.

In many situations, the sympathy of the children is with the child being punished, because they have not accepted the particular standard being enforced or the right of adults to punish for its violation. In situations of this sort, they lend emotional support to the punished child.

NEUROTIC REASONS FOR NONCONFORMITY

The maturity of an individual, whether adult or child, is sometimes put to a severe test in matters of conformity. There are two important reasons why we may not want to conform: the first is immature and neurotic, and the second is mature and emotionally healthy.

The immature and neurotic forces within us (and we all have them to a greater or lesser degree) lead us to seek the acceptance and support of the group, without taking any responsibility in return. Thus, a four-year-old may expect others to give him gifts, but he may have no intention of sharing his toys or his candy. Or, he expects others to consider his wishes and feelings, but he is inconsiderate of the feelings and wishes of others. The immature person in the middle grades would like to be accepted as a member of the groups he sees about him, but he is unwilling or unable to give up his own ways of doing things and is more concerned about his own feelings than he is about the feelings of others. In effect, he has decided that he would prefer to remain alone, rather than make the compromise which the group would require. Yet he is not completely happy with this decision; he would like to be accepted by others, but he is not ready to meet his responsibilities to the group. The group is aware of this, and they either reject or ignore him.

The adolescent who has his troubles with adults is caught on a similar dilemma. He would like to be free from the domination of adults, free to make his own decisions. Yet he is not ready to take the responsibility for the results of these decisions. When he exceeds the speed limit and is fined by the traffic court, he expects his father to pay the fine. In short, he would like to retain the acceptance and support of the adult world, without adhering to the standards set for the conduct of members of society.

HEALTHY REASONS FOR NONCONFORMITY

But there is also a mature and mentally healthy reason for being concerned about conformity. As long as groups make rules and establish standards that are beneficial, there is no great cause for alarm. But often groups exceed reasonable limits and use their power to exact more and more conformity to more and more rules and standards. This often occurs when the group or its leaders feels threatened or anxious. When this occurs, there is a tendency for requirements to be made more severe and more exacting. Therefore, the teacher who fears that his class may get out of control is likely not only to punish every whisperer but also to look with disfavor on any child whose ideas differ from his. Or a gang may insist that no member talk to a teacher outside of class as a result of one of the members being humiliated by a scolding in front of his class.

When an individual who is capable of doing original thinking is continually forced to suppress his ideas for fear of offending an individual or group who insists on complete conformity, there is likelihood that he will become discouraged and will abandon originality in favor of complete and unthinking conformity. Thus, when we as teachers and parents insist on strict compliance to our ways of thinking, we should be aware that we run the risk of discouraging children who are ready to start thinking for themselves.

Let us consider the situation faced by Miss Watson when she tried to teach long division to the fourth grade.

Miss Watson did not enjoy teaching arithmetic. She had never been particularly good at it, and, in a way, she resented having to teach it at all. Still, there it was in the curriculum, and there was no honorable way of avoiding it. Actually, she felt a little guilty about her resentment because she disapproved of people shirking their responsibilities, and, goodness knows, she wanted to be a good teacher. She wanted her fourth graders to be as well prepared for the fifth grade as possible. And the remarks that Mrs. Wilson and Miss Dickson, the sixth-grade teachers, were constantly making in faculty meeting about the faulty preparation of the pupils they were getting did not help the matter any. She often wondered whether they were talking about preparation in arithmetic fundamentals, but she was afraid to ask.

Miss Watson worked hard on preparing her presentations in arithmetic. She knew the textbook by heart, and could tell you what rule was on what page. Memorizing the textbook was a big help, she felt, particularly when the time came to teach long division. Fourth graders had so much trouble with long division.

Miss Watson's fourth grade this year was nothing special— the usual number of behavior problems, two or three nonreaders, and a couple of children with IQs over 120 who were not working nearly up to capacity. Ronald Pearson was one of these children. He never said much or did much in class. Miss Watson suspected that he spent most of his time daydreaming. Often she had to speak sharply to him because he had failed to respond when called on.

And so it happened that on the day that Miss Watson presented long division to the fourth grade that she did not notice that Ronald, instead of looking out the window with a dreamy look on his face, was actually watching the steps she was outlining on the board. Perhaps ordinarily she would have noticed his changed expression, except that she was so very intent on seeing that the children had a clear idea of the steps they followed in doing a problem in long division. In fact, she had just written a "7" when she meant a "9" and had to go back and retrace some of the steps in order to emphasize certain points.

In the midst of this, Ronald's hand shot up. Miss Watson

wanted to ignore it and finish her presentation, but there was such a sense of urgency on his face. She nodded at him: "Ronald?"

"Miss Watson—I just thought of this! Long division is a kind of subtraction!"

Miss Watson felt the anger and irritation rise within her. To be interrupted at such a time by a stupid remark like that! But when she spoke, her voice was cold and hard.

"Ronald," she said, "if you would pay more attention to what goes on in this class and spend less time in daydreaming, you would be much better off. If you expect to pass in arithmetic in June, I suggest you put those wild and silly ideas out of your head and apply yourself to learning the steps in long division!"

Ronald dropped his head and twisted his pencil, nervously, and Miss Watson knew that she had struck a telling blow. Later in the morning she wondered vaguely whether she had been too hard on Ronald, but when she had to speak to him three times when it was his turn to read, she wished she had spoken more severely. It seemed to her that what the boy needed was a good shaking up.

It will be a long time before Ronald will dare to do his own thinking in one of Miss Watson's classes again. The chances are that he will retire to his dream world for the rest of the year. If he is fortunate to have teachers in later years who recognize his marked ability to analyze abstract situations, his capacity for original thinking may grow and develop in spite of this momentary setback. On the other hand, if his attempts to think for himself are frustrated and ridiculed at every turn throughout school, he may become afraid to do anything beyond following directions. Conformity of this sort amounts to complete intellectual dependency, a form of immaturity. The mature person is one whose capacity to think for himself is continually growing, and this is true of fourth graders as well as of adults.

There are, of course, many students in school whose emo-

tional health is better than Ronald's (note that he daydreams too much) and whose capacity for independent
thought and action will continue to grow in spite of attempts
of well-meaning adults to enforce unnecessary conformities.
It is fortunate that this is so, inasmuch as one of the great
resources of our nation is our ability to foster and utilize
original thinking. However, this is a resource which could
be developed more fully. Our concern here is not with the
unusual individual whose intellectual powers develop in
spite of our teaching, but rather with those many students
whose attempts to think for themselves are discouraged and
thwarted by adults more concerned with forcing children
to adhere to strict routines than with helping them to grow
intellectually as well as socially and emotionally.

MAINTAINING A BALANCE BETWEEN FREEDOM AND CONTROL

The problem of conformity is one of several which the
teacher must face in his work of helping children to develop
in ways which are mentally healthy. It is one which is both
perplexing and exasperating. Teachers need to have control
over their classes, and children need to be able to follow directions and observe reasonable limitations on their behavior. Yet at the same time children also need to learn how
to think and act for themselves and to observe limits and
standards of their own making. In order to carry out this
dual responsibility, the teacher needs to maintain a fluid
balance between direction and control on the one hand, and
freedom for self-expression and self-determination on the
other. And, as we shall discover in a later chapter, this will
involve some risks and some hazards. It is the teacher who
feels that he cannot afford to take such risks who usually decides that it will be all direction and control and no freedom.
In carrying out such a decision, he is more likely to develop
rebelliousness or an apathetic form of conformity among his

students than he is to develop an enthusiasm for learning and a capacity for self-expression and self-direction.

REFERENCES

1. H. C. Lindgren, "The Problem of the Adolescent: Its Roots and Origins," *The Clearing House*. 27:195–202;1952.
2. M. H. Appel, "Aggressive Behavior of Nursery School Children and Adult Procedures in Dealing with Such Behavior," *Journal of Experimental Education*. 11:185–99;1942.
3. A. T. Jersild, *Child Psychology*, 3d ed. New York: Prentice-Hall, 1947. P. 153.
4. H. H. Jennings, *Sociometry in Group Relations*. Washington: American Council on Education, 1948. Pp. 69–71. Reprinted by permission.
5. *Ibid*. P. 71.
6. C. Lambert, *Understand Your Child—From 6 to 12*. New York: Public Affairs Committee, 1948. Pp. 3–4.
7. M. M. Reynolds, *Children from Seed to Saplings*, 2d ed. New York: McGraw-Hill, 1951. P. 124. Reprinted by permission.
8. H. Taba, "Communication," unpublished lecture delivered at the Pre-Summer Session Conference on Group Processes, San Francisco State College, June 20, 1951.
9. F. Redl, "Pre-Adolescents—What Makes Them Tick?" *Child Study*. 21(2):44–48, 58–59;1943. Reprinted by permission.
10. Association for Supervision and Curriculum Development, *Growing up in an Anxious Age*. Washington: National Education Association, 1952. Pp. 203–04.
11. Reynolds, *op. cit*. Pp. 179–80.
12. F. Redl and W. W. Wattenberg, *Mental Hygiene in Teaching*. New York: Harcourt, Brace, 1951. P. 88. Copyright, 1951, by Harcourt, Brace & Co., Inc. Reprinted by permission.
13. A. V. Keliher, *Life and Growth*. New York: D. Appleton-Century, 1938. P. 185.
14. L. H. Meek *et al.*, *The Personal-Social Development of Boys and Girls with Implications for Secondary Education*. New York: Progressive Education Association, 1940. P. 70.
15. K. Young, *Personality and Problems of Adjustment*, 2d ed. New York: Appleton-Century-Crofts, 1952. P. 395.
16. P. M. Symonds, *Adolescent Fantasy: An Investigation of the Picture-Story Method of Personality Study*. New York: Columbia University Press, 1949.

17. C. M. Tryon, "The Adolescent Peer Culture," *Forty-Third Yearbook of the National Society for the Study of Education,* Part I. Chicago: University of Chicago Press, 1944. Pp. 227–28.

18. M. C. Jones, *Institute of Child Welfare Interest Record.* Berkeley: Institute of Child Welfare, University of California, 1944.

19. W. E. Martin and C. B. Stendler, *Child Development.* New York: Harcourt, Brace, 1953. Pp. 455–56.

20. J. H. S. Bossard, *The Sociology of Child Development.* New York: Harper, 1948. Pp. 495–96.

21. A. T. Jersild, *et al., Child Development and the Curriculum.* New York: Bureau of Publications, Teachers College, Columbia University, 1946. P. 175.

22. G. Wilson and G. Ryland, *Social Group Work Practice.* Boston: Houghton Mifflin, 1949. P. 107.

SUGGESTED READINGS

Association for Supervision and Curriculum Development, *Growing Up in an Anxious Age.* Washington: National Education Association, 1952. Chapter 12, "The Normal Progression."

A. W. Blair and W. H. Burton, *Growth and Development of the Preadolescent.* New York: Appleton-Century-Crofts, 1951.

P. Blos, *The Adolescent Personality.* New York: Appleton-Century-Crofts, 1941.

C. M. Harsh and H. G. Schrickel, *Personality: Development and Assessment.* New York: Ronald, 1950. The first half of the book is devoted to the nature and development of personality through the various stages of childhood and adulthood.

A. T. Jersild, *Child Psychology.* 3d ed. New York: Prentice-Hall, 1947. Chapters 5 and 6, "Development of Social Behavior."

I. M. Josselyn, *The Adolescent and His World.* New York: Family Service Association of America, 1952.

R. G. Kuhlen, *The Psychology of Adolescent Development.* New York: Harper, 1952.

W. E. Martin and C. B. Stendler, *Child Development.* New York: Harcourt, Brace, 1953. Chapter 13, "The Child in the Family;" Chapter 14, "The Child in School;" and Chapter 15, "The Peer Group."

H. J. Otto, *Principles of Elementary Education.* New York: Rinehart, 1949. Chapter 11, "Growing Up and Learning."

C. E. Skinner, ed., *Educational Psychology,* 3d ed. New York:

Prentice-Hall, 1951. Chapter 3, "Emotional Development," and Chapter 4 "Social Growth and Character Formation."

G. C. Thompson, *Child Psychology: Growth Trends in Psychological Adjustment.* Boston: Houghton Mifflin, 1952.

F. M. Thrasher, *The Gang.* Chicago: University of Chicago Press, 1936.

K. Young, *Personality and Problems of Adjustment,* 2d ed. New York: Appleton-Century-Crofts, 1952. Chapters 12, 13, and 14, "Infancy and Childhood," "Some Other Aspects of Child Training," and "Adolescence and Problems of Physical and Social Maturation."

C. B. Zachry, *Emotion and Conduct in Adolescence.* New York: Appleton-Century-Crofts, 1940.

See also items 6, 7, 9, 12, 14, 17, and 21 listed in the References for this chapter.

SUGGESTED FILMS

Life with Jimmy. March of Time.

Social Development. McGraw-Hill.

Study in Human Development: Part IV. Three Years to Five Years. Available from Psychological Cinema Register, State College, Pennsylvania.

Children Growing Up with Other People. British Information Service.

Farewell to Childhood. Problems that arise during adolescence. Available through International Film Bureau.

9

FORCES OPERATING IN
CHILDREN'S GROUPS

ANXIETY

PRODUCT OF INTERACTION IN GROUPS

PERSONS who are keen observers of human behavior are sometimes aware of a kind of tension or brittleness which develops when individuals come together in groups. It seems more likely to be present when groups are composed of people who do not know each other very well, or when matters are proceeding in an unsatisfactory manner.

It is highly probable that what they are observing is the expression of a sort of anxiety which is produced when people try to "feel their way," as it were, into unfamiliar situations, or when they try to cope with situations which are vague or confused or which do not seem to want to solve themselves. According to one group of writers in the field of human relations, "Anxiety is a natural and universal phenomenon whenever a group of people are assembled. One of the easiest and most frequent mechanisms employed to handle this anxiety is hostility [1]."

Our problem in this chapter is, roughly speaking, a three-fold one—to explore the sources of this anxiety, to discover how it expresses itself, and to discuss a few of the ways in which groups attempt to cope with or reduce their anxiety. The role of the teacher in dealing with this problem we shall leave to a later chapter.

We have already touched on one possible source of anxiety—the ambivalence or mixed feelings we have with regard to becoming members of a group at all. On the one hand, we need the companionship and acceptance of others, for our basic needs cannot be met without them, but, on the other hand, we dislike giving up what we feel is our right to make our own decisions and follow our own inclinations. In other words, we would like to enjoy the privileges of group membership without having to give up anything in return.

Schools, too, produce anxieties knowingly or unknowingly, by requiring children to adopt patterns of belief or behavior which are at odds with the patterns followed by their families. Sometimes this conflict in patterns is inevitable and unavoidable, as when children learn democratic ways of life at school which are in marked contrast to the more autocratic values of the Old World which predominate at home. But at other times the problem is made unnecessarily difficult, as in the case of the midwestern teacher who criticizes the pronunciation of a student who has recently come from Alabama. More often it is the students themselves who pounce upon these differences and make life miserable for the child who is different.

CONCERN ABOUT THE OPINIONS OF OTHERS

The fact that we experience both satisfaction and frustration when we associate with groups would be cause enough for the anxieties and hostilities which arise. However, there are additional aggravating factors. Most of us are quite con-

cerned about what others think of us. To be in a group at all
is to be "on trial."

The opinions and attitudes of the leader also cause concern. In adult groups the attitudes of the leader often reflect
and represent the attitudes of the group, although this is
not always the case, particularly when the group has no
voice in the choice of a leader. In such cases, the attitudes of
the leader are often at sharp variance with the attitudes of
the group. This conflict is even more pronounced with school
children. Not only is there a wide gulf separating the child's
world from the adult, but also the goals and attitudes of
teachers are often at odds with the goals and attitudes of
children. The conflict between these two modes of thought
and feeling increases with the age of children, being at a
minimum in the primary grades and reaching a climax in
junior high and high school. It should be noted, however,
that it is less of a problem in schools which have developed
an active interest in the needs of children and are making
some progress in meeting them.

The point in this discussion which is of most concern to us
here is that the school child is placed in the midst of a situation which encourages the development of anxiety and
hostility. On the one hand, he is concerned about the opinions and attitudes of his teacher, and on the other, he is concerned about the opinions and attitudes of other children.
His task is often made difficult or impossible of solution by
the fact that he must try to satisfy two groups of people
whose demands on him often contradict each other.

As a result of these factors, the gathering of children into
groups and placing an adult in charge (in other words, putting them into a classroom) make them, as a group, less stable emotionally, less reasonable, and more sensitive than
they would be individually. Teachers often have the experience of "reasoning" with a child outside of class and arriving
at a good understanding with him, only to have him revert
to undesirable patterns of behavior when he rejoins the class.

This phenomenon would not be so puzzling if we would remember that the child in the group is to all intents and purposes not the "same child" as he is when he is separated from the group. And the wider the separation from the group in terms of time and space, the less effect the group has on his conduct and attitudes.

An example of how behavior differs from the group situation to the individual situation is provided by the experiences of Mr. LeBlanc and Mike Moreno.[1]

James LeBlanc, high school teacher of social studies, has a cross to bear this semester. The name of the cross is Mike Moreno. Mike is not a bad kid. He is a C plus student, usually turns his work in on time, is cooperative in group projects. He doesn't try too hard, and is obviously working below capacity. Perhaps the latter symptom alone would have merited Mr. LeBlanc's special attention, had it not been for another factor —Mike's annoying habit of talking to his neighbors during class.

Miss Witherspoon, the English teacher, does not have this kind of problem with Mike. She insists on "pin-drop" silence in her classes, and when Mike broke this silence the second time, she moved him up to the front row, where he was under constant scrutiny. True, she has problems with Mike, but talking in class is not one of them.

Mr. LeBlanc has deliberately precluded Miss Witherspoon's kind of solution by his decision to organize and operate his class democratically as possible within the restrictions prescribed by tradition and common sense for the conduct of the high school classroom. He has encouraged students to pick their own seats, to help plan the instructional program, and to conduct as many of the class sessions as possible. Yet whenever the group is in total session, an annoying buzz from the back of the room indicates that Mike is talking to one of his neighbors. Mr. LeBlanc attempted a number of techniques. At first

---

[1] The following eight paragraphs are taken from H. C. Lindgren, "The Effect of the Group on the Behavior of the Individual," *Education.* 73:383–87;1953. Reprinted by permission.

he tried to ignore Mike, on the grounds that to recognize the disturbance would be to magnify it and to create more distraction than actually existed. This did not succeed, for, as the buzz continued day after day, the class became restless and inattentive, and he himself became increasingly irritable. He tried making suggestions that all conversation cease. At first he made these suggestions pleasantly, but later he began to make them in a firm and incisive tone. It was no good. Mike would stop for about five minutes, and then would start in again. Mr. LeBlanc spoke to Mike about the matter casually outside the class; Mike was apologetic and appeared to be contrite, but the next day the subtle sabotage continued. There was nothing grossly delinquent about this behavior, yet Mr. LeBlanc felt that the morale of the class was deteriorating. It was almost as though the class were waiting for this impasse to be resolved before settling down to work.

Mr. LeBlanc's own morale was affected, too. He knew that he could achieve an administrative solution of the problem by means of some drastic action as sending Mike to the principal's office. Yet he felt that to do so would be to chill the pleasant, permissive working relationship he worked so hard to achieve with his classes. Furthermore, there was Mike himself to consider. Undoubtedly there were hidden reasons why he acted as he did. Unquestionably Mike had his problems, too, and it might well be that an abrupt handling would worsen his adjustment to them rather than help him. Yet, on the other hand, Mr. LeBlanc felt somewhat like the man who had been condemned to torture by the constant dripping of water. His patience, his emotional reserves, his smoothly efficient techniques were in danger of being worn away by the abrasive effect of the insidious and subversive murmur in the back row.

And so Mr. LeBlanc chose the obvious solution—he asked Mike to see him after school. Only by getting at the source of the problem could he help himself, the class situation and, of course, Mike.

The meeting, which was scheduled for thirty minutes, lasted two hours. It started with Mike being belligerent, resentful at having to give up a half hour out of his afternoon. Mr. Le-

Blanc was equal to this, he sympathized with Mike, and in the same breath stated that he, too, disliked giving up *his* leisure time. This took Mike aback, since he had expected a reprimand for his insolent tone. His immediate reaction was to break into tears. Such kindness was unexpected, he had not deserved this, he ought to be punished, he knew he had been doing wrong, he could not help himself. After the storm had subsided, he told Mr. LeBlanc about his home life, about a father who was seldom home, about a stepmother who hated him and doted on her own two sons, about the complete, instantaneous, and unquestioning obedience which was expected of him. And Mr. LeBlanc understood how the permissive atmosphere of his classroom had somehow upset Mike, how his latent hostilities had led him to "test the limits" of the situation. Although Mr. LeBlanc used most of the interview to understand Mike, he did not forget the purpose of the meeting. He ended the interview by carefully, yet pleasantly, discussing with Mike the importance of not disturbing the class. Mike understood and promised that the future would see a marked change in his behavior.

His promise was good for one week. In the very middle of an interesting discussion of race prejudice, a low buzzing in the back of the room indicated that Mike was at it again.

The point here is that individuals behave differently within the contexts of groups from the way that they do when they are operating on a person-to-person basis. When Mike was alone with Mr. LeBlanc, he was sincere in his good intentions not to disturb the class again. When he rejoined the class, this resolution continued for a short time, yet there was something about the group situation that made his continued obedience impossible. If Mr. LeBlanc continues to meet with Mike after school, it may be that he can help him to overcome his behavior problem. If so, he will be aided by the realization that the Mike he talks to after school is not the same as the Mike who sits in the back of the class. Different psychological forces play upon Mike, forces that make him behave quite differently in the two situations.

SYMPTOMS OF ANXIETY IN THE
CLASSROOM GROUP

The anxieties that grow out of the group situation express themselves by a variety of symptoms. Some classes never seem to "settle down." They are easily distracted and seldom can concentrate on one subject for any extended period. Some classes seem to have "a chip on their shoulder." They appear to resent anything the teacher says or does, whether it is part of the daily routine or whether it is a special favor that he has done to please them. Other classes are apathetic and seem to defy any attempts of the teacher to interest them in the curriculum.

These are relatively extreme, but not uncommon, instances of classes whose anxiety and hostility run high. More usually, classes demonstrate an "on-again–off-again" type of behavior. Sometimes they are interested and involved in the learning task which has been set them, and then at other times, for no discernable reason, they are apathetic, "mulish," disruptive, or otherwise "uncooperative." This is one of the chief reasons why the teacher needs to be an "artist in human relations." It takes much insight, understanding, and sensitivity to the needs of children to maintain one's emotional balance, to restore the emotional equilibrium in the class, and to help it "get back on the track." What happens all too often is that the anxiety and hostility expressed by the class infect the teacher as well, whereupon he responds according to whatever his characteristic pattern of handling anxiety happens to be. Usually this involves punishment of some sort, although some teachers surrender to what appears to be inevitable. Some teachers put the class on a strict routine; others outdo themselves in trying to get the class to like them. All of these techniques may be quite effective and desirable at appropriate times and places. The question is: Are they being used as a result of a genuine understanding of the difficulties of the group, or are they used because this is how this teacher usually responds to anxiety generated in him by a hostile class?

Although well-run classes are not immune to group-generated anxiety and hostility, the effects of these forces are held to a minimum because their teachers have been successful in creating situations which afford satisfactions for basic needs rather than neurotic ones and which provide stimulus for positive growth in the direction of emotional, intellectual, and social maturity. However, the experienced teachers who supervise these classes are well aware that their groups are vulnerable to external and internal pressures which provoke immature behavior, and that anxieties and hostilities will sometimes get out of hand, in spite of their best efforts to prevent this from occurring. At such times the skilled teacher is able to put aside the work planned for the day and devote himself to the task of restoring the emotional equilibrium of the class. Usually this is not a lengthy process and may require only a few minutes, although often he may have to play this therapeutic role repeatedly.

COHESIVENESS

THERE are three factors or conditions which vitally affect the feelings and attitudes of groups as well as their ability to "produce" in terms of learning. These are cohesiveness, morale, and climate.

A cohesive group is composed of members who are aware of the existence of their group and who are strongly motivated to become involved in its activities. The members of a group that is not cohesive are not much interested in the goals of the group and instead are more concerned about their personal goals and interests. They may not even be aware that the group has an identity as such. Furthermore, the actions of members of a class which is not cohesive are often marked by a disregard of the welfare of others.

By way of example, a group of eighth-grade boys began to disrupt the study period at the end of the history class by shooting wads of paper with rubber bands. Mr. Johnson, the history teacher, was helping a girl who did not understand one of the questions in the workbook. He had his back turned and did not see what was going on, although he realized that some-one was causing a disturbance. He turned around and spoke rather sharply to the class and said that if they did not behave themselves, the whole class would have to stay after school fifteen minutes. Then everyone settled down immediately and began to work diligently at the assignment—everyone, that is, except Ross Cutler, who had started the trouble in the first place. Ross was the class cut-up, and he seldom concentrated on anything unless it was some elaborate hoax or trick. This time, Ross waited till everyone had quieted down and Mr. Johnson had returned to his task of explaining the workbook questions. Then Ross took careful aim with a heavy wad of paper and succeeded in winging Mr. Johnson's right ear. Mr. Johnson flared up and said that the class would have to stay after school. Some of the students were angry at Ross for get-ting them into trouble with Mr. Johnson, and causing them to be late in getting home, but most of them were amused. They talked about this escapade for days. Mr. Johnson had an even harder job keeping the attention of the class after that.

The lack of cohesiveness in Mr Johnson's class is in marked contrast to that of Miss Peter's fifth grade.

On the day that Miss Peters had planned to start a unit on the health department, she received word that one of her stu-dents had contracted infantile paralysis. Although it was a mild case, it was improbable that the child would return to school during the remainder of the semester. Her announcement of this news had a subduing effect on the class. Usually, when they started a new unit they were quite active in asking all sorts of questions about the things they were going to do. But today, they were quite thoughtful and quiet. After Miss Peters had tried rather unsuccessfully to get their interest, she said:

"I seem to feel that we have trouble in starting this new unit. Could it be that you are worried about Julia? If so, I think I can understand that. Even though Julia has only a mild case, the thought that one of us could get polio is pretty frightening. Now the health department, which is the subject of our new unit, has something to do with polio, but maybe you'd like to talk about Julia first before we go much further with our new unit."

Within a short time, the feeling of tension lifted from the class and a lively discussion was in progress. It appeared that what was uppermost on the children's minds was to do something for Julia, to let her know that she was missed, and to keep her informed of what the class was doing. As a result of the discussion they decided that they would organize a "Julia Committee," which would make arrangements for someone to visit Julia every afternoon, if possible, during the rest of the term. After that matter had been settled, the class turned with renewed interest to the unit on the health department.

In Mr. Johnson's class the behavior of one boy so disturbs the class that it becomes difficult for them to settle down to their assigned task. There is very little "group feeling" in this class, unless it is the feeling of the group against Mr. Johnson. Miss Peters' class has a different feeling about their existence as a group. The absence of Julia saddens and upsets them because she is prevented from participating further in the group. Miss Peters' sympathetic understanding of their feeling makes it possible for the group to develop ways of including Julia as a member through symbolic means; their decision to do this means that their solidarity as a group is increased even further.

COHESIVENESS MAY HAVE A NEGATIVE EFFECT

A group can also develop cohesiveness in ways which are detrimental to learning and emotional growth. This often happens when the goals of the class and the teacher are far apart. The harder the teacher works to get the class to move in the direction of his goals, the more they resist him. If the struggle becomes intense, many members of the class who otherwise would be neutral or who would be inclined to follow the teacher come to resent the teacher and join with those who are opposing him. More usually, classes become apathetic and passive and refuse to learn, although they will go through the motions of completing assignments and passing tests in order to avoid punishment. Such classes demonstrate a high degree of cohesiveness in their steadfast refusal to accept the goals of the teacher.

Ruth Cunningham states that a group whose members have discovered common hostile interests or goals may develop a high degree of cohesiveness:

> It is interesting to note that there may be favorable climate in a group united in its hostility—against the teacher, against the school, or against society itself. In the classroom such a situation may be very uncomfortable for the teacher, but pleasant for the group. We quickly add, however, that this teacher has little chance to teach, in the broadest sense, for although the climate may be favorable, there is no teacher leadership [3].

Teachers are often aware that it takes a week or two of school before a class can begin to make any real progress in learning. This phenomenon probably results from the need of the class to "find itself" as a group or to develop some cohesiveness before it can turn its attention to the tasks at hand. It can be argued that a class does not need a high degree of cohesiveness in order to learn effectively; yet it appears that there is a minimum level which should be maintained, otherwise the group will be vulnerable to distractions. The minimum cohesiveness required appears to be related to the kind of activity. In general, those classes and subjects which require widespread participation in group work of various sorts demand a high degree of cohesiveness, whereas it is not so important in learning situations where students participate as individuals and do not interact very much with each other. Using physical education as an example, high cohesiveness would be desirable in team sports, like football and basketball, but would be less important in track and field sports.

Cunningham describes two situations that depict the elusiveness of the cohesive quality in classroom teaching:

> Miss Baxter had been trying all semester to develop a climate of group feeling, by helping the group toward group goals, trying to establish self-management, and similar means, with but nominal success. Then came the election of officers of the student council. . . . The group, a tenth grade, which had felt rejected because new to the high school, found itself bombarded with campaign propaganda. It discovered it had position, force, and influence in the political structure of the school. Almost spontaneously, or so it seemed, the group achieved unity in order to wield its power effectively. Another tenth grade group, however, with a teacher less interested in group living, found the election just another disintegrating factor. It split into factions and subfactions, warring among themselves. Miss Baxter's seemingly ineffectual attempts to develop group feeling found flower in an experience which was initiated by the group, but to which her earlier efforts had contributed. The line between unity and disunity is thin, yet carefully drawn in terms of previous as well as current experiences of the group [4].

MORALE

MORALE is related to cohesiveness, in that groups which have high morale are likely to be cohesive. Morale is the product of expectations. We say that a group has good morale when it expects something satisfactory and satisfying to result from its labors. A student has good morale when he believes that he is capable of learning and that the situation in which he finds himself will aid, rather than hinder, his learning. A class has good morale when it accepts the development of emotional, social, and intellectual maturity as its main task, is optimistic about its ability to attain such growth, and feels confident in the ability of the teacher to help it grow. To put this in more specific terms, this means that a first-grade class that has good morale will have confidence in its ability to learn to read during the year because they have the background and maturity required as well as the kind of teacher who will help them develop the required skills. Morale, for this first grade, will not entirely revolve around reading. They will also expect to learn other skills, including the ability to get along in a new, strange, and potentially frightening situation. From their initial experiences with their teacher, they feel that she is the kind of person on whom they can depend in time of need; they expect her to be a sort of unifying center of love and strength. And because they are optimistic about the outcome, we say that their morale is good.

Poor morale is indicative of individuals and groups who are discouraged. Because they have no genuine hope of succeeding, they make no real efforts to do so. Discouragement and poor morale display themselves in apathy, cynicism, or in a wide variety of "behavior problems," for the child who has lost hope is willing to try anything, particularly if he can "get back" at those whom he feels are responsible for his feeling of discouragement.

Rudolf Dreikurs' comment is particularly pertinent:

> . . . One factor stands out as the primary cause of deficient development; it is discouragement. Children who do not function to their full potential ability, either academically, socially, or morally, are all discouraged children. It is so much easier and more satisfactory to do well in all aspects of living. Every child would discover this satisfaction if he were not discouraged in his self-evaluation as to his abilities to do well or to measure up [5].

EMOTIONAL CLIMATE

THE third factor in this trio is "emotional climate," or what is sometimes called the "feeling tone" of the group. Emotional climate is very responsive to the attitudes of people who are significant to the welfare of the group, particularly those attitudes which are persistent over a long period of time and which encourage certain activities and discourage others. The emotional climate in a classroom is partly a function of the teacher and his attitudes and partly a function of the attitudes of the administration and the other staff members. The attitudes of these persons are in turn colored and influenced by the attitudes of the superintendent of schools, the school board, and the community at large.

There are many varieties of climate. Kurt Lewin, Ronald Lippitt, and Ronald K. White experimented with three types, which they called autocratic, democratic, and laissez-faire [6], but above and beyond these there are many subvarieties and variations. In some schools the prevailing attitude toward children is one of amused tolerance; in another it might be characterized as "no nonsense, mingled with kindness"; while in still another school it may be simply "you can't trust kids." But whatever the prevailing climate, it will have a powerful effect on the morale and cohesiveness of the classes in the school.

Fritz Redl gives some examples of the kinds of disturbances that sometimes occur in the emotional climate of the classroom:

> The *punitive climate* is perhaps the most destructive of group morale and discipline of any classroom climate. It invariably produces these . . . effects: teacher shows little respect for the persons of the children in her room, being so sure that she can manage their behavior by threat and fear anyway that she doesn't bother about them as human beings; the pupils usually expect absolute acceptance or rejection on the basis of the teacher's behavior code, and they usually fall into two groups—some rebel, hate, and fight back . . . and others identify themselves with the teacher out of fear and, therefore, have to become moral hypocrites in their attitudes toward the other children. They are suspiciously submissive as long as the teacher is present, squeal on neighbors when they

get a chance, and, in general, develop a holier-than-thou attitude toward their pals. . . .

The emotional blackmail climate is another distortion of healthy group living. It is a variation of the punitive climate but sails under a different disguise. In the emotional blackmail climate the teacher "loves" all children and says so at the rate of three times a minute. . . . In the emotional blackmail climate, you don't get punished if you do wrong, but you know you have to feel like a heel for three weeks afterward. The teacher in this climate produces a tremendous emotional dependence on her, exploiting it as the only source of influence. . . .

The group pride climate has a very healthy counterpart. What we mean here is the distorted case where the group leader tries to develop a strong emotional relationship of every group member toward the total group and then overfosters a feeling of vanity and conceit. . . . Good "teams" sometimes allow their team spirit to disintegrate into the climate I refer to.

The group pride climate usually develops a high degree of group consciousness of a classroom as a whole, with a variety of positive attributes connected with such development. At the same time it produces a whole host of potential group executioners who just wait for a moment when they can swoop down upon the unlucky devil who was a stain on group honor or reward [7].

Studies of group climate in educational situations have been made by J. Wayne Wrightstone, John G. Withall, and Hugh V. Perkins, Jr. [8, 9, 10, 11]. Wrightstone and Withall developed techniques and methods to measure certain aspects of group climate, while Perkins, using the method developed by Withall, investigated the effects of emotional climate on the participation and learning of six groups of teachers in in-service training near the University of Maryland. Groups where the leader's statements were categorized as reassuring, clarifying, or "problem-structured" [2] were

---

[2] Concerned with restating, describing, or explaining a problem growing out of the group discussion.

classified as "group-centered," whereas groups where the leader's statements were categorized as directing, reproving, or defending were classified as "leader-centered." (In general, the "group-centered" climate would most resemble the "democratic" climate created in the study of Lewin, Lippitt, and White, mentioned above, while the "leader-centered" climate would most resemble their "autocratic" climate.) Perkins found that teacher-students in the group-centered groups displayed more objectivity and friendliness toward children in their discussion, whereas the discussions of the leader-centered groups were characterized by emotionality, coldness toward children, and conventionality. The implication here seems to be that a superior type of learning takes place in situations that are group-centered than in those that are leader-centered.

THE EMOTIONAL CLIMATE OF THE SCHOOL AND ITS EFFECT ON THE CLIMATE OF THE CLASSROOM

Inasmuch as the classroom group does not exist in isolation, we can expect that it will be affected by the prevailing emotional climate of the entire school. Although the teacher will have more effect on the climate of his classroom group than any other person (because he has the most direct and most frequent contact), his efforts to change or produce climate may at times be nullified if they are contrary to the general direction of the prevailing emotional currents of the school.

The superintendent who hired Miss Schwarz to teach at Riverton High School was impressed by the report he received on her from the principal at Pinetop. When asked about Miss Schwarz, the Pinetop principal stated that in spite of the fact that she had been teaching only three years, he considered her the most able social studies teacher he had ever seen. He was sorry to lose her, he said, but he realized that he could not compete with the salaries at Riverton.

Miss Schwarz looked forward to her job at Riverton with

interest and optimism. She had a satisfied feeling about her work at Pinetop but she felt that she needed the challenge of a new situation. She was sure that Riverton would provide this challenge.

Toward the middle of October, during her first term at Riverton, she began to be aware that she was having difficulties of a sort she had never encountered before. The methods she was using required that students do research in the library with minimum supervision. She and the librarian had spent a great deal of time during the first three weeks showing the students how to look up material, take notes, and organize reports; yet, in view of the results she was getting, it seemed like time wasted. Students kept complaining that they did not know what to look for or where to find it. The reports they made were word-for-word repetitions of passages from encyclopedias and popular magazines. Often students were unprepared because, as they said, they just did not know what she wanted them to do. Furthermore, the discussions which were so valuable and interesting at Pinetop never materialized at Riverton. They usually deteriorated into question-and-answer sessions, with Miss Schwarz doing most of the questioning.

Her first reaction was to think that she was a failure as a teacher, yet she remembered the warm and satisfying successes which were hers at Pinetop. Her next thought was that the students at Riverton were less intelligent, yet she knew that a very high percentage went on to college and university— much higher than was the case at Pinetop.

It was the librarian, Mrs. Rossetto, who gave her the key to the problem. Because of their work together at the start of the semester, they had come to know each other very well. While they were eating lunch together one day, Mrs. Rossetto said:

"You know, I've been here five years, but during that time I don't think any teacher has had her students use the library as much as you have in the seven weeks you have been here."

Miss Schwarz was surprised. She didn't see how you could do a good job in social studies unless you got students to do extensive reading in the library.

Mrs. Rossetto's reply was that the other social science teachers did have their students use the library, but mostly it was for specific assignments. She knew because they would come in and ask for specific books, whereas Miss Schwarz's students came in asking:

"Where can I find out something about the Point Four Program?"

During the next week, Miss Schwarz thought a lot about her conversation with Mrs. Rossetto, and she asked some questions, both of students and other members of the faculty. And that was how she discovered that the emotional climate at Riverton was different from that of Pinetop.

At Pinetop, students were expected to do things on their own. They were encouraged to run their own clubs and committees. If you went into a Pinetop classroom, you usually found the class in small groups, studying or talking, or in a big circle, discussing some issue or listening to a report. Students often presided as chairmen. The teacher was usually in the background, sometimes working with a student, sometimes listening and observing. Even Mr. Jordan the boys' physical education teacher, used to say that he was only a straw boss since he had turned over most of the coaching to high school seniors.

But here at Riverton, it was different. Students sat in rows here and listened to lectures, did work at their seats, or recited. True, students were quieter than they were at Pinetop, but they were not as enthusiastic. Here the teacher was very much in the foreground and was expected to set the pace. It was no wonder she was having difficulty with her class, no wonder that they kept asking her what to do and how to do it!

The reader can supply his own ending to this story. One possible ending is for Miss Schwarz to go back to Pinetop where she was successful and happy in her work, even though it would mean a cut in salary. Another ending is for her to adjust her expectations of her students to those more consistent with the emotional climate which prevails in the school. It is probably too much to expect that Miss Schwarz undertake to change the emotional climate of the school all by herself. There is not much that a lone teacher can do against the opposition, or, what is more likely, against the apathy of an entire faculty. However, if she can find two or three like-minded teachers who are willing to speak up in defense of their professional beliefs, her chances for bringing about a change in the thinking of Riverton High School will be much improved. A faculty will usually ignore the efforts of a lone individual to get them stirred up, but the combined efforts of two, or, better still, three, or four courageous individuals will arouse their interest and, sometimes, their support in bringing about reform in curriculum or educational procedure.

ROLES WITHIN GROUPS

IN THE last few pages, we have been concerned with how anxieties are aroused and reduced by events and forces which affect the total group. There are also ways in which individual members of groups attempt to reduce or avoid the anxiety produced by interaction with the group. One of these methods is the playing of "roles."

A role, according to Theodore M. Newcomb, is "a set of behaviors which are expected of everyone in a particular position, regardless of who he is [12]." Thus, a teacher helps students to read, takes attendance, hands out report cards, and attends faculty meetings because these behaviors are expected of one who occupies the position of a teacher. A student attends classes, listens when the teacher talks to him, and works at learning to read because these behaviors are expected of the one who occupies the position of a student.

All of us, adults and children alike, play a variety of roles in our daily life. A woman may be a third-grade teacher, a wife, a chairman of the rummage-sale committee at church, and an active member of the Republican Party. A child may play the roles of student, son, second-class scout and member of the Wolverine Patrol, shortstop, and younger brother.

We have some choices about how we play our roles, but these choices are limited. A person who is a teacher may have a choice of being severe or permissive or of taking his summer-school course at the local college or the state university, but he does not have the freedom to go fishing on the first day of the season, if it is a school day, and he is not permitted to treat children with physical cruelty. A child who is a student has some latitude in whether he really believes what the teacher says, but he may not carry on a conversation with another child when the teacher is speaking directly to him.

The point is that the behaviors which are appropriate to our roles are largely prescribed by society or by the groups of which we are members.

The playing of roles is one of the ways in which we reduce or avoid the anxiety that would otherwise bother and upset us in a group situation. Knowing what others expect of us and acting accordingly helps take the uncertainty out of a situation. This reduces our anxiety, for anxiety breeds on uncertainty. Furthermore, by behaving in ways that are expected, we avoid the anxiety that would be aroused if we deviated from these expectations. Suppose that a teacher forgets to take attendance in the morning. A ripple of tension runs through the class. In a minute or so the monitor will appear at the classroom door to pick up the attendance report and the teacher will not be ready! Then she catches herself and says: "Oh, I'm forgetting to see who is absent," and the class relaxes.

One of the ways that groups operate as groups is to assign positions and roles to their members. This is another way of saying that group members develop more or less well-organized expectations of each other as a means of making member-to-member relations somewhat less disorganized and less unpredictable.

Teachers generally are unaware, however, of the roles that the members of their classes play as they fulfill their functions in the classroom or playground group. These roles have great variety and purpose, and identifying them can be very helpful in understanding the emotional background of the classroom group as well as the individuals who compose it.

Robert Delgado is a second grader who plays the role of a clown. Robert is the one who mimics the teacher when her back is turned, who draws pictures of her on the board when she is out of the room. In some ways the class accepts Robert because he can amuse them. When they are bored, they have little ways of "egging him on." Sometimes he is caught and scolded. The class enjoys this, too, because it breaks the monotony of the school day. Robert is a very lonely boy, for he has no close friends among the other children in the class. So he does his stunts again and again as a way of drawing some acceptance from the group.

Some roles are played on a temporary basis. Here is an example of a situation that was "saved" by a boy who played a temporary role:

The junior class decided, in the course of their regular spring meeting, that they wanted to hold an informal dance. The last Friday of the month seemed like the most logical evening, but that evening was already scheduled for a special glee club practice. Some of the class officers were members of the glee club and would have to miss either the practice or the dance. Furthermore, it was the practice of the school to avoid conflicts in scheduling extracurricular activities at night. It was evident that someone had to discuss the matter with the glee club and persuade them to change their meeting to another night, otherwise the dance would have to be postponed indefinitely. However, when the president tried to appoint a committee to negotiate with the glee club, he met with a series of refusals. No one wanted the job because the students were afraid of Miss Crawford, the glee club sponsor. She could be caustic and sarcastic on occasion. But if the class were to have its dance, someone would have to ask Miss Crawford to change her schedule. After three students had declined appointment to the committee, the president asked for volunteers. The class was silent for a few seconds, and then Louis Svensson stood up and said that he would see Miss Crawford, if two other students would go with him. Two students quickly volunteered, the class breathed a sigh of relief, and went on to other matters.

Louis is temporarily playing a leadership role. The situation calls for a leader. Louis sees himself as a person who can fill that role, and the group accepts him in that capacity. Perhaps he will not play such a role again in high school, or perhaps the class will recognize his leadership qualities and will elect him to some office. Or, very likely, they may accept him as one of their "unofficial leaders," as distinguished from their elected officers, and look to him from time to time for guidance and direction.

The actions of both Louis and Robert stem from anxiety. Louis' action helped to reduce the anxieties that were building up in the class meeting, anxieties produced by indecision and frustration. Robert's anxiety is more personal. It is hard to say how he came to develop the role of the clown. Perhaps it was because school was so strange and unfamiliar to him and he missed the friendly warmth of his family. He was afraid of the teacher; she scolded him when he was unable to stay in his seat. He was angry at the teacher for having shamed him in front of the other children. Some children would have become sullen, others would have wept, others would have shrunk back in their seats. But Robert's reaction was to wait until the teacher turned his back and then he pretended he was a teacher scolding a little boy—no words, just gestures. The class loved it. A snicker ran through the group, Robert felt the good, warm feeling of being appreciated, and the anxiety produced by the strange, new situation of school subsided somewhat. One success led to another, and before long, Robert had eased into the role which, to some degree, will be his for life. It will be one of his chief ways of coping with the anxiety which results from associating with others in a group.

STUDENT EVALUATIONS OF LEADERSHIP BEHAVIOR

Ruth Cunningham has gathered data to show that fourth and fifth graders are quite sensitive to how well their classmates play the role of leader. She cites the following examples:

1. *Leaders spread the participation in the group fairly.*
"Norma gives everybody a chance."
"She sees that everyone gets to give ideas."
"He got around to everyone."
"Sue is good in leading but plays favorites sometimes."

2. *Leaders act as representatives of the group.*
"She wrote down the plans the way they came from us."
"Don wanted what we wanted to do."
"Gordon didn't argue with us."
"I think Norma is a good leader, but sometimes she is too bossy."
"I liked everything Joan did except the way she told kids to shut up."

3. *Leaders are skillful.*
"He got straight to the point and didn't act silly."
"Marie was the best leader we ever had. She didn't have to be told what to do."
"She knew how to get started and got things done."
"He never talked all the time like some leaders. He let us talk."
"Some were silly but she didn't blow up. She is as good as any leader could be."

4. *Leaders learn as they lead.*
"Betty is improving."
"I thought she got some good experience out of it and she learned to stand on her own feet."
"He was good after he got into it."

5. *Leaders make themselves understood.*
"Sometimes she would write uphill and downhill and she would write so light you can hardly see the letters."

"She talks so everyone can hear her and she could talk awfully loud."

"She talked so soft nobody could hear her. She never talked loud enough."

6. *Leaders are free of personal mannerisms.*

"She was bashful and couldn't stand still."

"She didn't act silly."

"She didn't show off and was very good in front of the room."

7. *Leaders create a friendly atmosphere.*

"She was nice to us, and she never fought with us and we all liked her."

"I have enjoyed him very much and I think the other kids liked him very much."

"Mabel was nice to us so we had to be nice to her."

8. *Leaders overcome obstacles.*

"She's good for only a 4A." [That is, a good leader in spite of being younger than most group members.]

"Gary is a good leader, even if he is a boy."

"She can't write good so she had a scecktary [sic] but all but that she was good."

9. *Leaders achieve results.*

"She got things done."

"We done what we wanted and learned what we wanted when Gary was leader."

"When she was leader things went right."

10. *Leaders meet the general standards of the group.*

"I thought Marilyn was the worst planning leader we ever had and will ever have and I hope we never have one like her."

"Norma handled the planning as good as any child could."

"Patsy was a very good leader, and I don't think we will ever have a better one [13]."

OTHER ROLES

The roles of "leader" and "clown" that we have discussed so far are only two of the endless varieties and variations of roles that appear in children's groups. Here are some others.

The role of *follower* is perhaps the commonest. Groups cannot function unless someone follows, and any functioning group consists of more followers than leaders. Even in this common role there are many shades of differences. There is, for example, the *passive follower* who follows because he is unwilling or unable to think for himself. Followers of this sort are commonest in groups where the morale is low or where the emotional climate is highly leader-centered. *Active followers* participate through making contributions to the group's thinking, planning, and acting. Active followers are likely to play leadership roles temporarily, as they make contributions that are more significant. In a well-knit, cohesive group, where the morale is high and the emotional climate is group-centered, the leadership will not be centered in any one person but will be passed from member to member as the occasion demands. The higher the individual's status in the group, the more likely he is to be an active follower; the lower his status, the more likely he is to be a passive follower.

The role of *saboteur* is sometimes played by persons of low status who are inclined to express their hostility openly and aggressively or by persons of moderate or high status who want to wrest the leadership from the present leaders and who hope, by creating chaos, that they can take over the controls. If the leader is a teacher, saboteurs cannot, of course, actually take over controls, but they can set up a competitive form of leadership to attract the loyalties of the group members and to organize the group against the teacher. Saboteurs play their roles by making disturbing remarks, by objecting to everything that is proposed, by predicting that no good will come of the undertaking being discussed. Sometimes saboteurs express themselves with sincerity and even dignity and thus attract a large following. But if they are merely chronic saboteurs, whose chief abilities appear when there is something to oppose, it will be difficult for them to lead their group in anything constructive.

The role of *adult-interceptor* is one which is occasionally played by a child who has special skill in relating to adults. Louis Svensson's role of temporary leadership contains some elements of adult interception. Another example is that of a group of teen-agers who want to go on a picnic. Before plans can be carried through they must secure the approval of their parents as well as permission to use a family car or two. They will select as their ambassador one of the members of their group who has a reputation for steadiness and maturity with their parents or one whose social status is a little higher, the idea being that parents will be led to say to themselves: "Well, if the Hellman girl is going, it must be all right," or, "I don't worry when George Bright is along; he's *so* reliable." Sometimes when children or adolescents get into trouble one of them serves as spokesman because, by common agreement, he is more able than they to express himself easily and readily to adults.

No group can perform its functions if it is chronically disturbed by continued and violent differences among its members. When membership has lost patience with the wrangling of the dissident members, someone is almost certain to appear from the group to adopt the role of *peacemaker*. It is his task to adjust the differences between the warring members or at least get them to keep their hostilities outside the activities of the group. The more a group is characterized by high cohesiveness and morale, the sooner some member will take on the role of peacemaker in order to forestall group frustration and disintegration. Once a group member has played the role of peacemaker, he is likely to be called on again, when occasion demands.

THE ROLE OF THE "TEACHER'S PET"

The role of the *teacher's pet* is an interesting one, particularly because it is so often misunderstood by teachers. Many teachers assume that the children in their classes who always know the answers and who turn in their work on time and according to the proper form are also the ones that the children of the class accept as their leaders. It always comes as something of a shock to learn that this is not so.

The attitudes and actions of the teacher, the individual student, and the class as a whole need to be considered if the problem of the teacher's pet is to be understood. Some teachers create teacher's pets by complimenting individual students in front of the class. Sometimes this occurs because the student has done exceptionally good work, and sometimes it happens because the teacher somehow seems more favorably inclined toward the student, often for reasons unknown to himself. The latter situation is understandable in view of the fact that many teachers feel psychologically isolated from their classes. This isolation is brought about through the difficulties which teachers and students experience in trying to communicate with each other as well as by the mutual suspicion which adults and children display toward each other. We can picture the teacher as trying to communicate with the class, trying to get them interested in studying and learning the material assigned. All too often these efforts seem doomed to failure; yet now and then a student responds. Perhaps he responds by working hard at his assignments, perhaps he grasps some of what the teacher is trying to communicate, or perhaps he just looks sympathetic. Who, then, can blame a teacher who praises or favors a student under these circumstances?

But let us consider the student who becomes favored in this way. Children who play the roles of teacher's pets do not fall into them accidentally. Very often they have a strong need to identify themselves with persons in authority, such as parents or teachers. Sometimes this need arises because they are not popular with the group and thus come to look upon the teacher as a source of the love or acceptance they do not get from their peers. Sometimes we find this need in children who are highly competitive, who cannot become strongly identified with the group because it is more important for them to excel. Such children are drawn to the teacher because he is the standard of excellence in the classroom. Often parents enter the picture by setting high academic standards for their children. If children accept these standards as their own, it means that they must constantly strive for the teacher's approval.

School children as a group are likely to isolate or reject a student who is, in their opinion, "too close" to the teacher, even if that teacher is a well-loved teacher. In their eyes a child becomes a teacher's pet if it appears that the teacher favors him over the rest of the group. This may occur if the teacher compliments a child even casually in a way that somehow reflects unfavorably on the ability of the other children in the class. It may even occur if a child produces more "right answers" or gets better grades than the class thinks he should. Although this evaluation is unfair in many respects, it is not an unusual development in the field of human relations. For example, there is a tendency for factory workers to be suspicious of the employee who produces more than the average for the group [14]. There appears to be a deliberate attempt on the part of many groups of employees to hold production to a certain level in spite of the fact that they could double their wages under current piecework rates [15]. Both workers and school children appear to be motivated in this behavior by a common fear—that persons in authority (employers, teachers) would increase their demands if it appeared that present standards were achieved too easily. Since, in their eyes, their continued security and peace of mind depends on their ability to produce or learn no more than is required, we can understand how the individual who violates this tacit agreement by out-producing the other members or who threatens the solidarity and cohesion of the group by becoming a favorite of the bosses (or the teachers) would become the target of the group's resentment. The more insecure the group feels, the more they are likely to resent the performance of the member who produces too much, according to their standards, or who gets "too many" A's.

What this all means is that the teacher must learn to proceed judiciously in matters which involve the comparison of pupils with each other. In some schools this is no great problem, because evaluation is not merely a matter of assigning letter grades, and teachers, pupils, and parents have come to accept the principle that such evaluation constitutes appraisals of the skills and competencies of the child and is not a measure of the worth of the child as an individual. However, the problem of divorcing the appraisal of skills from the value of the individual is a difficult task, and one we shall discuss further in this text. (See Chapter 18.) The important point in the present discussion is that the teacher needs to be alert and sensitive to the attitudes, feelings, and behavior of the children in his classroom. If he is careless or ruthless in the ways he deals with the feelings of children, he is almost certain to create situations which will lead to his failure as a teacher. It may not be the kind of failure which comes to the attention of supervisors or principals, but it will be the kind of failure which causes children to lose interest in learning and to regard school primarily as an institution of restraint.

REFERENCES

1. R. A. Young, L. Miller, N. Verven, "Treatment Techniques in a Therapeutic Camp," *American Journal of Orthopsychiatry.* 21:819–26;1951.
2. H. C. Lindgren, "The Effect of the Group on the Behavior of the Individual," *Education.* 73:383–87;1953. Reprinted by permission.
3. R. Cunningham *et al., Understanding Group Behavior of Boys and Girls.* New York: Bureau of Publications, Teachers College, Columbia University, 1951. P. 47. Reprinted by permission.
4. *Ibid.* Pp. 47–48. Reprinted by permission.

5. R. Dreikurs, *Character Education and Spiritual Values in an Anxious Age*. Boston: Beacon Press, 1952. P. 9.

6. K. Lewin, R. Lippitt, and R. K. White, "Patterns of Aggressive Behavior in Experimentally Created 'Social Climates,' " *Journal of Social Psychology*. 10:271–99;1939.

7. G. Sheviakov and F. Redl, *Discipline for Today's Children and Youth*. Washington: National Education Association, 1944. Pp. 48–50. Reprinted by permission.

8. J. W. Wrightstone, "Measuring the Social Climate of a Classroom," *Journal of Educational Research*. 44:341–51;1951.

9. J. G. Withall, *The Development of a Technique for the Measurement of Social-Emotional Climate in the Classroom*. Unpublished Ph.D. Dissertation, University of Chicago, 1948.

10. H. V. Perkins, Jr., "The Effects of Climate and Curriculum on Group Learning," *Journal of Educational Research*. 44:269–86;1950.

11. H. V. Perkins, Jr., "Climate Influences Group Learning," *Journal of Educational Research*. 45:115–19;1951.

12. T. M. Newcomb, *Social Psychology*. New York: Dryden, 1950, P. 329.

13. R. Cunningham *et al., op. cit.* Pp. 124–27. Reprinted by permission.

14. L. Coch and J. R. P. French, "Overcoming Resistance to Change," *Human Relations*. 1:512–32;1948.

15. D. Roy, "Quota Restriction and Goldbricking in a Machine Shop," *American Journal of Sociology*. 57:427–42;1952.

SUGGESTED READINGS

S. E. Asch, *Social Psychology*. New York: Prentice-Hall, 1952. Chapter 8, "Knowledge of Persons and Groups," and Chapter 9, "An Introduction to Group Theory."

K. D. Benne and B. Muntyan, *Human Relations in Curriculum Change*. New York: Dryden, 1951. Part 3, Section A, "The Nature of the Group."

H. Bonner, *Social Psychology*. New York: American Book, 1953. Chapter 4, "Group Life and Socialization."

S. H. Britt, ed., *Selected Readings in Social Psychology*. New York: Rinehart, 1950. Part 4, "Behavior in the Presence of Others."

R. Cunningham *et al., Understanding Group Behavior of Boys and Girls*. New York: Bureau of Publications, Teachers College, Columbia University, 1951. Chapter 4, "The Individual in the Group," and Chapter 5, "Group Structure."

L. W. Doob, *Social Psychology*. New York: Holt, 1952. Part 2, "The Behavior of Groups."

E. L. Hartley and R. E. Hartley, *Fundamentals of Social Psychology*. New York: Knopf, 1952. Part 3, "The Individual and the Group."

H. C. Lindgren, *Psychology of Personal and Social Adjustment*. New York: American Book, 1953. Chapter 10, "What Happens in Groups."

T. M. Newcomb, *Social Psychology*. New York: Dryden, 1950. Chapter 9, "Role Behavior and the Self," and Chapter 14, "Effects upon Individuals of Membership in Groups."

F. Redl and W. W. Wattenberg, *Mental Hygiene in Teaching*. New York: Harcourt, Brace, 1951. Chapter 9, "Group Life in the Classroom."

S. S. Sargent, *Social Psychology*. New York: Ronald, 1950. Chapter 10, "Social Interaction and Social Groups," and Chapter 11, "Social Roles."

M. Sherif and C. W. Sherif, *Groups in Harmony and Tension*. New York: Harper, 1953.

G. E. Swanson, T. M. Newcomb, and E. L. Hartley, eds., *Readings in Social Psychology*, rev. ed. New York: Holt, 1952. See sections dealing with leadership and with groups.

SUGGESTED FILMS

Experimental Studies in Social Climates of Groups. Iowa Child Welfare Research Station, State University of Iowa. Depicts experiments with three kinds of social climates in boys' groups.

10

PATTERNS OF ACCEPTANCE

AND REJECTION

SOCIOMETRY

THE preceding chapter ended on a note of caution. We said, in effect, that teachers should become sensitive to the subsurface aspects of group behavior in their classes. Perhaps this admonishment does not help the classroom teacher very much. As he stands before his class, how is he to interpret the frowns and smiles, the whispered words, and most puzzling of all, the silences? And how is he to find out who is accepted and who is rejected in the class?

Part of the answer is that to some extent he will have to trust his own interpretations of what is going on. Sometimes reading books like this one will help, as will in-service courses and discussing some hunches with supervisors and other teachers. But these sources of help can carry him only so far—these people, expert as they may be, do not know the children in his class, the kind of situations which develop, and the effect which he himself has on his class. Indeed, a certain amount of this information will always be concealed

SOCIOMETRIC TABULATION FORM

Chosen → Chooser ↓	Ruth Allis	Irene Brown					Jos. Gold								John Smith		
Ruth Allis	•																
Irene Brown		•															
			•														
				•													
					•												
						•											
Jos. Gold	2	3					•								1		
								•									
									•								
										•							
											•						
												•					
													•				
														•			
John Smith															•		
															•	
																•
Chosen as:																	
1st choice															1		
2nd choice	1																
3rd choice		1															
TOTAL																	

FIGURE 1. Sociometric Tabulation Form. List names in the same order vertically and horizontally. Insert a "1," "2," or "3" in the proper squares to indicate the order of choice. Note example: Joseph Gold chooses John Smith first, Ruth Allis second, and Irene Brown third [5].

from him because it is so difficult to view one's situation objectively.

Nevertheless, there are some ways in which the teacher can follow up his hunches and determine how accurately and how sensitive he is in appraising the events and relationships within the class. One of the easiest and most reliable methods of appraisal is sociometry.

Sociometry is a way of measuring the social relationships in a class. It was developed by J. L. Moreno, an Austrian psychiatrist [1]. Its use in the public schools has been made possible through the work of such people as Helen Hall Jennings [2], Ruth Cunningham [3] and Hilda Taba [4], who have demonstrated how sociometry can be used as a means of understanding relationships among pupils.

There are many approaches to the sociometric testing of a class. One of the commonest is to ask members of the class to list on a piece of paper the children they would like to work with on a committee (or sit next to, or would invite to a birthday party, etc.). By tallying the results of these

←

Explanation and Interpretation. The spaces across the top of the Sociometric Tabulation Form are to be used to indicate the pupils chosen, and those along the left side are for entering the children making the choice; the names of all in the group should accordingly appear in both places. If Joseph Gold has chosen John Smith, Ruth Allis, and Irene Brown, in that order (to use the example on the form), the first thing to do is to find Joseph Gold to the left, and then, staying on his row, to insert a number "1" below the name of John Smith, a "2" below that of Ruth Allis, and a "3" below Irene Brown. The square under each pupil's own name across the top and on his own row from the left can be blocked out straight down the page, since the child will not choose himself. The sum of the choices received in each category (first, second, third) may then be recorded for each person at the bottom of the form in the spaces provided.

The tabulation form is mainly useful in giving a total picture of all children's responses and all positions in the group. Furthermore, it is easy to lift from it the information needed for further analysis [5].

choices or by diagramming them on a chart, the teacher is able to discover who the most popular children are, who are isolated from the group, who make up the cliques and mutual friendships, etc. If he asks the class members to list also those they would *not* like to work with, he can also learn who are the rejected ones in the class.

Those who have worked with this method have discovered that it is desirable to carry out the suggestion used by the teacher to serve as a basis for the testing—that is, if the question is, "Who would you like to sit next to?" the teacher should be prepared to change the seating arrangements in accordance with the requests of the children. Undoubtedly some teachers might have some misgivings about carrying out such a rearrangement for fear that disciplinary problems might be increased; however, children generally work more effectively with partners they have chosen than with partners who are assigned to them by someone in authority. And if an occasional grouping made on a sociometric basis does not work out, it is always possible to separate the disturbing individuals after they have had a chance to work together.

---->

Explanation and Interpretation. The sample sociogram (Figure 2) shows how data are entered. Choices between children are indicated by lines drawn in the following manner: An unreciprocated, or one-way, choice is shown by an arrow from the chooser pointing to the chosen person. The degree of this choice is indicated by placing the appropriate number at the base of the line from the symbol for the chooser. A one-way choice is illustrated by Paula King's choice of Saul Tonik. A mutual choice is shown by a line *touching* the symbols for both choosers with a small vertical bar at the center of the connecting line and the appropriate choice number placed at the base of the line of the chooser; arrows are not needed in this case. This is illustrated by Gale Keyne and Janet Toll. A dotted symbol should be used for any absent person. This situation is illustrated by Joe Brown. If rejections are obtained, they may be indicated in the same way except that the lines are made in small dashes or in a different color [6].

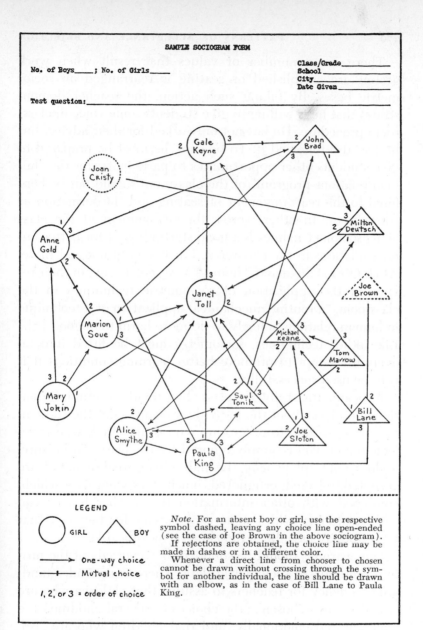

FIGURE 2. *A Filled-in Sociogram Form, Presenting Graphically the Choice Patterns. Blank forms, with empty circles and triangles, may be mimeographed so that the teacher may fill in the names and draw in the choice lines after the test has been given* [6].

There are a number of values that result when work groups are established or seating is rearranged on sociometric bases. By taking such action, the teacher demonstrates that he is willing to give students some voice in classroom procedure. He has not only asked for their advice, but he has also followed it. To be sure, he must be prepared to give students other opportunities to participate, for the "human relations program" of the classroom should not be confined to the rearrangement of seating and the formation of committees. In other words, the realignment of the class along sociometric lines is a good starting point for better human relations in the classroom, but it should not end there. As H. Otto Dahlke and Thomas O. Monohan say, in their review of the application of sociometric techniques in the classroom, "a routine, mechanical application of a technique in human relations is likely to do more harm than good [7]." Like other techniques, sociometry must be fitted into an over-all attempt to promote better learning conditions if it is to be used successfully.

A sociometric study of a class also provides useful information and clues about the individual members of the class, in that it is possible to determine who is accepted, who is rejected, and who is simply ignored by the class. To be sure, it does not explain *why* the individuals so designated are accepted, rejected, or ignored, but it does yield data which, combined with other information the teacher has or can gather, often provides some explanations for behavior that hitherto may have been puzzling or inexplicable.

One warning should be sounded, however, about the misinterpretation of sociometric data. There is an understandable tendency for teachers to assume that children who are "stars" or "overchosen" (the choices of several children) are well-adjusted emotionally, and that children who are "isolates" or "underchosen" (rejected or ignored by other children) are poorly adjusted. Although there may be a relationship between sociometric choice and emotional health,[1] there are so many factors that enter into the assignment of sociometric status and the state of one's emotional health, that the former cannot be used as a valid measure of the latter. A child may be chosen sociometrically because his antisocial and rebellious qualities make him attractive to the others, or a child may be rejected or ignored because he belongs to a minority group, or has a handicap of some sort, or is simply not interested in the same things as the rest of the class.

Another warning has to do with the changes that may take place in the social structure of a class. Although sociometric ratings are relatively stable [10], it is possible for shifts in popularity to occur. Therefore, one should not ascribe greater permanence and authority to a sociometric record of a class than it actually possesses. The probability of changes occurring can be increased if the teacher selects as one of his goals the promotion of better group feeling (higher cohesiveness and better morale). If he is at all successful, one would expect that the resultant changes would be reflected in sociometric studies done at a later date. Hilda Taba and Deborah Elkins used this method in assessing the improvement that took place in an eighth-grade literature class which was taught with an emphasis on human relations. Sociograms drawn in September and again in May showed that the number of rejections in the class was reduced from forty-three to eleven. In September there were three cliques that operated as "closed corporations," with no choices going out into the group. Intimate clusters still appeared in an April sociogram,

---

[1] Robert L. French, for example, found that naval recruits who ranked high in sociometric status were less likely to seek medical attention and less likely to become disciplinary cases [8], and Raymond G. Kuhlen and Howard S. Bretsch found, in a sociometric study of 692 ninth graders, that children who were "unaccepted" were more likely to have personal problems than were "accepted" children [9].

but they were composed of different children and none of them was closed to the rest of the group [11].

From the standpoint of better mental health in the classroom, there are two main reasons why sociometry is a useful tool: it can be used to help teachers understand children better, and it can be used to help teachers promote and evaluate efforts aimed at developing better human relations in the classroom.

RELATIONSHIP BETWEEN COOPERATION AND EMOTIONAL HEALTH IN THE CLASSROOM

WHEN we as teachers fall into the habit of thinking of a class as a collection of individuals rather than as a group, we are inclined to overlook the importance of helping children to learn how to work together. If we adhere to the former pattern of thinking, we are likely to stress a competitive approach to learning, whereby each child is encouraged to do better than the others. One of the difficulties of this approach to education is that it breaks down many of the ties which help to make the class a cohesive group. Communication is made more difficult, and anxieties are aroused. Being present in a class that is dominated by competition does not provide the satisfying experiences that group membership should give. Competitive situations are likely to produce frustrations for class members. The student who produces to the best of his ability, but who makes only a "C," is likely to feel inferior to the "B" student. Even the "A" student is unhappy and insecure—he cannot afford to relax an instant, because the students who make only "B's" are eager to take his place. And then there are those students who are made so anxious by competition that they are unable to work or learn effectively.

Fred T. Wilhelms notes that the schools are more competitive than we think they are:

It can hardly be thought necessary that the schools should be more competitive than the society for which they train. Yet nowhere else in our society is everyone forced to compete against everyone else—regardless of ability or goal. The school is actually unique in America in its stress on competition [12].

One of the difficulties which arise when teachers try to motivate students entirely on the basis of competition is that children are likely to be more concerned about getting better or poorer grades than other students rather than with what should be the chief business of the class—namely, learning. When grades become more important than learning, children are inclined to forget rapidly once the grade has been awarded. This is probably the reason why high school teachers complain that students have not been taught spelling, arithmetic, or English, or whatever, by the grade schools, and why college teachers complain about the preparation of students they get from the high schools, as well as why employers register similar complaints about college graduates. Undoubtedly, teachers at each of these levels bring students up to adequate levels of competence in their classes, but because students feel that grade-getting is more important than real learning, the competencies painfully acquired in grade school in dealing with decimals and fractions have vanished by the time they meet the problems of chemistry and physics in high school or the problems of everyday life as adults.

MUST CHILDREN BE TAUGHT HOW TO COMPETE?

Criticism of the overemphasis on competition in the schools often raises the question: Since children will have to compete when they become adults, should they not learn to compete in the school? The answer to this question is that a realistic appraisal of the world in which we live should demonstrate that it is virtually impossible to grow up without learning to compete. Almost every aspect of our social and personal life is touched by competition in some way—it reaches into recreation, politics, social life, and employment. Most children have learned about competition before they are old enough to go to school. They have learned to compete with their brothers and sisters for the attention of their parents. Even the only child learns how to divert his parents' attention from matters which interest them to matters which interest him, and this, too, is a form of competition.

It appears, therefore, that the real problem facing the school is not how to teach competition, but rather one of how to teach cooperation. This is a far more difficult skill to learn; yet, it is the more basic of the two. Unless people cooperate at the most basic levels, according to Emory S. Bogardus, they would not be free to compete [13]. Viewing the matter from another aspect, Ashley Montagu presents a well-documented argument that cooperation is the chief criterion of living as a civilized person [14].

The effect of cooperativeness on the functioning of small groups was studied by William Haythorn, who, reported, as a result of his experimentation, that

> effective group functioning was facilitated by cooperativeness, efficiency and insight, while behavior which we have called "striving for individual prominence" [that is, competitiveness] reduced group cohesiveness and friendliness [15].

Morton Deutsch conducted an experiment with groups of college students, half of whom were taught under conditions encouraging competition, the other half being taught under conditions encouraging cooperation. He reported that students in the cooperative sections were more strongly motivated by group goals than were students in competitive sections. He states further,

> Our results suggest that the intercommunication and pride in one's group which are basic to group harmony and effectiveness appear to be disrupted when students see themselves to be competing. . . . There is some indication that competitive-

ness produces greater personal insecurity (expectations of hostility from others) than does cooperation. In addition, it is evident that greater group productivity will result when members of a group are cooperative rather than competitive in their interrelationships [16].

Individuals who feel threatened or insecure are likely to express their anxiety through competition or some other form of aggressive behavior. In many respects, the problem of teaching cooperation is one of reducing this insecurity and anxiety, and the problem of teaching competition is one of increasing insecurity and anxiety. The teacher who is concerned about teaching cooperation will be interested in such factors as improving the cohesion of his class and making classroom work a satisfying experience for his students, whereas the teacher who feels that learning can take place only on a competitive basis will want to break down what cohesion there is in the group so that he can deal with his students as individuals. He will accept the principle that school work can be satisfying for only a few—those few who excel at their studies.

This is not to say that competition should be eliminated from schools. It would be highly unrealistic for a school to exist in a competitive culture without incorporating the culture's value standards into its curriculum. Children, living in a competitive society, will expect the school to help them compete better. Yet we should recognize that many functions of life—marriage and family life, community service, and even most of the activities involved in earning a living —are effective only if they are conducted on a cooperative, rather than a competitive, basis. The fact that our divorce rate is so high is due to a large extent to the fact that marriage partners are unable to cooperate. Many communities lack essential services because citizens do not know how to cooperate in matters of civic importance. Knowing how to compete is important, but first one must know how to cooperate.

HOW GROUPS AROUSE THE ANXIETIES OF
SOME OF THEIR MEMBERS

IN THE previous chapters we discussed some of the reasons why individuals develop anxiety when they become members of a group or attempt to gain and maintain the acceptance of other members of the group. In addition to these general sources of anxiety, there are conditions and special situations that provoke anxiety, feelings of inferiority and threat, and insecurity.

One of the commonest of these situations is faced by the new member of the group. The new arrival usually feels anxious and insecure. He does not know where he stands in the group's estimation; he is not sure whether the group will accept him or reject him. Of course, some of the other members of the group are already rejected or ignored by the group as a whole, but they at least know what to expect. Furthermore, they may have worked out some ways of dealing with rejection, or they may know to whom they might turn for comfort, acceptance, and security. Even if these expedients are not wholly satisfactory, their relations with the group do not have the unpredictable quality that is characteristic of the experiences of the new members.

Although some of the anxiety experienced by the recently arrived person is due to his own apprehensiveness regarding an unknown situation, some of it is also stimulated by his awareness of the attitudes of other, more established members toward him. The arrival of a new person in a group is often perceived by the other group members as a threat. Whether this is a mild or a severe threat depends on many factors, such as the security or insecurity of the group, the prevailing emotional climate, and the relationships among the members of the group. In any case, the accommodation of a new member into the group means that the social structure of the group must be adjusted and, to some extent, reformed. Perhaps a friendship or two will dissolve, perhaps the leader's favorite will be displaced. In other words, the arrival of a new member means change of some kind for the other members of the group. Since they do not know what the extent and nature of this change will be, they, too, are made somewhat anxious, although this anxiety is usually not nearly as great as that experienced by the new member. Their anxiety expresses itself in various ways, depending, again, on the kind of group and the nature of its problems. It may express itself as hostility, curiosity, extreme attentiveness, or even as a studied attempt to ignore the new person. Often various members will display differing symptoms: some of the boys will try to pick a fight with the new member; some will ask him endless questions about himself, his family, and the school he came from; some will play tricks on him; and some will ignore him.

Fortunately the attitudes and behavior attendant to the ritual of accepting new members into the group do not last very long, and, after a few weeks, most children have been accepted into the group and have found or are in the process of finding their roles, positions, and functions.

BEING "DIFFERENT" FROM THE GROUP

One of the chief reasons why a child encounters difficulties in becoming a part of a new group is that his newness gives him a quality of being "different" from the other members of the group. Furthermore, the fact that he has not been accepted by the group, and particularly by the leaders or the spokesmen for the group, means that he is weaker and more vulnerable than the others. This means, further, that those members of the group who have a need to attack, bedevil, or tease other children find that they can annoy the new child with relative freedom.

This same pattern of being different, lacking group support, and being vulnerable also applies to children who are established members of the total group, but who are regarded by the rest of the group as "different." Thus, being "different" may be accompanied by lack of group support, which, in turn, leads to vulnerability. Now, in reality, each child is "different" in *some* way; hence, when we say "different," we mean "different in the eyes of the group." In Miss Frank's fifth-grade class, Gary Bell is the one who is "different"—he is the only one who cannot read. At George Washington High School there are a dozen students of Mexican parentage among a student body of three hundred—*they* are "the different ones." Sylvia, Joanne, and Dennis are the "teacher's pets" in the sixth grade; in their class, *they* are "different." Wendell is a second grader; you have to shout at him in order to make yourself understood, even though he wears a hearing aid. In his class *he* is the one who is "different."

PREJUDICE AND THE AWARENESS OF "DIFFERENCES"

WHAT we have been talking about, of course, is prejudice. You will find prejudice in most classes, just as you will find it, in some form, in most communities. Most people are prejudiced in some ways, even though they may deny it or even be totally unaware of it. This is not to say that we as educators should accept the existence of prejudice as inevitable and hence incurable. Since one of the important purposes of education is the eradication of ignorance, it must inevitably be concerned with the elimination of prejudice, which is based on ignorance. Indeed, prejudice expresses itself as a desire to *remain* ignorant.

There are many forces and factors in the lives of children (and adults) that contribute to prejudice. One of these is the desire to feel superior to someone else—not superior in the sense of being more expert in some things, but superior in the sense of being essentially "better" than someone else. This is frequently offered as a "reasonable" basis for prejudice, as though the need to feel "superior" were a normal human need. Although it is true that we will go to great lengths to avoid feeling *inferior*, this does not mean that the feeling of superiority is a natural antidote for feelings of inferiority. Those who have had much experience in working with the problems of emotionally disturbed persons know that the individual who is plagued by feelings of inferiority and who tries to counteract them by competing with others and defeating them is rarely successful in ridding himself of his problem. Any relief that he gains is likely to be temporary, and he is led into an eternal round of "proving" his "superiority" again and again. It therefore appears that the "need to feel superior" is more on the order of being a "neurotic need" rather than a normal one. Instead of being directed at the establishment of satisfying and satisfactory relationships with others, it is directed primarily at the reduction of anxiety. This means that the "cause" of prejudice will be found in the anxieties of the prejudiced person, rather than in the behavior of the person or group that serves as the target for his prejudice.

WHERE CHILDREN LEARN PREJUDICE

This brings us to one of the sources of prejudice—that concept, which children learn from adults, playmates, and the mass media of communication (newspapers, magazines, television, movies, etc), that concept which says that each of us should try to improve himself at the expense of those around him. The concept of prejudice is of course in direct contrast to another widely accepted concept—that we should work together in harmony and cooperation to build a better world. It is not unusual for two contradictory ideas to exist side by side in a culture. What happens is that whenever we feel threatened, anxious, and frustrated, we are likely to be governed by the need to dominate and defeat others. Therefore, the more a group feels threatened, the more likely it is to want to feel superior to someone, or even to attack someone. Again, victory is not likely to bring relief. In the case of the dozen or so children of Mexican parentage at George Washingon High School that we mentioned above, the other children in the school were able to "prove their superiority" by getting better grades. But this did not satisfy their neurotic needs for superiority. They also strove to establish their superiority in other ways—by excluding them from parties and clubs, by snubbing them, and by making pointed remarks in their presence.

The establishment of a state or condition of superiority is plainly not an antidote to feelings of inferiority. The best solution is, of course, a growth in the awareness of the essential equality of individuals—the idea that we are all of equal worth as individuals, in spite of the superiority in skill or social status or personal charm or power which one or another of us possesses. This is the central idea of the democratic tradition. It is a difficult idea to teach, to help children to accept, partly because of the insecurities and neurotic anxiety that exist in most groups of children and partly because we have not completely accepted the idea ourselves.

FRUSTRATION AS A SOURCE OF PREJUDICE

The need to develop an antidote to feelings of inferiority is not the only factor which produces prejudice. Prejudice is a form of hostility, and hostility develops from the experience of being frustrated. There are many ways in which children experience frustration. Merely to live in a complex culture like ours is to experience some frustration; merely to be something less than an adult is frustrating. There are so many reasons why students should have frustrating experiences in school, and it is understandable why they should develop hostile feelings. Often the adults in the situation are the target for these hostilities, partly because the adults are often the ones who have caused the frustration, and partly because children have a tendency to blame adults for all their problems. In a school where adults and children can communicate with each other with relative ease, children find it easier to tell adults about their bruised feelings, real or fancied acts of injustice, and the like. Since in such schools there is better understanding, there is less prejudice, less of a tendency to behave aggressively toward children who are "different." In other schools, where the communication between adults and children is more difficult, children do not find it easy to tell adults that they think they (adults) are unfair. As a result they cannot express their feelings of frustration and inferiority in healthy ways. The children see themselves as the victims of an unjust system from which they cannot escape. Since they cannot easily express their hostility directly to the adults who, they believe, are responsible, they do what all groups do when they feel a need to express frustration and hostility but are prevented from expressing to or against those in authority—they turn on those who are weaker, those who cannot retaliate. If the group feels strongly, it will seek out differences and exaggerate them in order to create a small group of individuals who can serve as scapegoats.

Usually, however, society "pre-selects" the kinds of individuals who are to serve as scapegoats or the victims of prejudice—children of foreign parentage, the handicapped, those who come from "the wrong side of the tracks," children of different races or who attend different churches, and so forth. Children who belong to the dominant group learn from their parents and playmates what the differences are that "really count." Sometimes they learn about these differences from teachers who are careless about expressing or revealing their prejudices.

Thus far we have said little about the effect of prejudice on the groups who are made the targets for the hostility of the dominant groups. J. W. Tait made a study of two thousand eleven- to fifteen-year-old children of Italian-born parents living in New York City. As a result of his investigation he decided that the prejudice faced by these children had produced more than average trends in the direction of inferiority feelings, poor social adjustment, awareness of rejection, and emotional instability [17]. Radke, Trager, and Davis found both Negro and Jewish children suffering from feelings of insecurity because of prejudice [18].

These are but two studies of many that make similar findings: the emotional health of children (and adults) who are the targets of prejudice suffers as a result of the climate of rejection in which they must live. Rejection, as we have tried to stress in this book, is a primary source of anxiety. And the anxiety that we arouse through prejudice returns to plague us in the form of noncooperation, hostile competition, and apathy. In the classroom it presents a special problem in that it interferes with learning and normal emotional and intellectual growth. Thus the whole educational situation suffers because of prejudice. Not only is the work of the teacher made more difficult, but he often feels helpless and inadequate when he sees the mental anguish that prejudice produces.

The *Fact-Finding Report* of the White House Conference describes the effect on children of minority groups as follows:

> As minority group children learn the inferior status to which they are assigned, they react with feelings of inferiority and humiliation; they lose self-esteem. As a consequence of being almost universally regarded as inferior, they become confused concerning their own personal worth. On the one hand, like all other human beings, they require a sense of personal dignity; on the other hand, almost nowhere do they find their own dignity as human beings recognized and supported. Almost inevitably, then, the minority group child is thrown into a crucial situation in his own feelings about himself and in the way he estimates himself. Is he the person he feels himself to be? Or is he a person worthy of no more respect than he gets? . . .
>
> When any individual is surrounded by pervasive hostility and rejection, and has become ambivalent in his feelings about himself, he is likely to react to the ambiguous or even the ob-

jectively non-threatening aspects of his experience with defensiveness and protective hypersensitivity. Minority group children tend to be hypersensitive and anxious concerning their minority status; hostile toward the members of the dominant group, their own group, and other minority groups; and to exhibit a generalized pattern of personality difficulties that seems to be associated with the humiliation to which they are subjected [19].

Nor are children of minority groups the only ones injured by prejudice. To quote from the *Proceedings of the Midcentury White House Conference on Children and Youth*, "prejudice and discrimination are harmful to the development of healthy personality in *all* children, and hence to the welfare of the *whole society* [20]." (Italics ours.)

The role of parents in the formation of prejudice is described in an intensive study by Helen G. Trager and Marian Radke Yarrow of prejudice in young children. In their interviews with parents they found that parents' attitudes toward various ethnic and religious groups affected and controlled the social relationships of their children at home, in the neighborhood, and at school. In the course of these interviews, parents told how they placed restrictions upon friendships and how they created experiences that helped to influence the attitudes and behavior of their children. Some of the parents were aware of how they were influencing their children in this respect; others were either unaware of their role or were unwilling to acknowledge it. Only a few parents stated that they were trying to help their children resist the prejudices that surrounded them. None of the parents interviewed appeared to have any understanding of what caused prejudice. When they did attempt to account for it, they explained it as being due to the bad characteristics of the group that was the object of prejudice. However, the parents did give verbal support to the teaching of democratic values and intercultural education in the school [21].

The extent of the pressures that play upon many children,

pressures that almost inevitably direct their attitudes into ways of prejudice, is recognized by Gordon W. Allport, who writes:

> In some localities intolerable ostracism or ridicule would fall upon the adolescent if he were friendly with Mexicans, Japanese, or Jews . . .

And, further:

> A prejudiced attitude is not like a cinder in the eye that can be extracted without disturbing the integrity of the organism as [a] whole. On the contrary, prejudice is often so deeply embedded in the character structure that it cannot be changed unless the entire inner economy of the life is overhauled [22].

Allport goes on to say that this, in part, is why piecemeal efforts to eliminate prejudice are not more effective than they are. You do not eliminate prejudice by working on the prejudice itself; it is necessary to change a great many other attitudes also.

Yet, since the task of education is that of changing attitudes, or rather, of helping children to develop attitudes that will lead to positive emotional, social, and intellectual growth, and since the attitude of prejudice is one that interferes in many ways with this kind of growth, it follows that education must include the elimination or reduction of prejudice among its several goals.

Within recent years much progress has been made in developing curricula and methodology in what is known as intercultural or intergroup education. When these approaches are used under the direction of skilled and sympathetic teachers and supervisors, they meet with marked success. In essence, this type of education stresses:

1. The development of a classroom situation or atmosphere that permits free exchange of ideas and discussion of feelings [23].

2. The understanding and acceptance of differences among people and respect for these differences.

3. An understanding of some of the causes of prejudice and discrimination.

4. Various attempts to translate course content into practice through acting out or trying out ideas and approaches in the classroom, using a medium like sociodrama, combined with the "unfinished story [24]."

5. The relating of antiprejudice material to other courses in the curriculum—e.g., literature, composition, and social studies.[2]

In most of the communities of the world, prejudice permeates the everyday way of life. Perhaps it is too much to hope or expect that we as teachers can eliminate it within the next generation or so. However, it is reasonable to expect that we can reduce or control some of the forces and factors which produce and aggravate prejudice. By making it possible to discuss prejudice frankly and openly in the classroom, by helping students to search into its causes and effects, by helping students to accept the fact of their own prejudice (which means that the teacher must be prepared to accept the fact of his *own* prejudices), it may be possible to reduce some of the unfortunate results of prejudice. If teachers are successful in reducing the expression (and perhaps the amount) of prejudice among school children (as well as among teachers) they will not only improve the mental health of the children they supervise, but they will also help to develop classroom groups which are more receptive to what the school has to offer. Children in such groups should be more amenable to learning since they would be less likely to be plagued by anxieties and frustrations which arise in groups that are not cohesive, for the group that is ridden by prejudice is the group in which children war one against the other. Groups of the latter type do not provide satisfactory experiences for children; they discourage, rather than en-

---

[2] See H. Taba, ed., *Elementary Curriculum in Intergroup Relations*, Washington: American Council on Education, 1950; and H. Taba, E. H. Brady, and J. Robinson, *Intergroup Education in Public Schools*, Washington: American Council on Education, 1952.

courage, learning. Reducing the amount of prejudice in classrooms not only improves the mental health of children, but it also helps to create an atmosphere or a climate which promotes learning.

REFERENCES

1. J. L. Moreno, *Who Shall Survive?* Washington: Nervous and Mental Disease Publishing Co., 1934.
2. H. H. Jennings, *Leadership and Isolation*, 2d ed. New York: Longmans, Green, 1950.
3. R. Cunningham, *Understanding Group Behavior of Boys and Girls.* New York: Bureau of Publications, Teachers College, Columbia University, 1951. Chapter 5.
4. H. Taba and D. Elkins, *With Focus on Human Relations.* Washington: American Council on Education, 1950. Chapter 7.
5. H. H. Jennings, *Sociometry in Group Relations.* Washington: American Council on Education, 1948. Pp. 17–19. Reprinted by permission.
6. *Ibid.* Pp. 22–24. Reprinted by permission.
7. H. O. Dahlke and T. O. Monahan, "Problems in the Application of Sociometry to Schools," *School Review.* 57:223–34;1949.
8. R. L. French, "Sociometric Status and Individual Adjustment among Naval Recruits," *Journal of Abnormal and Social Psychology.* 46:64–72;1951.
9. R. G. Kuhlen and H. S. Bretsch, "Sociometric Status and Personal Problems of Adolescents," *Sociometry.* 10:122–32; 1947.
10. H. H. Jennings, "Leadership and Sociometric Choice," in G. E. Swanson, T. S. Newcomb, and E. L. Hartley, eds., *Readings in Social Psychology,* rev. ed. New York: Holt, 1952. Pp. 312–18.
11. Taba and Elkins, *op. cit.* P. 190.
12. F. T. Wilhelms, "Meeting Inevitable Feelings about Competition," an unpublished address made to teachers of Vallejo, California, April 23, 1953. Reprinted by permission.
13. E. S. Bogardus, "Gradations of Cooperation," *Sociology and Social Research.* 35:356–62;1951.
14. A. Montagu, *On Being Human.* New York: Henry Schuman, 1950.
15. W. Haythorn, "The Influence of Individual Members on the Characteristics of Small Groups," *Journal of Abnormal and Social Psychology.* 48:276–84;1953.

16. M. Deutsch, "Social Relations in the Classroom and Grading Procedures," *Journal of Educational Research*. 45:145–52;1951. Reprinted by permission.
17. J. W. Tait, "Race, Prejudice, and Personality," *School: Secondary Edition*. 34:795–98;1946.
18. M. Radke, H. Trager, and H. Davis, "Social Perceptions and Attitudes of Children," *Genetic Psychology Monographs*. 40:327–447;1949.
19. Midcentury White House Conference on Children and Youth, *A Healthy Personality for Every Child*. Raleigh: Health Publications Institute, 1951. Pp. 48–49. Reprinted by permission.
20. E. A. Richards, ed., *Proceedings of the Midcentury White House Conference on Children and Youth*. Raleigh: Health Publications Institute, 1951.
21. H. G. Trager and M. R. Yarrow, *They Learn What They Live*. New York: Harper, 1952. Pp. 226–27.
22. G. W. Allport, *The Resolution of Intergroup Tensions*. New York: National Conference of Christians and Jews, 1952. P. 36. Reprinted by permission.
23. M. Heaton, *Feelings are Facts*. New York: National Conference of Christians and Jews, 1952.
24. G. Shaftel and F. R. Shaftel, *Role Playing the Problem Story*. New York: National Conference of Christians and Jews, 1952.

SUGGESTED READINGS

T. W. Adorno *et al.*, *The Authoritarian Personality*. New York: Harper, 1950. The report of an intensive piece of research at the University of California, the results of which show that prejudice is associated with the personality of persons who seek power over others.

H. Bonner, *Social Psychology*. New York: American Book, 1953. Chapter 13, "Group Tensions and Conflicts."

Bulletin of the National Association of Secondary School Principals. 33:1–204;(Feb.)1949. The entire issue is devoted to "Curriculum in Intergroup Education."

H. H. Cummings, ed., *Improving Human Relations*. Bulletin No. 25, National Council for the Social Studies. Washington: National Education Association, 1949. A compilation of brief articles on intergroup and intercultural education.

L. W. Doob, *Social Psychology*. New York: Holt, 1952. Chapter 12, "Group Prejudice."

E. L. Hartley, *Problems in Prejudice*. New York: King's Crown, 1946.

W. H. Kilpatrick and W. Van Til, eds., *Intercultural Attitudes in the Making*. Ninth Yearbook of the John Dewey Society. New York: Harper, 1947.

K. Lewin, *Resolving Social Conflicts*. New York: Harper, 1948. Part 3, "Intergroup Conflicts and Group Belongingness."

G. Myers, *The History of Bigotry in the United States*. New York: Random House, 1943.

The National Conference of Christians and Jews publishes a series of twenty-five-cent pamphlets that deal with various aspects of prejudice and intergroup education. (See items 22, 23, 24 in the References.) Pamphlets and lists may be obtained from local offices of the Conference or by addressing: The National Conference of Christians and Jews, 381 4th Ave., New York 16, N. Y.

G. E. Swanson, T. M. Newcomb and E. L. Hartley, eds., *Readings in Social Psychology*, rev. ed. New York: Holt, 1952. Part V, "Some Psychological Approaches to Public Issues."

H. L. Witmer and R. Kotinsky, eds., *Personality in the Making*. New York: Harper, 1592. Chapter 6, "The Effects of Prejudice and Discrimination."

Also see items 2, 3, 4, 5, 14, 21, 22, and 23 in the References for this chapter.

SUGGESTED FILMS

Boundary Lines and *Picture in Your Mind*. Colorful, artistic arguments for greater tolerance and understanding among nations and ethnic groups. Available through McGraw-Hill.

The High Wall. Prejudice among teen-agers, its causes and effects. Available through McGraw-Hill.

Learning Through Cooperative Planning. Bureau of Publications, Teachers College, Columbia University.

Whoever You Are. How citizens in a community got together to control race violence and prejudice. Available from New York University Film Library.

11

THREE APPROACHES TO TEACHING

OUR plan in this chapter is to discuss the mental-hygiene aspects of the prevailing philosophies of education under three headings, which we shall call the directive, laissez-faire, and guidance approaches. We realize that in doing this we shall, for the moment, ignore the fact that the methods of many, if not most, teachers defy absolute classification by these standards. Most of us, indeed, are blends of the three types. Some teachers "talk a good line" of guidance, but observation of their classroom practices makes it clear that they are wedded to the directive approach. Other teachers sound as though they believe in the toughest form of directive teaching, yet their classrooms are examples of the laissez-faire system.

The threefold classification we are using resembles that of the autocratic, laissez-faire, and democratic climates created by Lewin, Lippitt, and White in their famous experiment [1]. However, we have not used the terms "autocratic" and "democratic" because they are "loaded words"—that is, they have emotional values for most of us which might interfere with our evaluation and appraisal. Instead we have used "directive" and "guidance" which we feel possess connotations that are more neutral.

THE DIRECTIVE APPROACH — THE METHOD OF TRADITION

WE SHALL begin with the directive approach to learning; it is the oldest system and the one most likely to be understood and accepted by teachers as well as by laymen.[1]

In its extreme form, the directive approach to education assumes that adults know what is best for children; hence, there is no need to find out how children feel about any aspect of the curriculum. It also assumes that, if left to their own devices, children would turn out badly. Education is therefore seen as a corrective measure, one of the main purposes of which is to keep children in line. The person who subscribes to directive education in its extreme form does not believe that children can be trusted, even when supervised by adults.

REWARD AND PUNISHMENT

Directive education subscribes to a theory of learning which depends on conditioning and influencing the behavior of children by the use of rewards and punishment. The idea is that if good or satisfactory behavior is rewarded and bad or unsatisfactory behavior is punished, good behavior will be strengthened and bad behavior will be weakened and may drop out. Children are thus said to be "conditioned" in favor of good behavior and against bad behavior.

As far as can be determined experimentally, there is some truth to this theory. Apparently learning does take place through a process of conditioning. People do tend to con-

---

[1] This approach is sometimes characterized as "autocratic," "authoritarian," or "paternalistic," particularly by those who do not approve of its philosophy and methods.

tinue behavior which they associate with satisfactions and to discontinue behavior which they associate with frustrations and lack of satisfaction.

However, the theory does not explain why children can grow up in an environment where they are punished for their bad deeds and rewarded for their good ones and still behave in ways which are unsatisfactory according to any standard of conduct. And this is where the directive system runs into a major difficulty. It overlooks the fact that what is "reward" and what is "punishment" is a highly personal matter. What is a reward to one child is punishment to another. The teacher praises Marion for giving the right answer in class. Marion is proud and happy; she likes the teacher to praise her. But if the teacher should praise Dora, the effect would be quite different. Dora is a tomboy. Her chief aim in life right now is to prove to the gang of boys she goes with that she can beat any boy at his own game, that she is, in effect, more of a boy than the boys themselves are. She does not want the teacher to praise her because she is afraid that she will lose status with her gang.

What we are saying is that in order to determine what is reward and what is punishment, we have to understand the self-concept of the child in question. Marion likes the teacher's praise because it fits in with her concept of herself as someone who resembles the teacher. As we say, she "identifies" with the teacher and would like to be more like her. Praise from the teacher does not fit into Dora's self-concept because she sees herself as someone who would like to be more like the boys she goes around with and less like the teacher.

The examples we have given are highly individualized and hence do not tell us what children in general are likely to regard as rewards and punishment. We shall not explore further at this point the attitude formation of children in general because we have discussed it at other points in this text. The point is that the adult who adheres rigidly to the

directive approach to education is not concerned with finding out what children's attitudes or self-concepts or frames
of reference are. He is satisfied that he, as the adult in
charge, is competent to decide what the rewards and punishments should be. He needs no guidance or help from children.

THE MIND AS A STOREHOUSE FOR KNOWLEDGE

Another concept which appears to be common among people
who subscribe to the directive school of learning is what
might be called the "quantitative" approach to learning. Persons holding this concept see education as a process of filling
children with knowledge. Children are seen as coming to
school empty of knowledge, whereupon the school under-
takes the task of filling them full. At various periods the
teacher checks on the effectiveness of this process by measuring the amount of knowledge children have absorbed.

The directive teacher is likely to feel that education is doing its job well if children are storing away large quantities
of information. However, he overlooks the fact that unless
children find use and value in the information they acquire,
they are likely to keep it in mind only long enough to pass
the required tests. After examinations are over and final
grades have been assigned, forgetting is very rapid. And, of
course, there are many children who refuse to be bothered
with studying information which, they feel, has no relation
to their lives and interests. The followers of the directive
school of learning would like to exclude these children from
school, but this does not fit in with our philosophy of education today, which may be stated in two propositions: (1) the
modern world needs educated citizens; and (2) every child
is entitled to an education.

Research in the field of learning demonstrates rather con-
clusively that learning does not occur as an accumulative or
additive process, as the quantitative approach to learning

would lead us to believe. Instead, it indicates that learning is a process of reorganization, whereby each new skill or concept learned affects in some way what the individual has already learned. Learning may also be seen as a process of growth, whereby the individual is enabled to gain increased competence in dealing with his social and physical environment, as well as with himself. However, if the educator sees learning in terms of reorganization and growth, he is forced to look upon education as an infinitely complex and difficult process. The quantitative approach to learning, as well as the reward-and-punishment approach, makes learning seem simpler than it actually is. This appearance of simplicity makes these theories very attractive to harried educators in search of easy solutions to complex classroom problems.

AUTOMATIC TRANSFER OF TRAINING

There is still another concept which is likely to be favored by persons who follow the directive line of reasoning, and that is that an individual's general competency to deal with the problems of life can be improved or strengthened by studying certain specific studies that are isolated from the main currents of everyday life. And the more difficult and the more traditional the subject matter, the greater the improvement in general competency. This idea appears in the arguments which are put forth to defend the continuance of such subjects as Latin and plane geometry as requirements for high school graduation. It also appears in the educational philosophy which holds that students should spend long hours with Aristotle and St. Thomas Aquinas if they are to have adequate preparation for dealing with the problems of the world. These arguments are often proposed by persons who want to keep the curriculum just as it is at all costs, or by those who are aware of inadequacies in the present curriculum, but who see the solution as one of reviving the curricula and methods of former days.

Research in the field of learning partially supports and

partially negates the point of view expressed in the preceding paragraph, which, in psychology, is termed "the theory of automatic transfer of training." There is no evidence to support the proposition that mere difficulty of subject matter aids an individual by "strengthening his mind" or by improving his general competency. Nor is there much value to be gained studying books and subjects whose content is unrelated to the problems which students face. However, there *is* some point in children learning general principles which can be applied to a variety of situations, and if a teacher is able to help children draw out these principles and apply them to the problems of life as they see it, the experience will be a worth-while one. The important factor here is the competence of the teacher. Some teachers are well able to help children draw conclusions from subject matter which, at first glance, is unrelated to their everyday experience. Other teachers who attempt this, however, are baffled by the dissimilarity between the experiences of children and the subject matter they are supposed to teach and hence would prefer to employ concepts and materials which are more obviously related to the lives of children and the events of the world today.

INTELLECTUALISM

The directive approach to learning attempts to stress the intellectual processes to the exclusion of the emotional. The teacher who subscribes to the directive philosophy is likely to feel that emotions and feelings "get in the way" of learning and that matters would be better off if the learning situation were de-emotionalized. However, this concept overlooks the fact that the willingness of the individual to learn is a prerequisite to successful learning. In other words, unless an individual is emotionally toned to be receptive to what is taught, little positive learning is likely to take place. And if he is negatively disposed, the emotional atmosphere must be changed before learning can proceed. Lawrence K. Frank has this comment to make on our tendencies to overintellectualize education:

> The dilemma of education arises from belief in man as a rational being in whom emotion can be controlled by reason and intelligence. Educational programs shrink from any frank acceptance of the underlying personality make-up and emotional reactions of students as entering into the educational situation because to do so would bring a widespread collapse of the whole educational philosophy and undermining of approved pedagogy [2].

Although Frank's criticism is directed to education as a whole and is certainly to some degree applicable to most educational programs, it applies most especially to directive education.

THE TEACHER AS AN AUTHORITY

The directive method of teaching would be characterized as "leader-centered" or "teacher-centered" rather than "group-centered" because the activities of the class center around the teacher's wants, plans, and demands, rather than those of the children. The teacher initiates all discussion, answers or poses questions, and "runs the show." He is the active, dominating leader; the children are the passive, submissive followers. As far as the directive teacher is concerned, the class does not exist as a group. It is, instead, a collection of individual children, and he sees his relationship as one existing between him and each individual child. John Dewey believes that this is why the commands of the teacher and the submission of the students play such an important part in the scheme of traditional education. Because teachers do not see the school as a community held together by participation in common activities, he says, the normal and proper conditions of group control are lacking. Therefore, it is necessary, in such schools, for the teacher to "keep order." Order is thus the teacher's to keep, instead of being a part of the work to be shared [3].

Another of the difficulties of the directive form of education stems from the attitudes toward authority that children bring from home. Nathaniel Cantor describes child-rearing practices in most homes as being largely characterized by punishment and the arbitrary authority of parents. He says:

> The net effect of punishment and arbitrary authority as the means of rearing children is to develop in them a pervasive sense of fear, anxiety, and hostility. To fight off the threat of punishment children develop many defenses. . . . These defenses are built into patterns which become the accustomed ways by which the growing child meets the challenges of schools and . . . the challenges of society, whenever he feels threatened by authority. . . .
>
> . . . Children bring to the classrooms the patterns of avoiding or meeting authority which they developed in the home. By listening, generally remaining silent, and being told what to do, when and how to do it, they can avoid conflict and the consequences of disobeying the teacher, the substitute for the authority of the parents. "Tell us what to do, we'll do it. Only leave us alone." What happens to them during the classes? Their vivid curiosity is dulled into a stubborn resistance, and their creativity into a fear of being themselves. . . . Watch an average group of children leaving school at the end of the day. They are escaping from the school [4].

THE LAISSEZ-FAIRE APPROACH [2]

THE laissez-faire approach to learning is opposed to the directive approach in almost every way. Whereas the directive approach assumes that children cannot be trusted to make their own decisions or to direct their own efforts, the laissez-faire approach assumes that if children are placed in an environment that is free from all restrictions and from adult domination, they will develop in ways which are basically sound from the standpoint of mental health and

[2] The "laissez-faire" approach is called the "permissive" approach by some and the "anarchic" approach by others.

general effectiveness in living. One might say that the assumption of the *directive* school of learning is that children are basically "bad"—that is, that they will turn out badly unless they are under constant supervision, direction, and control—whereas the assumption of the *laissez-faire* school is that children are basically "good"—that is, that they will turn out well if only they are given the freedom and opportunity to work out their own destinies.

ARGUMENTS PRO AND CON LAISSEZ-FAIRE EDUCATION

Actually there are some elements of truth in both of these ideas. A number of writers in the field of personality development believe that each of us possess "a drive toward health" which serves as a corrective factor and which maintains the mental health of most of us at a high enough level to keep us out of difficulties and to help us operate effectively most of the time [5, 6, 7, 8]. Otherwise we would not be able to withstand the insecurities, shocks, and unfortunate occurrences which are the everyday lot of all of us, adults and children alike. Therefore, we undoubtedly do not give children enough opportunities to exercise their own potentials for emotional, social, and intellectual growth. We probably overprotect and overdominate them more than is necessary or even desirable for their own good, and many of the problems we experience as adolescents and young adults may be traced to such child-rearing practices, which serve, in the final analysis, to create children and adults who are too dependent and who have difficulty in making decisions independently or in meeting responsibilities.

Yet, there is some evidence that children (and adults, too) are basically "bad," if by "bad" we mean "antisocial" or "asocial." As we have indicated in previous chapters, young children are highly self-centered; they want to do what *they* want to do, irrespective of the rights and privileges of others. If their self-oriented tendencies are not limited, controlled, and redirected, they may continue in this immature orientation toward life. Therefore, it appears that control and direction is necessary, both for the welfare of the child and the welfare of society.

One of the basic requirements of the laissez-faire school of education is that the environment of the child must be completely free in order that the more positive and healthy drives which control his life may be free enough to have their maximum beneficial effect. However, the difficulty here is that it is impossible to create situations which are completely free from the interference of forces and conditions outside the school. Children bring into the school the conflicts, frustrations, and anxieties which are a part of life outside the school. For example, a child who feels that he is overdominated and overcontrolled at home may try to express some of this feeling by attempting to become a sort of junior dictator in school. If the school or the classroom is run on a completely permissive basis, he may actually succeed in setting up a tyranny more rigid and severe than that of the most authoritarian teacher. Ideally, the group should be strong enough to resist him, yet the other members of the group have their problems, too, and it may meet their more or less neurotic needs to permit the dictator to dominate. In actual practice, the laissez-faire approach to education usually creates more anxieties than it prevents or cures because it does not provide help and direction for children when they need it—only when they ask for it. This, too, is unrealistic, psychologically speaking, for children will often ask for help and direction when they do not need it or, on the other hand, they may need help and direction and not be aware of it.

THE COMPLETELY PERMISSIVE SCHOOL IS A RARITY

There are very few schools and classrooms which operate on an avowedly laissez-faire basis. Virtually the entire educational profession is aware of the deficiencies of this approach to education. (Indeed, they are far more aware of the short-comings of laissez-faire education than they are of the deficiencies of directive education.) When one does discover a laissez-faire situation, it is usually the result of the policies of a teacher who lacks the courage or the ability to control and direct his class or who does not care whether his students get any direction or control. Very rarely does one find a teacher who is a laissez-faire educator by philosophy and conviction. Nevertheless, there are such teachers, and some of them are quite successful, particularly with preschool children. Even in the most orthodox laissez-faire situations, however, there are elements of direction and control, which, in the final analysis, may be a factor in their success.

THE GUIDANCE APPROACH

THE guidance approach to education is not a compromise between the directive and the laissez-faire approach, although it contains elements which are typical of both schools. Whereas the *directive* approach holds, in effect, that when in doubt you must *always* direct and control children and the *laissez-faire* approach holds that you must *never* direct and control them, unless they request it, the guidance approach holds that the decision to direct and control or to "keep hands off" depends upon the situation. This means that persons who subscribe to the guidance philosophy are likely to be in an occasional quandry and may even make wrong decisions. While persons who subscribe to either the directive or the laissez-faire point of view never need to be in doubt as to whether to direct and control or not, the guidance person is very often in doubt. As he watches the tensions wax and wane in the groups he supervises, he must ask himself again and again: "Should I step in and take over? Or will they work it out without my help?" Sometimes he will take over and will realize later that the children would have worked it out without his help and that actually he spoiled what could have been a real opportunity for learning and positive growth. Or he will not interfere in a certain situation and on later evaluation will realize that the children needed his help and support rather badly. However, if the guidance-oriented person is basically a competent teacher who has a good relationship with his classes, an occasional error in judgment will not seriously impede the progress of his students nor disturb his relations with them. Actually, children often find it easier to accept a teacher who makes an occasional mistake and who is willing to admit it than one who "never makes mistakes" or is unable to admit to himself and to others that he has made one.

ARE CHILDREN BASICALLY "GOOD" OR "BAD?"

The guidance approach to the question of whether children are basically "good" or basically "bad" varies somewhat according to the individual teacher. However, most guidance-oriented teachers believe that children are basically "good" and hence can be trusted to make decisions, carry out responsibilities, and work out their own problems far more than they are permitted in most classrooms. Such teachers are realistic enough to know that children often display antisocial (or at least asocial) behavior which, if left unchecked, would disrupt the everyday activities of the classroom. Some guidance-oriented teachers attribute these negative tendencies to forces and situations outside the classroom, such as quarreling parents, living in slums, unmet needs for love, and the like. Others feel that while these factors are important, there *are* elements in every child which make him want to behave in antisocial ways and which are opposed by other elements within him which impel him to act in ways which are essentially healthy. Regardless of what theory of personality guidance-minded teachers subscribe to, they are inclined to view children realistically and to realize that sometimes they need freedom to develop and grow and that sometimes they need direction and control. Hence, they would reject an approach which said that you must always direct and control children to keep them from turning out badly or an approach which said that you must never direct and control if you want them to turn out well.

THE RELATIVE IMPORTANCE OF THE TEACHER

The guidance approach to education differs from the other two approaches in the importance assigned to children and to teachers. The directive approach makes the teacher *the* important figure. *His* ideas and decisions are the ones which count and which must be considered. The ideas and feelings of children are not worth considering, according to this formulation, because children are too immature, too inexperienced, and too biased by their emotions. The laissez-faire approach emphasizes the importance of the child. His needs, wishes, decisions, and demands dominate the school. The school adjusts to the student, instead of the student adjusting to the school—the latter being the pattern in the school dominated by the directive educator.

In the guidance approach, the relative importance of teacher and pupil approaches equality. This does not mean that the children and the teacher will each have one vote and that the class can then outvote the teacher. It *does* mean that the teacher will remember that the children will have "something to say" about the kinds of educational experiences they are undergoing or are about to undertake. But they will not usually say this "something" through the medium of voting. Instead, the guidance-oriented teacher will create a permissive relationship between teacher and group so that children will feel free to express themselves. But he will also remember that since children are less skilled in verbal communication than he is, he will have to develop some highly sensitive skills in order to determine how children feel, how they are reacting to their educational experiences, and how they view or perceive what is going on in the classroom. This means, further, that the guidance-minded teacher must become a keen and sensitive observer and a perceptive listener, otherwise he will not know how to give children an opportunity to participate in the plans and conduct of their education.

Again, this does not mean that the teacher completely remakes and redesigns each curriculum for each class or for each individual. For one thing, it would be inefficient for the teacher to discard techniques and materials which had become useful parts of his repertoire. For another thing, the teacher has responsibilities to the community, the administration, his profession, and to himself. The job of the guidance-oriented teacher is to maintain a good balance among these responsibilities over a period of time. However, he *will* expend a large portion of his energy in making it possible for children to participate in the educational process *in accordance with their level of maturity*. Another way to put this is to say that the guidance-minded teacher *shares* his leadership with the class, whereas the directive teacher retains the leadership for himself alone, and the laissez-faire teacher assumes virtually no leadership at all, but abdicates his leadership.

Margaret Heaton has this to say about the teacher's role as a leader:

. . . The teacher who does a great deal of "telling" may be interesting to the students, may intrigue them with new terminology, but may leave them quite passive and with no useful insight into their own problems. The teacher, on the other hand, who sets the stage for students to talk about their own experiences and trains them to draw their own conclusions and to experiment with new ways of meeting their needs can make students sensitive to their own emotional problems and active in finding ways to deal with them. The success of such teaching can be evaluated in terms of whether students become more responsive to the emotional needs of others and more experimental in planning ways of dealing with their own feelings [9].

SENSITIVITY TO STUDENTS' NEEDS

It is often difficult to identify persons who are genuinely sensitive to the needs and feelings of students because so many directive people firmly believe that they know what students want. They sincerely believe that they have made an accurate reading of the feelings and needs of their students, and that this now serves as the basis for their choice of curricula and methods. However, what usually has happened is that they have confused their own feelings and needs with the feelings and needs of the students.

One of the basic requirements for good communication is a sense of equality on the part of the persons involved (a kind of mutual "self-respect"). Since the directive teacher cannot regard students as equals, as persons with anything worth while to communicate, he is unable to develop true perspective with regard to what they really think and feel. Therefore, he is free to believe in his (erroneous) analysis of students and their needs, insulated as he is against the corrective influences of the truth. When one suggests that perhaps he has misinterpreted the wishes of students, he is likely to react as though a question had been raised about his integrity and sincerity, since he is unaware that his students are unable to communicate effectively with him, or even that, basically, he really does not want to make it possible for them to communicate.

DIRECTIVE EDUCATION AND ITS APPEAL TO THE LAYMAN

Probably the great bulk of the people in this country, or, for that matter, in the Western world, are sympathetic to directive forms of education. For one thing, the principles which underlie the directive viewpoint are very simple. (Actually, this simplicity is deceptive; any situation which involves human relations is in reality highly complex.) Furthermore, the emphasis, in the directive approach, on the dominant and important teacher as contrasted to the subordinate and relatively insignificant students is very similar to the state of affairs existing in business and government organizations in the world outside the school. The man in the street is so used to living in an environment where someone is always controlling and others are always taking orders, that he is made uneasy by any situation which seems unfamiliar, which differs in any way. He does not understand that ordering or directing someone to learn does not make for the best conditions for learning, and he does not understand that people learn most effectively in situations where they are stimulated, encouraged, and helped to find out things for themselves (granting, of course, that younger children need far more help in this than older ones).

Because of this tendency to look unfavorably on permissiveness or any kind of freedom in learning situations, the man in the street tends to lump under one heading all systems which differ from a clear-cut directive approach. The usual label he applies is "progressive education." Progressive education can be understood to mean those forms of education which attempt to use the ideas of educators like John Dewey and William Heard Kilpatrick, but the term has become so heavily charged with emotion that it has lost much of its original meaning, as far as the lay public is concerned. Like so many emotionalized terms, it has come to mean whatever the speaker wants it to mean.

CONFUSION REGARDING GUIDANCE AND LAISSEZ-FAIRE APPROACHES

To the man in the street, a "progressive" school is one in which the children are permitted to "run wild," where they are not required to meet any standards, and where few if any limits are imposed. In actuality, this picture comes closer to laissez-faire education, although it does not take into consideration any of the philosophical bases for this approach. Although the teachers who adhere to what we have in this

text termed the "guidance approach" do maintain standards
and employ direction and control (although their approach
to both these matters differs markedly from that of directive
teachers), they have so far not met with much success in
helping lay persons to see that their methods of education are
quite different from those of laissez-faire teachers. Grace
McLean Abbate has this to say on the subject:

> For some time, child psychiatrists have been concerned
> about the way in which psychoanalytic theory, as well as the
> teachings of Dewey, Kilpatrick, etc., have been distorted in the
> rearing and education of children. Thus, to psychoanalytic
> concepts and teachings have been attributed the idea that any
> frustration causes neurotic disturbances, that any deprivation
> imposed upon the child is necessarily evil, and that any inter-
> ference from the world of the adult damages the child's proc-
> ess of emotional growth. In accordance with these misconcep-
> tions, the atmosphere of child education, which includes parent
> and school influence, must be permissive, non-thwarting, and
> non-restrictive.
>
> It is true that there was a period two or three decades ago
> when early psychoanalytical concepts as then applied to the
> education of children, particularly those of the middle class,
> gave impetus to the removal of most controls; but psychoana-
> lytic experience soon revealed that the uninhibited, undis-
> ciplined child developed many anxieties and disturbances.
> This knowledge, however, was integrated into the teaching
> and guidance of parents and educators only partially or not at
> all. Today, we know that for the development of an adequately
> adjusted personality it is necessary for the child, and particu-
> larly the young child, to be exposed to the control of his par-
> ents and teachers. Nevertheless, we still find, all too often, per-
> missiveness and an "adult-hands-off" attitude the prevailing
> philosophy both in homes and schools [10].

In the eyes of the directive educator and the lay public,
the question of freedom in the classroom is "all or none"—
either the teacher dominates the class or the class dominates
the teacher. Thus, it is relatively easy for them to assume

that because laissez-faire and guidance educators have similar points of view in one respect, their approach must be identical. Interestingly enough, the laissez-faire educator often classifies the guidance-oriented educator with the directive because both believe in using controls and are concerned about discipline.

This confusion in the minds of both educators and the lay public makes the task of the guidance-minded educator all the more difficult. Not only must he devote a major portion of his attention to the energy-consuming task of maintaining a classroom atmosphere which is friendly to learning, but he must also struggle to keep his form of education from being taken over, crippled, or dominated by educators of the directive or the laissez-faire persuasion. Since the latter constitute such a minute proportion of the educational profession and since the former are not only numerically large, but also have the support of most of the lay public, the guidance-minded educator must very often cope with severe pressures in order to keep his methods from becoming more directive and to continue to provide the kind of education he believes in.

WHERE DO MOST TEACHERS FIT IN?

As WE stated earlier in this chapter, most teachers do not fit neatly into the three classifications we have described. Most teachers use a combination of at least two of the three approaches. Although both the guidance and laissez-faire approaches have been attacked severely during the last few years by the more conservative elements in the profession, there has, nevertheless, been a trend in the direction of greater permissiveness and greater freedom in the classroom. Some teachers, whose *attitudes* readily identify them as directive, use some teaching methods which appear to be borrowed from the guidance approach to education, while other teachers, whose *methods* are still largely directive, have adopted a point of view toward education which is decidedly more sympathetic to the guidance approach. These gaps between theory and practice may be symptoms of accelerating change in educational practice, or they may be a reflection of the indecision, shifts, and swings which have characterized the public's attitude toward all manner of things during recent years. Whatever the cause, the result is an emotional climate which has its advantages and disadvantages—it makes the task of the guidance-minded educator more difficult, but it also renders the fixed positions of the directive and the laissez-faire educators less tenable.

It should be clear from the foregoing discussion that the sympathies of the mental hygienist are largely with the guidance approach to education, inasmuch as it appears to provide the conditions most favorable to mental health in the schools. Yet, one must grant that good teaching is more than being guidance-minded, and, furthermore, that there are thousands of effective teachers who are not particularly guidance-minded. And the classification we have made of directive, laissez-faire, and guidance are not the only ways of classifying and describing approaches to education.

Leland B. Bradford and Ronald Lippitt identify four types of leaders: the hardboiled autocrat, the benevolent autocrat, the laissez-faire leader, and the democratic leader. Although their characterization of these leaders is oriented primarily to an industrial setting, nevertheless, it is pertinent to education.

> The hardboiled autocrat gives orders and employees carry them out. He believes that he must constantly check up on everyone to maintain production. He is careful not to spoil employees with too much praise. *Results:* Some submission, but accompanied by an undercurrent of resentment and incipient rebellion; no one assumes any more responsibility than he is forced to take; buck-passing is very common; employees are irritable and unwilling to cooperate with each other; there is much backbiting; the works slips badly when the supervisor is not present.

The benevolent autocrat would be shocked to learn that he is autocratic. He is interested in his employees, wants to see them happy, praises as well as criticizes, is seldom harsh or severe, tries to think he is developing a happy-family type of group. His praise is always phrased in terms of his own standards: "That's the way I like to see it," or "That's the way I want it done." He tries to make employees dependent upon him and him only for their standards of work. Failure to live up to these standards is taken as evidence of disloyalty. *Results:* Most employees like the supervisor, but those who see through him dislike him intensely; no one shows much initiative about his work until he can check with the supervisor; the tone of the group is characterized by submissiveness and lack of individual development; production is good as long as the supervisor is on hand to give directions.

The laissez-faire leader may be one who lacks confidence in himself and hence buries himself in paperwork or stays away from his employees. Or he may feel that being a "good fellow" means avoiding demands or restrictions. He does not set any clear goals, he avoids making decisions, and he lets things drift. *Results:* Lowest morale and productivity; work is sloppy and output low; employees have little interest in their jobs; much buck-passing, irritability, and unrest; no teamwork or cohesion; no one knows what to do or what to expect.

The democratic leader shares decision-making or work-planning whenever or wherever possible. When he must make a decision, he is careful to explain the basis of his decision to the group. He is careful to develop as much participation, opinion-giving, and responsibility as possible. Praise and criticism are delivered in terms of work and results. *Results:* Group shows high degree of enthusiasm; quality and quantity of work are highest of all types of groups; employees show more emotional involvement in their work; there are fewer problems involving disputes between employees; the supervisor can devote more time to planning and constructive leadership [11].

The applicability to teaching of Bradford and Lippitt's description of the four types of leaders is apparent if we substitute the word "teacher" for "leader" or "supervisor" and the word "student" for "employee."

Ruth Cunningham describes five patterns of interaction between teachers and classroom groups:

1. *Adult Rule, Child Obedience.* The teacher employing this pattern assumes that he holds absolute authority and that pupils should comply unquestioningly with his demands. The reaction to this pattern is either one of docile obedience or open hostility.

2. *Planless Catch-as-Catch-Can Pattern.* There is no attempt by the teacher to control or organize the group. The reaction here is one of confusion, insecurity, and keen competition for the control of the group among class members, among small groups in the class, or between the total group and the teacher.

3. *Teacher Planning with Individuals.* Teachers using this approach interpret planning as a process of individual pupil-teacher interaction. Each student in turn plans a course of action with the teacher. Some groups appear to like this, particularly if they like the teacher. But it does not provide opportunities for classes to make progress and to interact as total groups.

4. *Adult-directed Group Planning.* Teachers using this pattern permit group interaction and planning within rigidly defined boundaries. Groups in this situation are able to plan short-range, limited projects, but cannot plan for long-range goals.

5. *Group Self-Management through Group Planning.* This is the ideal. A group that is able to develop goals, plan attainment of goals, cooperate in achieving them, and evaluate its progress in a group that will learn, grow, and develop.

Cunningham notes that good teachers in a democratic society do not limit the scope of their classroom activities to patterns 4 and 5, but rather, are inclined to use whatever pattern happened to be appropriate to the situation at hand. "Thus seemingly less desirable patterns may provide important experiences (if used appropriately), even though patterns 4 and 5 are the ideal [12]."

The patterns we have described so far have a similar basis, in that they involve some elements of autocracy, laissez faire, and democracy. However, Robert N. Bush uses a threefold description of teacher behavior that cannot be fitted easily into these categories. Although the types of teachers he describes are more often found in secondary schools, some of their characteristics typify a great many elementary teachers:

Type A. This type might be called the *academic teacher.* He is primarily interested in subject matter. He would have liked to continue study in his own field. Meanwhile, he tries to keep up with new developments in it. When he goes back to summer school, he much prefers to take courses in his own subject field than in further professional courses. He is often a brilliant teacher of his subject. He is very sensitive about maintaining high standards of workmanship and scholarship; his criteria are usually of college-preparatory level. He does his best job with college-bound students, since they are more likely to do well in his subject and to find it interesting. He does not do much counseling with his students; often knows very little about their home background; is impatient with psychological explanations for poor student work which he is prone to term "excuses." He flunks students with a clear conscience.

Type B. This type might be called the *counselor-teacher.* He is first of all interested in students. He uses subject matter mainly as a way of working with young people; in fact, he often throws traditional subject matter out the window if he finds a substitute that comes nearer to the interests or needs of students. Sometimes his teaching is a little dull in the classroom because he did not spend enough time preparing for it. Most of his attention is devoted to students and their problems and only incidentally to the chores of teaching. He would rather pass all students than fail anyone. He gives grades almost intuitively, because of the effect on the student than for any measurable attainment. He is apt to drive Type A teachers mad on this account, since they can never understand each other's different view of the function of grades and standards. Type B teachers are sometimes extroverts who seem happiest when with a group of people. Sometimes they are sensitive and easily hurt because of their awareness of people, their emotions and motives.

Type C. This kind of teacher might be called the *inspira-*

tional type. Like Type A, he loves his subject field, but on an emotional basis primarily. He is convinced that if people only loved to play music, to paint, to play on the team, then all the ills that troubled them would probably fade away. This is the kind of teacher who will put on marvelous plays and have constant wrangles with the rest of the faculty . . . [because he insists] that the students be released from any and all classes for rehearsals. Obviously taking part in a dramatic production (or playing on the team, or being in the band, or participating in a debate, or putting out the school newspaper, or decorating the gym for a fiesta) is more rewarding to the student's total personality than any class! These teachers are likely to get support from Type B teachers, but Type A teachers resist them to the last breath. A running battle usually goes on all year between this kind of teacher and those who have the students in other academic classes. The inspirational-type teacher usually asks only that students feel the spark, share his enthusiasm for the activity. Then even lack of skill may be forgiven. This teacher, however, may sometimes be impatient with the unskillful and devote most of his time and energy to those who are enthusiastic and talented [13].

Of the three types of teachers described by Bush, Type B is more likely to be group-centered and guidance-minded, but only if he works to promote interaction among members of his group. Otherwise, he may proceed no further along the scale of group-centered behavior than Cunningham's Type 3 (teacher planning with individual students). Bush's types of teachers are extremes, of course, and most teachers in secondary schools represent a blending of the traits and qualities he lists.

Good teachers will be found under any and all of the classifications we have used, provided good instruction is our chief criterion. But if we are deeply concerned about the emotional health of students and the development of classroom conditions favorable to emotional and social maturity as well as intellectual maturity, we shall in future years be looking more to the teachers who may be characterized as guidance-minded, group-centered, and democratic to provide children with the kinds of educational experiences we believe they should have.

REFERENCES

1. K. Lewin, R. Lippitt, and R. K. White, "Patterns of Aggressive Behavior in Experimentally Created 'Social Climates,'" *Journal of Social Psychology.* 10:271–99;1939.
2. L. K. Frank, "The Dilemma of Leadership," *Psychiatry.* 2:343–61;1939.
3. J. Dewey, *Experience and Education.* New York: Macmillan, 1938. Pp. 60–61.
4. N. Cantor, *Learning through Discussion.* Buffalo: Human Relations for Industry, 1951. Pp. 18–20. Reprinted by permission.
5. W. B. Cannon, *The Wisdom of the Body,* rev. ed., New York: Norton, 1939.
6. G. W. Allport, "The Psychologist's Frame of Reference," *Psychological Bulletin.* 37:1–28;1940.
7. D. Snygg and A. W. Combs, *Individual Behavior.* New York: Harper, 1949.
8. K. Goldstein, *Human Nature in the Light of Psychopathology.* Cambridge: Harvard University Press, 1940.
9. M. Heaton, *Feelings Are Facts.* New York: National Conference of Christians and Jews, 1952. Pp. 54–55. Reprinted by permission.
10. G. McL. Abbate, "The Mirror of Children," *Saturday Review.* 36:19; January 31, 1953.
11. L. P. Bradford and R. Lippitt, "Types of Group Leadership," *Personnel.* 22(3):142–48;1945.
12. R. Cunningham, *Understanding Group Behavior of Boys and Girls.* New York: Bureau of Publications, Teachers College, Columbia University, 1951. Pp. 25–30.
13. R. N. Bush, quoted in J. D. Grambs and W. J. Iverson, *Modern Methods in Secondary Education.* New York: William Sloane, 1952. Pp. 520–21. Reprinted by permission.

SUGGESTED READINGS

T. Brameld, *Patterns of Educational Philosophy.* Yonkers-on-Hudson: World Book, 1950. Part 2, "Three Educational Philosophies in Their Cultural Settings."

L. E. Cole and W. F. Bruce, *Educational Psychology*. Yonkers-on-Hudson: World Book, 1950. Part 3, "The Psychology of Learning in a Free Society."

R. A. Davis, *Educational Psychology*. New York: McGraw-Hill, 1948. Part II, "Directing Learning."

J. Dollard and N. E. Miller, *Personality and Psychotherapy*. New York: McGraw-Hill, 1950. Part II, "Basic Principles of Learning."

A. I. Gates *et al.*, *Educational Psychology*, 3d ed. New York: Macmillan, 1948. Chapters 9 and 10, "The General Nature of Learning," and Chapters 11 and 12, "Principles of Guidance in Learning."

J. Grambs and W. Iverson, *Modern Methods in Secondary Education*. New York: Sloane, 1952. Chapter 3, "Developing Democratic Behavior in the Classroom."

N. B. Henry, ed., *Learning and Instruction*, 49th Yearbook, Part I. Chicago: National Society for the Study of Education, 1950.

E. R. Hilgard, *Introduction to Psychology*. New York: Harcourt, Brace, 1953. Chapter 10, "Nature of Learning," and Chapter 11, "The Management of Learning." Easier reading than *Theories of Learning*. Recommended for the reader who wishes a brief overview of learning theory.

————, *Theories of Learning*. New York: Appleton-Century-Crofts, 1948. A scholarly review of learning theories in psychology.

C. Pratt, *I Learn From Children*. New York: Simon and Schuster, 1948. The experiences of a teacher who made her first venture into progressive education fifty years ago.

A. D. Woodruff, *The Psychology of Teaching*, 3d ed. New York: Longmans, Green, 1951. Chapters 15 through 17 deal with the learning process; Part 4 is concerned with the factors that modify learning.

See also items 3, 4, 12, and 13 in the References for this chapter.

SUGGESTED FILMS

Broader Concept of Method: Part 1. Developing Pupil Interest. Contrasts teacher-dominated techniques with ways of achieving broader educational objectives. Available through McGraw-Hill.

Motivating the Class. Available through McGraw-Hill.

12

THE TEACHER AS A PERSON

OF POWER AND AUTHORITY

THE most important person in the classroom, in terms of determining what kinds of experiences children will have, is the teacher. Most of what goes on in a classroom is with direct or indirect reference to the teacher: "Because the teacher wants me to . . ." "What will the teacher think?" "Let's pin this sign on George's back and see what happens." "Did you hear that Sue got an A out of Miss Turlock?" "Come on, kids, we have to make a report on this tomorrow!"

In all these statements the teacher is in evidence. Sometimes the statement is about him, as in the case of the child who is concerned about what the teacher might think; and sometimes he is a psychological force very much in the background, but nevertheless present, as in the case of the boy who wants to pin a sign on George's back. To be sure, the boy wants to see what George will do, but he also is interested in what the teacher will do. Furthermore, his desire to play a prank at this particular time is conditioned by the psychological atmosphere which the teacher has played a part in creating.

Another way of describing this situation is to say that the

teacher is the most powerful person in the classroom, psychologically speaking. His ability to reward and punish is usually greater than that of any individual in the room; he sets the pace; he takes the initiative, or rather, the initiative is his if he wants to take it. The teacher's power is such that even when he does *nothing,* he does *something* to the class. He even has an effect on the class when he is not present.

In psychological terminology, the teacher is "an authority figure." He is a repository of power because other persons of greater power and authority have assigned him the role of supervising children and have given him the power and freedom to carry out his responsibilities. And many of his successes and failures as a teacher are the result of how he uses his power.

There are a number of roles which teachers play in using their power. There is the role of the parent, the role of the supervisor or "boss," the role of the professional expert, and the role of the guidance worker and therapist.

Many teachers, particularly in the lower grades, are aware that they have parent-like qualities, at least in the eyes of the children in their classes. For example, children often accept the teacher's evaluations and pronouncements with a kind of finality— "It's so because the teacher says it's so." Sometimes this blind acceptance of the teacher as an authority figure produces a conflict in the mind of the child, particularly when parents and teachers are in disagreement. In some respects parents and teachers are conflicting authority figures to the extent that they compete for the control of the child. In this way they enact the drama of society versus the family, with the teacher representing the demands of society. In other respects—and this is more common—the teacher represents an extension of parental authority to the child. The child sees the teacher as making the same sorts of demands that his parents make and therefore tends to view them in the same light. This leads many children to behave toward teachers much as they do toward their parents.

CHILDREN REGARD PARENTS AND TEACHERS IN THE SAME LIGHT

THE psychological term which is applied to this kind of development is "transference." In effect, the child is "transferring" the attitudes and behavior which he displays toward his parents to the teacher; he is acting as though his parent and his teacher were the same person. In reality, of course, they are not. Even though his teacher's attitudes resemble those of his parents in some respects, it is certain that they do not resemble them in every respect. Because the teacher is a different person with a different personality, his expectations of a given child are bound to be different from those of the child's parents. Yet many children, particularly children who are emotionally disturbed, insist on making this mistaken identification.

Robert was a child of this sort. The youngest child of three, he was his mother's favorite. She always had the best of intentions. She really did not mean to indulge him, but always found herself giving in when he put up any fuss. When Robert went to school, the teacher made demands on him. She asked him to copy the numbers in the workbook. Robert tried this for a while, but it was hard and he found it more interesting to write his name instead. The teacher was disappointed and said so. Robert just smiled at her because he knew that it wasn't very important and that she would get over it. After all, she was his "mother" at school.

But the teacher did not get over it. As the days wore on, she made more and more demands on Robert. She asked him to try to read and to spell. She asked him to pick up the blocks and to help the other children put away the things in the doll corner. Sometimes Robert would try for a while, but usually he would wander off and do as he pleased because he "knew" that the teacher would not mind.

Inevitably, Robert was punished. He had to stay in during recess. He had to stay after school till he had picked up the blocks. He could not go with the other children to see a puppet show. But Robert's faith in his "school mother" never wavered. He was puzzled and unhappy when he was punished, but he consoled himself with his steadfast belief that she didn't mean it and that next time it would be different.

When Robert arrived in the third grade, he had not learned to read and had not developed fundamental number concepts. He was causing more difficulty in the classroom because he was demanding more and more of the teacher's time and had developed the technique of teasing other children until he received the attention he craved. His third-grade teacher was less tolerant and permissive than his first- and second-grade teachers. She scolded him when he refused to try and sent him to the principal's office when he played tricks on the other children and refused to carry out the tasks she assigned. But Robert's attitude did not change. He still acted as though he expected the teacher to change her mind at the last minute and not require him to finish his assignment or learn the words on the spelling list. He always seemed surprised when she insisted that he complete his work and live up to his responsibilities. Apparently he could not understand why she was angry and reprimanded him.

Although Robert's inability to differentiate adequately between his teacher and his mother is extreme, it is not unusual. However, most children are more realistic than Robert, and although they may halfway hope for or expect the same treatment from their teachers that they receive from their parents, they recognize the more essential differences in the two kinds of relationships. Robert's problem is a difficult one; it will not be solved either by permitting him to "get away with it," or by punishing him for being disobedient. Very likely he needs the professional attention he would get in a child-guidance clinic.

Another form of transference is the tendency of children to regard the other children in the classroom as brothers and sisters with whom they must compete for the attention and approval of the teacher. A certain amount of this sort of "sibling rivalry" is the norm in most families, and usually it is held in check by sensible parents or even by the children themselves. Since children are used to this pattern of life at home, it is probably inevitable that they should transfer this relationship to the classroom, particularly if they already tend to look upon the teacher as a sort of substitute parent. However, the sooner children realize that the classroom is not a family and that the skills which are useful in sibling rivalry are not appropriate to the more group-oriented activities of the school, the sooner they will be able to profit from their classroom experiences.

TEACHERS HAVE TROUBLE WITH
TRANSFERENCE TOO

THE problem of transference is one which is not confined to children, although it is easier for the teacher to observe children in the act of "transferring" than it is for him to realize that he, too, has transference difficulties. These difficulties appear in a variety of forms. One of the commonest is that of "counter-transference." Mr. Bledsoe's clash with Robin will serve as an example.

Before Mr. Bledsoe met his new fourth grade, he had been warned about Robin.

"Robin," Mrs. Larue, the principal, told him, "is a bitter, sullen child. Her parents were divorced when she was three, and she went to live with her father. After a year or two he married a woman who had two boys, both older than Robin. Robin's stepmother does not give Robin one-tenth the attention she gives her boys, and her father is away from home much of the time. When he does come home, he usually takes his stepsons golfing or fishing. Robin has never heard from her own mother since the divorce."

Mr. Bledsoe interrupted at this point. "Haven't we been able to get her parents to give her a little more attention?"

Mrs. Larue was silent for a moment. "We have asked them to come in several times to discuss Robin's work. We didn't want to mention her behavior, because we were afraid that we would get her into trouble, and she has trouble enough, poor child. Well, her father never came. Her stepmother came twice, but she really wasn't very interested. She feels that Robin is a very stubborn little girl and that no one can do much with her."

She paused and then continued. "The reason I wanted to talk to you about Robin, Mr. Bledsoe, is not only that she has these difficulties at home and will therefore need a lot of understanding from the school, but also that she is a child who will say and do things which seem deliberately aimed at getting other children and the teacher angry. She doesn't do this very often, but she seems to pick a time when a chance remark of the wrong kind will cause the most difficulty."

During the first few weeks of the term, Mr. Bledsoe tried to be friendly to Robin, but without much success. There was no question about it, she was a difficult child to work with. She just would *not* communicate. As the weeks rolled by, he became immersed in other problems. Robin's work was about average for her grade and she gave him a little trouble, though not enough to notice. He was somewhat irritated when she refused to recite, but remembering her difficulties, he yielded to her refusals and called on someone else.

One morning the fourth grade got a new student, a Negro girl from an out-of-state school. Mr. Bledsoe seated her next to Robin and then went about the business of conducting class. After recess, the new girl came to him in tears and said that Robin had been making fun of her color and her way of talking.

Now, for the first time, Mr. Bledsoe was genuinely angry at Robin. If there was anything he could not stomach, it was race prejudice. No sooner had the class assembled, than he called them to order and gave them a lecture on tolerance and the evils of race prejudice. He did not mention Robin by name, but he looked at her a couple of times. She did not look at him, but stared at her desk. Thinking back on the incident, he wondered whether it was the best thing to do. The new girl seemed very uncomfortable when he was talking, and all the class craned their necks to look at her when he had finished.

An hour or so later, the class was on a social studies unit

which involved some writing on the board. As they were discussing the material on the blackboard, Mr. Bledsoe noticed that one of the children had mispelled the word "separate," using three "e's" and one "a." He started to correct the word and then realized, to his horror, that he could not remember whether the "p" or the "r" should be doubled or not. He tried writing it with two "p's." That didn't look right either. He was just starting to erase it again, when he heard Robin say:

"I don't think you know how to spell that word."

Mr. Bledsoe felt as though something had exploded inside his brain. He wanted to hit her. Fortunately, he was able to control himself, and his voice had almost no emotion in it as he said:

"Robin, leave the class and go down to see Mrs. Larue."

Mr. Bledsoe himself dropped into Mrs. Larue's office after school. He had to force himself to do it, yet he knew it was the only thing under the circumstances. On the other hand, he felt as though he wanted to talk to someone about the incident. He felt as though he was very much to blame—after all, he *knew* what Robin was going through at home, and Mrs. Larue had warned him about her. Furthermore, he had promised himself that he would try to succeed with Robin where other teachers had failed. And now he, too, had failed.

When he had finished describing the events of the morning, he sat back and waited for Mrs. Larue to confirm his feeling that he was entirely to blame for the incident. Instead, she said mildly,

"I *could* tell you that you ought to know that when Robin acts this way, she is not attacking you, but the parent she thinks you are. It is her way of getting back at her parents. I *could* say that you should therefore not be angry. Yet I know that it is very difficult to keep this in mind when you are in front of a class and a child makes a verbal attack on you when you have not yet recovered from the jolt she gave you an hour previously. No, Mr. Bledsoe, as long as we teachers are human, we are bound to make some mistakes, and I think I know you well enough to say that I don't think you make many mistakes like this one. Furthermore, with the kind of relations you have with your class, you know this is not going to make any real difference to them."

"But I am more concerned about Robin. Life for her is very difficult, and as long as it is difficult, she is going to make trouble for other children and, of course, for teachers like you and me. I think I will ask the county psychologist to put Robin on her waiting list, although, frankly, I shall be surprised if it does much good—unless, of course, the situation improves at home."

Mr. Bledsoe's experience has been shared by many a teacher who has been irritated or angered by the verbal attack of a child who identifies and confuses the teacher with his parents. It is difficult for a teacher at such times to realize that the child is attacking not this teacher in particular, but authority figures or adults in general. Although the child's remarks may be "personal" in nature, there is nothing personal about his motivation. The reprimand or other form of punishment which usually follows such an attack does not help the teacher to understand the situation and seldom helps the student to improve his behavior. It may, of course, relieve the feelings of the teacher, and sometimes this is understandably urgent. However, once the incident is passed, it should not be allowed to stand in the way of the development of better relations and improved communication.

MISINTERPRETING CHILDREN'S BEHAVIOR

An important thing, then, for us to understand about transference is that it leads teachers to misinterpret the behavior of the children in their classes. An extreme example of this is that of the teacher who believes that children can never be trusted. An equally extreme example is that of the teacher who believes that children never cheat. Each of these evaluations is unrealistic and is a distortion of the real situation. A common example of such distortion is that of the teacher who says that all the girls in her class love her, but the boys must hate her because they act like demons. When we observe her classes, we come to the conclusion that her pupils are all afraid of her, but the girls, being more submissive than the boys, express their fear by asking her questions and by making a show of being pleasant to her, whereas the boys express their fear through rebellion.

Because transference is so much a part of us, it is very unlikely that we shall see how we tend to make certain consistent misinterpretations of children's behavior even when these tendencies are pointed out to us. Only too few of us have the insight and humility displayed by Mr. Bledsoe following his difficulties with Robin. One hopeful note is that as we become more mature and more experienced as teachers, we may become more aware of our tendencies to misinterpret the behavior and attitudes of children and thereby become more objective. Hence, we must not be too unsympathetic when we observe that children consistently misinterpret *our* attitudes and intentions.

Such misinterpretations are not limited to the relations between teachers and students. Mason Haire and Willa Grunes conducted an experiment whereby they asked college students to write paragraphs describing a factory worker, basing their description on a list of characteristics supplied by the experimenters. One group of students was supplied with a list that included the word "intelligent"; the other list was identical except that it did not include the word "intelligent." Students who were supplied with the first list had difficulty in describing the worker because the concept of intelligence did not fit in very well with their stereotyped preconception of a factory worker. Some reacted by omitting the idea of intelligence from their descriptions; others used the concept but felt called upon to explain why an "intelligent" person would be working in a factory; and still others made large alterations in the personality of the worker. In general, students attempted to maintain their original stereotyped concept of a factory worker and resisted inclusion of the idea that he could be intelligent [1]. The students in this experiment are like teachers who have fixed ideas of what children are like and maintain these concepts in spite of evidence to the contrary, or like children who endow teachers with the personal qualities of their parents and who maintain these concepts in spite of the fact that their teachers may behave quite differently from their parents.

Another study which is of interest here is the experiment conducted by Harold H. Kelley, who introduced a substitute instructor to several economics classes in college by informing half the students in each section (using a mimeographed description) that the instructor was "a rather cold person" and the other half that he was "a very warm person." During the discussion that took place, it was observed that students who had been informed that the instructor was "warm" participated more than those who were informed that he was "cold." After the discussion period, students were asked to evaluate the instructor. Their reactions here showed that the two groups viewed the instructor quite differently [2].

This study shows the importance of first impressions in subsequent reactions to people. No one knows how much of what goes on in groups is conditioned by first impressions, but they doubtless play a large part in the kind of interaction that takes place between students and teacher and in the evaluations that both teachers and students make of each other.

SHARING POWER AND RESPONSIBILITY

One of the problems experienced by most persons who have power and authority is that of motivating the individuals they supervise. This is a problem which is shared by parents, teachers, administrators, army officers—in short, by anyone who controls, directs, or guides the activities of others. One reason why this problem is so difficult is that the person in authority is repeatedly faced by the need to decide how much freedom to allow his subordinates. The usual practice followed by persons in authority may be phrased, "When in doubt, restrict freedom." Any person who has had the supervision of children knows that there are times when freedom must be restricted in order to help them establish better controls. The question in this discussion is whether freedom should *continually* be restricted.

Some "authority figures" are always in doubt, always insecure. This means that the freedom of those they supervise is constantly restricted. Indeed, it can be predicted that the greater the insecurity of the person in authority, the more likely he is to restrict the freedom of those he supervises. One of the best examples of this is the reluctance of many parents to permit adolescents to make any decisions or to take any actions on their own responsibility. When such parents begin to see that their children have reached an age at which they can begin to make decisions and act independently, they become anxious and worried for fear that their children might make some mistakes, overlooking the fact that making mistakes is a necessary part of the learning process. To be sure, parents are often plagued by other worries, not the least of which is fear of getting old. Thus a common pattern is for the parent of an adolescent to take a tighter grip, so to speak, on the life of his child, partly because he needs to reassure himself that the fact that his child is growing up does not mean that he (the parent) is growing old, and partly because he does not trust the child to learn how to make proper decisions and take responsibilities.

Nor are parents the only offenders. Supervisors and administrators in business, industry, and government service are often afraid to give their subordinates any responsibility. Again, the rule holds true: the greater the insecurity of the person in authority, the more likely he is to limit the freedom and responsibility of the persons he supervises. Insecure authority figures appear to get a sort of perverse neurotic pleasure out of deciding that their underlings cannot be trusted, which means that the person in charge ends up by making all decisions. However, before we become too unsympathetic, we should realize that being an administrator means subjecting oneself to the kinds of pressures and demands that produce insecurities. In other words, not all the insecurity experienced by persons in authority is of a neurotic origin.

HELPING CHILDREN TO LEARN RESPONSIBILITY

It is an important part of the job of the teacher to help children learn how to make decisions for themselves, to accept responsibility for their own decisions and actions, and to make constructive use of increasing amounts of freedom. This task calls for a great deal of skill, understanding, and emotional maturity. Each teacher has to decide for himself how much freedom he wants his class to have. His problem is complicated by the great variation among individual children as to their readiness for freedom, as well as by the variation among the classes he teaches. Since most of us have some minor neurotic problems which keep us from being as effective and as emotionally mature as we would like to be, we must cope with our own tendencies to restrict the freedom of children more than is necessary or desirable. Still another factor which operates to make our situation even more difficult, is that there are citizens in every community who believe that the way to help children grow into responsible citizens is to restrict their freedom for thought and action more than whatever the local practice happens to be. In other words, even if the schools in the community restrict children more than is desirable, these people will want even tighter and more rigid restrictions and controls. Indeed, their remedy for any educational problem is to impose even greater restrictions. Fortunately, most persons of this persuasion are a minority in most communities; however, they are usually a highly vocal minority. Since they do not hesitate to speak up and make their views known, they are likely to exert more influence with school boards and administrators than their number would lead one to expect.

Thus the teacher who is trying to give children opportunities to think and act for themselves is hampered by the great variability among children and classes, his own more or less neurotic tendencies, and the feeling of some members of the community that school children have too much freedom anyhow. It is little wonder that most children get insufficient opportunity to practice the skills of democratic living.

THE TEACHER AS A PERSON OF POWER AND EXPERTNESS

WE HAVE said that the teacher is a person of power and authority in his classroom, whose success will depend on how he uses his power and authority. Erich Fromm points out in *Man for Himself* that authority which is based solely on power, that is, solely on the ability to control and direct others, is not a healthy kind of authority, whereas authority which is based on competence, that is the ability to help others to grow emotionally and intellectually and to become more productive and useful, is a healthy type of authority [3].

S. A. Szurek, noted psychiatrist, has expanded on Fromm's concepts of authority as follows:

In one type of relationship—which might be called *authoritarian*—coercive power, whatever its nature, is exercised by the dominant person primarily for his own rather than the subordinate's immediate gain. The power is exercised to the end that the status quo of the relation in these terms be continued forever, or for as long as possible. In simpler terms it is an enslavement, an effort by the dominant person to maintain control of the slave's services, deference, admiration, or whatever is demanded. Only such care is given, only such concessions or attention to the inferior person's welfare and needs are made by the dominant one as will enhance or assure the continuation of the benefits and profit to the latter. Certainly there is no concern or interest in the development of the inferior's potential abilities or strength, for this might endanger the relationship or lead to freedom for the inferior [4]. . . .

Szurek contrasts the authoritarian relationship with the opposite approach, which he calls *authoritative*. He describes this more democratic relationship in the following terms:

> Coercion is absent. The authority derives from superior competence and skill. As in the best teacher-student or ideal parent-child relations, the purpose of both persons in the situation is to promote and foster the acquisition by the subordinate of the competence and skill of the authority. Their common effort is to grow more alike in respect to the power which the competence brings and eventually to achieve equality and genuine freedom of each other. Admiration and deep respect is mutual. . . . Rather than envy, the good teacher or ideal parent manifests genuine delight if the student or child approaches or even begins to surpass his own competence [5]. . . .

If Fromm and Szurek are to be believed, it appears that teachers who operate by power alone are not likely to be effective teachers, whereas teachers who depend upon their skill as artists in human relations and as experts in organizing and presenting the curriculum are likely to succeed—that is, children are likely to learn under their direction and guidance.

This does not mean that the teacher should avoid the use of power, for there are times when children need direction and control. Perhaps the test should be: Why is power being used here—on whose behalf? Is the teacher using power to help children, or is he using it for his own convenience or to reduce some of his own anxieties? Sometimes, of course, the anxieties of the teacher are of immediate, though temporary importance, whereupon he invokes controls in order to maintain his own equilibrium or peace of mind. However, the more that the teacher considers his needs to control the class and the less he makes his decisions on the basis of the *real* needs of children, the more difficulty he will have in creating a classroom situation conducive to learning. This principle is applicable to any sort of human relationship— the more we are concerned about our *own* feelings (which means that we become proportionately less concerned about the feelings of others), the less effective we become.

Kenneth D. Benne indicates two of the ways that a skilled teacher exercises skill and authority in helping a group become more mature:

> A group of children planning a party may get into a snarl of competing ideas as to what games should be played. An immature group may give up and leave it to teacher to decide or may break into aggressive griping and name-calling. A mature group would probably stop and see that it had run into its snarl when John and Mary had started calling each other's ideas crazy and then start over to reach a common decision or some acceptable compromise. In this case, a leadership function in the immature group is to help the group look at its own ways of working and to see the relationship between these and the making of satisfactory plans.
>
> Again, members of an immature group in choosing members to do some job find it hard to distinguish between persons they like or dislike and persons with the abilities required to get the job done well. A mature group is able to distinguish between "personalities" and the roles required for productive group work. The group of children which chooses members for a committee to make posters not because they can draw but because they are likeable and "popular" has not attained much maturity as a group. A function of leadership here is to help the group see that contributions are to be judged in terms of their relevance to getting a job done well, not in terms of the person who happens to make the contributions [6].

Nathaniel Cantor suggests three generalizations that describe the behavior of the skilled teacher-leader who uses his skill and authority in working with groups that are emotionally and socially mature. His ideas, somewhat paraphrased, are as follows:

1. The teacher-leader is essentially a helper, not a master. He is not there to control the class or be controlled by it, but to be used by it. Both the teacher-leader and the class have responsibilities: his is to direct the movement of learning, inasmuch as he is the one who understands the learning process; the responsibility of the members of the class is to use the class situation and the leader to further their development. Cantor says: "Responsibility for the course cannot be forced upon or demanded from the members without perverting their growth. Genuine learning is always, in the final analysis, self-motivated."

2. The teacher-leader must remember that the class members' feelings and problems are important, not his own. "The need to be right, to have one's way, to play God, is unfortunately so much a part of most adults and leaders that it becomes the outstanding obstacle in acquiring professional discussion skill."

3. The teacher-leader who recognizes that constructive effort must come from creative forces within the individual member, will recognize the importance of the needs of that member and will accept his differences. In other words, he will not attempt to force needless conformity to some pre-conceived pattern [7].

ROLES PLAYED BY TEACHERS

TEACHERS employ a variety of roles in dealing with the situations which the teaching day presents. Some of these roles involve more of the expert and some involve more of the authority figure or power-wielder.

One of these roles is that of the *group conscience*. In this role, the teacher reminds students of moral standards, responsibilities, and accepted norms of behavior. Sometimes he plays this role by lecturing students about cheating on tests, sometimes he raises a discreet question at a strategic point in a group discussion, a point that causes students to stop and re-examine what they have been saying or proposing, and sometimes he plays this role merely by being present in the classroom.

Another role is that of the *evaluator*. The teacher plays this role when he gives tests and examinations, assigns grades, and discusses learning problems with individual students. These are the more obvious expressions of this role and are a part of the behavior pattern of most teachers. A less obvious way of playing this role, but one that is highly desirable from the standpoint of promoting learning, is in helping students to evaluate themselves—to find out how far they have come in their learning and how far they must go, to find out what their strengths and weaknesses are. Criticism by another person (e.g., a teacher) is hard to accept; there is a natural tendency to defend oneself against the criticism and to reject it as a basis for self-improvement. However, if students can learn to evaluate themselves objectively, they stand a better chance of promoting real self-improvement.

Most teachers can readily see themselves in the role of the *academic expert,* since everyone expects the teacher to be the best-informed person in the classroom. However, this, too, is a role that is played with a difference. For some teachers, being an expert means that one goes out of one's way to impress children with the extent of one's knowledge. Usually this is a mild form of exhibitionism that, like other forms of exhibitionism, is a way of compensating for feelings of inferiority. Being an expert to some teachers means that the teacher is always right and never wrong. For others, the role of the expert is a subdued one because the teacher believes that it is better for students to find out things for themselves, rather than being told by the teacher. Consequently, the expert knowledge of the teacher appears in the guidance given students in helping them to find out things for themselves, or, on occasions, it appears when the superior knowledge of the teacher would aid children in organizing their information into larger concepts.

Most teachers do not like to think of themselves as *policemen,* yet this is a role that must sometimes be played. It is sometimes necessary to restrain physical aggression, to prevent the destruction of property, and to ferret out information leading to the identification of culprits in order to prevent continued misbehavior. Even among the best behaved children rules are broken or injuries inflicted, whereupon everyone expects the teacher to take action. Like the other roles we have described, the role of policeman can be overplayed; some teachers apparently regard it as their most important role. Other teachers make the mistake of trying to avoid the unpleasant responsibilities associated with the role and may even endanger morale by overlooking obvious misbehavior that is raising the anxiety level of the group to dangerous heights.

Another role with unpleasant associations is that of the *scapegoat.* It is inevitable that teachers be blamed occasionally for mistakes and deficiencies that are no fault of their own. Yet this is a role that teachers share with all leaders, inasmuch as there seems to be a universal tendency for subordinates to blame leaders for things that go wrong. If teachers can accept this as part of the inevitable price that leaders must pay for power and status, it may help them to avoid feeling martyred or that their students are unusually unappreciative of their efforts. It is somewhat reassuring to know that there is really nothing personal about such undeserved blame and criticism—it is a more or less normal part of being a teacher. According to Redl and Wattenberg,

. . . . Many teachers must cope with some juvenile ill-will that has nothing to do with the teacher's personality or procedures. Because it may be undeserved, it often hurts badly, unless its origin is realized. There is no escaping this role; the best we can do is to play it in such a way that children learn how to express hostility feelings in more socially acceptable and conflict-free ways [8].

Many teachers see themselves in the role of a *friend* to students who need help with personal problems. However, as we learned from the study of Jenkins and Lippitt we discussed earlier, students are not very likely to perceive teachers in this role [9]. Ruth Cunningham found that only three students out of a group of thirty-three fourth- and fifth-grade children said they would go to a teacher with their personal problems. Only two students in an eighth-grade group said they would discuss their problems with a teacher [10].

The list of teacher roles is endless, inasmuch as there is such a variety of behavior patterns which students, parents, administrators, and teachers themselves expect of teachers. Some of the roles that Ruth Cunningham describes show penetrating insights into the personal and professional lives of teachers:

> *Enemy:* This is a teacher who is identified by students as one to be fought and outwitted in battle. Elaborate strategies are developed to outwit and plague the teacher who plays this role.
>
> *Kill-joy.* A teacher earns this label by continually opposing or preventing pleasurable activities of students by interposing some demand or objection that appears to have no reasonable basis.
>
> *Devil.* Teachers who harass students by making petty, annoying requests, who insist on conformity to meaningless rituals earn the respect, fear, and hostility that goes with this role.
>
> *Security-giver.* The teacher who is perceived in this role is one who is able to convey to a group the feeling of his faith in them or who has been able to meet the frustrated needs and interests of his students. The power of a teacher to provide reassurance to his group is great when he plays this role successfully. However, the teacher who overplays it is likely to develop overdependent attitudes and behavior in his students.
>
> *Hero.* Children often designate a well-liked teacher as a hero, often on the basis of personal attractiveness or local fame but sometimes because of deeper and more enduring qualities.

The likelihood of such a role being assigned to a teacher depends on the extent to which the teacher exemplifies or personifies the values deemed important by the group [11].

One of the concepts we have attempted to stress in the last few chapters is the importance of the teacher playing the role of the group leader, a function that parallels or, at times, even supersedes the role of the adult helping individual children to learn. This is one of the reasons why teachers need such a good understanding of what happens in groups. Because every teacher is a group leader, the following comment of Rudolph M. Wittenburg, writing from his extensive experience as a leader of youth groups, is pertinent:

> Group leaders need more knowledge of behavior—more knowledge of mental hygiene—more than most people, because they do not work with one individual, but always with several. All leaders agree that the real secret of success is in their awareness of the interactions that take place among the members of their group [12].

Trow, Zander, Morse, and Jenkins, in an analysis of the classroom situation from the standpoint of the psychology of group behavior, identified three kinds of roles that teachers must play in order to develop and maintain the participation of group members in the learning process: (1) the instructional role, (2) the role of the democratic strategist, and (3) the role of the therapist.

The *instructional role* is much like that of the *academic expert*, described above. Trow and his co-workers point out that this role has changed, in the last generation or so, from that of a drillmaster or taskmaster to that of a "resource person" who explains, tells, and demonstrates, who helps to foster the students' power to think and reason.

In the role of the *democratic strategist* the teacher helps his classroom group to clarify their goals and objectives and to evaluate and appraise their accomplishments, failures, and progress. Playing this role also includes arranging situations that help the group experience democratic goals and relationships in their everyday classroom experiences.

In the role of *therapist* Trow and his co-workers see the teacher as a combined clinician and group worker. In this role, the teacher manages the group to the end of helping children toward social and emotional adjustment. Successful playing of this role involves permissiveness, establishing rapport with children, and not permitting one's feelings and sensitivities to get in the way of one's relations with children. Trow and his collaborators feel that teachers play this role least adequately of all, and that they tend, rather, to be moralists, policemen, or punitive agents who expect good character to be developed by decree. It is the inability to play the role of the therapist properly, say these writers, that leads to failure [13].

CONTRADICTIONS IN ROLES

Many of the roles which teachers find themselves playing are inherently contradictory. For example, a teacher may serve as the friend and confidant of a child one day and the next day become a policeman who reprimands or punishes the same child. Or the teacher may serve in one instance as a democratic group leader, helping children to take some responsibility for working out the solution of a problem which concerns them, and then, later in the same day, he may be forced to adopt the role of an autocratic leader, who has to enforce a rule which allows for no exceptions and which neither the teacher nor the children had any part in making. Contradictions of this sort are inevitable in teaching. Sometimes they seem wholly illogical, and they certainly are one of the chief sources of tension and anxiety in our somewhat nerve-racking profession. One of our tasks in maintaining psychological balance and thus preserving our mental health is to look for some of the basic similarities in the several roles we play—to resolve some of the contradictions, so to speak.

For instance, perhaps these roles are not so contradictory. Perhaps they are just some of the different ways we must behave in our attempts to help children to learn, to help them to grow up to be useful and mentally healthy citizens.

THE DIVIDED RESPONSIBILITIES OF TEACHERS

There is an additional reason why teachers must play roles which seem to be in conflict. The teacher is responsible to several groups, agencies, institutions, and individuals, whose aims are similar in some respects but differing in others. At any given moment, the teacher's behavior is likely to be dominated by one sort of allegiance to the partial exclusion of his other responsibilities.

Perhaps the chief responsibility of the teacher is to the children under his supervision. Their welfare is paramount. Yet, he cannot base all his decisions on their welfare alone, for the welfare of others is also involved. Or, rather, let us say that he cannot base his decisions on *his interpretation* of the welfare of his pupils because his view of their needs will differ somewhat from the view held by the administrators of the school, and this, in turn, may be somewhat at variance with the view of pupil needs held by the community. So far we have four considerations which enter into the making of a decision regarding what is done in the classroom: How do the children view this situation? How do I view the situation? How would the administrator view it? How would the community view it?

Actually, we can see five elements because the teacher may have one reaction as an individual and a somewhat different reaction as a member of the educational profession.

Usually we do not break our decisions down into precise classifications according to the nature of our responsibilities; most of us "do our duties as we see them." Nevertheless, the variations in our roles and the apparent contradictions in emphases reveal our awareness of the different kinds of responsibilities which are ours. Let us take Miss Clements as an example of how a teacher may alter his roles and general behavior without violating the essential unity of his teaching.

Miss Clements' second grade started the day with pledging allegiance to the flag. There was no conflict in roles here as she led the group in the pledge. It gave the children something familiar with which to begin the day; it sounded a note of security, so to speak. Furthermore, it helped give children a feeling of unity and identity with that larger community which is the nation. And certainly the administration and the community were in accord here.

A half hour later, the children were engaged in their reading lesson. Miss Clements played a dual role here—she presented the material which had been selected for the grade by persons in higher authority and she helped children who were having difficulty with their reading. But she did not feel that the reader was an appropriate one for her class. Its subject matter was focused on the lives of upper-middle-class children, children who have lawns to play on, who go to the mountains and the seashore for vacations, and whose fathers are business and professional men who wear suits and white collars. The children in *her* class are drawn almost entirely from the industrial section of a large city. They have no grass around their flats and apartments; vacations in the country are almost unknown, and their fathers do not wear business suits and white shirts to work. Miss Clements often wondered what they really got out of books which presented such unfamiliar concepts. The vocabulary of the text seemed difficult for most of her pupils, too.

In this instance, the aims of the administration and the needs of the children are somewhat at variance. Miss Clements does all she can by sympathizing with children who find the text too difficult, by giving them as much help as possible, and by providing temporary relief for a few children through giving them brief periods of reading easier materials. But in the main she has no real choice—she must play the role of presenting this part of the curriculum to the children very much as recommended by the administration.

An hour or so later found Miss Clements in a different role. Three of the children came in from recess crying. A bunch of sixth-grade boys had chased them in back of the school and had pushed them down. A dozen or so of the second graders had observed the incident but were afraid to intervene. As the children entered the room, they were quite wrought up about the matter. Miss Clements made a mental note to report the incident to the principal, but she knew that little could be done with the school as overcrowded as it was. The lesson plan called for a review of basic number concepts during the half hour after recess, but Miss Clements could see that the children were so upset by the incident that little learning would result. She decided that it was more important to help the children calm down, so she conducted a discussion for a while: How does it feel when someone in the group is being attacked by a larger child? How do you suppose this happened? Why do you suppose the bigger boys did this? What should second graders do when something like this happens?

At first the children all wanted to talk at once, to say how bad the big boys were and what should be done to punish them, but after a while they seemed to be aware that second graders probably shouldn't have been wandering out on the basketball court and that if teachers who supervise the recess play period do not happen to see an occurrence like this, it is legitimate for a group of children to call their attention to what is going on. Miss Clements was pleased with her discussion because she had to say very little. The children seemed quite capable of working out good solutions to their problem—at least in the classroom. And she had hopes that someday some of them would be able to put into practice the kinds of solutions they would develop through such discussions.

We note that in this instance, Miss Clements is playing the role of the group leader as well as that of a friend of children. She feels that for the moment the welfare of the class is more important than the prescribed curriculum. In the final analysis, the curriculum will be better off because of her choice. To have forced the children to review numbers at that particular moment would probably have awakened the hostility of the group. To be sure, their response would only have been one of apathy, but Miss Clements knows that apathy may be a form of hostility and that no one learns who is apathetic.

Miss Clements is not deeply disturbed because she has to play conflicting roles at various times during the day. She might wish that she could always play roles which were attuned to the needs of her children, yet she is realistic enough to know that this can never be. True, she is annoyed that she has to use reading materials which are inappropriate for her children, and perhaps, if she has the opportunity, she will speak up in favor of a change. Yet she knows that she can do an adequate job in spite of the inadequate reader. And because she is a flexible person and can keep her main objective in mind (helping children to learn) while playing her many roles, she is a succesful teacher.

REFERENCES

1. M. Haire and W. F. Grunes, "Perceptual Defenses: Processes Protecting an Organized Perception of Another Personality," *Human Relations.* 3:403–12;1950.
2. H. H. Kelley, "The Warm-Cold Variable in First Impressions of Persons," *Journal of Personality.* 18:431–39;1950.
3. E. Fromm, *Man for Himself.* New York: Rinehart, 1947. P. 9.
4. S. A. Szurek, "Emotional Factors in the Use of Authority," in E. A. Ginsburg, ed., *Public Health Is People.* New York: Commonwealth Fund, 1950. P. 212. Reprinted by permission.
5. *Ibid.* P. 213. Reprinted by permission.
6. K. D. Benne, "Leaders Are Made, Not Born," *Childhood Education.* 24:203–08;1948. Reprinted by permission.
7. N. Cantor, *Learning through Discussion.* Buffalo: Human Relations for Industry, 1951. Pp. 48–50. Portions reprinted by permission.
8. F. Redl and W. W. Wattenberg, *Mental Hygiene in Teaching.* New York: Harcourt, Brace, 1951. P. 241. Copyright, 1951, by Harcourt, Brace and Company, Inc. Reprinted by permission.
9. D. H. Jenkins and R. Lippitt, *Interpersonal Perceptions of Teachers, Students, and Parents.* Washington: National Education Association, 1951. Chapter 4.

10. R. Cunningham, *et al., Understanding Group Behavior of Boys and Girls.* New York: Bureau of Publications, Teachers College, Columbia University, 1951. P. 148.

11. *Ibid.* Pp. 142–46.

12. R. M. Wittenberg, *So You Want to Help People.* New York: Association Press, 1947. P. xiii.

13. W. C. Trow, A. E. Zander, W. C. Morse, and D. H. Jenkins, "Psychology of Group Behavior: The Class as a Group," *Journal of Educational Psychology.* 41:322–38;1950.

SUGGESTED READINGS

D. Baruch, *New Ways in Discipline.* New York: McGraw-Hill, 1949.

A. W. Gouldner, ed., *Studies in Leadership: Leadership and Democratic Action.* New York: Harper, 1950.

H. Guetzkow, ed., *Groups, Leadership, and Men.* New Brunswick, N. J.: Rutgers University Press, 1951.

E. L. Hartley and R. E. Hartley, *Fundamentals of Social Psychology.* New York: Knopf, 1952. Chapter 19, "Leadership-Followership."

C. Kluckhohn, "Student-Teacher," in I. Leighton, ed., *The People in Your Life.* New York: Knopf, 1951.

H. C. Lindgren, *The Art of Human Relations.* New York: Hermitage, 1953. Chapter 11, "Why We Strive for Power and Status."

M. Sherif and C. W. Sherif, *Groups in Harmony and Tension.* New York: Harper, 1953.

G. Sheviakov and F. Redl, *Discipline for Today's Children and Youth.* Washington: National Education Association, 1944.

G. E. Swanson, T. M. Newcomb, and E. L. Hartley, eds., *Readings in Social Psychology,* rev. ed. New York: Holt, 1952. Part IIID, "Leader-Follower Roles."

P. M. Symonds, *Dynamic Psychology.* New York: Appleton-Century-Crofts, 1949. Chapter 13, "Identification."

See also items 3, 7, 8, 10, 12, and 13 in the References for this chapter.

13

THE RELATIONSHIP OF THE TEACHER TO THE CLASS-ROOM GROUP

PROBABLY most persons who are charged with the supervision of others wish, at times, that they had more power. They feel that if they only had more power, they could do a better job. For example, in the anecdote that ended the previous chapter, Miss Clements probably wishes that she had the power to select her own reading materials for her class. Or she wishes that she had the power to remove her class from their overcrowded school to one where they would not have to play in the proximity of sixth-grade boys. Mr. Dial, who teaches the fifth grade, wishes that he were permitted to "tan the hides" of some of the boys in his class. He has tried everything—bribes, flattery, scolding, bad marks, letters to parents, dismissal from class—and he is at the end of his rope. He does not see how he can get the results that are expected unless he can take forthright measures of his own. Mrs. Kindler wishes she had the power to "hold back" a quarter of her second graders, but the policy of the school is that all children shall be promoted automatically. "After all," she says, "they can't read, and what's the sense of letting a child go on to the third grade if he can't read?"

There are various reasons why teachers have less power and authority than they would like to have. Some administrators and school boards are reluctant, for one reason or another, to share their power with teachers; hence teachers in many schools have no voice in the development of the curriculum or the selection of textbooks or the formulation of rules to govern the everyday life of the school. Administrators also restrict the power of teachers as a way of protecting the welfare of children. This is the intent behind rules forbidding teachers to flog children or the regulation which requires that all children be "passed" to the next grade. These are some of the ways in which the community and the administrators of the school limit the power of teachers. But there are other factors that limit the power of teachers. One of these factors lies within the classroom group, and the other lies within the teacher himself.

POWER WHICH COMES FROM WITHIN THE GROUP

WHEN we think of the power which leaders possess, we usually overlook the fact that much of their power comes from the groups they lead or supervise. This is true to a greater extent of the leader who is elected by the group and who may, by the same token, be deposed by the group who made him their leader, but it is also true of the leader who is appointed by an outside authority—like the teacher. One of the ways we know that leaders possess power is that people follow them. When a leader is no longer followed, he is a leader in name only. The teacher possesses power as a leader if he is able to get children to "follow" him—that is, if he is successful in getting children to learn. The teacher who is unable to promote learning in his class is neither a successful leader nor a successful teacher, no matter how much power and authority have been given him by the administration. The teacher in the latter instance has failed because the power of the group was opposed to him. Perhaps, through exercise of the powers given him by the administration, he was able to get children to go through the motions of following the curriculum, or perhaps he was unsuccessful even in this. At any rate, little learning of a positive nature took place under his tutelage. It may even be that the morale of the class deteriorated somewhat, to the extent that future teachers will have difficulty in helping the group to learn.

Many teachers first become acquainted with the power of the group through their own failure—that is, they try to get the group to do something or learn something or perhaps they try to motivate the group, and they do not succeed. For some teachers, this is the frightening thing about a classroom group—it can cause teachers to fail. Usually, the teacher does not fail because the group has actively opposed him or openly defied him, although this, too, may occur. More likely it is a passive sort of resistance. Then there are various kinds of noncooperation: the bewildered hopelessness of a class that does not believe in its own ability; the bored apathy of a group that is tired of doing things merely to satisfy teachers; the good-humored tolerance of a class that is past caring about school and now is only interested in getting an occasional laugh.

THE FEAR OF FAILURE

FORTUNATELY these conditions are temporary stages for most normal groups that work under the guidance of a competent teacher. However, when teachers who are inexperienced or inept in human relations meet with a noncooperative, nonconforming class, they find the experience unduly frustrating, upsetting, and even frightening, particularly if they are afraid of failure. Experienced and competent teachers are well-acquainted with the taste of failure. One of the reasons they are successful is that they have developed what the psychologists call "a high frustration tolerance," which means, in this case, that their morale is good in spite of repeated failure. They realize that learning is a slow and often painful process—painful for the teacher as well as the class. They realize also that many setbacks and reverses will occur before children are ready to accept the demands and responsibilities which come with increased maturity. But the teacher who is inexperienced or inept is not prepared for failures, large or small. For him, every lesson must be a winner, every day must show evidence of improvement. Hence, when he sees that the class is solidifying against him, he is gripped by the fear that he is about to fail again, whereupon he may redouble his efforts to succeed. However, what is likely to happen is that the more anxious the teacher becomes, the more the group resists him, until he feels forced to use drastic measures, punishing the group, as it were, for his failure to motivate them. These measures often take the form of threats to fail students who do not learn certain skills or knowledge by a certain time, or they may take the form of unusually difficult tests and quizzes. In effect, the teacher who is thwarted by the power of the group is tempted to depend more and more on the power and authority granted him by the school administration and less and less on his skill as a leader or as an artist in the field of human relations. The chief difference between ineffective and effective teachers is that the former are likely to yield to this temptation and the latter are more likely to resist it. The more emotionally insecure the teacher, the more he will depend on power, status, and authority and the more he will fear failure; whereas the greater the emotional security, the more likely the teacher will depend on his sensitivity to good human relations and his skill in promoting them and the less he will fear failure.

THE TEACHER AS AN "ARTIST IN HUMAN RELATIONS"

IN THE preceding paragraph we have used the term "artist in human relations" in describing the competent teacher. This concept is somewhat at variance with older concepts of the teacher. During the nineteenth and early twentieth centuries the teacher was thought of as a scholar —primarily a bookish person—or a disciplinarian. Interest in children was less important than interest in academic learning. Curricula were laid out specifically and rigidly; children either learned what was required or were punished or taken out of school. During the earlier years of the twentieth century we developed doubts about the existing objectives and methods of education and began to apply some of the principles of the newly developing science of psychology to the problems of the school. Although the teacher of the 1920's continued to be somewhat of a scholar, he developed a greater interest in results and became somewhat the scientist. We are still interested in science today, but we are beginning to realize that the process of helping children to learn cannot be accomplished solely on the basis of formulas, no matter how scientifically respectable they sound. Whereas some educators in the 1920's rather hoped that science had solved the problem of how to educate, there is a general realization today that the teacher cannot depend entirely on science and hence cannot avoid the responsibility of working out his own solutions to his own problems. To help him in this, he has the findings of the psychologist, as well as the advice and counsel of other educators.

Perhaps the position of the teacher can best be described by comparing the artist with the technician. The technician is someone who analyzes and diagnoses problems and applies solutions on a formulalike basis. If his diagnosis is correct and if he uses the correct formula, success is his. His results are completely predictable, provided, of course, he operates in a situation that does not possess unpredictable elements.

When we use the term artist in this discussion, we are using it in the broadest sense. Essentially, any person who works with such dynamic, changeable, and complex media as human relationships is, or ought to be, an artist. An artist may use formulas and techniques to help him with his work, but he uses them in a highly individualized manner. A technician decides what to do about a problem because of what his rule book or his manual tells him. An artist makes *his* decisions on the basis of what *feels* like the right thing to do. He may be aided by scientific knowledge, but he knows better than to operate through the rigid application of formulas.

THE USE OF TECHNIQUES

Teachers often get together and compare notes on techniques. It is a commonplace for one teacher to describe a method he uses to put across a certain principle in arithmetic, whereupon another teacher will comment: "I tried that and it didn't work." Now, these two teachers may be very competent; hence the fact that the method worked for one but not the other is no reflection on their ability.

I shall always remember a parent-education meeting over which I presided as discussion leader. One of the parents asked me a direct question: "What should you do when a three-year-old child bites you? Do you bite him back?"

I fell neatly into the trap and said, "No, this would be regressing to the child's level. After all, you are more mature than the child; you have other ways of expressing your displeasure and disapproval."

"Well," said the mother, "my daughter used to bite me all the time, so one day I bit her back and now she doesn't bite me any more. I just wanted to know if that was all right."

What could I say? She had me and I knew it. All of which goes to show that parents and teachers who are dealing directly with a child are often in a better position to work out solutions to their problems on the basis of what *feels* right than are psychologists who analyze and prescribe for the situation from afar.

This does not mean that teachers should forget all they have learned from psychologists about children and about the processes of learning and make all their classroom decisions according to the whims of the moment. However, it does mean that teachers should, when at all possible, employ methods and techniques with which they are "comfortable" and which have been effective for them. This is true particularly for experienced teachers who have had opportunities to try various approaches and techniques and have developed patterns of skills which are effective. Less experienced teachers may find themselves uncomfortable in using almost any of a wide variety of methods because they have not as yet had a chance to test their strengths and weaknesses on a variety of children and classes. And, as we are well aware, it is the unknown which fills one with anxiety.

THE IMPORTANCE OF THE "HUMAN FACTOR"

It is significant that today the teacher is becoming an artist in human relations rather than an artist in subject matter. This is the result of our growing awareness that it is the human factor in any situation that is the important one. It is interesting to note that there are some indications that business and industry, too, are coming to realize that productivity is often improved more by such human considerations as the friendly interest of the supervisor or the worker's ability to communicate with management than it is by bonuses and improvements in working conditions [1, 2, 3]. Educators, likewise, are beginning to see that it is necessary for children to become actively involved in the learning process, which means that the emotional climate of the classroom must be sympathetic to such involvement. The creation of such a climate cannot be done by formula. It takes empathy—the ability to sense the feelings of students—as well as the ability to help the classroom group to use its powers constructively and effectively. This calls for real artistry in the broadest and deepest sense.

RAPPORT

One of the ways in which the skill of the teacher who is an artist in human relations expresses itself is in the development of the empathic and permissive relationship that we call "rapport."

The concept of rapport is one that has come into education from clinical psychology. One of the most important, if not the chief, functions of the clinical psychologist was, at one time, the administration of diagnostic tests to mental patients. In order to perform his duties adequately, the psychologist was put to some pains to see that the patient was put at his ease so that he would cooperate with the test administrator. "Establishing rapport," then, was largely a matter of putting the patient in a cooperative frame of mind. In more recent years, when counseling and psychotherapy have become more accepted as a major function of clinical psychologists, rapport has come to be associated with more of a *mutual* relationship. Carl Rogers describes the situation which leads to rapport as follows:

> First is a warmth and responsiveness on the part of the counselor which makes rapport possible, and which gradually develops into a deeper emotional relationship. From the counselor's point of view, however, this is a definitely controlled relationship, an affectional bond with defined limits. It expresses itself in a genuine interest in the client and an acceptance of him as a person [4].

Robert I. Watson, another clinical psychologist, describes rapport as a "warm, positive, cooperative relationship" and says that it is inspired in the client when the attitude of the clinician is characterized by "acceptance, friendliness, interest, and personal understanding [5]."

The function or purpose of rapport in a clinical setting is to free the patient or client from some of the anxieties that block his ability to express himself and that keep him from seeing himself and others objectively. As long as the client is worried about what the clinician thinks of him, he will have difficulty in developing the understanding and insight that are necessary to good mental health. The clinician, therefore, maintains an attitude of friendly permissiveness and acceptance in the hope and expectation that the client will not see him as a threat—that is, will not see him as someone whose opinion he ought to worry about. Rapport is therefore a very necessary prerequisite to helping clients to learn how to understand and accept themselves and others, in other words, how to grow in the direction of emotional maturity.

As educators have come to see that education, too, is concerned with helping children to become more mature, they have borrowed a number of concepts and ideas from clinical psychology. In pursuing these ideas they have discovered that in classes where students are learning to become more mature, emotionally and socially speaking, the relationship between teachers and students is characterized by rapport. They learned, too, that when a condition of rapport exists in a classroom, students feel free to express themselves and to communicate with the teacher because they do not look upon the teacher as a threat, as a person who would express personal dislike or disfavor toward a child who did not learn or who did not conform to behavior standards. It appears also that the teacher who is able to establish rapport is most likely one who is permissive and understanding, one who respects the individuality and the personality of the student, and one who is able to communicate these feelings to his class.

When we use the concept of rapport in an educational setting, we should be fully aware that there are some major differences between the functions and goals of the teacher and the psychotherapist. (We shall discuss some of these differences in Chapter 17.) For example, the mere fact that the teacher must deal with twenty-five to forty-five students at one time and must be concerned about such a wide variety of activities and objectives means that he cannot give as much attention to the development of rapport as the clinician can. Nor is it always necessary that he do so. After all, the clinician must work with persons whose relations with other persons are badly warped and damaged and whose psychological defenses are stronger than the average person. The teacher, on the other hand, deals with children who, as a general rule, are much easier to work with and more responsive than the clients seen by psychotherapists. In general, we may say that rapport is a quality likely to be present in classrooms where children are being helped to develop in the direction of emotional and social maturity and absent in classrooms where the emphasis is on conformity, submission, and memorization.

The value of good rapport is illustrated by a study undertaken by Elinor L. Sacks of the scores made on the Stanford Binet intelligence test by three groups of nursery school children. After the test had been given to the children, Sacks established a good relationship with one group, a poor relationship with the second group, and had no contact with the third group. A different form of the same test was given ten days later. Although all three groups raised their scores on the occasion of the second administration of the test, the group with whom she had established a positive relationship received scores that were significantly higher than those of the other two groups [6]. Sacks' study seems to indicate that the establishment of good rapport with children affects their behavior favorably; whether this is produced by lowered anxiety or increased desire to do well is not revealed by her study. The significant fact is that rapport affects almost any leader-follower situation where motivation, effort, and performance are important.

As we might expect, rapport enters into those aspects of the curriculum which are concerned with attitudes and feelings. In her work in the field of eliminating prejudice, Margaret Heaton has found that there is a relationship between a sense of emotional security and the shifting of feelings. In other words, students are more likely to feel free to change or to shift their attitudes if they do not feel psychologically threatened—that is, if they do not have to worry about whether the teacher or the class will reject them [7]. If the teacher has rapport with his class, if he has been able to encourage the development of a sense of security in the group, the members of the group will then feel free to take some steps toward building those attitudes that are mentally healthy.

An important factor in building rapport is the amount of talking the teacher does. Inasmuch as rapport is characterized by the ability of the child to communicate, it follows that a teacher who is developing rapport, let us say, in a discussion setting, will do very little talking. Such talking as he does will be with the two purposes of (1) encouraging students to talk and to contribute to the discussion and (2) providing a sort of "relatedness" between the contributions so that they are not too scattered or disjointed. As the teacher learns how to do these things effectively, he will find that he talks less and less. Students, on their part, are then more likely to take the teacher at face value when he says that he expects them to speak freely and to participate in the discussion. Some classes need more help in talking freely than do others, and the level of rapport that a given teacher is able to achieve will vary from class to class, but the point here is that the best results will come from the teacher talking *less* instead of more. The more he talks the less opportunity the student has to express himself.

THE TEACHER'S EFFECT ON EMOTIONAL CLIMATE

THE group of experiments by Lewin, Lippitt, and White involving the creation of autocratic, laissez-faire, and democratic climates that we have referred to elsewhere was one of the classic studies in the field of social psychology and one which served to inaugurate a new era in the scientific study of human relations. Lewin, Lippitt, and White organized four clubs of eleven-year-old boys. Each of these clubs was supervised by one adult group leader for seven weeks, whereupon a different leader took his place for another period of seven weeks. This was followed by a third period of seven weeks under a still different leader. Each of the leaders played a different role with each club in such a way that each club was subject to the influence of each of three different philosophies of leadership. Each of the four leaders in turn acted the parts of autocratic, democratic, and laissez-faire leaders with the three groups they supervised.

Four distinct climatic conditions were observed during the period of this study. The experimenters labeled them: democracy, laissez-faire, aggressive autocracy, and apathetic autocracy. The democratic groups were characterized by free discussion, growth in self-direction, and greater cooperation among group members. Laissez-faire groups were characterized by a general feeling of frustration and discontent, lower cohesiveness, and lower morale. Under conditions of apathetic autocracy, the boys became dependent on the adult leader and showed little initiative. When the climate was aggressively autocratic, the boys directed much hostility toward the leader. When autocratic leaders were absent from their groups for short periods, the amount of work done by the boys on their projects declined markedly. This was in sharp contrast to the similar situation in the democratic groups, where boys continued to work when the leader was out of the room [8, 9, 10].

This study demonstrates not only that group members behave differently in different kinds of social and emotional climates, but also that a change in the behavior of the leader can alter the climate. The results of the study also seem to indicate that teachers who behave "democratically" (like our "guidance-minded" teacher of Chapter 11) are likely to create conditions that are favorable to cohesiveness and self-direction, whereas teachers who behave autocratically (like our "directive-minded" teacher of Chapter 11) are likely to create conditions leading to (1) apathy and submission, with much dependency on the teacher and little self-direction and initiative, or (2) hostility and rebellious behavior. From what we have said about rapport, it also seems likely that better rapport will develop in the "democratic" (guidance-minded) classroom.

The ability of teachers to influence the emotional climates of their classrooms is further demonstrated by a study by Boynton, Dugger, and Turner, who discovered that after only two or two-and-one-half months of association between teachers and pupils, children began to show the emotional effects of the contact [11]. Ruth Cunningham and her associates observed the behavior of a single junior high class as it went from teacher to teacher throughout the day. With one teacher, the class was quiet and submissive; with another, it was noisy and rebellious. In a third classroom, the students voluntarily and spontaneously engaged in group-centered activities even before the teacher came into the room [12]. As the class entered each teacher's "climate zone," its behavior changed radically, thus demonstrating the great power a teacher exerts in creating emotional and social climate, as well as the effect that climate can have in changing the behavior of group members.

THE TEACHER AS A "GROUP-BUILDER"

THE chief contribution of the democratic or guidance-minded teacher appears to lie in his ability to make the class a group. This involves helping children to be interdependent —that is, dependent on each other, rather than being entirely dependent on the teacher-leader. David H. Jenkins suggests that the teacher, too, should become a part of this group and share this interdependence. He points out that the teacher is dependent on the student for information regarding the latter's progress and that the student does most of his learning when he participates in an interdependent relationship with the teacher, whereby "he shares his present understandings and confusions, and the teacher helps him through the processes of making progress in meeting his learning needs." Jenkins also believes that teachers should use this interdependence as a means of evaluating the effectiveness of his teaching. He states, further:

> There would seem to be an important increase in the morale of students if they could feel that while the teacher was making a contribution to their learning, they were also able to contribute to his learning. To face frankly the potentialities of the mutual learning situation in the classroom and to utilize them fully should make the greatest contribution to classroom processes. By this token, the students would be able at a given point to let the teacher know that he seemed to be interfering in their learning. This would give the teacher an opportunity either to explain what he was trying to do and get greater acceptance of the method and involvement in it, or he could revise the method in order to help this particular class [13].

Although Jenkins notes that few of us have developed enough security in our classrooms to be able to face such problems as these frankly with our students, his approach does seem, nevertheless, to suggest some of the ways in which teachers can develop a more democratic atmosphere in their classes.

The satisfying effect of group-centered activities on the feelings of group members was noted by Everett W. Bovard, Jr., who studied the differences between leader-centered and group-centered groups. He found that the members of group-centered groups were more inclined to like each other and to like the group itself as compared to the members of leader-centered groups [14].

The idea of the desirability of group activities being satisfying to the members is also discussed by Nadine I. Clark and Gertrude M. Aitchison:

> The relations of students one to another affect most, if not all, of their emotional needs. The learnings which result from these relations greatly influence their growth as persons, since the satisfaction of common emotional needs is a part of the developmental tasks which are the most pressing and immediate concerns of youth. . . .
>
> In attempting to promote a good group spirit, a teacher should continually be aware of the central importance of the group as a possible source of the approval and recognition which each individual seeks. The group will affect its individual members for good or ill. Their status in the group will either aid or inhibit their learning. The group can enhance the importance of the individual by making him feel wanted. If the group feeling is strong enough, it can absorb individual hostilities. . . . Hence, the teacher will regard his efforts to promote desirable group processes as fundamental to the success of the year's work.
>
> One of the teacher's first objectives, then, should be to create an atmosphere of friendliness and belongingness to aid the growth of the "we" spirit which will make the class become a group [15].

THE PLACE OF TECHNIQUES

HELPING children to organize themselves and develop group feeling calls for a high degree of artistry in the field of human relations, because the situations and relationships with which the teacher must deal are so fluid and sensitive, and because, even at best, they possess a certain quality of unpredictability. For these reasons, the development of a group-centered classroom calls for far more than the mastery of a few tried-and-tested techniques. It calls for the ability to use the proper techniques in the proper setting and with the proper emphasis.

However, although artistry in human relations calls for more than the application of techniques, techniques are necessary. Without them, the artist would be unable to translate into action his understanding of children and groups and his insight into the learning process.

The following paragraphs present a few of the methods or techniques used by teachers in sharing their leadership and in encouraging group participation.

FREE DISCUSSION

This is one of the commonest methods, although most discussions are not as "free" as the teacher thinks they are. As we have noted previously in this chapter, it is hard for teachers to limit their own participation. Free discussions go best when they stem from some topic that is of controversial interest and in which children are deeply involved. The trick is to get children to interact with each other, rather than with the teacher. At first they will direct most of their comments and inquiries to the teacher, but as the teacher keeps saying: "I wonder what the rest of you think about this idea," and "If I understand what you mean it is . . ." (making a brief paraphrase of the student's words, instead of a reply or comment), the class begins to see that the teacher meant what he said when he told them that this discussion was to be theirs and not his.

BUZZ SESSIONS

It is difficult to get maximum participation in a large group. A partial remedy is to break up the class into small groups of four to seven individuals and have them discuss the issue at hand for five or ten minutes. Then the total group is convened and each group reports on its discussion. This is sometimes a good way to start off a general discussion because it involves almost every individual in the class. Furthermore, many who are too shy to speak up in a meeting of the entire class feel free to participate in a small group discussion.

SOCIODRAMA

This is an informal type of role-playing, whereby students enact the parts of individuals who are involved in various kinds of situations. No parts are memorized, and individuals participate more or less spontaneously, trying to behave and speak as they think the characters they are portraying would behave or speak. For example, students might role-play what happens when an individual from a minority group applies for a job and is not hired. Another situation that lends itself to role-playing is the problem of the boy or girl who has come home later at night than he or she should have. Role-playing the part of a parent often helps adolescents get an insight into parental problems that they could not have gained otherwise. The introduction of role-playing into the classroom calls for much skill, and the teacher who plans to use it must expect some failures as well as successes. However, when it is used properly and is followed by free discussion, it can be a stimulating and valuable adventure in helping children understand human behavior.[1]

SOCIOMETRY

Since we covered this subject in detail in Chapter 10, we shall not pursue it further here, except to note that committees and work groups that are organized sociometrically usually succeed better than those that are organized by the teacher.

TEACHER-PUPIL PLANNING

If the teacher is permitted sufficient latitude to develop his own curricular approaches, he can involve the entire class in

---

[1] If you are tempted to try sociodrama, it is recommended that you read up on it first. See "Suggested Readings" at the end of this chapter.

the development of an "experience unit" to meet the goals and purposes of the course.[2] This approach lends itself best to such subject-matter areas as English, social studies, and general science and has the advantage of giving students maximum opportunities to participate in and to direct their own learning experiences.

SELF-EVALUATION

This method can be a part of teacher-pupil planning or it can be used in courses conducted along more traditional lines. It is properly used at several points in the school term in order that students may make comparisons of their progress and attainment. Unless students make evaluations, they become immersed in the details and day-by-day tasks of education—the forest becomes obscured by the trees, as it were. However, through a discussion of the goals and objectives of the course and the progress that has been made or not made, students may be helped to become reoriented to the broader and more basic purposes of their activity.

CONTROL-AND-INFLUENCE TECHNIQUES

So FAR, we have discussed a few of the methods that teachers use in creating an emotional climate favorable to group-centered learning. There are other techniques that are used for more specific purposes, such as the emergency situations that inevitably develop in the best run classrooms. These are control-and-influence techniques that are a part of the repertory of most teachers. A few are discussed here.

DIRECT COMMAND

This varies from the mild "Please keep your eyes on your own paper," to the urgent and abrupt "Stop that at once!"

---

[2] For an example of such an experience unit, see N. I. Clark and G. M. Aitchison, "Adapting Classroom Activities to the Needs of Youth," in the *Fifty-Second Yearbook of the National Society for the Study of Education.* Pp. 240–43 [15].

In the first instance, the command is hardly recognized as such because it is phrased and intoned so mildly. The second instance is that of a command supposedly to be used in a state of emergency. Commands like these are used every few minutes in some classrooms, whether an emergency exists or not. After a while, they lose their force. Of course, if a *real* emergency *does* occur every ten minutes in a certain classroom, the situation has probably gone too far to be remedied by sharp commands.

REMINDER OF CONSEQUENCES

Sometimes boys and girls become overinvolved in a situation or get carried away by enthusiasm or anger so that they forget or overlook the limits that society or the school or common decency has imposed on behavior. At such times, the teacher can frequently bring the class back to reality by raising a question about the appropriateness of the conduct: "What would happen if you actually carry through the plan that you are thinking about?" or "Let's stop and think about what we're doing," or "What do you think the principal would say about that?" These are, of course, relatively mild exhortations. A teacher who is upset and has lost his air of professional detachment would express himself more strongly. However, regardless of the strength of such expression, the teacher does, occasionally, have to remind children of the consequences of their behavior.

GIVING AND WITHHOLDING AFFECTION

In general, the use of personal acceptance and rejection impedes or thwarts the development of democratic or group-centered climate. On the other hand, teachers are human and have human failings; hence, they are all too likely to use on others the methods used on them by their administrators and supervisors and by their own parents in former years. Often teachers will show their feelings even when they think they are concealing them. Since, in the long run, personal acceptance and rejection do not provide firm bases for building sound relationships with classroom groups, the teacher who is working for the development of more effective relations with his classes will try to develop methods that are less personal and autocratic and more objective and democratic.

PRAISE AND CRITICISM

These are techniques that usually accompany the giving or the withholding of affection. However, they often cannot be divorced from evaluation, a function that every teacher must perform. The problem is how to keep praise and criticism on as objective a plane as possible, and how to keep from depreciating or inflating the individual in the eyes of his peers. Sometimes praise *and* criticism can be used together as a means of controlling the less-than-satisfactory behavior of a group. First, telling a group what it is doing well often helps take the sting out of the unfavorable evaluation that sometimes must be made.

PURPOSEFUL IGNORING

This technique is sometimes useful when a student engages in mild misbehavior, the purpose of which is to challenge or annoy the teacher. When such manifestations are temporary or sporadic, they usually can be safely ignored. Often, however, a student will persist in his attempt to "get a rise" out of the teacher. The teacher must then decide what the limits of the situation are and what action he can take that will reduce, rather than raise, the level of anxiety in the total group.

TENSION RELEASING

Often negative behavior can be avoided or forestalled by giving children an opportunity to "get things off their chest" by holding a "gripe session." If the teacher has been able to create an atmosphere in which children can express themselves freely, this technique will serve as a handy safety valve. It is better for children (and adults) to say things harmlessly than to engage in destructive behavior or physical aggression. Often such gripe sessions can serve as the basis for real gains in insight and understanding of human relations.

SHOWING ENTHUSIASM OR CONCERN

These are less direct but often highly effective ways of communicating with groups. If the teacher is enthusiastic or excited about learning, there is a good chance that the group may catch some of this enthusiasm. If anything, it reminds the group that learning can be an exciting affair. On the other hand, a note of concern in the teacher's voice or a worried look can at times be more effective as a deterrent than mere words. Like the other methods we have mentioned, these techniques lose their effectiveness if they are overworked or if they are not genuine.

RESTRUCTURING THE SITUATION

Redl and Wattenberg suggest this approach as a means of dealing with such situations as the restlessness that sometimes appears in a group of children that has been sitting too long, or the wildness that sometimes gets into children when they are overstimulated or overexcited. By "restructuring the situation" it is sometimes possible to change the nature of the activity or to give the group something else on which to focus their attention. Thus a boring review can be turned into a quiz program or a straggling group of first graders can be brought back into line by the suggestion, "Let's pretend we're soldiers on parade [16]."

A complete list of techniques for influence and control would be endless. The reader would do well to make up his own list and evaluate them—observing a single class over an hour's time may reveal a dozen or more.

We have been concerned in this chapter about the ways

in which teachers carry out their functions as persons of power and authority. Probably teachers are most effective when they do not have to use their power; yet there are times when the combinations of forces and events are such that power must be used and authority invoked. What counts most in the lives of children is the general day-to-day atmosphere that prevails in the classroom, not the occasional recourse to power. A teacher who has rapport with his students, who has created an atmosphere that is conducive to learning, does not need to be overly concerned about the occasional use of power, particularly if he is continually learning how to deal with students in ways that do not require him to depend solely on power and authority.

REFERENCES

1. F. J. Roethlisberger, *Management and Morale*. Cambridge: Harvard University Press, 1941.
2. ——— and W. J. Dickson, *Management and the Worker*. Cambridge: Harvard University Press, 1939.
3. S. Chase, *Roads to Agreement*. New York: Harper, 1951.
4. C. R. Rogers, *Counseling and Psychotherapy*. Boston: Houghton Mifflin, 1942. P. 87. Reprinted by permission.
5. R. I. Watson, *The Clinical Method in Psychology*. New York: Harper, 1951. P. 94.
6. E. L. Sacks, "Intelligence Scores and Social Relationships between Child and Examiner," *Journal of Abnormal and Social Psychology*. 47:354–58;1952.
7. M. Heaton, *Feelings Are Facts*. New York: National Conference of Christians and Jews, 1952. P. 32.
8. K. Lewin, R. Lippitt, and R. K. White, "Patterns of Aggressive Behavior in Experimentally Created 'Social Climates,'" *Journal of Social Psychology*. 10:271–99;1939.
9. R. Lippitt and R. K. White, "An Experimental Study of Leadership and Group Life," in T. M. Newcomb and E. L. Hartley, eds., *Readings in Social Psychology*. New York: Holt, 1947. Pp. 315–30.
10. ———, "The 'Social Climate' of Children's Groups," in R. G. Barker, J. S. Kounin, and H. F. Wright, eds., *Child Behavior and Development*. New York: McGraw-Hill, 1943. Pp. 485–508.

11. P. L. Boynton, H. Dugger, and M. Turner, "The Emotional Stability of Teachers and Pupils," *Journal of Juvenile Research.* 18:223–33;1934.

12. R. Cunningham *et al., Understanding Group Behavior of Boys and Girls.* New York: Bureau of Publications, Teachers College, Columbia University, 1951. Pp. 42–43.

13. D. H. Jenkins, "Interdependence in the Classroom," *Journal of Educational Research,* 45:137–44;1951. Reprinted by permission.

14. E. V. Bovard, Jr., "The Experimental Production of Interpersonal Affect," *Journal of Abnormal and Social Psychology.* 46:521–28;1951.

15. N. I. Clark and G. M. Aitchison, "Adapting Classroom Activities to the Needs of Youth," ch. 13 in N. B. Henry, ed., *Adapting the Secondary-School Program to the Needs of Youth,* Fifty-Second Yearbook of the National Society for the Study of Education, Part I. Chicago: National Society for the Study of Education, 1953. Pp. 231–32. Quoted by permission of the Society.

16. F. Redl and W. W. Wattenberg, *Mental Hygiene in Teaching.* New York: Harcourt, Brace, 1951. P. 289.

SUGGESTED READINGS

Association for Supervision and Curriculum Development, *Fostering Mental Health in Our Schools.* Washington: National Education Association, 1950. Chapter 13 deals with sociometric grouping; Chapter 16, with sociodrama; Chapter 17, with understanding group processes; and Chapter 18, with accepting and clarifying children's feelings.

D. Baruch, *New Ways in Discipline.* New York: McGraw-Hill, 1949.

B. Baxter, *Teacher-Pupil Relationships.* New York: Macmillan, 1941. Chapter 3 contrasts the behavior of successful and unsuccessful teachers. A shortcoming, however, is the lack of exploration of psychological bases and causes of the unsatisfactory behavior.

C. Buhler, F. Smitter, and S. Richardson, *Childhood Problems and the Teacher.* New York: Holt, 1952. See Chapters 9, 10, and 11, "The Teacher's Methods of Working with Individual Children," "The Teacher's Approach to Frequent Problems of Children," and "The Teacher's Management of Situational Difficulties."

M. W. Clark, "Role Playing in a Group Guidance Class," *California Journal of Secondary Education.* 26:24–26;1951.

R. Cunningham *et al., Understanding Group Behavior of Boys and Girls.* New York: Bureau of Publications, Teachers College, Columbia University, 1951. Chapter 3, entitled "Group Goals," discusses ways of helping classroom groups to develop controls of their own by making them aware of goals and objectives related to their needs.

E. Fromm, *Escape from Freedom.* New York: Rinehart, 1941. A philosophical and psychiatric discussion of how man is tempted to solve his problems through the use of power and authoritarian methods.

————, *Man for Himself.* New York: Rinehart, 1947. See particularly Fromm's discussion of power and of authoritarian ethics.

J. Grambs and W. Iverson, *Modern Methods in Secondary Education.* New York: Sloane, 1952. Chapter 7, "Discussion, Sociodrama, and Related Techniques;" Chapter 8, "Group Techniques in the Classroom;" Chapters 13 and 14, "Adjustment to School Life: Discipline."

K. Horney, *The Neurotic Personality of Our Time.* New York: Norton, 1937. Chapter 10, "The Quest for Power, Prestige, and Possession."

J. L. Hymes, Jr., *Discipline.* New York: Bureau of Publications, Teachers College, Columbia University, 1949.

H. J. Otto, *Principles of Elementary Education.* New York: Rinehart, 1949. Chapters 12 and 13, "Living with Children" and "Working with Children."

F. Redl and W. W. Wattenberg, *Mental Hygiene in Teaching.* New York: Harcourt, Brace, 1951. Chapter 9, "Group Life in the Classroom."

G. and F. R. Shaftel, *Role Playing the Problem Story.* New York: National Conference of Christians and Jews, 1952. One way to use sociodramatic techniques in the classroom.

G. V. Sheviakov and F. Redl, *Discipline for Today's Children and Youth.* Washington: National Education Association, 1944.

M. J. Sobel, "Socio-Dramas: An Aid in Classroom Discipline," *Clearing House.* 26:235–38;1951.

B. and F. Strauss, *New Ways to Better Meetings,* New York: Viking, 1951. Chapter 11, "Role-Playing."

R. M. Wittenberg, *So You Want to Help People.* New York: Association Press, 1947. "A mental hygiene primer for group leaders."

See also items 2, 3, 4, 7, 12, and 16 in the References for this chapter.

SUGGESTED FILMS

Broader Concept of Method: Part 2. Teacher and Pupils Planning and Working Together. Available through McGraw-Hill.

Maintaining Classroom Discipline. Available through McGraw-Hill.

14

RELATIONS WITH PARENTS

THE main emphasis in this book has been on understanding children. Inasmuch as the effectiveness of the teacher depends so much on the extent to which he understands the children he works with, it follows that anything that has a major effect on the behavior of children is worthy of careful attention. As we have indicated earlier, the behavior of a child is conditioned to a large extent by his relations with his parents. Even if the teacher never has an opportunity to meet a parent face to face, he is bound to become directly or indirectly concerned about the kinds of relationships that children in general have with their parents or the specific relationships that certain children have with their parents.

PARENTS' ATTITUDES
TOWARD EDUCATION

Let us start with children's attitudes toward the school and toward education in general, for these are very likely to be influenced by parental views. Some parents look upon schools as a nuisance and a waste of time. If their children have any feelings of this sort—and almost every child feels this way occasionally—they come to feel that their parents will lend them moral support in any attempts to resist the demands of the school. Other parents look upon education as the chief means of advancing socially and economically. Foreign-born parents often feel this way. Indeed, one study indicates that students with at least one foreign-born parent tend to receive better grades than students whose parents are natives of this country [1]. Some parents have a good opinion of education generally, but are highly critical of curricula, textbooks, or methods. Of course, such criticism should be expressed openly where it can be discussed by school personnel or members of boards of education, for this is one of the ways that citizens "have their say" about education.

All too often, however, unfavorable comment about the school is like a whispering campaign that never gets out into the open. Children who live in homes where adults continually criticize the schools in a destructive manner are almost certain to develop distorted and biased viewpoints. It is difficult for teachers to motivate and help those children who hear only critical and negative things about school from their parents. Children cannot develop confidence in teachers who are constantly criticized by their parents as inept. One of the prime requisites of learning is that the learner must feel that the task at hand is worth while and that he has a reasonable chance of success. Hence, the child who believes that school work is not worth while or that teachers are not competent to help him learn will not be motivated to try very hard.

Sometimes religious beliefs make school adjustment difficult for a child. Merle Bonney tells of how the parents of some religious sects believe that motion pictures are sinful and hence request school authorities not to permit their children to view them [2]. This creates a problem when it is desired to show visual aids in the classroom or when the student body is assembled to see a worth-while film. Parents certainly have a right to hold such beliefs and to bring their children up according to the tenets of their faith. On the other hand, we would be less than objective if we did not note that such practices do interfere with the regular school program and help to set children off from the others as "different," thus creating problems of adjustment.

TOWARD THEIR CHILDREN

The attitudes of parents toward the learning activities of their children also have marked effect on school performance. There is the parent who consistently underestimates the difficulties experienced by his child in making progress at school. His reaction to the child's performance is one of chronic disappointment. Some children react to an attitude of this sort by becoming convinced that there is not much use trying. Since they expect nothing but failure to result from their experiences at school, they are discouraged before they start. One sixth grader had this to say about the demands made on him:

> They always seem to be expecting me to be a smart person and get all A's or something like that. They also expect me to be able to do everything. My dad tries to show me how to do school work that is all different. When I don't understand, he gets mad at me. I just do my best and that's all I can do. It makes me feel like a little kid that doesn't know anything at all [3].

Some parents look upon education as a form of intense competition—a series of competitive trials in which one must succeed before he is ready to tackle the problems of adult life. As education operates today, this attitude has often some basis in fact, inasmuch as teachers, too, frequently see education in this way. However, as we have indicated elsewhere, the competitive aspect of education can be overemphasized to the detriment of real learning. Parents often help children to make such an overemphasis by continual discussion of the necessity to make the best grades in the class, to become class president, and to play leading roles in as many activities as possible. In some cases, the child feels that he must succeed for his parent's sake, rather than his own, that it is his parents who are on trial in classroom competition as well as himself. The way in which parents affect children's attitudes toward cooperation and competition is revealed by the statement of ·a first grader who repeatedly protested against cooperative games, saying "You are supposed to see who can beat. That's what my Daddy says. See who can beat. He's the best one." His attitude was in marked contrast to the attitudes displayed by other children in the room who were quite happy to engage in activities where no child would emerge as winner [4].

There are, of course, many parents who have a sympathetic understanding of problems faced by children and by teachers in the course of the educational process. They appear to be aware of their children's abilities as well as their shortcomings, and they seem to understand the strengths and limitations of the school. Often, these parents are the ones who provide the chief support in the community for the program of the school.

THE EMOTIONAL CLIMATE OF THE HOME

IN UNDERSTANDING a child, it helps to know about the emotional climate of the home. Do the parents insist that children take responsibilities and do things on their own initiative? Or do they insist on making all the decisions? Do children get some opportunities to grapple with their environment more or less on their own? Or do they lead sheltered lives, "tied to their mother's apron strings?" Is the atmosphere one of continual fault-finding and negative criticism? Are the parents a sure source of guidance? Or are they so wrapped up in their own troubles that they can give little attention to the problems of their children?

Then there are the conditions, factors, and events which tend to have a disintegrating effect on family life. One of the commonest of these conditions is the broken home. Another is the addiction of one or both parents to alcohol, drugs, or gambling. Some parents are completely preoccupied with parties, entertainment, or lodge work. In some families, life always seems to be a desperate struggle—the father cannot seem to keep a job, the mother is always ill, and life seems very grim indeed. There is usually some sibling rivalry or dissension among the children in most families. Usually it flares up only occasionally or is kept at a low pitch of intensity by the common sense of all parties concerned. However, in some families, the warfare among siblings (brothers and/or sisters) assumes violent proportions, to the extent that it has a marked and disturbing effect on the lives of all participants. In still other families, an even more difficult problem is created by continual dissension between mother and father. A child can usually tolerate a certain amount of sibling rivalry, but frequent disputes between his parents can be extremely upsetting because they strike at the foundations of the child's emotional security.

POTENTIAL CONFLICTS BETWEEN PARENTS AND TEACHERS

DIFFERENCES IN HOME AND SCHOOL STANDARDS

The child's emotional security is threatened whenever there are sharp or severe differences of opinion among or between significant people in his life—that is, between his parents or between his parents and his teacher. Unfortunately for the child, it is not unusual for conflicts to develop between parents and the school.

Sometimes disagreements develop because the parents and the school differ in their expectations regarding the child. Perhaps the parents expect a certain child to make better progress than he is making or to come home with a "perfect" report card. The school, basing its expectations on this child's measured aptitudes, expects average but not out-standing performance. Many parents interpret a "poor" re-port card as a reflection on them, the implication being that they have done a bad job in raising their children or that their children have perhaps inherited defective mentalities. Usually, attitudes of this sort are more indicative of parental insecurity than anything else. Indeed, Jean S. Grossman sug-gests that a good home is a place to which a child may bring a bad report card [5].

Sometimes difficulties develop when parents encourage the very sort of behavior the school is attempting to elimi-nate. Faith Smitter describes a case of this sort:

> Nine-year-old Peter . . . had a chip on his shoulder and al-ways seemed to be itching for a fight. One day after school the principal saw a crowd of children gathered about what ap-peared to be a cloud of dust. When he investigated, he found Peter pummeling another boy and the crowd fascinated by the brutal scene. The boys were separated, and when Peter was questioned, his explanation was, "My father says when a guy hits you, you got to hit him back [6]."

The problem here is obviously a delicate one. On the one hand, the school wants to help children learn better ways of solving problems than through physical violence, but on the other hand, it does not want to jeopardize the father-son re-lationship that is so important for Peter's development. These are the kinds of dilemmas that render relations with parents difficult, indeed.

PROBLEMS IN DISCIPLINE

Another source of conflict is the difference in standards of behavior and discipline. Parents may be permissive and in-dulgent, and the school may be demanding and strict. Or the parents may be dominating and exacting, expecting com-plete conformity and submission from their children, and the school may be trying to get children to develop in-dependence and initiative. Then there are the parents

who have difficulty in controlling their children and in
getting them to do the ordinary things which are important
or desirable in everyday living, such as getting to school on
time, being considerate of the feelings of others, respecting
law and order, and so forth.

Such difficulties are not unusual. Rudolph Dreikurs points
out that parents today have more problems than formerly,
partly because today's parents have doubts about the efficacy
of punishment, partly because children are being given
greater equality with adults (hence have more rights and
privileges), and partly because today's children often lack
the motivation to do the right thing. These are all symptoms
of the transition from an autocratic, paternalistic, power-
oriented culture to a democratic culture, a transition that
has been going on for centuries and that is now approaching
a climax. Dreikurs says that we are now at a point in our
cultural development where we cannot, in good conscience,
apply the punitive methods of yesterday but have not found
ways to express the democracy of tomorrow. As a result, we
are confused and anxious, particularly when it comes to relationships with children. The point is that parents who are
dissatisfied with their success in controlling their children
often expect the school to succeed where they have failed
[7]. However, such expectations are usually doomed to disappointment because schools have the same problem as the
parents and for the same reasons. Nevertheless, some parents
persist in this hope. It appears in the case of the parent who
suggests to the teacher that his child be spanked if he misbehaves or if he fails to get his lessons. Some parents bring
pressure on the school to assign children more homework,
with the thought that it is easier to control a child and limit
his activities if the school is requiring him to spend his free
time doing homework. This is a way of saying, "*I* am not
very successful in getting my child to spend his spare time
in socially useful activity, but *you,* the school, can do this
for me by assigning homework." Indeed, one might say that

the chief purpose for assigning homework very likely is that of using it as a way of controlling children because research does not show that it has any particular value as far as improvement in learning is concerned [8].

The danger of the situation we have described in the foregoing paragraph is that parents may come to believe that the school can do more in the way of disciplining or controlling their children than they (the parents) can themselves. Such an expectation has no firm foundation in fact. It is bound to lead to disappointment and, perhaps, to resentment. The parent who entertains such expectations has no real grasp of the function of the school, and the school which encourages parents to entertain such expectations is, in effect, asking for trouble. When a large number of parents in a given community are depending on the school to do their disciplining for them, this is a sign that neither school personnel nor parents have thought through their functions and goals or that there is poor communication between the school and the community.

"SOCIAL DISTANCE" BETWEEN PARENTS AND TEACHERS

A third source of potential conflict between parents and teachers lies in an attitude which might be characterized as the "snobbishness of the expert" or an attempt to maintain a polite "social distance." Many educators look upon parents as potential intruders—persons who interfere with the educational process, persons who hinder more than they help. Such educators look upon the efforts of parents to help their children to read or do long division as bungling attempts to compete with the school. Education, as these teachers see it, is a specialized and highly technical business—no field for amateurs. One should note, in passing, that this attitude is by no means confined to educators. For example, doctors depreciate attempts of laymen not only to diagnose and treat themselves but even to learn anything about the nature of

their illness, and lawyers are quick to point out that people
are likely to get themselves into difficulty in legal matters if
they do not seek the advice of a lawyer. It is evident that
there is a sound basis to this attitude—uninformed persons
are likely to make unnecessary mistakes if they venture too
far into the field of the expert, regardless of whether the
field of expertness be medicine, law, or education. However,
if the professional practitioner presumes too much on the
ignorance and incompetence of lay persons, and deals with
them in an arrogant and unfeeling manner, he is likely to
gain only noncooperation and hostility instead of the support
and cooperation he needs. Perhaps we may say that educators are less likely to err in this than are members of other
professions; nevertheless, the danger does exist wherever
parents feel that the school is trying to exclude them from
participation in any phase of the educational program.

Teachers who are overly conscious of their professional
status and training are probably compensating for feelings
of insecurity or inadequacy, feelings that for them may be
beyond the limits of their immediate awareness. Often they
express these neurotic needs by trying to make parents feel
inferior. As Jean S. Grossman says,

> Parents are often made to feel like colossal failures. In
> many cases they are summoned to their children's schools only
> when something is wrong; rarely do they have opportunity to
> hear about their youngster's worthiness, charm, intelligence, or
> success [9].

On the other hand, some parents make it difficult for
teachers and children alike by their unwillingness to "let go"
of their children. It is normal and natural for children to
find teachers that they like and admire, and if the parent is
at all emotionally insecure, he is likely to resent sharing even
a little of the spotlight of his child's love and admiration.
Probably most parents feel a little of this when their children

come home from school and speak glowingly of a new teacher, or when their children say, "You're wrong about that, Dad, because Miss Fenwick says such-and-such," or, "Mr. Hoffman says you're not supposed to say that, Mother." However, most parents are mature enough to swallow their temporarily injured feelings and write off the experience as part of living with a child who is growing up. It is the parent who cannot accept this feeling who causes the difficulty. Perhaps he feels that his authority has been challenged when his child momentarily places his faith in the teacher rather than in him, or perhaps he bears emotional scars from encounters with punitive and unsympathetic teachers when he was a child. The chances are that he will not know what the *real* factor is that is bringing him into conflict with his child's teacher. All the parent knows is that he does not like the teacher, his methods, and the things he is trying to teach his child.

There is something to be said for the teacher and his side of the conflict. It is true that parents sometimes "spoil things" by teaching children some things, deliberately or otherwise, things which are contrary to what is being taught in school. This not only confuses the child by exposing him to contradictions in authority, but also it makes for difficulties in classroom management. Then there is the parent who teaches his child material which *is* in harmony with the school's curriculum, except that he teaches it ahead of time so that the bloom is taken off what would normally be the teacher's satisfaction in having helped the child to discover some new fact or learn some new skill. A common example of this is the tendency of some parents to teach their five-year-olds how to read. This may not be a very serious problem, yet many teachers resent this as an invasion of their professional domain. Another example of parental interference resented by teachers is that of the parent who does his child's homework—and not always correctly. These are all more or less legitimate reasons for teachers to become concerned about the attempts of parents to interfere in the education of their children.

TEACHERS TEND TO BE OVERLY SENSITIVE

It should also be noted that teachers are rather quick to go on the defensive when they sense that parents may be interfering. They sometimes get upset over a minor instance of interference which might easily be ignored or worked out in friendly fashion by dealing directly with the parent himself. It is difficult to say why teachers are so sensitive. Perhaps it is because they are under constant pressure from all sides— from the administration, from students, from parents, from the community, from fellow teachers, yes, and even from themselves. One writer describes the teacher's situation as follows:

> Teachers are pressured from all sides to teach this, not to teach that; to individualize instruction and help children socially and emotionally as well as intellectually and to do it in large classes of thirty-five or more; to use democratic methods and maintain a permissive atmosphere but not let children "get out of hand" or, for that matter, out of their seats; to give children materials which they can handle and let them progress according to their ability and maturation but cover the course of study and be sure that the class is up to grade level on the "national norm." Teachers are told to make the curriculum functional and to adjust instruction to meet the personal-social needs of children and then are given a standardized test to administer and are criticized if the children fail to demonstrate achievement in the traditional content material [10].

A teacher works under constant observation; his mistakes and failures are for the most part public knowledge. This is truer of teaching than it is of almost any other profession. Therefore, the possibility of failure and criticism assumes enormous importance; teachers are likely to feel that they are always in danger of failing and of being criticized whether or not they have failed. This helps to make teaching a nerve-racking occupation. It is no wonder that teachers tend to be quick to defend themselves against real or fancied attacks or to blame the interference of parents for some of their mistakes.

Although there are extenuating circumstances which help to explain some of the bases for the conflict between parents and teachers, the detrimental effects of this rivalry cannot be overlooked. As we mentioned earlier, some children feel insecure when disagreement develops between tachers and parents—the important adults in their lives. Other children recognize the situation as a weak spot in adults' defenses and proceed to stir up trouble by playing teachers off against parents and vice versa. This has the apparent purpose of getting adults to take some of the pressure off children and direct it instead against each other. Usually the teacher comes off the worse in such conflicts because the parent has the psychological and moral advantage. Some children react to parent-teacher rivalry by becoming discouraged or cynical. In any event, the result is deteriorated morale and increased difficulties in learning.

Fortunately, there are some solutions to this problem. Parent-teacher disputes are not inevitable and, even when they do develop, they can usually be resolved on the basis of the indisputable fact that, in the final analysis, parents and teachers are together on at least one point—they are both interested in promoting the welfare of children. And they can be ever so much more effective if they work on these problems together, cooperatively, than if they work on them separately or at cross purposes. Parents and teachers need to regard each other as partners, rather than as competitors. If they are divided by suspicion, competition, or other forms of hostility, everyone will suffer—teachers, parents, schools, and particularly the children.

PARENTS AND EDUCATIONAL POLICY

STILL another reason for concern about better parent-teacher cooperation is the fact that parents have much to say about school policy. The power that parents exercise varies widely from community to community. In some communities they virtually elect and staff the school board; in others, they have little effect because they are unorganized. But even in the latter communities the unorganized parents possess great potential power. If they disapprove of school policies, they can quickly mobilize against the existing administration and bring about drastic changes. On the other hand, educators have been able at times to interest lethargic and apathetic parents in educational reforms that have captured their imagination, whereupon they have organized themselves into groups which have brought about great gains for the schools of the community.

It is sometimes difficult for the classroom teacher to see what part he can play in the over-all improvement of education in his community. But as he works with parents in helping them to get a better understanding of what is going on in his classroom, and as he helps to change passive, indifferent, or hostile attitudes into feelings that are constructive, sympathetic, and supporting, he is not only doing something which will make it easier for him to continue to do his job effectively, but he is also helping to bolster and improve the whole school program.

PROMOTING COOPERATION BETWEEN PARENTS AND SCHOOL

The surest way of enlisting the support of parents is to involve them actively in the actual administration and operation of the school program. This type of involvement has perhaps been brought to its greatest height in the cooperative nursery school program where parents make the policies of the school and help to operate it by serving as mother-helpers to the teachers, by repairing or building equipment, and by actually constructing and maintaining school buildings. These activities give the parents a sense of identity and involvement that they could not otherwise gain. There is no problem of enlisting the support of parents who are already involved in operating and administering a school—after all, it is *their* school.

We probably are not ready to go to such lengths in seeking the support of parents for schools above the nursery level —it may be inappropriate or unfeasible to involve parents in the more complex skills and problems which are part of administering and operating elementary and secondary schools. But the basic principle remains: parents will lend their support to the extent that they feel identified with the school. Some schools help parents develop this feeling of involvement by consulting with them when changes are contemplated. One school wanted to change the report card system and spent a year discussing the problem with groups of mothers and fathers and did not go ahead with the change until it was evident that the parents understood the proposed method of reporting and that most of them were in sympathy with the proposed change. Other schools get parents to act as co-sponsors of various extracurricular activities. Some teachers enlist the interest of parents by having them discuss their jobs with classes in occupations or senior problems.

Norman Fenton, in a discussion of parent participation in the life of the school, states that too many obstacles have been placed in the way of cooperative action.

> From the standpoint of mental hygiene, elementary and secondary schools have before them a challenge to match the accomplishments in the integration of school and home which have been achieved by teachers and parents of preschool children. The greatest handicap to progress here is the conservative attitude of educators and parents [11].

He continues by saying that administrators are likely to object, not only because the idea is original and radical, but also because they are afraid that parents may assume too much authority in the management of the school. Some administrators have had experiences with emotionally disturbed parents that make them shy away from any collaboration that promises to be too close. On the other hand, says Fenton, many parents would feel anxious and insecure about working with educators, others would feel hostile, and still others would be too apathetic and passive to want to do anything original or important. Furthermore, a large number of parents welcome the opening of school because it provides a partial means of escaping from the cares and worries of full-time supervision of their children. In spite of these objections and difficulties, Fenton believes that the values to be obtained from collaboration and cooperation are great and he suggests some approaches which would lead to better and closer working relationships. For example, a school that wishes to promote cooperation between parents and educators should start by hiring administrators who are sympathetic to the idea of sharing their power and responsibilities; minor issues and problems should be taken up first; and teachers and parents should be encouraged to get together and share their knowledge.

THE NEED FOR BETTER RELATIONS WITH THE COMMUNITY

Teachers should also be concerned about relations with parents because of the need for better communication between the school and the community. It is important for members of the community to be informed about the needs, activities, and policies of the school partly because the school needs financial and moral support from the community and partly because there is a danger of the school's becoming too isolated from the main currents of community life. The school that is out of touch with the community can easily become the target for attacks by the uninformed or the irresponsible. Prejudice thrives on ignorance. And let us be realistic about this—among laymen almost a tradition of prejudice exists where school matters are concerned. Look at this stereotype of the teacher, as compiled by the American Association of School Administrators:

1. The teacher is an old maid.
2. Teachers are aloof, snobbish, unwordly.
3. Teachers are querulous, irritable, generally unsympathetic, and lacking in understanding of young people and their problems.
4. Teachers are ineffectual.
5. Teachers have no interests outside of school and schoolwork.
6. Teachers are paid too much and have too long vacations.
7. Teachers get their jobs through political, racial, or religious connections.
8. Teachers are inclined to be "bossy" in relationships with others—they carry over classroom manners into adult contacts.
9. Teachers are fussy, picayune, and trivial in their attitudes.
10. Men teachers are timid, queer, eccentric, or sissyish; a "real" man does not go into teaching [12].

The report goes on to say that much of the blame for this stereotype lies with school administrators who "trivialize" school methods, routines, and teachers' outlooks, and with "legislatures, boards of education, and community groups, which, through restrictive legislation and social and economic discrimination, have forced teachers to function as second-class citizens [13]. . . ."

Perhaps some of the above can be dismissed as overly prejudiced or as inapplicable to more enlightened communities. Nevertheless, the attitudes described are prevalent enough to cause concern among educators who are seeking community support and cooperation for the school program. And this is where the parent enters the picture.

The parent is the lay person who is most immediately concerned with the school. Its success is as important to him as it is to teachers and school administrators. If the school communicates effectively with parents, it can depend on parents to carry some of its message to the community and to act as its allies when the support of the total community is needed, as, for example, during a school bond election. Of course, this does not preclude the school's communicating directly with the community through advisory committees of laymen, through newspaper publicity, or through the devices mentioned previously. The important principle to be observed is that communication, to be really effective, must be two-way: it is necessary for the school to give careful and sympathetic attention to what parents and other lay people have to say if it expects to receive the same kind of attention from the community.

In the research into the interpersonal preceptions of junior high students, parents, and teachers that we have mentioned elsewhere in this text, Jenkins and Lippitt found that one of the major areas of potential and probable difficulty involved the gaps between the self-concepts of parents and teachers with respect to their relationship. Parents felt that their major contact with teachers should grow out of their mutual concern for the welfare of children whose supervision they shared, whereas teachers looked for more contact with parents on a more friendly basis, as members of the adult community. In other words, teachers wanted acceptance as fellow participants in the life of the community, not merely a relationship based on their professional roles. Jenkins and Lippitt also noted that there was opportunity for a closer relationship between parents and teachers growing out of the teachers' desire that parents visit and consult with them at school. Parents are relatively unaware that teachers want this. The authors felt that as parents begin to see that teachers want their participation and not just their cooperation, some of the barriers to closer contact and better communication will disappear [14].

Recent developments in the field of parent education are very encouraging in this regard. Public school departments in a number of communities throughout the country are providing a great variety of educational experiences for parents who want to learn how to play their life roles more effectively, who are looking for ways to improve their ability to help their children develop in ways that are emotionally and socially mature. The experiences that are made available include small-group discussions, panels and forums, workshops and conferences, and cooperative nursery schools. Although the proportion of parents benefiting from these experiences is still quite small, the number is growing, and many school departments find that the demand for these services exceeds their ability to meet it. Parents who take advantage of this kind of education help to reinforce the mental-health experiences their children receive in school and in the playground. It is easier for teachers to communicate with such parents because both teachers and parents have a common area of understanding in the area of child development—they both possess a common vocabulary of terms and concepts. Furthermore, parents who participate in this kind of education are likely to have developed more favorable attitudes toward the school and its educational program because they have become a part of this program and are receiving direct personal benefits from it.

HOW TO COMMUNICATE WITH PARENTS

THIS brings us to a consideration of some rather technical aspects of communicating with parents and other lay people with whom the teacher has contact. We shall discuss these points in terms of dealing with parents, bearing in mind that these principles are applicable to communication with other lay people.

The first and foremost rule is to be a good listener. This holds true even if one of the purposes in the meeting is to tell the parent something. Very often a parent has something on his mind, something which has been bothering him. If he wants very much to express himself but has not had a chance, he may not even hear what you are trying to say. Some parents, of course, do not have much to say at first because they are more interested in hearing what the teacher has to say. However, once they have grasped the main points, they may wish to express themselves at length. The point is to be alert and sensitive to parents' needs to communicate. The advantage is usually with the teacher—even if he does not know "all the answers," the conversation is largely concerned with education, and in this field he is the trained, professional expert. Therefore, he can afford to discipline himself to defer to the parent in such conversations, secure in the feeling that his prestige and status will be undiminished. Redl and Wattenberg have this to say on the subject:

> The first principle of good interviewing is to let the other fellow talk when he wants to. Let him say what he wants to get said. Having spoken his piece, he is more likely to feel appreciated. The more he can explain his problem, the better we can understand him, and the more he feels understood. Time spent listening attentively saves time which would otherwise be wasted in futile arguments and blunders due to misunderstanding. Having to hold their tongues may be frustrating to the teachers but, as professionally trained people, they can get their satisfactions from long-term accomplishment. This principle should not be carried to the extreme, where a teacher would feel compelled to be passive and show absolutely no reaction in an interview [15].

It is hard to be a good listener with parents who are dominating and aggressive or even truculent. However, this type of behavior is often an attempt to compensate for feelings of insecurity and inferiority. Such parents are, very likely, steeling themselves in anticipation of the teacher's criticism. When, instead, the teacher listens sympathetically and respectfully, this often helps to reduce their tension, whereupon attention can be directed more profitably to the main purpose of the interview.

The second principle is to be cautious with criticism and advice giving. There is a feeling on the part of most clinicians that many parents cannot profit by advice or information that is given to them directly [16]. However, sometimes the giving of advice is most appropriate, particularly when it can take the form of a friendly discussion of the problem with possible ways of handling it. Timing is an important factor here. If the teacher gives advice, he should also be prepared to accept advice from a parent, and the trading of suggestions in a friendly give-and-take is one of the many good ways of establishing satisfactory communication with parents. Yet, until such a relationship is established, it is wise to proceed carefully. The parent who is not prepared to accept advice can easily be put on the defensive by the teacher's criticism. Even parents who *ask* for advice are often not ready to use it. Often this is a way of getting the teacher to commit himself, whereupon the parent says to himself, in effect: "Hmph. Just like all teachers—ready to tell me how to run my family at the drop of a hat. Who does he think he is, anyway?" Naturally, such an attitude is highly illogical in view of the parent's request for advice, but parents are no different from the rest of us—we all do illogical things occasionally and are completely unaware of them, particularly during moments of stress or when we feel that our pride and reputation are at stake.

Lois H. Meek indicates some other problems that may lead to unwarranted advice giving during interviews with parents:

> If the child is not successful or happy in school, [mother and teacher may] each . . . look to the other as the source of the

difficulty. The mother is likely to be protective of her methods when confronted with the clinical training of the teacher. . . .

Too often teachers do not sense these feelings. They feel somewhat superior because of their professional training and expect the mother to appreciate this and accept advice readily. In some cases the teacher identifies herself with the child and is in a manner jealous of the mother's position. She may herself long for the experiences in family life that the mother is having. Her criticisms are likely to be harsh because they spring from yearnings she herself scarcely realizes exist [17].

The difficulties described by Meek obviously do not apply to all interviews between teachers and parents. The point here is that unconscious and sometimes neurotic needs can interfere, often when we are least aware of them, with the establishment of rapport and the attempt to develop good communication in an interview.

A third principle is not to betray confidences. Children often tell teachers things they would not tell anyone else, particularly their parents. It is a breach of professional ethics to share information received in this manner. The same principle applies to anything that parents tell teachers in confidence. An exception to this rule is the case conference. Sometimes a serious problem develops and the information which the teacher has held in confidence may be used by qualified persons to aid the child, assuming, of course, that the persons concerned will also handle the information as confidential. Teachers have to use their judgment at such times to determine whether the sharing of such information would be a violation of confidence.

The principles that Nathaniel Cantor has drawn up as applicable to every well-handled discusion are also pertinent to interviews with parents:

1. Do not argue.
2. Do not give advice.
3. Do not direct the discussion.
4. Do not force answers.

5. Do not take sides.
6. Listen rather than talk.
7. Try to grasp what lies behind what a speaker is saying.
8. Do not make moral judgments.
9. Above all, try to communicate to the speaker your appreciation of what he says and how he feels [18].

Perhaps the most important principle of all is to trust parents to do the right thing and to let them know that you trust them. When parents discover that the teacher listens to what they say, accepts them at face value and is not prone to give unwanted advice, their tensions, anxieties, and hostilities melt away. They see the teacher as "one of us"—someone with whom they can identify, someone who is deeply interested in the welfare of their children, someone whom they can trust and respect, and, finally, someone whom they will aid and support.

REFERENCES

1. R. C. Myers, "Biographical Factors and Academic Achievement: An Experimental Investigation," *Educational and Psychological Measurements*. 12:415–26;1952.
2. M. Bonney, "Counseling Youth for Social Living," in *General Lectures, Counseling Workshop, Chico State College, Summer, 1950*. Chico, Calif.: State College, 1950. P. 74.
3. Association for Supervision and Curriculum Development, *Fostering Mental Health in Our Schools*. Washington: National Education Association, 1950. P. 23. Reprinted by permission.
4. *Ibid*. P. 22.
5. J. S. Grossman, *Life with Family*. New York: Appleton-Century-Crofts, 1948. P. 11.
6. C. Buhler, F. Smitter, and S. Richardson, *Childhood Problems and the Teacher*. New York: Holt, 1952. P. 213. Reprinted by permission.
7. R. Dreikurs, *Character Education and Spiritual Values in an Anxious Age*. Boston: Beacon, 1952. P. 6.
8. P. J. DiNapoli, *Homework in the New York City Elementary Schools*. Contributions to Education No. 719. New York: Bureau of Publications, Teachers College, Columbia University, 1937.

9. Grossman, *op. cit.* Pp. 10–11.
10. Association for Supervision and Curriculum Development, *Growing up in an Anxious Age.* Washington: National Education Association, 1952. P. 10. Reprinted by permission.
11. N. Fenton, *Mental Hygiene in School Practice.* Stanford: Stanford University Press, 1943. P. 360. Reprinted by permission.
12. American Association of School Administrators, *Public Relations for America's Schools,* Twenty-Eighth Yearbook. Washington: National Education Association, 1950. P. 157. Reprinted by permission.
13. *Ibid.* P. 159. Reprinted by permission.
14. D. H. Jenkins and R. Lippitt, *Interpersonal Perceptions of Teachers, Students, and Parents.* Washington: National Education Association, 1951. Chapter 3.
15. F. Redl and W. W. Wattenberg, *Mental Hygiene in Teaching.* New York: Harcourt, Brace, 1951. Pp. 368–69. Copyright, 1951, by Harcourt, Brace and Company, Inc. Reprinted by permission.
16. M. J. Fitzsimmons, *Some Parent-Child Relationships as Shown in Clinical Case Studies.* New York: Bureau of Publications, Teachers College, Columbia University, 1935.
17. L. H. Meek, *et al., The Personal-Social Development of Boys and Girls with Implications for Secondary Education.* New York: Progressive Education Association, 1940. P. 104. Reprinted by permission.
18. N. Cantor, *Learning through Discussion.* Buffalo: Human Relations for Industry, 1951. P. 66. Reprinted by permission.

SUGGESTED READINGS

D. S. Arbuckle, *Teacher Counseling.* Cambridge, Mass.: Addison-Wesley, 1950. Chapters 4 and 5 depict contrasting types of interviews conducted by the traditional teacher and the "new" teacher. Some of these interviews are with parents.

Association for Supervision and Curriculum Development, *Fostering Mental Health in Our Schools.* Washington: National Education Association, 1950. Chapter 2, "Children Bring Their Families to School," and Chapter 9, "The Child Patterns Himself After His Favorite Models," and Chapter 13, "Informal Talks with Children and Parents."

D. W. Baruch, *Parents and Children Go to School.* Chicago: Scott, Foresman, 1939.

M. W. Brown, *Partners in Education*. Washington: Association for Childhood Education International, 1950.

C. Buhler, F. Smitter, and S. Richardson, *Childhood Problems and the Teacher*. New York: Holt, 1952. Chapter 12, "The Teacher's Work with Parents."

R. Cunningham, *et al., Understanding Group Behavior of Boys and Girls*. New York: Bureau of Publications, Teachers College, Columbia University, 1951. Chapter 10, "Parents as Co-Researchers," deals with an interesting and novel approach to enlisting the participation of parents in the educational program.

K. D'Evelyn, *Individual Parent-Teacher Conferences: A Manual for Teachers of Young Children*. New York: Bureau of Publications, Teachers College, Columbia University, 1945.

N. Fenton, *Mental Hygiene in School Practice*. Stanford: Stanford University Press, 1944. Chapter 20, "The School's Relation to Mental Hygiene in the Home."

Helping Teachers Understand Children. Washington: American Council on Education. Chapter 3, "Seeing the Child as a Member of a Family." Discusses home visits.

L. J. Luker, "Working with Home and Community," in C. E. Erickson, ed., *A Basic Text for Guidance Workers*. New York: Prentice-Hall, 1947.

F. Redl and W. W. Wattenberg, *Mental Hygiene in Teaching*. New York: Harcourt, Brace, 1951. Chapter 15, "Working with Parents."

C. R. Rogers, *The Clinical Treatment of the Problem Child*. Boston: Houghton Mifflin, 1939. Chapter 7, "Family Attitudes as a Focus of Treatment."

H. Witmer and R. Kotinsky, *Personality in the Making*. New York: Harper, 1952. Chapter 4, "The Importance of Parent-Child Relations," and Chapter 9, "The Family."

See also items 5, 7, 10, 12, 14, and 18 in the References for this chapter.

SUGGESTED FILMS

Family Circles. Available through McGraw-Hill.

A Guidance Problem for Home and School. Available through Columbia University, Division of Audio-Visual Aids.

Individual Differences. Parents help a teacher to gain a better understanding of their son. Available through McGraw-Hill.

School and Community. Available through McGraw-Hill.

15

DISINTEGRATIVE

INFLUENCES IN EDUCATION

EDUCATION AS AN INTEGRATIVE PROCESS

THIS chapter and the one following will discuss certain factors and forces in present-day education in terms of whether they help children to achieve "integration" in their personalities.[1] In using the concept of integration we have reference to the process of becoming more mature. A person who is more mature is better "integrated" than one who is less mature. There is greater harmony and efficiency in the actions of the mature person; he is not so likely to work at cross purposes with himself. He is less confused, less disturbed by neurotic anxiety, better able to go about the business of meeting his normal needs. He is more capable of thinking through problems intelligently and independently, and he

---

[1] For discussions of integrative and disintegrative factors in personality development see: H. C. Lindgren, *Psychology of Personal and Social Development.* New York: American Book, 1953. Chapter 19, "Integrative and Disintegrative Factors in Mental Health." Also, see Chapter 14, "The Therapy of Everyday Life," in *The Art of Human Relations,* by the same author. New York: Hermitage, 1953.

can apply himself to the task of learning without being hampered unduly by neurotic needs.

The mental-hygiene task of the school can thus be seen as one of helping children to achieve a better integration. In order to work in the direction of this goal, it is necessary that we be aware of those forces and factors in the school that promote integration and those that discourage it. Integrative influences and forces are those conditions or factors that aid, stimulate, or encourage the child's growth and development in the direction of better mental health and emotional, social, and intellectual maturity. They would thus include influences that aid the child in becoming more aware of the realities of life, in establishing satisfying relationships with others, and in meeting his basic needs. Disintegrative influences and forces are those conditions or factors that prevent or discourage the child's growth and development in the direction of better mental health. These are factors that make children feel insecure, that arouse neurotic needs, that stimulate overrebellious or overdependent behavior.

It should be noted, however, that not all negative aspects of a child's environment are disintegrative, for some of them constitute challenges he must learn how to handle if he is to grow emotionally and intellectually. In attempting to minimize or eliminate disintegrative forces in the classroom we must therefore not commit the error of shielding the child from all forms of anxiety, normal as well as neurotic. This is one of the most vexing problems in teaching: how to permit enough *normal* anxiety to exist in the classroom to stimulate learning and growth and how, at the same time, to eliminate the factors and reduce the forces that stimulate the *neurotic* anxiety which interferes with learning and growth.

In this chapter we shall be concerned principally with some of the conditions and situations existing in the school that may be characterized as "disintegrative." Some of these factors have already been discussed elsewhere in this textbook. Where this is the case, we shall but mention them briefly, with reference to the chapters where fuller discussion may be found.

CULTURAL INFLUENCES

THERE are disintegrative conditions and influences which are a function of the cultural and social atmosphere of which the school is a part and which, therefore, are inescapable. Inasmuch as the school is the instrument of society, it is bound to inculcate those values and standards which are part of the culture, often without regard to whether they have an integrative or disintegrative effect on mental health.

EMPHASIS ON CONFORMITY

One of these factors is the emphasis and insistence on conformity and submission which is characteristic of the emotional climate of many schools. This often has the effect of discouraging originality and independence in thought and action. To be sure, a certain degree of conformity is necessary in all social situations, otherwise groups lack cohesion and purpose and are unable to operate effectively. But when conformity becomes an end in itself instead of the means to an end, when it becomes a central value in the child's personality, there is a dying out of the capacity for originality and the desire for self-direction. It is almost as though the individual is afraid to be himself.[2] (See discussion in Chapter 8.)

EMPHASIS ON REWARD AND PUNISHMENT

The attempt to translate all learning into reward-and-punishment situations commonly does violence to the principle that learning is a natural outgrowth of the child's attempts to

---

[2] For a discussion of personality pattern of the "overconforming" person see the description of the "marketing orientation" in Erich Fromm, *Man for Himself*, New York: Rinehart, 1947; and the description of the "other-directed" person in David Riesman, *The Lonely Crowd*. New Haven: Yale University Press, 1950.

meet his needs for growth and development. Persons who utilize the reward-and-punishment approach to education exclusively assume that children will not learn unless the situation has been rigged by the teacher to punish failure and reward successes. Some children who are subjected to situations of this sort over the years come to believe that the rewards of learning are not the pleasure and satisfaction of practicing a new skill or discovering a new bit of information but are instead the praise of the teacher. Or, even more commonly, children come to feel that learning is something one does to avoid punishment or criticism. In effect, an overemphasis on the reward-and-punishment aspects of the educational situation produces a distortion which causes students to substitute a rather hollow and insubstantial type of goal for the deeper satisfactions that result from greater personal adequacy—such things as improved relations with others, greater skill in dealing with the problems of one's environment, greater effectiveness in self-expression, and the like. (See discussion in Chapter 11.)

EMPHASIS ON COMPETITION

The third influence we wish to discuss under this heading is the overemphasis on competition. There is no quarrel here with the friendly sort of competition which often helps to stimulate interest in the classroom. What we are concerned with is a situation that causes children to subordinate all other considerations in favor of an intense drive to get the best marks. In the worst of the competitive situations, children no longer care about what they learn—whether it is useful, whether it is worth remembering over the summer vacation, whether it helps make the world around them more understandable—their only concern is to defeat each other. One writer comments:

> The kinds of pressures used by middle-class teachers and parents to make children conform to adult expectations are not always desirable. To please his parents and to be accepted by

them, it is not enough for a middle-class child to do well in school; he must do as well or better than other children in the neighborhood. If Johnny Jones is getting 4 A's, then Tommy Brown's family expects him to get 4 or more A's on his report. Both parents and teachers frequently make the mistake of thinking that getting better marks in school is simply a matter of effort and will power. "If Johnny would only *try* harder" or "If Mary would just make up her mind to learn" expresses a commonly held viewpoint. Yet Johnny and Mary may be doing the best that their mental powers will permit, or may not be doing their best, not because of lack of effort or will power but for some reason which is rooted in Johnny's or Mary's personality structure [1].

Nathaniel Cantor indicates how the school situation develops and encourages competition through its system of rewards and through its policy of ignoring or denying the existence of peer-group relationships of the classroom:

> The school rewards individual, not cooperative effort. Grades and reports are given to the individual student for the acquisition of intellectual and verbal skills. The classroom, generally, consists of a group of children each of whom is in an insulated individual relationship with the teacher. The "I" growth, not the "we" development, is emphasized [2].

Another effect of the overemphasis on competition is that it makes students too fearful of failure. Preoccupation with failure induces an unrealistic and somewhat neurotic orientation to life. In the first place, a certain amount of failure is inevitable in life. Ofttimes the overly competitive person is so afraid of failure that he tries to cover up or deny to himself the fact that he has failed. Or he might indulge in self-condemnation and self-recrimination for not having lived up to his expectations. In the second place, failure can be a useful experience in learning. The emotionally mature person is one who can accept the fact that he has failed, analyze and appraise the situation, and determine what he should do next. The overly competitive person is often so overcome by anxiety or the inability to accept the reality of his failure that he is unable to profit from his experience. (See discussion of competition in Chapter 10.)

Sheviakov and Redl describe the emotional climate of a classroom dominated by competition that has gone beyond the "friendly stage:

> The hostile competition climate is a distortion of an otherwise healthy phenomenon in our society. Normally, a good deal of competitiveness is unavoidable, even liked, by the children growing into a society where there can be little doubt of the presence of competitiveness. However, there are two things that can go wrong with a normal competitive climate: one is that there may be more competitiveness than children need or can stand without developing negative character traits or defeatism; the other is that competitiveness may deteriorate into hatefulness.
>
> The hostile competition climate can be characterized thus: everybody is whipped into aggressively competing with everybody else all of the time. Reward is given to him who proudly tramples under his feet whoever dares to compete with him. Shame falls upon the head of the child who would rather get a lower grade than feel holier-than-thou toward his best pal. The hostile competition climate turns a classroom into a dog race. It is highly doubtful that love and friendship is instigated in the participants while the race is going on [3].

There are other conditions and forces in our culture which have an adverse effect on the mental health of children in the schools; our purpose here has been to describe three which are most likely to affect the atmosphere of the school. It should be noted that in each case the forces stem from trends in our culture which are basically healthy, but which are likely to be exaggerated and overemphasized.

A similar point is also made by David C. Wilson, who points out that neurotic trends may affect the behavior of a whole social group or even a complete society. He terms this type of trend a "neurosis of everyday living":

A neurosis of everyday living occurs when socially-accepted behavior is exaggerated to such a degree that it interferes in an injurious manner with interpersonal relations, and the performer is unaware of the actual cause for his behavior, or—if he becomes aware—is unable to modify the exaggeration [4].

Wilson says that persons suffering from a neurosis of everyday living are not aware that they are behaving in ways that are detrimental to their mental health, nor is their behavior considered unhealthy by others in the group who observe them. Thus a child may engage in hostile and destructive competition in the classroom and on the playground to the detriment of his normal emotional and social development without his teachers, parents, or classmates being aware that such an overemphasis is unhealthy because competition is an accepted mode of behavior in our culture.

INFLUENCES RESULTING FROM THE ORGANIZATIONAL STRUCTURE OF THE SCHOOL

UNDER this heading we shall consider a variety of conditions that largely develop within the school itself and that have a negative effect on the mental health and normal development of children.

DIFFICULTIES IN COMMUNICATION

One of the chief problems is the difficulty which children experience in trying to communicate with adults and vice versa. We discussed this at length in the chapter on communication, so shall not belabor the subject further here. However, we should be aware that the organization of the classroom makes it easy for the teacher to talk to the class but not for the class to talk to the teacher. Furthermore, the tradition is that it is the role of the teacher to talk and the role of the student to listen. This not only stifles the self-expression of students, but it also impedes the free operation of the learning process. Learning is facilitated by the free operation of two-way communication; it is blocked when we attempt to maintain communication on a one-way basis.

THE AUTOCRATIC TRADITION

The organizational structure of the schools prescribed by convention and tradition is one which is best suited for the distribution of power in an autocratic atmosphere. It is an arrangement that makes it easy for one person to make most of the decisions on behalf of the staff and the students. This type of organization may seem desirable for purposes of economy and efficiency, but it makes the development of democratic practices a difficult one. If the principal happens to be of a democratic turn of mind, he can share his power and responsibility and thus tacitly permit and encourage teachers to do the same in their classrooms. But the system also permits an insecure person to hoard his power and to monopolize decision-making. Teachers usually react to this treatment by becoming more authoritarian and autocratic in their classrooms.

Some of the insecurities of the principal may be the direct result of the pressures brought to bear on him by the superintendent, the school board, or the community. Unfortunately, we do not appear to have any easy way of getting school boards and communities to see that schools operate more effectively under democratic leadership than under autocratic. Until enough people, within the schools and without, are willing to dedicate themselves to changing the prevailing climate in schools from autocratic to democratic, children must continue to attend schools in which the emotional climate is one which is, in many respects, unfriendly and unsympathetic to emotional health.

DIVORCEMENT OF THE CURRICULUM FROM REALITY

One of the most difficult problems which schools must face is that of developing a curriculum which has reality and life for children. What happens all too often is that children fail to see any connection between what they study in school and life in the world outside. Merely because the connection between the curriculum and life is obvious to an adult does not mean that it is obvious to a child. After a while, children get the idea that nothing that the school teaches is of any practical use, and that the curriculum is a series of uninteresting tasks which do not bear any real relationship to each other. This situation is most likely to develop in schools where no one is interested in involving teachers in curriculum development; but it can also occur in schools where the curriculum has been democratically evolved, but where teachers have forgotten or neglected to help students make the connections between the various segments of the curriculum and between the curriculum and life itself. In the schools which are doing this job most effectively, the curriculum becomes part of the student's life, and he becomes as much involved in it as he is in the other activities of everyday life.

In his analysis of frustration in adolescent youth, David Segel comes to the conclusion that the organization of the curriculum in the typical high school creates difficulties for some students who attempt to use it as a means of helping them meet their basic needs for self-enhancement—that is, their normal needs for status, self-expression, and creativity. He feels that the core curriculum and the "common learnings" courses are more helpful than the patchwork of unrelated and segmented courses in the traditional curriculum, but that the only effective way in which the basic needs of students can be met is through courses that are based on and grow out of these needs [5].

The great danger is that if the student views the curriculum as uninteresting and sterile, he is likely to become cynical and discouraged about school, about education, perhaps even about *any* kind of learning or *any* activity operated by adults. If he develops these attitudes, his growth in emotional and intellectual maturity may halt far short of capacity; he may even become antisocial. In any case, his effectiveness as a citizen and his ability to participate adequately in society may be impaired. Most students who develop attitudes of this sort drop out of school at the earliest opportunity. Teachers and administrators often rejoice at seeing them leave, saying, "There goes one who cannot benefit from the program." The implication, of course, is that the program is right and the student was wrong. However, one of the main purposes of the school is to help children. If the children drop out of school, they can no longer be helped by the school. We commonly think that it was the student who failed; more than likely it was we who failed.

EXAMINATIONS AND MARKS

The question of academic failure brings us to a consideration of marks and examinations, a chronic source of tensions and anxieties. Since we have discussed these aspects of curriculum elsewhere, we shall not explore them extensively here.[3] Most teachers agree that our present systems of grading leave much to be desired, but they also agree that we have not found acceptable substitutes for grades. One of the reasons for this difficulty is that our grading system is suited to an educational organization which emphasizes competition, often to the detriment of learning. If competition were no problem, grading would be much less of a problem. If grades were merely the evaluations of learning, devoid of any emotional considerations, they would present no real difficulties, but as long as an A is an honor, a reward, and a designation of high status, and an F is a disgrace, a penalty, and a designation of low status, tensions and anxieties are inevitable.

INEPTNESS IN HANDLING CHILDREN

Many of the difficulties which develop in some schools are the direct result of what might be called "chronic mishan-

---

[3] See discussion in Chapter 18.

dling"—the seeming inability of the teachers and administrators to do the right thing where children are concerned. A school of this type is likely to be divided into two camps: a group of determined teachers and administrators on one side, together with a few students who identify with authority, and an equally determined and defiant group of students on the other. Much of the teachers' time is taken up with planning strategies to control or trap students into doing the work assigned, and much of the student's time is taken up with the devising of ways and means to defeat teachers. Sometimes the adults win these skirmishes, and sometimes they are won by the children. But in the end, the adults always lose the "war"—assuming, of course, that the prime objective of the struggle has been to help children learn. Any learning which takes place under such situations occurs in spite of the school program, rather than because of it.

The "divided camp" situation is perhaps an extreme (although not too unusual) development of what happens when relations with children are chronically mishandled. Mishandling, on the face of it, appears to be the result of selecting the wrong techniques or using good techniques but applying them in the wrong way or to the wrong situations. This brings us to the problem we have mentioned repeatedly in this text; if we were more concerned with understanding children, we would have to worry less about techniques. The teacher who chronically mishandles his class is usually one who does not understand the motivation of children; he does not seem to grasp the effect that certain of his actions will have on their behavior. Perhaps, on a deeper level of consciousness, he does not understand himself; for, as we watch him in action before a class, we wonder whether he has an unconscious need to antagonize and frustrate children or whether he is trying, unconsciously, to arrange matters so that he will fail. We wonder about these things because we see him try, again and again, techniques and approaches which have already failed with the same children. One of the earmarks of the chronic mishandler is that if a certain method does not work with children, he is likely to try it again, only with more force.

There are other imbalances and stresses in our schools that are likely to have warping effects on the mental health of children. We have covered only a few of the principle ones. There is a recurring theme which runs through them all: when we become dedicated to maintaining a certain prescribed form or structure, or when we become concerned with preserving our own power and allaying our own anxieties—in short, when we become preoccupied with anything but the welfare of the children we supervise—then we are likely to impair our effectiveness as teachers. This happens, in effect, because we have turned our backs on our main objective.

THE UNMET NEEDS OF INDIVIDUAL CHILDREN

THE NEEDS OF THE GROUP VERSUS THE NEEDS OF THE INDIVIDUAL CHILD

The greater portion of this text is concerned with meeting the needs of the classroom group, recognizing that as long as the teacher must operate within the context of mass education, his main problems will be the problems of dealing with groups of children. Even when he deals with individual children, he must always keep the group in mind and must ask himself: "Am I neglecting the group to work with this child? Must the group wait until I am finished? How will the group feel about me if I give this child so much individual attention? How will they feel about him?"

Sometimes a compromise must be made because the problems of the group and those of the individual are in both cases pressing and urgent. Sometimes unmet needs of individual children pile up to the point where the educational progress of the group is jeopardized. A common example of this is the disturbance created by children who are emotionally upset. And very often the educational program is threatened because of the unmet needs of a large group of students. In this section we shall consider both types of problems.

BOYS: A "DEPRIVED" GROUP

In terms of the magnitude of the problem, probably the largest "deprived" group in the schools is the boys. Boys begin school at a disadvantage—socially and linguistically their development lags, on the average, behind that of girls [6, 7]. The cultural norm is for boys to behave in ways which are aggressive, destructive, individualistic, and physically active, whereas girls are expected to be submissive, cooperative, and more anxious to please. Since the school situation places a high premium on linguistic skills and the ability to conform, girls are likely to adjust to the situation more readily.

The superior linguistic ability of girls is revealed by such studies as the one by J. Louise Despert, who studied the background of fifty stuttering children. She confirms the findings of other researchers to the effect that there are more boys than girls among stutterers [8].

Dorothea McCarthy reviewed the research on the linguistic development of boys and girls. She attributed the development of superior linguistic behavior among girls to their more favorable emotional environment. She states further:

> The average boy is more likely to enter school feeling somewhat insecure and rejected and to have had a less healthy relationship with his mother than the average girl. His predisposition therefore toward the female teacher is more likely to be fraught with a great degree of anxiety, which may interfere with effective learning; and hence he is somewhat more likely

to have difficulty with reading and other . . . skills in the academic situation than the average girl [9].

Linguistic development and social adjustment appear to go hand in hand. The superior social adjustment of girls is demonstrated in a sociometric study of high school youth conducted by George A. Lundberg and Lenore Dickson. They concluded that the girls in their sample were better adjusted socially than the boys in that they were more likely to make sociometric choices of persons who also chose them. Furthermore, they were more likely to know who reciprocated their choices [10].

Further evidence of the better adjustment of girls is provided by a study made by Joseph Jastak and Lois G. Gilliland, who explored the personality problems of juvenile delinquents. They report that boys display their delinquent tendencies earlier than girls and that they are more overt and more aggressive in their offensive behavior. For example, four times as many boys as girls in their sample were charged with stealing [11]. Similar evidence pointing to the greater social maladjustment in boys appears in a survey made by the Children's Bureau of the Federal Government in 1949, covering 413 courts and over 70,000 children and youths. Among this group of delinquents, boys outnumbered girls better than four to one [12].

In reviewing evidence compiled in a study of personality problems of 810 ninth-grade students in Prince Georges County, Maryland, Charles A. Ullman concluded that boys demonstrate the problems they do because they tend to turn their drives outward and are concerned with doing something active about life situations as a means of releasing their tensions, regardless of whether these acts involve sex, school, teachers, or religion [13].

The almost inevitable result of this inequality in the ability to adjust to the academic and social demands of the school is that girls are more likely to succeed and be rewarded and boys are more likely to fail and be punished. In effect, girls are approved and accepted, and boys are rejected. Taking into consideration the level of linguistic skill and social adaptibility, the needs of girls are likely to be met more readily by the school as it exists today, and the needs of boys, less readily.

This problem is not one which can be met easily. Perhaps it involves re-educating an entire culture to the end that our expectations for boys and girls become more similar. Separate schools for boys and girls suggests itself as a solution, yet most educators, as well the public, feel that there is much to be gained by having boys and girls work and play together. In a commencement address, Lynn White, president of Mills College, suggested that girls start school at five years of age and boys at seven. Probably none of these proposed solutions should be attempted until we know more about the processes of growth, learning, and the interaction among children of both sexes. There is no question about the problem being serious. We noted above that four times as many boys as girls are arrested for delinquency. This is a rough measure of the extent to which the school, along with other agencies of society, has failed to motivate boys in the direction of mental health. In this writer's opinion, one of the ways in which we could begin to attack this problem is to recognize that in our culture there are differences in the needs of boys and girls and that part of the job of understanding children is to be aware of these differences. In some ways this poses an extremely difficult problem for teachers in the primary grades. It is more difficult for women teachers to empathize with boys and to deal with their problems sympathetically; yet it is important that this be done because the basic attitudes that children develop toward school are laid down in these early years. Indeed, this is a problem which requires much study. Unfortunately it is one which has been largely neglected both by the educational psychologist and the mental hygienist.

CHILDREN FROM LOWER SOCIOECONOMIC GROUPS

There is another group of children whose needs are for the most part unmet in most schools. These are the children who come from environments variously described as "lower class," "working class," "deprived," or "slum." Not all these labels apply to the same children—that is, a child who comes from a working-class home may not live in a slum and may not even come from a lower-class environment. However, there are common factors that apply to the behavior and problems of a great many children who come from such environments, factors which interfere with their ability to benefit from the kinds of educational experiences that are commonly offered them in conventional schools. We explored some of the aspects of this problem in Chapter 6. Allison Davis believes that our inability to meet the needs of these children constitutes a major lack in our educational system. He says:

> The fate of our nation, industrially, politically, and in case of war, depends primarily upon the ability of the public schools to help large numbers of children from these slum and farm-tenant groups to learn the basic skills of our society. The schools have not learned to do this. Our public schools for the lowest third of our population, the schools in the slums, are almost a complete failure. The staffs of these schools generally are aware of their basic failure, and are demoralized [14].

Davis goes on to say that one of the difficulties is that we as teachers know very little about the values which are uppermost in the lives of children from lower-class groups, that we need to study them and get to know them better to the end that we might develop curricula which would meet their needs more effectively. He says that "the present curricula are stereotyped and arbitrary selections from a narrow area of middle-class culture," and that "the greatest need of education is for intensive research to discover the best curricula for developing children's basic mental activities. . . . [15]"

Although not all educators would agree that the schools are as deficient as Davis claims they are, there is much that he says that cannot be denied. The fact that the vast majority of children from lower-class and working-class environments drop out of school as soon as the law permits, if not before, is clear-cut evidence that they do not find much in school to meet their needs.

CHILDREN WITH LOW IQ'S

There are two other groups of children whose needs are unmet by the conventional curricula. These are the children of low and high academic aptitude—say, with IQ's of less than 80 or more than 125 or 130. Not all children who get low IQ's on standardized intelligence tests lack what might be called "general intelligence" or "effective intelligence." Most of the standardized, group tests used in schools are concerned with measuring and predicting the ability (and often the inclination) to do school work—that is, work in the conventional school curriculum.[4] Incidentally, children from lower-class groups tend to score lower on tests of this sort than do children from middle-class environments. Motivation toward school tasks and interest in linguistic problems may very likely be a factor here.

In a discussion of goals for mentally retarded children, Harold A. Delp recommends that any work done with children of lower mentality be preceded by adequate diagnosis. Then there must be an understanding of the problem. Because the thinking of the retarded child takes place at a lower level, some things must be taught in a manner different from that used with children in the normal range of intelligence. According to Delp:

---

[4] For a discussion of the differences between "effective intelligence" and academic aptitude, see H. C. Lindgren, *Psychology of Personal and Social Adjustment.* New York: American Book, 1953. Chapter 15.

Parents and teachers must understand fully the need for concrete training and for always giving training in its simplest elements. Consideration must be given all other characteristics of the retarded, such as short attention span and the lack of ability to make generalizations. Everyone must understand that the 10-year old who has obtained a test mental age equal to 5 years is NOT like the average 5-year-old child. He will show certain different ways of approaching and solving problems. He will differ in many of his ideas and concepts [16].

In dealing with children classified as mentally retarded, teachers should always remember that most of them turn out to be useful, law-abiding citizens. Don C. Charles followed a group of 127 individuals who had been classified as mentally deficient some thirty years previously. Of this number, only nine were institutionalized, and twelve had been institutionalized; seven were unemployable. Eighty percent of the group were employed, and over half owned their own homes. Although, as a group, they tended to violate the law somewhat more than most people, their offenses were, for the most part, minor in nature, consisting mostly of traffic violations and drunkenness. The majority of their children proceeded through school without retardation and achieved at least a grade school education before leaving. Charles' general conclusions are that his subjects fared better, as a group, than early predictions might have led one to expect. Although he was unable to find any actual improvement of intelligence, he suggests that

> psychologists, educators, and parents may gain encouragement in the knowledge that many children whose test scores and academic performance suggest mental deficiency develop into self-sufficient and desirable citizens as adults [17].

However, regardless of whether children with low IQ's are really deficient in "effective intelligence" or will be successful as adults, the fact remains that most of them have some difficulty in keeping pace with other children in the class. Some schools attempt to deal with this problem by "homogeneous grouping"—setting up classes on the basis of children's intelligence test scores. For example, a school might have enough students for three fourth-grade classes. All students with IQ's of 90 and below might be put into the "Z" section, the "Y" section might consist of students with IQ's between 90 and 110, and students with IQ's over 110 might be placed in the "X" section. Many teachers like this system because it seems more "efficient"—that is, the teacher does not have to arrange or supervise work for children of so many different levels of ability. However, other teachers point out that children become aware of the basis for the groupings, with the result that those in the "Z" section become more discouraged. The Fact-Finding Committee of the Midcentury White House Conference on Children and Youth reported as follows:

> Homogeneous grouping, originally designed to protect children from unfair competition, has created at least as many problems as it has solved, largely by giving rise to a kind of invidious distinction. The sense of discouragement, failure, and unworthiness which so frequently befalls children who find themselves in groups designated "opportunity," who are counseled to take vocational rather than academic courses, or who discover that they are in the "slow" reading group in the first grade has been well established [18].

Homogeneous grouping also helps to break down friendliness and cohesiveness among classroom groups. Elva E. Kinney found, in a sociometric study of fifth grades, that there were significantly more children who were psychologically isolated from their group in classes where ability grouping was employed [19].

Other criticisms of homogeneous grouping are that the ungrouped class is more realistic and lifelike; the ungrouped classes enable slower children to learn from brighter ones; that there are other variables which are just as important as IQ—for example, social, physical, and emotional maturity—and that teachers do not like to work with slower groups.

Some schools make special provision for children whose IQ's are so low (70 or below) that they cannot benefit from regular class instruction by setting up special ungraded classes of limited enrollment for them. Some of these classes are indeed "opportunity classes" in the very best sense, but some teachers, because of the lack of training in or understanding of the problems of these children, attempt to teach the same curriculum that is taught other children, except that they teach it more slowly and with more repetition. In the best of the classes for the mentally retarded the curricula are completely reworked with the idea of providing experiences that are meaningful and useful for children who are handicapped in this way.

CHILDREN WITH HIGH IQ'S

The problem of the child with the high IQ receives even less consideration than that of the child with the low IQ, for he is usually left to shift for himself. The everyday tasks of school are too easy for him—they do not constitute any real challenge. Often his level of academic achievement is two or three or more years ahead of his grade; hence much of what he has to do in school is "busy work" for him. Some bright children become bored with the unstimulating tasks that are assigned them with the result that they become disruptive or spend their time in daydreaming. Others may actually have poor academic records because they do not bother to work at their assignments. One solution is to advance the child with the high IQ a grade or so ahead, but this takes him away from children of his level of emotional, social, and physical maturity, and this separation, in turn, may serve to isolate him even from the other children. Another problem the bright child poses is that he is often likely to argue with the teacher or criticize him in class or raise questions which are beyond the comprehension of the rest of the group.

Many children with high IQ's do nothing in class which

distinguishes them from other children. It is not until they are given intelligence tests that they reveal their true abilities. Unless they are stimulated into using their superior abilities, they may remain in step with the rest of the group, content only to maintain passing grades. Like the other children with high IQ's, they can be helped and "salvaged" by being given special assignments or special problems that will give them opportunities to develop their talents and that will make school work more interesting and stimulating [20, 21, 22, 23, 24].

In this chapter we have reviewed some of the deficiencies of the conventional school situation. These shortcomings are more typical of some schools than they are of others. Other conditions which have a warping effect on the mental health of children are peculiar to certain localities or to certain schools. What we have tried to do here is to describe some of the forces, conditions, or situations which are commonly found in all or most schools. The reader is encouraged to make his or her own list of deficiencies, keeping in mind that there may be mitigating or compensating forces which help to bring the educational situation into balance as far as mental health is concerned, although there are times when the weight appears to be largely on the negative side.

When we examine any social institution, we must remember that there are good as well as bad features. For example, we are naturally concerned about the high rate of divorce in this country, not only because it is a rough measure of the mental health (or the lack of it) among our citizens, but also because divorces result in broken homes, which in turn create serious problems of mental health for children. On the other hand, we should also remember that most marriages endure and most families remain intact. Thus, while we attempt to do something about reducing the number of broken homes we should not forget to facilitate or develop the conditions that help to integrate the family life of those which remain intact. Similarly, in education we should not only be concerned about eliminating or alleviating disintegrative forces and conditions, but we should also study the integrative factors so that we may strengthen and improve them as well.

REFERENCES

1. Association for Supervision and Curriculum Development, *Growing Up in an Anxious Age*. Washington: National Education Association, 1952. P. 94. Reprinted by permission.
2. N. Cantor, *Dynamics of Learning*. Buffalo: Foster and Stewart, 1946. P. 285. Reprinted by permission.
3. G. Sheviakov and F. Redl, *Discipline for Today's Children and Youth*. Washington: National Education Association, 1944. Pp. 49–50. Reprinted by permission.
4. D. C. Wilson, "The Neuroses of Everyday Living," *Psychiatric Quarterly*. 26:387–98;1952.
5. D. Segel, *Frustration in Adolescent Youth*. Washington: Federal Security Agency, 1951. Pp. 44–47.
6. D. McCarthy, "Language Development in Children," in L. Carmichael, ed., *Manual of Child Psychology*. New York: Wiley, 1946. Pp. 551–55.
7. W. C. Olson, *Child Development*. Boston: Heath, 1949. Pp. 134–35.
8. J. L. Despert, "Psychosomatic Study of Fifty Stuttering Children," *American Journal of Orthopsychiatry*. 16:100–13;1946.
9. D. McCarthy, "Some Possible Explanations of Sex Differences in Language Development and Disorders," *Journal of Psychology*. 35:155–60;1953.
10. G. A. Lundberg and L. Dickson, "Inter-Ethnic Relations in a High-School Population," *American Journal of Sociology*. 58:1–10;1952.
11. J. Jastak and L. G. Gilliland, "Personality Problems of Juvenile Delinquents as Revealed in Psychological Tests," *Delaware State Medical Journal*. 22:225–28;1950.
12. U. S. Children's Bureau, *Juvenile Court Statistics, 1946–49*. Statistical Series No. 8. Washington: Government Printing Office, 1949.

13. C. A. Ullman, *Identification of Maladjusted School Children.* Public Health Monograph No. 7. Washington: Federal Security Agency, 1952. Pp. 32–33.
14. A. Davis, *Social-Class Influences upon Learning.* Cambridge: Harvard University Press, 1948. P. 23. Reprinted by permission.
15. *Ibid.* P. 97. Reprinted by permission.
16. H. A. Delp, "Goals for the Mentally Retarded," *American Journal of Mental Deficiency.* 55:472–78;1951.
17. D. C. Charles, "Ability and Accomplishment of Persons Earlier Judged Mentally Deficient," *Genetic Psychology Monographs.* 47:3–71;1953.
18. Fact-Finding Committee of the Midcentury White House Conference on Children and Youth, *A Healthy Personality for Every Child.* Raleigh: Health Publications, 1951. Pp. 114–15. Reprinted by permission.
19. E. E. Kinney, *A Study of Peer Group Social Acceptability at the Fifth-Grade Level in a Public School.* Unpublished Ed.D. dissertation, Pennsylvania State College, 1951.
20. H. J. Baker, "An Experiment in the Education of Gifted Children," *Journal of Exceptional Children.* 9:112–14, 120;1943.
21. L. H. Burnside, "An Experimental Program in Education of the Intellectually Gifted Adolescent," *School Review.* 50:274–85;1942.
22. J. E. Downes, "An Experiment in Meeting the Needs of Superior Students," *Social Education.* 4:247–49;1940.
23. B. B. Greenberg, "The Education of the Intellectually Gifted," *Journal of Exceptional Children.* 5:101–09;1939.
24. P. Witty, "Some Considerations in the Education of Gifted Children," *Educational Administration and Supervision.* 26:512–21;1940.

SUGGESTED READINGS

American Youth Commission, *et al., What the High Schools Ought to Teach.* Washington: American Council on Education, 1940.
Association for Supervision and Curriculum Development, *Fostering Mental Health in Our Schools.* Washington: National Education Association, 1950. Chapter 11, "Shall We Use Rewards and Punishments?"
L. Carmichael, ed., *The Manual of Child Psychology.* New York: Wiley, 1946. Chapter 17, "The Feeble-Minded Child," and Chapter 18, "Gifted Children."

R. E. Eckert and T. O. Marshall, *When Youth Leaves School.* New York: McGraw-Hill, 1938. Presents the results of an inquiry into the deficiencies of schools in the State of New York; indicates how schools failed in many of their objectives.

N. B. Henry, ed., *The Education of Exceptional Children,* 49th Yearbook, Part II. Chicago: National Society for the Study of Education, 1950.

A. A. Hollingshead, *Elmtown's Youth.* New York: Wiley, 1950.

C. M. Louttit, *Clinical Psychology of Children's Behavior Problems,* rev. ed. New York: Harper, 1947. Part 2, "Problems Correlated with Abilities."

See also items 1, 2, 3, 4, 5, 14, and 18 in the References for this chapter.

SUGGESTED FILMS

Feelings of Hostility. National Film Board of Canada. Available through McGraw-Hill.

Problem of Pupil Adjustment. Parts 1 and 2. The story of a boy who drops out of school and his consequent inability to "find himself." Available through McGraw-Hill.

16

INTEGRATIVE INFLUENCES

IN EDUCATION

IN THE preceding chapter we discussed some of the conditions and forces which have a disintegrative effect on the welfare of children in the school. If there were nothing to counteract these forces, the school would be a very bad place for children, indeed. However, the advantages of schooling generally outweigh the disadvantages. It is our purpose in this chapter to discuss the nature of those advantages which weigh most heavily in favor of mental health.

THE SCHOOLS AND CHILD WELFARE

As THEY exist today, schools are the visible expression of our concern for the welfare of children. Although we have reason at times to complain about the attitudes of adults toward children—in fact, we have been quite critical in this text—we should be aware that even the most authoritarian aspects of the lay public's attitudes and opinions regarding children are quite enlightened as compared to what they were in past centuries. Bossard points out that during the Middle Ages and the centuries which immediately followed, the prevailing attitude toward children was marked by harshness and physical cruelty. For example, during the eighteenth century children were hanged in England for theft and even for less serious offenses. Child labor was regarded very favorably during the nineteenth century both in England and America. During these years, children generally were regarded as nuisances, and childhood was looked upon as an uncomfortable, awkward period which should be gotten over with as quickly as possible. Although some vestiges of this attitude remain today, there has been a marked change in the status of children during the last two hundred years [1].

Bossard describes this change as follows:

. . . . The essence of the change is the child's shift from a subordinate and incidental position in a family group dominated by an autocratic parent to one of acceptance as an equal with his own personality, needs, and problems of development. More tersely stated, it is a change from a position of subordination to one of equality, both in the family and in the larger social group. . . . The fact of the matter is that for centuries the child was dominated by his elders to be exploited in their interests. He had no rights, except as they fitted into the interests of his elders or his kinship group. . . .

Today the child is recognized as a human personality in a peculiarly vital stage of development. He is a co-equal in the emerging democracy of the family. The guarding of this personlity is the child's precious right, and the dangers which threaten it are recognized social problems; the development of this personality is his most precious opportunity, and the furtherance and guidance of that development are the concern of his elders [2].

DEMOCRATIC IDEALS AND AUTHORITARIAN PRACTICES

As THE child has gained more status, and as adults come to recognize and accept responsibilities for furthering and guiding the development of the child's personality, the emphasis in the schools has shifted from one of preparation for adult life, supported by harsh and rigid discipline, to one of concern for the more immediate needs of children, accompanied by a doctrine of increasing permissiveness. Thus the school has become the main agency for implementing a point of view which is more enlightened and more humanitarian than that of previous centuries or even previous decades. However, the democracy of our ideals has advanced far beyond the autocracy of our methods. Hence, there is a large gap between our concepts and our everyday practice. The schools also reflect this discrepancy, for the organization and methods of the school, as we have noted in the last chapter, are largely autocratic, even though our philosophy is becoming increasingly democratic and permissive. Nevertheless, even though our current practice is somewhat autocratic, it is a distinct improvement over the methods of even twenty or thirty years ago.

Because our ideals are essentially humanitarian and democratic, we are deeply concerned whenever we come upon conditions in our schools which are contrary to the best interests of child welfare. We do not always know what we ought to do in the way of reform, but we are made anxious enough by these discoveries to want to do something about the deficiencies that are revealed. Even if we do not eliminate these deficiencies because of conditions beyond our immediate control, we are nonetheless made sensitive and self-critical by them. And the changes which have been made in our schools during the last 150 years are the result of countless numbers of such discoveries and repeated self-examinations. The underlying attitude that has made these changes possible is a genuine and deep concern for the rights and feelings of the individual—and particularly those of the individual child. There is much evidence that the schools are moving closer toward the goal of being concerned primarily with the welfare of children (as contrasted to the previous emphasis upon the convenience of adults). Thus the school is a healthier place for children than it used to be, and the evidence indicates that it will become even healthier.

HELPING CHILDREN TO BECOME MORE MATURE

SATISFYING THE NEED TO LEARN

One of the more specific contributions which the modern school makes toward the mental health of children is the opportunity it provides for satisfying their normal curiosity, their natural desire to learn more about themselves and their environment. As we have said earlier, learning is a natural expression of growth toward emotional, social, and intellectual maturity, and the school performs its most valuable function by helping children meet this need. The school has probably always done this to a certain degree, to the extent that it stimulated the imagination and intellectual powers of a few students. However, the modern school is in a better position to meet this need because it encourages greater freedom of the intellect, because its curriculum includes a deeper and broader portion of human experience, and because it provides a richer variety of activities.

MEETING THE NEED TO PARTICIPATE WITH OTHERS

One of these activities or experiences is the opportunity to develop relationships with others outside the family sphere. The child at home is almost never on an equal basis with his brothers and sisters because of differences in ages, parental expectations, and family preferences for certain children over others. At school the child consorts with children who are more or less his physical and intellectual equals. Classrooms and playgrounds provide new opportunities to develop status independently from that of the home. A child may have inferior status at home because he is the middle child, or the youngest, or perhaps because his parents are disappointed in him. At school he has a chance to win status and acceptance on his own merits. If he succeeds in doing this, the school is providing an atmosphere for him which is, in many respects, healthier than that of his home. Another child may have extremely high status at home. He may be the favorite child or the only child. At school he is on a par with others. School may be less pleasant for him because of his proportionately reduced status, but even this is emotionally healthy, since it introduces him to the realities of a world in which the value of an individual is measured by his accomplishments and by the kinds of relationships he is able to develop with others, rather than by his being a favorite son or daughter. Though not unusual, these are special cases; the chief value of a social nature that the school has for children lies in the opportunities it provides for children to learn how to cooperate, cope, and even compete with a variety of adults and children. This is an experience which would be denied them to a great degree if they remained within the family circle or were put out to work, as was the practice in bygone days.

LEARNING SOCIAL NORMS AND CUSTOMS

By participating in a social situation removed from that of his family, the child is enabled to have a dual experience in learning how to deal with the problems of life. At school he learns the ways that society has developed for dealing with such problems, ways that may be different from those of his family. For example, his family may belong to a religious group which insists on the strict observance of the Sabbath. If he were to live in close contact with only his family and friends, he might develop the idea that this form of behavior was the only standard by which people live, that the behavior of all people was, in effect, the observance of or deviation from this standard. By coming in contact at school with children of other modes of belief, he is in a position to discover that the essential worth of the individual has nothing to do with the form of his religion. By playing, working, and becoming friendly with children of various religious sects, he will discover something about the variety of beliefs which go to make up a democratic community. The normal effect of such experience is for children to develop a more liberal attitude toward the observance of the Sabbath for themselves, one which is closer to the "norm" of the community, or to maintain an attitude similar to that of their family, but also to be tolerant of other modes of belief. Unfortunately, some children, usually those who are more insecure, maintain their own beliefs and at the same time develop a deep prejudice against children of different beliefs. Such casualties are part of the price we pay for religious freedom and for the maintenance of free schools in a rapidly changing society; yet the advantages of such freedom outweigh the disadvantages for most children.

Another example of such learning may also be seen in the case of the children of immigrant parents who have certain attitudes towards social institutions that they have brought with them from their native land. For instance, the prevailing attitude in their homeland might be that of having as little to do as possible with the government, and especially with the police. If it were not for the possibility of learning at school what the functions of the government are, children from these families might develop and persist in attitudes similar to those of their parents. However, from their formal and informal contacts with adults and children at school, they learn about ways of dealing with certain kinds of problems by using the services provided for everyone by the government. More often, what children learn is a different attitude toward government—an attitude which expects government to be the servant of the citizen rather than vice versa.

A specific case is that of Anthony's father, who received a notice in the mail from the traffic court stating that inasmuch as he had ignored a parking tag some three months before, he was directed to appear in court or to forfeit twenty-five dollars bail. The license number listed on the notice was that of an automobile which the family had sold six months previously; hence, it was the new owner who had parked the car illegally and who had ignored the ticket. Anthony's father was very much upset at receiving the notice. He would have willingly paid the twenty-five dollar penalty, because he remembered that the police in his native land were arbitrary, corrupt, with no concern for the rights of the individual. It was easier to pay what they asked, because if you crossed them or became involved with them in any way, your life was made miserable. But Anthony felt differently. He knew that in a democracy the rights of the individual were what counted; if an arm of the government made a mistake, the individual who was innocently involved could not be held accountable. This was what he had learned in school. It was nothing he had read in a book or had heard from the lips of a teacher, but it was part of a general attitude about the individual and the government which he had learned indirectly, through years of association with teachers and fellow students. Against his father's protests, he wrote a letter to the traffic court, explaining the situation. A few days later, they received a reply from the court, accepting the explanation and apologizing for any inconvenience which may have been caused.

Participating in group experiences with other children also helps to "socialize" the child. He learns to share, plan cooperatively, lead and follow, and to participate in group decision making. And the more opportunity his school provides for experiences of this sort under competent guidance, the better he will learn these social skills.

He also learns to cope with some difficult problems. Not only will some of the values and standards he learned at home come into conflict with the norms of his peer group, but there is also likely to be differences among the several peer groups with whom he associates, not to mention the disparities between the standards of the student world and the world of teachers and other adults. Learning to socialize means, in part, being able to maintain a satisfactory balance between being an individual and being a member of the family group, the peer group, and the larger group that is the school.

LEARNING TO BE SELF-DIRECTIVE

We said earlier that the school afforded the child an opportunity to have a dual experience in learning to deal with the problems of life. The first type of experience was learning to use and adjust to the patterns of society. The second type of experience is learning to think for oneself, to take responsibility for one's own actions, to become self-directive. Although there is much progress to be made by the schools in this regard, the very fact that the school presents the child with a new experience which he must meet largely on his own means that he must develop some resources for independence and self-reliance. And although the school tends to provide ready-made solutions for many if not most of the problems it presents to children, there are still situations, particularly in the informal aspects of the curriculum, that give children opportunities to work out solutions for themselves. Some schools give children more opportunities to work out solutions than others; some teachers do more with this than others. Most teachers are aware of the need to help children to become self-reliant and self-directive, yet are not sure exactly how to go about it. This is an area of learning which demands much sensitivity from the teacher because children have to be ready to take the initiative and to do their own decision making. If the teacher's attempts to put children "on their own" are poorly timed, they are likely to backfire, and the class is made apathetic, rebellious, or resentful by the seeming abdication of decision making on the part of the teacher. Nevertheless, the modern school has made some progress in this regard; teachers are more concerned about helping children become self-reliant than they used to be, and the atmosphere is friendlier to the develop-

ment of independent thinking than it was, say, fifty years
ago.

PROVIDING EMOTIONAL SECURITY

In our last chapter we discussed some of the dangers inherent in our tendency to overemphasize conformity in the
schools. We also said or implied that conformity was a useful and valuable part of the school program, provided it was
not overstressed.

The fact that schools maintain standards of behavior and
develop certain routines and rituals as a way of "structuring"
the school day means that the daily experience of students
will have a certain quality of stability and predictability.
When a child goes to school on a given morning, he knows,
within certain limits, what will happen during the day. The
certainty that reading will follow science, that social studies
will follow reading, and that the first recess will come at
10:30 makes some of the unknown and unexpected events
of the day easier to bear. A little of the unknown and unexpected helps to arouse interest and anticipation—normal
anxiety, if you like—but an absence of structure and predictability and a lack of familiar elements mobilizes neurotic
anxiety with all its accompanying difficulties. A child who
knows pretty well what will happen next and what is expected of him is able to attain a measure of emotional security that would be difficult to maintain in an "unstruc-
tured" situation. Ruth Cunningham states these principles
very concisely:

> Routine has a very important place as a security-giving de-
> vice. It is much easier to feel at home in a group where many
> of the casual aspects of daily living have become routinized
> and are thus predictable. No one feels at home in an entirely
> strange and unpredictable situation. One of the early tasks in
> any group is to establish purposeful routines which can pro-
> vide a partial basis for group security [3].

Routine should not, however, dominate the scene to the point where emotional and social growth, problem solving, and real learning are subordinated to it. Perhaps a good rule of thumb to use is that when the leader or the group are continually preoccupied with routines and the conformity to behavioral standards, little real learning is taking place because the situation or the emotional atmosphere is not conducive to mental health and growth toward maturity.

For many children, going to school is the most stable and most predictable thing that happens in their lives because life away from school is rendered precarious, as a result of family problems, economic difficulties, or the instability of life in deprived surroundings.

Evidence for the contribution that the school makes in the way of stability and security is provided by W. W. Wattenberg, who analyzed nation-wide juvenile delinquency rates on a month-by-month basis throughout the year. He found that there was a tendency for delinquency rates to rise during the summer when school is not in session. His data indicate that although schools may aggravate the tendencies of a few children to get into trouble, it serves as a deterrent or preventive function for a greater number during the months it is in session. He concludes his study with this significant statement:

> Without the stabilizing influence of school routines, some children appear to find that leisure, unorganized and undirected, is a frustrating experience [4].

THE CURRICULUM AND THE EXTRA-CURRICULUM [1]

STUDENT GOVERNMENT

There are a number of ways in which schools help children to think for themselves. One of the most important of these

---

[1] Some authorities prefer the term "cocurriculum" to "extracurriculum," because the former term indicates the close identity of these activities to the aims and goals of the school.

is student government. At its best, student government can be a way of enabling children (particularly at the secondary school level) to participate in the operation of their school, to help make policy, and to help enforce rules of their own making. At its best, student government can build morale and cohesiveness, can give students a sense of identity with the school, and can make the school psychologically attractive. All of these factors are important both from the standpoint of good mental health and the learning of subject matter. For instance, students can accept the assignment of studies in a course which normally might seem senseless to them (like Latin or mathematics or any other course which does not fit in directly to their interests as they perceive them), if they feel that the school really has their best interests at heart, if they feel that the administration of the school thinks that their opinion counts for something, and if they feel that the adults in charge are not trying to keep them out of something which really concerns them.

However, student government, like all good educational techniques, can be subject to abuse. Some administrators use the student government principally as a "kangaroo court" —that is, they turn over to the student courts all students who break the rules—because they have discovered that the punishment meted out by student courts is more severe than the penalties exacted by adults. Having student courts handle certain types of discipline cases can be a useful learning process, but the point here is that the administrators in question do not really share any of their power or policy-making functions. As far as they are concerned, the rest of the structure of student government is there only for show.

Then there is the principal who insists on having students set up a student government, but who delegates no powers or functions. Or the principal who submits problems to the student council for recommendations and then repeatedly ignores the council's suggestions and goes ahead and does what he originally planned. Some principals turn the entire matter of student government over to a few faculty advisers and proceed to wash their hands of the whole business. And some student governments are entirely dominated by faculty advisers. Chase Dane, a student-council sponsor himself, says on this subject:

> . . . . The sponsor must be exceedingly careful that the student council does not become a teacher council. This is a very easy, and perhaps natural, error for teachers to fall into. A sponsor, especially during a meeting, must keep in the background as much as possible. He should seldom impose himself or his opinions on the council. This is sometimes extremely difficult for a teacher to do; he is so used to commanding his class that he finds it not unnatural not to command the council also. But as soon as the sponsor takes over the council and runs it, he deprives the students of the very experience they so sorely need. It is often tempting for a sponsor, when, for example, the order of a meeting becomes lax, to assume command and correct the situation himself. But when he does this, he prevents the president from learning how to solve the problem himself. Learning by doing is probably even more important in a student council than it is in the classroom. And a sponsor must often allow students to work out their problems for themselves, even though such a method takes time and prevents the speedy execution of council business. A sponsor must be a guide and not a crutch to his council [5].

Many teachers and administrators are favorable to the idea of giving student governments responsibilities, but they are not sure that students can carry through the plans they undertake. The following example illustrates what can be done in a school where students are given responsibilities and receive proper guidance:

> Our campus clean-up problem is intensified by the fact that our campus is in the heart of town, and by the fact that we do not have either adequate or attractive eating areas. . . . The problem was discussed in council and turned over to the senior class to tackle. Their method was to clean up the campus

themselves after each lunch period. Whole groups would swoop over the campus and pick up papers. The campus was spotless, but of course the seniors soon felt they were simply doing the work of custodians. The next year . . . a group set out to study plans of other schools. Finally, they evolved a plan whereby each student was to clean up his own lunch debris or suffer the consequences. The consequences were that if a committee found the campus dirty, the entire student body had to stay after school for as many minutes as it took the custodians to clean up. This plan was first presented to the principal by a group of students and, although he was very dubious about its success, he agreed to a trial, provided a two-thirds majority of the entire student body passed it. Much to his amazement two-thirds did pass it, and the plan went into effect. . . .

In the last eight weeks of school, the pupils stayed in about five times. Many of the teachers did not like this type of plan and there were lots of complaints from students, especially those who went to work at 3 o'clock. However, the campus was cleaner than it had been for years . . . and all had to admit that the pupils had accomplished what administrators and teachers had not been able to do [6].

WILLINGNESS TO EXPERIMENT WITH THE CURRICULUM

Another factor that has helped to make the atmosphere of the school more conducive to mental health has been the willingness of some administrators and teachers to try experimental educational programs that in some cases are radical departures from traditional curricula.

One such experimental program was that sponsored by the Progressive Education Association and commonly known as the Eight-Year Study. This was a large-scale research project devoted to studying students in thirty "progressive" high schools and their graduates who went to college. In college the graduates from these high schools were matched and compared with graduates from conventional and traditional high schools who were equivalent in every important respect. The graduates of progressive schools did slightly better in academic studies than the graduates of traditional schools in almost every instance. Their record in the non-academic areas of college life was even more outstanding [7].

Although the Eight-Year Study demonstrates that a reorganization of the traditional high school curricula is desirable from the standpoint of both academic and social competency, it has not brought about any marked revolution in secondary education. It may be years or even decades before the results of this study have an effect on high school curricula. However, the point here is that a group of educators was interested enough in improving the quality and effectiveness of educational experiences for children to revise the curriculum and to undertake this study. Even though a fraction of one percent of educators are willing and able to undertake experimental programs of this sort, the stimulation that results from their research findings may eventually change the educational pattern for the entire world.

HUMAN RELATIONS IN THE CLASSROOM

Another experimental program which has attracted widespread attention is the project sponsored by the Delaware State Society for Mental Hygiene under the direction of H. Edmund Bullis and Emily E. O'Malley [8]. Bullis and O'Malley have developed a curriculum entitled "Human Relations in the Classroom" for the seventh and eighth grades which reaches 200,000 children annually in the state of Delaware, as well as in Nassau County and Brooklyn, New York. The aims of this course, according to Bullis, are as follows:

> I have been convinced for many years that it is possible for most young people to build up a robustness of personality so that in their later lives—when emotional crises come up—they can face up to them without breaking down mentally. The purpose of these human relations classes is to help our boys

and girls to become more robust from an emotional and personality standpoint [9].

The course is, then, a direct attempt to teach principles of mental health at the grade school level. Although it represents a willingness to break with the traditional curriculum and an attempt to improve the quality of educational experience made available to children, a committee of psychiatrists that evaluated the approach raised a number of questions regarding certain aspects. For example, they pointed out that the authors and sponsors provide little training for the teacher, that the training courses which do exist are so brief that "the individual biases of the teachers may continue and thus invalidate the material in many instances," and that much of the course "attempts to convey the ideas that control and conformity to the existing mores leads to happiness." The committee wondered also whether it was desirable to moralize in a course of this sort and whether some children would be made overly anxious by the material discussed [10].

USING THE "CAUSAL APPROACH" TO HUMAN BEHAVIOR

Another experimental program involving a sizable number of teachers and children is the Ojemann Project, conducted and supervised by R. H. Ojemann of the State University of Iowa.[2] Ojemann is concerned about the fact that curriculum and instruction in the schools deal with the surface aspects of human behavior rather than the causes which underlie it. He believes that by teaching the student the causal factors in human behavior—the emotional processes and motivations within himself and others—we can develop adults who are emotionally mature. He has therefore developed curricular materials to be used in grades four through twelve in connection with courses involving human relations: litera-

---

[2] See discussion of Ojemann's approach in Chapter 1.

ture, civics, history, and social problems. The committee of psychiatrists which reviewed the Bullis and O'Malley project also examined Ojemann's work. They felt that the material was effective and noted that both students and teachers found the material interesting. In the committee's opinion, the curricular material devised by Ojemann was more suited than that of Bullis and O'Malley to conventional pedagogical methods; hence special training of teachers did not appear to be necessary. They also felt that there was less likelihood of Ojemann's material arousing the anxieties of children, thus forcing teachers into the role of professional psychotherapists [11].

Further evidence of the efficacy of the causal approach is provided by the research of Frances S. Stiles, who found that the use of Ojemann's materials and methods produced decided improvement in the ability of fourth, fifth, and sixth graders to make decisions based on an understanding of causal factors involved in certain social situations [12].

Still another study that shows what can be done to improve the mental health of a classroom through developing a more permissive atmosphere and using techniques designed to encourage self-understanding is one conducted by Sheldon Rosenthal. Rosenthal used sociodrama combined with some ideas from Bullis and O'Malley [8]. Over a two months' experimental period the amount of hostility and rejection was reduced in a class of children coming from a slum area in New York's Harlem, scores made on a personality questionnaire were improved, and there were positive changes in the amount and distribution of friendship [13].

SCHOOL CAMPS

These programs are doing pioneer work by trying out methods and materials in the field of mental health. If they are successful, their findings may eventually be incorporated into standard educational practice, with the result that all children will benefit. There are, however, programs which are less directly concerned with the subject of mental health, but which also bear promise. One of these is the school camping program which has been adopted in a few localities. School camps provide children with opportunities to learn in a laboratory situation, to develop new skills in group living, and to participate in an experience which helps to heighten interest in the educational program of the school. The school camp also helps to meet the needs of children who are too much "cooped up" in cities. Much petty juvenile delinquency is the result of children not having adequate play space—space to run, jump, shout, and wrestle. While the school camp is not a cure-all in this respect, it does help to alleviate some of the pressure.

An outstanding and successful example of a school camping program is that of the San Diego City and County Schools in California, where thousands of elementary and secondary pupils have participated actively in various kinds of camping programs [14].

The foregoing glimpses of "things to come" are admittedly only a patchwork discussion of curriculum reform in this country, but they nevertheless indicate how educators in various parts of the country are working and experimenting in order to develop programs which will eventually make schools healthier for children—and for teachers as well. If education follows the pattern of development which has typified its progress, changes in the desired direction will come slowly, perhaps imperceptibly. But twenty or thirty years hence, as we look back, we shall then be aware of the amount of progress which has taken place.

THE ACTIVITY CURRICULUM

One of the advances education has made in recent decades is the development of courses outside the traditional college-preparatory sequence. Because these courses are less "intellectual"—that is, less verbal, less formal, and less concerned with the acquisition of information—there is a tendency to assign them a lower status. The usual basis for such an evaluation is that such courses do not constitute adequate preparation for college. The unwillingness of some colleges to accept such courses is apparently based on tradition and custom rather than on sound experimental evidence because research so far has failed to demonstrate any recognizable relationship between the pattern of courses taken in high school and success in college. However, more and more colleges are coming to evaluate high school records in terms of the general level of ability that they indicate for each student, rather than in terms of the extent to which they adhere to a rigid pattern of required courses. As colleges become more liberal in this respect, public schools will feel freer to develop courses that are more attuned to meet the needs of students rather than the specifications of institutions of higher learning.

There is an impressive list of courses in this transitional stage of respectibility: home economics, band and orchestra, industrial arts, animal husbandry, printing, radio, speech, physical education, arts and crafts, and dramatics. Many of these courses have an emotional appeal to students because they involve such a wide variety of skills and experiences over and beyond those required for the highly verbal, traditional curriculum. This is not to say that students do not need development of verbal skills. The difficulty seems to be that the traditional curriculum concentrates on the latter to the exclusion of other kinds of skills and experiences. What happens is that students get saturated with verbal material while other needs are frustrated or ignored. This makes it particularly difficult for those students whose best abilities lie in fields other than verbal.

These are more or less negative reasons for including activity-type courses in student's programs. But the chief value of these courses lies in the opportunity they provide for creativity. Intellectual pursuits can be creative, too, and students need to learn this as well, but they also need the reassurance that comes with completing a dress or a bookcase, singing a round in close harmony, presenting a play, or breaking one's own record at the shot-put. These are tangible evidences of adequacy in areas of endeavor that are as much a part of life as foreign languages, biology, and English.

Because many of the activity courses are related to or are extensions of the everyday experience of children, they are likely to develop more interest and motivation. Some of the courses, like music, drama, and athletics, provide opportunities for students to work together in close cooperation and to develop a spirit of group unity and teamwork that is difficult to achieve in other classes. It seems likely that schools which provide a rich and varied curriculum not only do a better job of meeting student needs and promoting growth in emotional and social maturity but also are able to hold students longer than more traditional schools, thus reducing the drop-out rate that plagues so many secondary schools.

Another type of course that helps to retain students in school longer and is related to their needs and interests is the work-experience program. Under one form of this program, a student's day or term is divided into equal periods of school study and of on-the-job training under supervision away from school. Another type of work-experience program provides work at the school, such as student library assistance, clerical or janitorial work, or operation of motion picture projectors. In some schools students are paid; in others they are not [15].

One of the advantages of the work-experience program is that it helps students explore various fields of work preliminary to making decisions about the choice of an occupation. It gives students practical experience under supervision, experience that will stand them in good stead when it comes time to seek full-time employment. When work-experience programs operate at their best potential, they provide educational experiences that supplement and enrich classroom learning. When they are not well supervised or are poorly conceived and coordinated, they are merely a way of permitting students to enter the labor market while nominally still attending school.

EXTRACURRICULAR ACTIVITIES

During the last decade or two teachers have come to recognize that there is much that can be gained, educationally speaking, from a well-organized extracurricular program. The awareness of the importance of this part of the school program is reflected in the term "cocurricular," that some educators prefer instead of the more traditional "extracurricular." Students are well aware of the benefits to be obtained from the extracurriculum. When J. Lloyd Trump asked 3,525 secondary students what personal gains they obtained from these activities, the following results received the highest rating: developed new friendships, made school more interesting, helped one to learn to win and lose in a sportsmanlike manner, promoted greater loyalty to the school, gave one something worth while to do in leisure time, developed more friendly relations with teachers, developed a willingness to accept criticism, and received information not available in a regular course [16]. Earl Graham Pogue asked 6,817 high school students to rate the following activities in terms of personal satisfaction: school subjects, extraclass activities, home activities, activities centering around service agencies (the church, the YMCA, and the like), activities centering around commercial agencies (movies, soda fountains, skating rinks, and so forth), and unplanned peer-group activities. When data from all thirteen schools surveyed were combined, extraclass activities ranked second, just below activities centering around commercial agencies; in five schools, extraclass activities ranked first [17].

Extracurricular activities afford outstanding opportunities

for students to learn social skills and to meet basic needs for status, acceptance, creativity, and self-expression. In many schools they supplement the more formalized courses of the traditional curriculum by providing students with ways and means to develop the skills of cooperation, self-reliance, planning in groups, and developing friendly relations with others. Children readily recognize the improvement in social skills that results from participation in extraclass activities. Ruth Fedder asked several groups of adolescents to discuss what they had gained from their experiences. On the basis of her analysis of their discussion, she concluded:

There seems to be a growing ability among these boys and girls to understand themselves and to face their limitations without feelings of guilt, because a knowledge of their limitations is being balanced by a sense of accomplishment and a growing consciousness of their abilities. This fact makes possible the gradual development of what adolescents call "ability to take it"—a sincere welcoming of criticism and an ability to give it in a friendly fashion. There seems to be less necessity for reacting to unpleasant situations by being offended, developing hostility, blaming someone else, or resorting to futile argument. These negative attitudes are gradually being replaced with a reasoning technique for handling worries, dislikes, deprivations, feelings of guilt, and prejudices. There is some acceptance of the thwarting of one's own desires without temper, resentment, or infantile expressions.

Many individuals volunteered the statement that their group experience was freeing them from some of their tight ideas and preconceptions. One individual said, "In club, you sometimes have to work with people you thought you didn't like. Then you find out that you do like them. Sometimes I think it was something the matter with me, not with the other person." Another individual said, "I think you grow up better *together* because you get ideas from other boys and girls." These people are beginning to recognize the fact that it is the way in which an individual is different that makes him or her valuable [18].

It is clearly apparent that the students in these groups are having experiences that are promoting development in the direction of greater emotional and social maturity.

Extracurricular experiences may also help the adjustment and development of individual students. The case of Joseph, as told by Fred McKinney, illustrates how this may occur:

Joseph had no playmates until he first entered school at six years of age. His mother and father were quiet, serious hard-working people. The father was a lawyer, the mother had been a teacher. Both had a very good vocabulary and read widely. Joseph could read before he attended school. School was a very unpleasant experience for him. He cried for many weeks when he first attended. The other children recognized him as a tense, awkward boy, and often teased and physically mistreated him. All through his prepubic years, Joseph stayed as far away from other children as he could. He only spoke when he was spoken to. He avoided their approaches, since most of the time other children were critical of him. He participated in no activities, had very few playmates and no friends.

Joseph went to a large city high school. At first, he was somewhat uneasy about leaving home, but having entered this large school he soon saw possibilities of losing himself in the crowd and thereby not becoming the butt of jokes. Previous to his entrance into high school, his only pleasant moments had consisted of lone reading sessions, times spent with his family, and quiet absorption of the teacher's remarks in certain classes. He remembered his English classes very positively. When he had to write his first theme, his English teacher remarked to him in the class that it had been the best thing she had ever read from a student his age. This impressed him. He relived, over and over again these complimentary moments in his daydreams. He felt somewhat at ease in high school, although he still did not feel free to approach other children on his own. One matter that impressed him in high school was a school paper. He noted that practically all its content had been contributed by students. There were by-lines on some of the articles and students names were listed. He read the issues of the paper completely.

While wandering around the building one day, he noticed the office in which the writers for the paper congregated. He speculated as to how students became members of this staff. He could not muster enough courage to walk into the office himself and inquire. However, he contrived to pass this office every day, and to walk slowly beside it, looking carefully at each of the students he saw there. One day he noticed that one of the boys who belonged to the staff of the paper was a member of his classes. He wanted to become friendly with this boy but did not know how to bring it about. He lingered often as the class walked out the door. One day he noticed that this boy did not have a pencil and was looking around to borrow one. Quickly he offered him a pencil. When the boy returned the pencil, Joseph said what he had rehearsed for many a day: "I see," he stumbled, "that you are on the school paper." "Yes," the boy replied, and to Joseph's great surprise added: "Are you interested in writing?" Joseph flushed and became slightly incoherent, but managed to make it very clear that he was very much interested. "Well, drop around sometime." This upset Joseph. If his friend had said: "Come in Tuesday, at 12 o'clock," he could have complied. "Drop around sometime" was too vague. A week transpired. Finally Joseph got up enough courage to ask his new friend when he might come around. The boy said: "Meet me there today at noon." At first, Joseph did odd jobs in the paper office. One day he built up enough nerve to submit one of the many stories that he had written and then stored away in his desk. It was accepted immediately and appeared with a by-line.

In time, Joseph began to show traits that had never appeared before. He began to volunteer remarks in the student paper office. This was unprecedented in Joseph's behavior. After six months he began to joke rather tentatively. All this was preceded by carefully watching the others in the office, getting to know them, and receiving their respectful remarks and overtures. Before long he became accepted as the most outstanding writer on the paper. He had many by-lines. He found that people recognized him in classes, in school; many talked to him who had not spoken to him before. It was very confusing and puzzling to him to have to assume this role, yet he enjoyed it greatly. He also found that he began talking to people on each side of him in class, something that he had not done before. He felt self-conscious about this, felt that he was awkward in social contact. Sometimes he felt that he was too excited . . . and said things which he did not mean and that these were inconsistent with himself, as he knew himself. He would re-live these experiences with great embarrassment later. His entire view of himself slowly began to change. Whereas previously he would never have thought of admitting mistakes and shortcomings, he found that, around the office, he could allude obliquely to his shyness, his lack of aggressiveness. Finally one day he had a long talk about himself with the sponsor of the paper when they were in the office together.

The most striking aspect of the story of Joseph's development in high school is the fact that many of the processes that occurred are what is usually found in connection with effective counseling and psychotherapy. He began to *accept* himself, began to assume a new role. He found a warm, accepting environment in which he could release tendencies and attitudes which had been bottled up previous to this time. He was able to see the negative aspects of himself, and talk about them and air them, something that he previously had been unable to do. Then he began to grow as a person. This occurred because of the warm, accepting environment, the release of previously repressed tendencies, the view of himself in a new perspective, and finally the use and integration of behavior which previously had been inhibited [19].

THE GROWTH IN GUIDANCE SERVICES

MOST of this chapter has been concerned with the existing conditions and potential changes in the school that affect the mental health of all children—children as a total group. We should also be aware that we are in the midst of a quiet revolution in the ways and methods we employ in dealing with the problems of individual students. In the last chapter, we mentioned the unmet needs of children who have certain special problems. Although we must continue to plan and provide for these unmet needs, we should be aware that many schools have already developed facilities which have done much to individualize the relations of the school with the child. One of the most important phases of this development has been the growth in the number of trained school psychologists, counselors, and guidance workers. In schools where there is an effective guidance program, children do not feel so alone with their problems. They know that they have some place to go for help. To be sure, they have always been able to take their problems to their teachers, and probably just as many children go to their teachers as ever before, but there are many children who have difficulty in communicating with a teacher. Perhaps it is that the teacher is too much like a parent; the teacher, as we have said, is an authority figure—he can punish and reward. The counselor is more of a neutral figure; one can talk things over with him and preserve one's privacy. Often teachers simply do not have the time to see all the students who would like to see them; one of the big advantages of a well-organized guidance program is that there are people who have time to meet with children individually. We shall have more to say about how the counselor operates in the next chapter. We mention him here because he makes a large contribution to those educational situations that are helping children to develop in ways that are healthy and emotionally mature.

SPECIAL EDUCATION

SCHOOLS in increasing numbers are making provisions for children with special problems—mentally retarded, hard of hearing, cerebral palsied, and so forth. Schools and classes for these children are expensive—they require special facilities and specially trained personnel. Community after community is coming to realize that it must provide special education for those who need special handling. The reasons for providing this special aid are not primarily financial, although one may argue that children with handicaps are less likely to be burdens on the community if they receive proper education.[3] Rather, the important motive where such programs have been organized seems to be the recognition by the community that it has a responsibility to *all* children, not merely to those who are able to benefit from the conventional school situation. This awakening awareness on the part of communities is further evidence of the changing attitude toward children, evidence that we are coming to realize that children have status and value for their own sake and not for their contributions to the convenience and welfare of adults. Or to put this in a little different way, children who need special help and attention should get this service as one of their rights as free individuals and not because of the generosity and charity of adults. For it is as we come to regard children as equals that we can begin to build educational programs that are really integrative and rewarding in terms of mental health.

REFERENCES

1. J. H. S. Bossard, *Sociology of Child Development*. New York: Harper, 1948. Chapters 25 and 26.
2. *Ibid*. Pp. 642–43. Reprinted by permission.
3. R. Cunningham *et al.*, *Understanding Group Behavior of Boys and Girls*. New York: Bureau of Publications, Teachers College, Columbia University, 1951. P. 212. Reprinted by permission.
4. W. W. Wattenberg, "Delinquency during Summer Months," *Journal of Educational Research*. 42:253–67;1948.

---

[3] The possibility of measurable gains being produced by programs of special education is demonstrated by research such as the study of Margaret L. Healey, who found that an experimental group of retarded second-graders who received special attention showed improved health and scholastic attainment as compared to a control group that did not. The extra cost per pupil in the experimental group was less than $10 for the five-month period covered by the experiment [20].

5. C. Dane, "Some Hints on Student Government," *California Journal of Secondary Education.* 25:149–54;1950. Reprinted by permission.

6. L. McMonies, "A Positive Plan of Student Government," *California Journal of Secondary Education.* 25:142–48;1950. Reprinted by permission.

7. D. Chamberlin *et al., Did They Succeed in College?* New York: Harper, 1942.

8. H. E. Bullis and E. E. O'Malley, *Human Relations in the Classroom.* Wilmington: Delaware State Society for Mental Hygiene, 1947.

9. Committee on Preventive Psychiatry of the Group for the Advancement of Psychiatry, *Promotion of Mental Health in the Primary and Secondary Schools,* Report No. 18. Topeka: 1951. P. 4. Reprinted by permission.

10. *Ibid.* P. 5.

11. *Ibid.* Pp. 8–11.

12. F. S. Stiles, "Developing an Understanding of Human Behavior at the Elementary School Level," *Journal of Educational Research.* 43:516–24;1950.

13. S. Rosenthal, "A Fifth-Grade Classroom Experiment in Fostering Mental Health," *Journal of Child Psychiatry.* 2:302–29;1953.

14. E. E. Pumala, "Secondary School Camping," *California Journal of Secondary Education.* 25:281–84;1950.

15. W. H. Ivins, "Providing for Work Experience and Outdoor Activities," in N. B. Henry, ed., *Adapting the Secondary-School Program to the Needs of Youth,* 52nd Yearbook, Part I. Chicago: National Society for the Study of Education, 1953. Chapter 10.

16. J. L. Trump, *High School Extracurriculum Activities.* Chicago: University of Chicago Press, 1944.

17. E. G. Pogue, *Participation in Extraclass Activities as Related to Socio-economic Classification.* Unpublished Ed. D. dissertation. University of Illinois, 1949.

18. R. Fedder, *Guiding Homeroom and Club Activities.* New York: McGraw-Hill, 1949. Pp. 335–36. Reprinted by permission.

19. F. McKinney, "Counseling for Emotional Stability," *Workshop in Counseling and Guidance.* San Francisco: San Francisco State College, 1951. Reprinted by permission. (Joseph's case has also been published in *Education.* 73:241–44;1952.)

20. M. L. Healey, "Report on the Supplementary Care Program," *Journal of Educational Research.* 42:201–08;1948.

SUGGESTED READINGS

P. W. L. Cox *et al.*, *Basic Principles of Guidance*. New York: Prentice-Hall, 1948. See chapters entitled: "The Club Program as an Instrumentality for Guidance"; "Guidance through Athletics and Health Education"; "Guidance through Dramatic Arts"; "Guidance through Student Participation in School Management"; "The Subjects of Instruction—Their Place in the Modern Curriculum and Their Value in Guidance"; "Guiding Youths of Special Artistic Talent"; "Guiding Mentally or Physically Defective Youths."

F. G. Davis and P. S. Norris, *Guidance Handbook for Teachers*. New York: McGraw-Hill, 1949. Chapter 27, "Guidance through Extracurricular Activities."

C. E. Erickson, ed., *A Basic Text for Guidance Workers*. New York: Prentice-Hall, 1947. See chapters entitled: "Group-Guidance Activities," "Organized Group-Guidance Activities," "The Community Occupational Survey," "Self-Appraisal and Career Courses," "The Role of Work Experience," and "Placement and Follow-Up Services."

H. H. Giles *et al.*, *Exploring the Curriculum*. New York: Harper, 1942. How the thirty high schools participating in the Progressive Education Association's Eight Year Study built their experimental curricula.

A. J. Jones, *Principles of Guidance*, 4th edition. New York: McGraw-Hill, 1951. Chapter 7, "Tryout and Exploratory Experiences in Studying the Individual," and Chapter 24, "Guidance for Individual Development and for Leisure Time."

A. Meiers *et al.*, *Let's Look at the Student Council*. Detroit: The Citizenship Education Study, 1949.

National Association of Secondary School Principals, *The Student Council Handbook*, rev. ed. Washington: National Education Association, 1950.

C. M. Smith and M. M. Roos, *A Guide to Guidance*. New York: Prentice-Hall, 1941. Chapter 13, "Cooperative Education—A Guidance Laboratory."

J. Warters, *High School Personnel Work Today*. New York: McGraw-Hill, 1946. See chapters entitled: "Socializing the Individual: Student Activities"; "Group Guidance"; "Helping the Individual to Progress through Supplementary Services: Health Orientation and Student Aid"; "Work Experience, Placement, and Follow-Up."

B. H. Wright, *Practical Handbook for Group Guidance.* Chicago: Science Research, 1948. A book for teacher-advisers of homerooms, common-learnings classes, and clubs.

W. A. Yeager, *Administration and the Pupil.* New York: Harper, 1949. Chapter 11, "Administering to the Needs of Exceptional Pupils." See also items 5, 7, 8, 15, 16, and 18 in the References for this chapter.

SUGGESTED FILMS

The Teacher as Observer and Guide. How teachers deal with slow learners and problem solving, how they stimulate personality growth and artistic expression. Bureau of Publications, Teachers College, Columbia University.

We Plan Together. How students participate in a core course. Bureau of Publications, Teachers College, Columbia University.

17

THE SCHOOL AS A THERAPEUTIC ENVIRONMENT

EDUCATION AND PSYCHOTHERAPY

PSYCHOLOGISTS and educators occasionally become involved in debates as to whether there is any real or basic difference between education and psychotherapy. Such discussions frequently end with one or both parties saying something like this: "Well, maybe it's therapy or maybe it isn't. It depends on how you define therapy."

If we define psychotherapy as a process whereby one person attempts to bring about changes in the personality and the emotional life of another person or persons, education is certainly an attempt to perform therapy. Under this definition, almost anything that one does to a child is an attempt at therapy. If we define therapy as an attempt to create a relationship whereby an individual (or individuals) will become emotionally more mature, more in touch with reality, and more effective in his relations with others, then education is still an attempt at therapy. If, however, we say that therapy is an attempt to alleviate emotional difficulties or problems of internal conflict, then it is more difficult to say whether education is a form of therapy. In other words, if we think of psychotherapy as a form of treatment, then it is clear that our usual conceptions of education do not include psychotherapy. On the other hand, psychotherapy is itself actually a form of re-education or relearning, as J. Dollard and N. E. Miller [1], and E. J. Shoben, Jr., [2], have indicated.

As the terms education and psychotherapy are commonly employed, education usually refers to changes that are primarily intellectual, while psychotherapy refers to attempts to bring about changes that are primarily emotional. Yet, as we have pointed out elsewhere in this text, it is difficult or impossible in actual practice to distinguish between emotional and intellectual factors. There is much that we do in education which is therapeutic, and much that is done in psychotherapy that is educational.

Dorothy W. Baruch states that education is therapeutic: (1) when teachers recognize that the thwarting and frustrating experiences of childhood create tensions, fears, and aggressive feelings that demand an outlet; (2) when teachers provide nonharmful channels for the expression of these emotions; and (3) when teachers recognize children's need for affection, attention, and personal friendly contact [3].

Perhaps, for the purpose of this discussion, we can characterize as therapeutic any attempts to deal constructively with the emotional aspect of life. The more that a given process is concerned with emotional adjustment, the more it takes on the nature of therapy, or the greater and deeper the emotional disturbance of the client or child, the greater the need for therapeutic handling. If we can accept these criteria, then we can examine various phases of education in terms of the amount and kind of therapeutic activity.

DIFFERING LEVELS OF THERAPY

A USEFUL approach to this problem is that formulated by Charlotte Buhler in analyzing problem behavior. There are the "trivial, everyday disturbances" that teachers cannot study in detail and that must be dealt with on the spot. Buhler classifies such treatment as problem solution on the "behavior level" or "level one." She notes that this kind of treatment is adequate for many classroom problems, but that it is often applied inappropriately to problems which require more study and deeper understanding.

She also calls "level-one" treatment "supportive therapy,"

> a technique which does not attempt a fundamental change of the person's personality, but is content with the removal of anxiety and other incapacitating emotions and with the providing of encouragement and confidence [4]:

Buhler feels that all *repetitious* disturbances should be given more careful examination because they cannot be dealt with adequately on the "behavior level" ("level-one"). Repetitious behavior is not produced by momentary release of temporary tension but is an indication of deeper and more chronic emotional disturbance. There are other clues to the kinds of behavior that cannot be handled on "level one." Sometimes a single disturbance will give indication of a deep-seated emotional disturbance and will call for further study. Or a child may produce a succession of seemingly unrelated disturbances:

> A child may today wriggle restlessly, tomorrow poke his neighbors, the next day sit and stare into space, another day masturbate openly, and still another complain of headaches. Each of these behavior disturbances may be different expressions of the same deep conflict or frustration in the child [5].

According to Buhler, these various types of behavior should be handled on "level two" or "level three."

"Level two" consists of "treatments which attempt to

achieve, beyond the support of encouragement and release, a degree of *insight* which brings acceptance of prevailing difficulties [6]." In other words, the person working with the child tries to help the child to "live with" or adapt himself to whatever difficult problem he has to face at school or at home or elsewhere. "Level two" is an approach that is within the scope of the teacher or the guidance worker who has had sufficient training and experience to deal with emotional problems of this sort.[1] Ideally, a teacher with this training would not undertake the responsibilities of helping a child with such a problem unless he had sufficient time to carry out the responsibilities involved. It should be admitted, however, that all too often teachers discover that a child needs help with a pressing problem, and there is no one on the school staff who has the time or the training to take the referral. This is not unusual, inasmuch as only a minority of school districts and communities have trained guidance workers. What often happens in such cases is that the teacher tries to fit appointments with the child into an already over-crowded schedule. This practice is admittedly far from satisfactory, but under present circumstances this may be the only solution.[2]

---

[1] There is a growing feeling that every teacher should have this kind of training. Lyman B. Owen, Superintendent of Schools in Wellesley, Massachusetts, writes, for example:

"Probably none of us want teachers to become little psychiatrists or mental health specialists. However, it is reasonable that every teacher should have basic training as a guidance counselor. For example, parents and children might expect a teacher, either in elementary or secondary schools, to have a rather complete knowledge of existing intra- and extraschool services which pertain in social and emotional adjustment. Should not a teacher have developed a reasonable amount of skill in using the techniques of interviewing? . . .

"I wonder if it is too much to expect our teachers to have familiarity with the case study and its possibilities? Is it too much, also, to expect a teacher to possess an ability to use and interpret cumulative and anecdotal records of her pupils? Should she not also be familiar with the literature on school mental health or at least possess facility in locating and using such literature [7]?"

[2] A useful book for the teacher who finds himself in this kind of a predicament is D. S. Arbuckle, *Teacher Counseling*. Cambridge, Mass.: Addison-Wesley, 1950.

Buhler sees "level-two" therapy as appropriate for

children who live in unhealthy home conditions, whose parental demands cannot be corrected. . . . Because they are always under the pressure of acute situational conditions, these children need *emotional release.* Simultaneously, the therapist endeavors to *improve* the *objective conditions* as far as possible by working with the parents, if they are accessible. Furthermore, the therapist uses the close relationship he has developed with the child to help the child *understand, accept,* or *cope* in some way with those difficulties which cannot be eliminated [8].

"Level-three" therapy goes much deeper than the preceding levels. It is required by children whose difficulties are intimately involved with their parents' personal problems of adjustment and who are under the strong influence of one or both parents. Such treatment requires the dynamic restructuring of children's relationships with their parents. Hence, it should be undertaken only by psychologists, psychiatrists, or psychiatric social workers.

Buhler also identifies a fourth and a fifth level of psychotherapy, which involve closer relationships between psychotherapists and their patients, as well as long-term treatment [9].

In this chapter we shall be concerned with what Buhler would term the first three levels of therapy because these are the levels which concern classroom teachers with regard to both treatment and referral.

THERAPEUTIC HANDLING AT THE "BEHAVIOR LEVEL"

MOST behavior problems get no further than the classroom door; they are handled on the spot. As Buhler says, the teacher's role here is largely supportive. By censuring or limiting behavior which is likely to disrupt the classroom activities and by encouraging behavior which is likely to promote the general welfare, the teacher plays a dual role: he supports those forces within the group (1) which operate to keep children from indulging in antisocial behavior and (2) which make children want to do things which are in the best interests of the class. A common difficulty here is that we tend to be more concerned about the negative aspects of support than we are about its positive aspects. The fact is, of course, if children are progressing in the direction of goals which are emotionally healthy, they will require fewer reprimands and punishments.

DISCIPLINE

Some of the teacher's therapeutic functions come under the heading of discipline. Unfortunately, discipline is a term whose use has come to be limited to punishment and restrictions—something that the teacher does to children in order to make them behave properly. Yet discipline has a function which is more in harmony with the principles of mental hygiene. What we really want is that children become *self-*disciplined. What we really want is to help children develop inner controls which keep them from behaving in ways which are antisocial or immature when they are not under our supervision.[3] Only if children develop these controls properly can we trust them out of our sight. What happens so often is that we lose sight of this goal and settle instead for control through fear—that is, we get children to behave properly not because they feel the need for proper behavior but because they are afraid of what we will do to them if they do not behave. This external sort of discipline is getting more difficult to apply as the years go by, for, as we have pointed out elsewhere, we are developing more and more misgivings about dealing with children in harsh and punitive ways. Therefore, when children "step out of line," we are often pre-

---

[3] For an excellent discussion of a mental-hygiene approach to discipline see G. V. Sheviakov and F. Redl, *Discipline for Today's Children and Youth.* Washington: National Education Association, 1944.

vented from taking drastic action by our own humanitarian impulses, as well as our good sense. Since we are discovering that harsher, more traditional methods are unsatisfactory, we really have no choice but to find more effective ways of motivating children. Parents and children often have difficulty in accepting the fact that they have little choice in this.

IMPROVING COMMUNICATION BETWEEN STUDENTS AND TEACHERS

The first step we must take if we are to motivate children in the proper directions—that is, if we are to help them to *want* to do what is right—is to establish good relations with them. This implies an improvement in communication between the teacher and his students—rapport, if you like. One of the problems growing out of the traditional relationship between teacher and pupil is that the "social distance" between them is so great they have difficulty in communicating.

Taba and Elkins describe how an eighth-grade teacher improved the communication among her students and between herself and her class by "focusing on human relations." As a result of the changes she introduced, her students gained better understanding of themselves and their social environment, they became more interested and more involved in the processes of education, and the atmosphere of the classroom became more therapeutic, more conducive to mental health—more "human." She brought about these changes by first diagnosing the needs of her students through such devices as sociometry, interviews with students and their parents, and student diaries based on the activities of selected two-day periods. Then she counseled individual students who had pressing problems, she arranged for special experiences (one boy gained self-assurance by helping out in the kindergarten), she helped the children organize panel discussions on problems about which they were deeply concerned, she reorganized the reading program so that it would reflect individual interests of children, and she experimented with a variety of techniques which enabled children to work with various situations in the field of human relations.

As a result of these experiences, "children grew in their ability to work in groups and to relate themselves to each other [10]"; hostility was markedly reduced (rejections, according to sociogrammatic studies, dropped from forty-three to eleven between September and May) [11]; children learned to settle conflicts through reaching common agreements; and they "grew in their ability to think through a problem, to consider a variety of solutions, and to apply them with some measure of personal satisfaction [12]." An example of the latter type of learning is as follows:

> One child . . . found weekends very difficult. She learned to analyze what caused the confusion and contention at home. Mother, grandmother, and stepfather were all home together in crowded quarters. All three of them were weary from the monotony of machine labor in the factory; all three were good cooks, anxious to do the cooking. This task was a bit more creative than the formidable dishwashing; hence everybody wanted to cook. One would start; the others would follow into the kitchen and begin stirring together ingredients for another recipe—and thereby hung a fight. By her insight the girl helped to forestall the up-to-now inevitable battles over the family menu. She led them to see that taking turns would solve the problem; she even helped them plan a schedule of hours. At each meal she learned to provide some satisfaction for each of them. Later she organized a clean-up crew; teamwork in cleaning up provided a measure of real fun. She even learned that there were times when all her efforts were futile; then she herself must stand ready to carry a greater share of the monotonous tasks [13].

The teacher learned from this experience also. She reports:

Perhaps the most dramatic single discovery for me was that an ordinary teacher can cut loose from cherished moorings of textbooks and curriculum outlines and chart a journey of her own. . . . Another dramatic discovery lay in the use of group work. By finding ways of making children comfortable with each other and with me, by setting assignments so that children could work with each other in small groups, and by allowing children to react to each other's ideas, I had apparently tapped a new source of creative thinking and learning [14].

LEARNING TO ACCEPT FEELINGS

The classroom atmosphere may become more therapeutic if the teacher can recognize and accept his feelings and help students to recognize and accept theirs. This may be difficult for some of us to accomplish, since in our culture we are so inclined to "play down" feelings and hence feel uncomfortable when they are discussed frankly and openly. However, as Robert S. Stewart points out,

. . . There are many feelings that we not only accept within ourselves but can also share with children—even negative feelings—and thereby ease ourselves and the children.

What is suggested here is very simply that the air can be cleared by everyone saying at times what he feels. The teacher, in this case, shares with the children the feelings that they are all conscious of, and thereby becomes not more but less the enemy. . . .

Bringing feelings out in the open may also be helpful to children and teachers on those days when one is irritable and cross —perhaps because of an outside difficulty. Verbal anticipation of a situation sometimes results in prevention of the situation. . . .

When a class is restless, it is likewise sensible to bring out the feelings indulging the restlessness. Expression of feelings naturally is not only psychologically sound for the teacher but also for the children [15].

Margaret Heaton makes the ability to express feelings easily a condition of the teacher's ability to establish a healthy group climate—that is, a climate in which students can communicate easily and freely. She describes the qualities of such a teacher as follows:

> First, he must be a person who has learned not to be afraid of feelings, however negative they seem, his own feelings or those of children. Second, he must be permissive about, not condemning of, negative feelings. While not attempting to perform the tasks of a therapist, the teacher must have some faith in catharsis—in letting feelings get out into the open and resolve themselves in interaction. Finally, he must understand that feelings cannot be changed directly—and that what is done about them must be a normal part of the on-going school program [16].

Heaton's list of desirable qualities receives partial validation in a study conducted by John C. Glidewell, whose data indicate that denial of feelings by a group leader tends to reduce his effectiveness, whereas acceptance of feelings helps to improve effectiveness [17].

In spite of the growing awareness in the educational profession of the role and importance of feelings, there are still a great many teachers who are afraid to express and to accept their feelings. As one writer in this field says,

> It is surprising how many teachers there are who still keep unexpressed even their warm and friendly feelings toward their children and who fear that expression of spontaneous liking will undermine their authority [18].

In this section we have described a number of different ways in which a teacher can create and maintain a therapeutic atmosphere. There are certainly no hard and fast rules to follow in this. What the teacher does will be dependent partly upon the grade or subject he teaches, partly on the emotional climate of the school, partly on the kind of relationship and the rapport he maintains with the children, partly on the amount of freedom he is permitted to experiment with curriculum and methods, and partly on the kinds of techniques he is able to develop comfortably and easily. Last, but certainly not least, it will depend upon the amount and kinds of problems that develop in his classes. Some of these problems he will be able to handle because they will fall within the scope and level of his skill but some he will have to refer elsewhere.

REFERRING DIFFICULT PROBLEMS

Referral of problems is also a technique which must at times be used in order to maintain an atmosphere conducive to emotional health. Some children are so disturbed emotionally that their presence creates chronic unrest or they demand far more than their share of the teacher's attention or both. These are the children who ought to be referred to specialists who have proper psychological training and who have the time and facilities to provide psychotherapy. Referral is not always easy. Sometimes teachers look upon referral as an admission that they have "failed" and therefore continue to try to work with a child for weeks or months in the face of evidence that they are really having little effect on his attitudes and behavior. What is even more difficult to accept, referring a child to a guidance worker implies that others may succeed where you have failed. Sometimes administrators have also taken the viewpoint that teachers should be able to handle all the problems that arise in their classrooms. And, of course, there is the very real likelihood that child-guidance facilities might be so badly overcrowded that they cannot deal with referrals, or, indeed, they may even be nonexistent. At such times it is very helpful for the school to have good working relations with parents and with the community at large, for it is completely unrealistic for anyone to expect that the classroom teacher function both as an educator and a psychotherapist. Not only is this too much responsibility to load upon the shoulders of an individual who has been employed to perform the functions of a full-time teacher, but also it is not fair to the class whose education may suffer while their teacher tries desperately to cope with the behavior of one or two disturbed children. It is the responsibility of the community to provide special services for children who need special help, although very often the school must go to great lengths to arouse the community to the need for meeting its responsibilities.

THE ROLE OF THE ADMINISTRATOR
IN MENTAL HEALTH

THE administrator can and should play a key role in helping the community to become aware of its responsibilities. One of his chief functions is that of interpreting the school to the community, and this duty includes informing the community of the school's unmet needs. Administrators have many ways of carrying out this function: speaking to Parent-Teacher Associations, making public reports at stated intervals, speaking to service organizations, socializing with the leaders of the community, holding special press conferences, taking advantage of times when the school gets into the columns of the local newspaper to remind the public of gaps in the resources of the community, and so forth. These are a few of the ways in which administrators stimulate citizens into taking more responsibility for solving the problems of the community which relate to the welfare of children and thus eventually improving the mental health of the school as a whole.

The administrator has an even greater responsibility to create an emotional climate within the school which is conducive to mental health. He can make a major contribution to this end by building and maintaining democratic relations with his teachers. This means sharing his powers with them, trusting them to do the right things, consulting them on matters which affect them, and treating them basically as equals.

An administrator can do all the things we have just mentioned and still be unable to provide his teachers with the emotional support they need. In other words, an administrator might do a good job of sharing his power and still be somewhat cold and remote—he may lack what has been called "the human touch."

Even the most effective teachers run into problems with which they need help, problems they would like to talk over with someone who understands teachers and the difficulties which they face. An administrator who has a human, friendly approach is an individual who will be sought out by teachers who need to discuss their problems. As the administrator performs this function, he is actually playing the role of a counselor for his teachers and thus providing them with a valuable service which they could not otherwise obtain. If the relationship is a sound one, if the teacher knows that the administrator values him as an individual and respects his ability as a teacher, he will have no real worries about discussing his problems or even his mistakes and failures with him.

If an administrator creates a democratic atmosphere and makes it easy for teachers to bring their problems to him, he will thereby improve the mental health of the entire school. Because the emotional climate of any social organization (including the school) is so dependent on the behavior and attitudes of the person in charge, the willingness of the principal to share power and to open up channels of two-way communication with his teachers is bound to have far-reaching effects.

Teachers need to be trusted with their share of power, but they also need someone who will serve as a professional leader—someone with whom they can identify. There will be times when the administrator, because of his position, will be able to see certain problems in clearer perspective than the individual teacher. At such times he may present his findings to them, together with certain recommendations. Unless he is accepted by his teachers as someone who can speak for them, he may be unable to influence their attitudes and opinions.

THE ADMINISTRATOR AS A COUNSELOR

In addition to this broader mental-health role, the administrator also may act as a counselor for disturbed children—that is, he may provide help on the first and second levels of therapy, as defined by Buhler. Sometimes he has the requisite time, facilities, and training to accomplish this function; sometimes administrators (particularly vice-principals and assistant principals) are hired with the intent that they provide such services. However, it should be noted that the very fact that a principal or vice-principal bears an administrative title may interfere with his ability to establish a good counseling relationship with students (just as it may interfere with his relationships with teachers). Some administrators are able to overcome this difficulty through sheer ability to establish rapport easily and quickly with children; others seem unable to bridge the social distance which separates administrators and students.

Traditionally, the principal is a disciplinarian; children who are unable to keep from disturbing others are referred to him for punishment. If the principal looks upon discipline from the mental-hygiene point of view, he may very likely use the referral as a basis for establishing a counseling relationship. On the other hand, he may take a more conventional approach and look upon his role as that of a person who administers punishment. Unfortunately, teachers often set the stage for such referrals by threatening children with the promise that if they misbehave they will be sent to the principal. Under such conditions, principals often feel that they have no course but to "back up the teacher." Some schools are fortunate in that they have principals who are able to keep several functions in an effective balance—they counsel some students, punish others, consult with parents and community agencies regarding some, and refer others to agencies and clinics for treatment. An example of the attitude and approach of the administrator who works for mental health is provided by the following statement from an article by William Chiverton, who writes from his experience as an elementary school principal:

> I believe that an effective school principal is one who guides the people with whom he works in finding solutions or working out procedures for themselves. I believe that good guidance is an absolute essential to effective teaching and that *guidance* is perhaps the most important task of the elementary school principal. The elementary school principal must realize that guidance does not involve the solving of problems for individuals but is the process of assisting others in finding solutions to their own problems [19].

THE ROLE OF THE SPECIALIST IN MENTAL HEALTH

INASMUCH as the administrative status and duties of principals and vice-principals often interfere with their ability to develop therapeutic relationships with individual students, the latter function often is made the responsibility of a specialist—that is, a counselor, a school psychologist, or a school social worker. Counselors usually operate within the framework of secondary schools, whereas school psychologists and school social workers usually operate from central offices of cities and counties and spend most of their time with elementary school children. There are many exceptions, of course. There are some elementary schools that have counselors, and some secondary schools are serviced by school psychologists, although the general practice is as we have stated it. In general, counselors are drawn from the regular teaching staff and assigned counseling duties because of their preference for this type of work, their experience, and/or their training. School psychologists are persons whose training is primarily psychological. As a general rule, they have more training than counselors in the specialized techniques of psychotherapy and diagnostic testing.

These specialists usually spend a large part of their time working directly with children in a counseling or therapeutic relationship. In the secondary school most of this service is concerned with vocational and educational counseling and with treatment of personal problems at the first or second level of therapy. In the elementary schools the relationship deals more with emotional problems and is conducted on the first, second, or even the third level of psychotherapy.

It is interesting to note that the trend in psychological services is for greater emphasis on counseling and therapy and less on diagnostic testing. Twenty years ago a much greater portion of the time of psychological personnel was taken up with the administration and interpretation of tests. Today, psychologists still continue to perform this function, but its importance has been superseded by consultations with children, teachers, administrators, and parents. This change has made the psychologist less of a test administrator and more of a worker in the field of human relations. One of the indications of this trend has been the change that has occurred in play therapy, which at first was often used by child psychologists as a projective test—a way of discovering and observing emotional trends and problems in children. Play therapy is still used to serve this function to some degree, but there is increasing emphasis on using it as a therapeutic device in its own right, as a means of helping children to accept themselves and to work out more satisfactory methods of expressing their feelings.

PLAY THERAPY

A child who is referred to play therapy is usually introduced into a room where there are many kinds of play equipment and play materials, including paints, clay, sand, and water.

Although therapists differ in their approach to this type of therapy, the usual method is to permit children to do anything they want during the therapy period—anything, that is, short of striking the therapist, breaking windows, and the like. Some children spend the time in dramatic activity, manipulating and talking to dolls and stuffed animals. Others work out their problems through the use of plastic materials, like clay and finger paint. Still others ignore the play materials and equipment and spend their time reading comic books or looking out of the window.

The ways in which children use play therapy differ widely, depending on the personality of the child in question and the problem he is trying to solve. This record of a play-therapy session by Elaine Dorfman, demonstrates how one ten-year-old boy, who was referred for his poor school-work and disruptive behavior in the classroom, was helped to express his hostility symbolically and harmlessly in his first session of therapy:

> (*The door opened and Bob literally leaped into the room.*)
> *Bob* (*making noise like machine-gun*): Rrrattatataaa! I'm Mr. District Attorney! (*Ferocious expression.*)
> *Therapist:* You're a very tough character?
> *Bob:* You bet I am! I'll mow you down!
> *Therapist:* You're so tough, you'll even shoot me down.
> *Bob:* Yes! And you! And you! And you! And you! (*He shoots at various unnamed parties with his imaginary gun.*)
> *Therapist:* Everybody's getting shot.
> *Bob:* I'll say they are! Rrrattattattaaa. All dead now!
> *Therapist:* You got them all?
> *Bob:* Yeah. (*He gets some clay from the table, rolls it into a ball, and tosses it into the air several times. As he does so, he talks to the therapist.*) Did you know I was a swop?
> *Therapist:* A swop, Bob? (*Uncomprehending.*)
> *Bob:* Yeah, my father says I'm a swop. He's one too. He likes spaghetti, he eats it every day. I like it too, oh boy!
> *Therapist:* You both like spaghetti and you're both swops?
> *Bob:* Yeah. I bet I can hit the ceiling.

Therapist: I bet you can too, and it'd be fun, but no clay on the ceiling, Bob.

Bob: Why not?

Therapist: It's too hard to get it off.

Bob: (*He tosses the ball several times. When it gets within an inch or two of the ceiling, he looks at the therapist.*)

Therapist: You want to see how I'm taking it?

Bob: I do! (*He tosses the clay ball again. It gets nearer and nearer to the ceiling.*) Heh heh heh!

Therapist: Bob, I know you'd like to throw clay at the ceiling. That's one of the things we can't do in here. You can throw it at the target or at the floor if you want to.

Bob: (*He says nothing, but goes to the table and begins to pound the clay ball flat.*)

Therapist: (*Comes and sits down opposite him, but says nothing.*)

Bob: Wait till you see what I'm making.

Therapist: You mean, it'll surprise me?

Bob: You'll see in a minute.

Therapist: I'll soon find out?

Bob: (*He makes a clay figure.*) It's a man.

Therapist: A man?

Bob: (*He puts a skirt on the figure, with great glee. He looks mischievously at the therapist.*) Guess who it is now.

Therapist: I don't know, Bob. Do you want to tell me?

Bob: My dear teacher, how do you do? (*He hits the clay figure with his fist.*)

Therapist: Teacher got socked.

Bob: Heh, heh. No, *you* did.

Therapist: Oh, I got that one.

Bob: (*He hits the clay figure another blow.*) There!

Therapist: I got another sock.

Bob: I'll say you did! And here's another one for you! (*Hits clay figure again.*)

Therapist: You hit me again.

Bob: And that's not all. Take that! And that! And that! (*He hits harder and harder as he pounds the figure quite flat.*)

Therapist: You're giving me an awful beating.

Bob: You bet I am! Take that one too! I'll mash ya! (*Hits.*) I'll smash ya! (*Hits several times.*)

Therapist: You are very mad at me and I am getting all pounded up.

Bob: Off goes your head!

Therapist: My head's off now.

Bob: There goes your arms!

Therapist: I have no arms now.

Bob: There goes your legs!

Therapist: No more legs left.

Bob: And there goes you! (*He throws the remnant of the clay figure into the basin.*)

Therapist: I am all gone now?

Bob: You're dead. I killed you.

Therapist: I am killed.

Bob: You're all washed up.

Therapist: I am very, very dead?

Bob: You sure are. (*Suddenly, he smiles*) I'll have you a game of catch now.

Therapist: You want to play with me now? O.K. (*The rest of the hour is spent in a quiet game of "catch" with a ball of clay.*) [20].

In interpreting this interview, Dorfman states that Bob's hostility was probably a reaction to the therapist's refusal to permit him to throw clay on the ceiling. Since Bob did not mention this as a cause, the therapist, too, did not refer to it. During the following sessions, Bob's behavior underwent marked changes. For example, he began to show consideration for the therapist and stopped cheating at the games he played with her, even though no mention had been made of his cheating. Dorfman feels that much of this improvement can be traced back to Bob's symbolic murder of the therapist in the first interview and her acceptance of both her fate and her executioner.

One of the amazing things about play therapy is that it works even when it appears to be failing. It is fairly easy to understand how a child who is troubled by a deep emotional conflict can "work it out" through dramatic play with dolls, or through talking over his troubles with an understanding and sympathetic therapist, or through working with plastic materials. These seem to be more or less obvious ways of getting rid of hostilities and anxieties through behavior that is directly symbolic. But even children who are apparently not participating benefit from the therapeutic situation. Dorfman describes the case of a fourteen-year-old boy who is referred because he waylays and robs smaller children, hits strange adults for no apparent reason, does unsatisfactory work in school, and executes cats by hanging. During fifteen weekly sessions with the therapist, he refuses to discuss anything, but spends the time reading comic books, raising and lowering window shades, and methodically searching closets and desk.

In the midst of these seemingly unprofitable contacts, his teacher reports that he has performed an act of unsolicited generosity, the first ever noted in his eight years at school. His teacher tells the therapist that he has used his printing press to print programs for a class skating party, and has distributed these to his classmates, although no one suggested it to him. As she puts it, "This is his first social act." For the first time, an interest in his schoolwork is noted. His teacher says, "Why, he's actually one of us now. We never even notice him now [21]."

Dorfman tells of another twelve-year-old who was referred for attempted rape and whose schoolwork was so poor that he had to receive special tutoring. He spent his therapy sessions doing his spelling homework or describing a recent movie he had seen. On one occasion he brought a deck of cards and played "war" with the therapist. This was apparently the total extent of their relationship.

When the semester is over, he is returned to his grade, where he is reported as "doing very well." Months later, he is walking along the street with a friend, when he accidentally meets the therapist. He introduces them and says to the friend, "You oughta go see her on accounta you can't learn to read. She helps kids who are in trouble [22]."

Undoubtedly the success of play therapy rests upon the freedom of the therapeutic situation and the accepting attitudes of the therapist. But there may be another element that is more basic. A child in a play-therapy situation comes in contact with an adult who treats him differently from any other adult he has ever met. He is treated as an equal, one whose feelings, thoughts, and wishes count for something. Here is an adult who has a different pattern of expectations, an adult who says, in effect, "I have confidence in your ability to develop mature behavior, and I believe that if I give you a free hand, during this hour of therapy, you will attain this maturity in your own way."

As the differences between the attitude of this adult and the attitude of adults-in-general begin to penetrate the child's awareness, a change takes place in his self-concept. He begins to see himself as a more adequate person, and his new-formed belief in himself is supported by the confident acceptance of his therapist.

The ability of play therapy to help children develop different self-concepts is a major contribution to their maturity and well-being. This is analogous to the contribution that can be made by good teachers who can make their classrooms truly therapeutic, in the broadest sense, and thus aid children in developing a greater feeling of adequacy.

DEALING WITH THE PROBLEMS OF RETARDED READERS

Some communities have entered the field of child psychotherapy through the establishment of reading clinics. Although such clinics are set up primarily to deal with the problems of retarded readers and nonreaders, the staffs of these clinics have found that reading problems and emotional maladjustments usually go hand in hand, and that when this occurs it does not pay to try to eliminate the reading problem without some alleviation of the emotional difficulty. A variety of techniques are used by such clinics in dealing with this dual problem. Worth J. Osburn describes an approach that makes use of semantics, nondirective therapy, and psychodrama (a "deeper" form of sociodrama) [23]. G. L. Persons and M. H. Grumbly report on a method that emphasizes group guidance [24]. Virginia Axline explored the use of play-therapy techniques over a three-and-one-half month period with a group of thirty-seven second graders diagnosed as retarded readers. She reported some remarkable gains in reading age, including some of sixteen and seventeen months [25]. Another study by Robert E. Bills confirms the effectiveness of play therapy with retarded readers [26], but a later study by the same author indicates that the method is chiefly effective when emotional problems accompany the reading difficulty, inasmuch as play therapy failed to produce gains in retarded readers who were well-adjusted [27].

There are few problems that perplex and baffle the teacher more than that of the child who cannot and/or will not read. Reading is the key to successful learning in school. A child who cannot read is automatically shut out of much of the daily class activity, and the areas of learning in which he cannot participate increase in size and importance as he is passed on from grade to grade. Even if the teacher decides that he cannot give the nonreader the time and special attention needed, he must still find some worth-while activity to occupy the child's time and attention; otherwise, discipline problems are likely to occur.

Nonreaders present a troublesome problem for the teacher not only because they require extra time and attention, but also because they symbolize the failure of the school system in general and the individual teacher in particular.

Mrs. Gladstone, the third-grade teacher, told Miss Hempel, the fourth-grade teacher, that she had literally "tried everything" to get David Prince to read, but it was all to no avail, even though David was "one of the smartest children in the group." As Miss Hempel listened, she promised herself that when *she* got David this coming year, things would be different. Perhaps Mrs. Gladstone hadn't tried hard enough or maybe she didn't use the right approach. After all, it is ridiculous for a bright boy to be in the fourth grade and not be able to read.

So, when Miss Hempel got the new class the following school year, she laid out a careful plan. She had David's eyes tested—they were normal. She gave him a nonverbal intelligence test—he was definitely above average. She then tried a variety of approaches—phonetic analysis, flash cards, and books with lots of pictures related to his interests. None of them worked. At first, David was cooperative and pleasant and tried very hard. He would learn the words assigned each day, but the next day they would be forgotten. Miss Hempel, too, was patient and friendly at first, but as the weeks went by and David was still unable to read, the atmosphere changed. David became petulant and irritable, and Miss Hempel became grim and determined. The problem which had intrigued and challenged her at the beginning of the year now assumed sinister aspects. It began to look as though David's inability or unwillingness to read was personal, an attempt to spite her. Whenever she had to make special assignments for David, she was reminded of her failure. The realization affected her morale; she was aware that she was sometimes inclined to deal more severely with the other children in the room after a frustrating session with David. Finally, she stopped giving David special attention. After that, her relations with her class improved, but whenever she looked his way in the classroom, she was aware of a sense of mingled guilt and hostility.

There is nothing very unusual in Miss Hempel's experiences with David. Many a teacher has hopefully taken up the task of helping a nonreader or a retarded reader to mend his ways only to meet with frustration and failure. Some teachers *do* succeed, of course, but the chances *against* success in the usual classroom situation increase with the age and grade of the child.

What we are saying here, and what the results of the studies we have cited indicate, is that the problem of the nonreader and the retarded reader in the upper grades is one that requires special care and attention—care and attention which are usually above and beyond that which can be given by the average classroom teacher. Such problems appear to find their best solutions in reading clinics and remedial groups supervised by specially trained personnel. Teachers in the upper grades can make their best contributions in two ways: (1) by looking for possible clues that can be shared with those who are working with the children in question, and (2) by trying to keep from putting too much pressure on children with reading difficulties.

The latter advice is the hardest to take because the normal reaction of the teacher to a child who has learning difficulties is to urge him to work harder, perhaps even to shame him a little. Yet, it is just this kind of pressure that produces and aggravates reading difficulties. The teacher feels anxiety and concern regarding the reading difficulty and urges the child to do better. The child is aware of the teacher's anxiety and reciprocates by developing anxiety of his own, which may express itself through irritation, complete passivity, resentment, or confusion, coupled with sheer inability to make sense out of the printed word. The greater the anxiety of the teacher, the greater the anxiety of the student. Indeed, much of the success with retarded readers reported by the nondirective therapists previously cited may be due to the fact that such methods tend to *reduce* anxiety by eliminating external pressures. It is also significant that many retarded readers of normal intelligence learn to read adequately once they are no longer in school. (Others, of course, are unable to overcome this handicap and sometimes develop elaborate means of avoiding situations involving reading.) The fact that some nonreaders learn to read "spontaneously" once they have left school does not mean that their unwillingness in school was subject to conscious control—that is, we should not assume that children with normal intelligence who have reading difficulties would improve if they would merely resolve to read. Unfortunately, the emotional factors that retard reading operate beyond the consciousness of the child. Since his anxiety keeps him from being aware of what forces or factors prevent his learning to read, he does not know how to cope with them. And as the therapist or clinician helps such a child to reduce his anxiety, the child is freer to cope with his problems, including that of reading.

RELATIONSHIPS BETWEEN SPECIALISTS AND TEACHERS

It sometimes happens that a school system will hire psychologically trained personnel for the purpose of providing services for emotionally disturbed children and then will find, after the service has been in operation for a number of years, that the psychologists or counselors are spending a major portion of their time working with teachers rather than with children. This is usually indicative of a healthy trend because it means that both psychologists and teachers have found that it is possible to forestall the development of major problems by dealing with smaller problems in the classroom in earlier stages. In this way, specialists are able to make a major contribution to the emotional climate of the classroom.

The work they do with teachers may take several forms. It may consist of direct consultation, whereby the teacher and the specialist sit down together to exchange ideas on a specific "problem child" or to discuss the relationships in a certain class. It may take the form of case conferences, whereby the specialist, the teacher, the school nurse, the principal, or any other person who has had to deal with a child, meet together for the purpose of talking over diagnosis and treatment. The advantage of this method is that it not only serves the purpose of drawing together more information about a child and thus makes it possible to form a well-rounded, objective picture of his problems, but it also helps to involve various school personnel in the process of working together under expert guidance to learn more about children's problems and how they develop. It is one of the most effective forms of in-service training.

An example of the kind of program that specialists can develop is the mental-hygiene project established at Public School 33 in New York City for children in kindergarten and the first grade who are shy or overly aggressive or who display other symptoms of maladjustment. Evelyn D. Alderblum describes the program as consisting of parent interviews, small-group play under observation, weekly group work with five children at a time, and conferences with teachers. Alderblum found teachers to be especially appreciative of this program because it gave them opportunities to discuss classroom programs with a "peer" (someone who was not in a supervisory position), it gave them relief with children who were sources of anxiety, and it did not threaten their status or trespass on their "rights" as teachers [28].

Other schools have used specialists to conduct in-service seminars devoted to problems of human relations. These courses feature free discussion of the interpersonal relations between teachers and their classes, the interplay of forces in the classroom group, the function and importance of feelings, and even the problems that arise from the relations among teachers themselves and between teachers and administrators. Many teachers have found such seminars useful as ways of ridding themselves of some of their anxieties and of developing greater effectiveness in their profession.

MAKING REFERRALS TO OUTSIDE AGENCIES

Psychological specialists also find it necessary to make referrals. Indeed, in schools where the specialists are well established, they may serve as the chief referral agents. In other words, teachers and administrators in these schools will follow the practice of referring children to the psychologist, social worker, or counselor, as the case may be, who will counsel with the child, consult with teachers and parents, hold case conferences, and, if appropriate, will use one of several community agencies as a source of further help. When the specialist becomes the chief referral agency of the school, this makes it possible for him to develop contacts and maintain close working relationships with social welfare agencies, the juvenile courts, child-guidance clinics, or any of the other agencies or organizations which provide specialized services for children.

THE CHILD-GUIDANCE CLINIC

SCHOOL psychologists and social workers often work within the framework of a child-guidance clinic. In some communities these clinics are part of the school system; in others, they are under the administration of public health or welfare agencies. They are usually staffed by psychiatric social workers, school psychologists, clinical psychologists, and psychiatrists. If they are under the supervision of the schools, they usually work closely with attendance officers.

There are not nearly enough of these clinics to provide the services which are needed by emotionally disturbed children in our schools, and those which do exist often have long waiting lists. There are several reasons for these deficiencies. Such clinics are expensive; they require the services of highly trained persons who spend long hours working with relatively few children. Trained personnel are in short supply. Psychotherapy is a slow and tedious process; it cannot be hurried and it does not pay to keep overloading the facilities of the clinic. As James L. Hymes, Jr., says, "it takes a long time to make a bully; it takes a long time to *un-make* one too [29]."

Not only are clinics expensive, but also the value of their services is often unappreciated. As we noted previously, some teachers resent having to refer children to clinics. The attitudes of these teachers are probably a reflection of a general public attitude which may be described as "fear of psychotherapy." The idea that psychotherapy is for "crazy people" and that psychologists and psychiatrists are themselves somewhat "peculiar" appears to be a delusion that is rigidly fixed in the folklore of our society. One might add that some clinical workers aggravate the situation by becoming overinvolved in the problems of the children they treat—that is, they see themselves as persons whose chief duty is to *protect* children from adults rather than to help both adults and children to get along better. However, if the relationship between the clinic and the school is a good one, if there is effective communication between these two agencies, none of these forms of misunderstanding need develop.

One of the major tasks of administrators of schools and clinics, then, is to interpret the work of child-guidance clinics to the general public. If the public is to pay for more of this very expensive service, it must know about the nature and the effectiveness of the kind of service being rendered. But more than financial support is required if a clinic is to operate successfully. The community must also accept and support the clinic from an emotional point of view. It must believe in what the clinic is trying to do and it must have faith in the ability of the clinic workers to perform the job they have set for themselves. If the community does not accept the clinic in this sense, its general negative attitude may serve to undermine the confidence of the teachers who refer children to the clinic and the parents who cooperate with the clinic as a necessary part of the treatment of their children.

Alice C. Henry, Supervisor of Child Guidance Services for the San Francisco schools, points up the delicate problem clinics face in getting parents to cooperate with them:

No matter how obvious the problem seems to be, you have to anticipate that parents will have mixed feelings about seeking help. Even the parent who agrees with you wholeheartedly, it seems, may go home and fail to follow through on an agreed-upon plan. This is because all of us are a little afraid of what these "experts" are going to do to us. All of us, unhappy as we may be, hesitate about submitting ourselves to a program which is supposed to change us [30].

Some communities report much success in the use of various methods of involving parents in group therapy as a way of treating children's problems. Buchmueller and Gildea describe a project in St. Louis whereby mothers of problem children meet together in group therapy. Roughly three-fourths of the children whose mothers participated showed improvement [31]. Rudolph Dreikurs describes a program in Chicago which uses group-therapy methods to work with children, parents, and teachers and which served 3,274 persons in a recent year [32].

Because of the interest in mental health which has grown up during and after World War II, communities are more favorable to the establishment of child-guidance services than was true previously. Although many city and county school systems have now provided such services, many more are needed and existing ones need expansion. This can only be done if we are able to demonstrate to the public that such services, though expensive, help children to grow up to be more effective employees, more enlightened parents, and better citizens (because of their better emotional health) and that they make for a more therapeutic, hence more educational, environment in the school itself. In other words, our viewpoint should be that if the public will pay out more money for counselors, school psychologists, and social workers to work in schools and in clinics and to give help to children, teachers, and parents as needed, it will then receive much greater value from its present expenditures for education.

REFERENCES

1. J. Dollard and N. E. Miller, *Personality and Psychotherapy.* New York: McGraw-Hill, 1950.
2. E. J. Shoben, Jr., "Psychotherapy as a Problem in Learning Theory," *Psychological Bulletin.* 46:366–92;1949.
3. D. W. Baruch, "Incorporation of Therapeutic Procedures as Part of the Educative Process," *American Journal of Orthopsychiatry.* 12:659–66;1942.
4. C. Buhler, F. Smitter, and S. Richardson, *Childhood Problems and the Teacher.* New York: Holt, 1952. P. 288.
5. *Ibid.* P. 13.
6. *Ibid.* P. 293.
7. L. B. Owen, Superintendent of Schools, Wellesley, Mass., "A Superintendent Looks at Mental Health and at the Psychiatrist." Address delivered before Group for the Advancement of Psychiatry, Asbury Park, N. J., November 1952. Reprinted by permission.
8. Buhler, Smitter, and Richardson, *op. cit.* P. 294. Reprinted by permission.
9. *Ibid.* Pp. 306–12.
10. H. Taba and D. Elkins, *With Focus on Human Relations.* Washington: American Council on Education, 1950. P. 190.
11. *Ibid.* P. 194.
12. *Ibid.* P. 202.
13. *Ibid.* P. 202. Reprinted by permission.
14. *Ibid.* P. 207. Reprinted by permission.
15. Association for Supervision and Curriculum Development, *Growing Up in an Anxious Age.* Washington: National Education Association, 1952. Pp. 77–78. Reprinted by permission.
16. M. Heaton, *Feelings Are Facts.* New York: National Conference of Christians and Jews, 1952. P. 27. Reprinted by permission.
17. J. C. Glidewell, "The Teacher's Feelings as an Education Resource." *Journal of Educational Research.* 45:119–26;1951.
18. Association for Supervision and Curriculum Development, *op. cit.* P. 75.
19. W. Chiverton, "Children in the Elementary School Look to the Principal for Guidance," *Education.* 73:462–67;1953. Reprinted by permission.
20. E. Dorfman, "Play Therapy," in C. R. Rogers, *Client-Centered Therapy.* Boston: Houghton Mifflin, 1951. Pp. 258–60. Reprinted by permission.
21. *Ibid.* P. 244. Reprinted by permission.

22. *Ibid.* P. 245. Reprinted by permission.
23. W. J. Osburn, "Emotional Blocks in Reading," *Elementary School Journal.* 52:23–30;1951.
24. G. L. Persons and M. H. Grumbly, "Group Guidance in the Program of a Reading Laboratory," *Journal of Educational Psychology.* 41:405–16;1950.
25. V. M. Axline, "Nondirective Therapy for Poor Readers," *Journal of Consulting Psychology.* 11:61–69;1947.
26. R. E. Bills, "Nondirective Play Therapy with Retarded Readers," *Journal of Consulting Psychology.* 14:140–49;1950.
27. ————, "Play Therapy with Well-Adjusted Retarded Readers," *Journal of Consulting Psychology.* 14:246–49;1950.
28. E. D. Alderblum, "Beginning School Guidance Early," *Mental Hygiene.* 34:600–10;1950.
29. J. L. Hymes, Jr., *Teacher Listen: The Children Speak.* New York: New York Committee on Mental Health of the State Charities Aid Association, 1949. P. 10.
30. A. C. Henry, "Where and How to Get Help," *Workshop in Counseling and Guidance.* San Francisco: San Francisco State College, 1951. P. 53. Reprinted by permission.
31. A. D. Buchmueller and M. C. L. Gildea, "A Group Therapy Project with Parents of Behavior Problem Children in Public Schools," *American Journal of Psychiatry.* 106:46–52;1949.
32. R. Dreikurs, "Family Group Therapy in the Chicago Community Child-Guidance Centers," *Mental Hygiene.* 35:291–301;1951.

SUGGESTED READINGS

F. H. Allen, *Psychotherapy with Children.* New York: Norton, 1942.

V. M. Axline, *Play Therapy.* Boston: Houghton Mifflin, 1947.

H. W. Bernard, *Mental Hygiene for Classroom Teachers.* New York: McGraw-Hill, 1952. Chapter 7, "Understanding and Helping Children with Problems;" Part 3, "Special Approaches to Mental Health."

B. Bettelheim, *Love Is Not Enough.* Glencoe, Ill.: Free Press, 1950.

R. Cassidy and H. C. Kozman, *Counseling Girls in a Changing Society.* New York: McGraw-Hill, 1947.

P. W. L. Cox et al., *Basic Principles of Guidance.* New York: Prentice-Hall, 1948. Chapter 5, "The Guidance Role of the Classroom Teacher."

Division of Research and Guidance, Los Angeles County Schools, *Guidance Handbook for Elementary Schools*. Los Angeles: California Test Bureau, 1948.

———, *Guidance Handbook for Secondary Schools*. Los Angeles: California Test Bureau, 1948.

C. E. Erickson, ed., *A Basic Text for Guidance Workers*. New York: Prentice-Hall, 1947. See chapters on the role of guidance services, case-study techniques, interviewing techniques, therapeutic counseling, the contributions and classroom teachers, and stimulating faculty growth.

———, *The Counseling Interview*. New York: Prentice-Hall, 1950.

———, *A Practical Handbook for School Counselors*. New York: Ronald, 1949. Chapter 3, "Interviewing and Counseling."

C. P. Froehlich, *Guidance Services in Smaller Schools*. New York: McGraw-Hill, 1950. See chapters on basic services of a guidance program, counseling, and teachers and the guidance program.

M. E. Hahn and M. S. MacLean, *General Clinical Counseling in Educational Institutions*. New York: McGraw-Hill, 1950.

L. Jackson and K. M. Todd, *Child Treatment and the Therapy of Play*, 2d ed. New York: Ronald, 1950.

A. J. Jones, *Principles of Guidance*, 4th ed. New York: McGraw-Hill, 1951. Chapter 3, "Meaning and Purpose of Guidance and Personnel Work," and Chapter 15, "General Methods of Guidance and Pupil Personnel Work."

F. Redl and W. W. Wattenberg, *Mental Hygiene in Teaching*. New York: Harcourt, Brace, 1951. Chapter 14, "Children Who Need Special Help."

C. R. Rogers, *Client-Centered Therapy*. Boston: Houghton Mifflin, 1951. An evaluation of the revolution started by his earlier book.

———, *Counseling and Psychotherapy*. Boston: Houghton Mifflin, 1942. A book that started a revolution in counseling and clinical psychology by proposing that psychotherapy should, in effect, be essentially a democratic relationship.

R. Strang, *The Role of the Teacher in Personnel Work*, 3d ed. New York: Bureau of Publications, Teachers College, Columbia University, 1946. Chapter 7, "The Teacher-Counselor."

P. M. Symonds, "Education and Psychotherapy," *Journal of Educational Psychology*. 40:1–32;1949.

A. E. Traxler, *Techniques of Guidance*. New York: Harper, 1945. Chapters 14, 15, and 17 deal with case study methods, the role of the teacher in guidance, and guidance in the adjustment of individuals.

J. Warters, *High School Personnel Work Today*. New York: McGraw-Hill, 1946. Chapter 5, "Helping the Individual to Be Understood," and Chapter 6, "Counseling the Individual."

R. I. Watson, ed., *Readings in the Clinical Method in Psychology*. New York: Harper, 1949. Part 4, "Methods of Treatment."

W. A. Yeager, *Administration and the Pupil*. New York: Harper, 1949. Chapter 18, "Guidance as an Adjustment Service," and Chapter 19, "Psychiatric and Clinical Procedures and Research."

See also items 1, 4, 10, 15, 16, and 29 listed in the References for this chapter.

SUGGESTED FILMS

Angry Boy. The story of a boy who steals money from his teacher's purse, how his behavior is related to emotional conflicts within his family, and how he is helped through psychotherapy. Available through Psychological Cinema Register, State College, Penna.

Counseling—Its Tools and Techniques. Carl F. Mahnke, 215 E. 3rd St., Des Moines, Iowa.

Why Can't Jimmy Read? The relationship between emotional conflicts and educational difficulties. Syracuse University.

18

EVALUATION AND

DIAGNOSIS

SCHOOL MARKS AND GRADES

AS FAR as most teachers are concerned, the processes of evaluation and diagnosis are concerned largely with school marks, examinations, tests, and quizzes. Since school grades or marks are the presumed final outcome of learning, in the eyes of most students and many teachers, we shall use them as a starting point for our discussion of this phase of human relations in the classroom.

It is difficult to determine exactly what a school mark means. We conventionally think of school marks as reflecting levels of competence in the subject matter of the courses for which they are assigned. However, it is fairly common to find a child who has superior competence in a variety of subjects, yet who has below average grades. On the other hand, almost every teacher knows of children whose subject-matter competence leaves much to be desired, yet who receive passing or even superior grades year after year. What we usually find, when we examine these two kinds of situations, is that the competent children who get poor grades are frequently the ones who are unwilling or unable to do the work assigned by the teacher or who disrupt the class-room proceedings, whereas the less competent children who continually get passing grades are those who always do their assignment, seldom create disturbances, and are obviously trying very hard. Therefore, we must conclude that school grades are not entirely based on competence but are also influenced by qualities that might be termed "effort" and "obedience." Even though teachers may conscientiously try to avoid being influenced by the personal qualities of children in assigning marks, they usually cannot rule out the subconscious effect of these factors.

These subconscious factors undoubtedly account for many of the differences that research workers have found among marks assigned by teachers asked to grade the same set of papers. Even when teachers do not know the child whose paper they are grading, they are apparently influenced by their own biases and frames of reference for there are vast differences in the marks they assign. In 1913 Starch and Elliott sent two English papers written by high school students to 142 English teachers throughout the state of Wisconsin and asked them to grade them according to the percentage system that was more popular then than it is today. The marks for one paper ranged from 64 to 90, and, for the other, from 50 to 98. The range of marks given by 118 teachers for a geometry paper was even greater—28 to 92. An examination paper in American history received scores ranging from 43 to 90 from 70 teachers [1]. Other research workers in this field report similar findings [2, 3, 4]. If teachers are so influenced by subconscious factors in grading the papers of children they do not know personally, how much greater are the biases that operate when the children in question are in their own classrooms?

What we are trying to show here is that there is nothing precise and scientific about the grades that teachers give children. Even though ability and competence are factors in giving grades, school marks are, in the final analysis, the product of the interaction between teachers and pupils.

In effect, the grade a child receives in a course reflects the amount of success he has been able to achieve in competing for the good opinion of the teacher. Implicit in this, of course, is the extent to which the child *wants* the teacher's good opinion. Children from lower classes, as Allison Davis points out, frequently do not value the opinion of the teacher very highly; therefore, they are less likely to try to get good grades.[1] Girls tend to get better grades than boys, even when achievement tests show that their subject-matter competence is nearly equal [5]. The superior grades of girls may be due, at least in part, to their being more highly motivated to secure the good opinions of teachers. There is some evidence that boys get better grades under men teachers [6, 7, 8]. Inasmuch as the competence of boys and girls is roughly equal, the differences in treatment received by boys from men teachers as compared to women may reflect greater tolerance of the traditional rebelliousness of boys on the part of men teachers. Or it may be that boys work harder for men teachers and are more anxious to please them. To translate this into attitudes as they would appear in the classroom, we would say that the boy who thinks it is "sissy" to cooperate with a woman teacher often outdoes himself to please a man teacher. Perhaps if the proportions of men and women teachers were more evenly balanced in the schools, there would not be such a wide gap between the average grades received by boys and girls.

SCHOOL MARKS AND COMPETITION

School marks and grades enter into many phases of the mental health of school children. For some children, com-

---

[1] "His gang teaches him to fear being taken in by the teacher, of being a softie with her. To study homework seriously is literally a disgrace. Instead of boasting of good marks in school, one conceals them, if he ever receives any." A. Davis, *Social-Class Influences upon Learning.* Cambridge: Harvard University Press, 1948. P. 30.

peting for school marks is a healthy thing—it helps add zest and interest to the problems of classroom learning. These children are usually the ones who learn with relative ease. However, there are many other children for whom school marks create many problems. Here are two examples.

According to the records, Michael Johns has received IQ's of 75 and 80 on the intelligence tests he took in the second and fourth grades. Although Michael is now in the fifth grade, achievement tests place him at the second- and third-grade levels. If it were not for the "automatic promotion" policy at his school, he would probably have been held back in the second or third grade. He is the fourth of four children, all boys. His brothers always received superior grades. His oldest brother is taking a premedical course at the University; the other two are on the high school honor roll. During the first three years of Michael's school career, his family tried every means at their command to prod him into doing better—punishment, encouragement, rewards, tutoring, supervised study. It was all to no avail. At first, when these devices failed, they were very angry with him. Now, they are more or less resigned to his repeated failures at school. But the resentment still smoulders, even though they are now aware that "it isn't Michael's fault."

Michael says that teachers pick on him. He feels that he has tried hard to do the things they have asked of him. Yet his only reward, as he sees it, are the D's and F's that appear on his report card with monotonous regularity. Lately he has come to hold the report card itself responsible for his troubles, for he has tried such obvious devices as losing it, trying to change his grades, and bringing the card back with his father's signature forged.

Jean Seaton's father is the principal of the junior high school she attends. Her IQ is somewhere in the 130's; yet her grades are less than adequate. Oddly enough, she made better-than-average grades in grammar school. Both her teachers and her parents complain about Jean's attitude. Whenever they try to talk to her about her school work, she changes the subject. She is not lazy, for all her out-of-school time is taken up in dramatics, Girl Scouts, and Christian Endeavor. But she will not complete the assigned work in her classes, nor will she try to do well on tests and examinations. Punishment does no good—when Jean is punished she acts as though she has been martyred and succeeds in making life miserable for all around her. When she is not being punished, she is good company, pleasant, vivacious, and cooperative—except that she neglects her school work and does not try to do well on her examinations.

The cases of Michael and Jean represent two of the many kinds of difficulties that are created or aggravated for children by school marks and grades. The list is endless, with problems differing according to the relationships and conditions which affect the lives of individual students. In defense of school marks, it can be said that they are but the natural outcome of the competitive situation that exists in most classrooms; therefore, it would be futile to eliminate them unless one were ready to do away with competition. The other argument is that even if we decide that grading is an undesirable practice, no suitable substitute has been found. However, many school systems have adopted a detailed oral "report to parents" in lieu of the traditional report card. This system is particularly useful in elementary schools, where teachers spend the entire day with one class and get to know the children quite well. It helps to provide opportunities for teachers and parents to get together to discuss their mutual problems. However, the method has not been adopted by secondary schools to any extent, probably because of the limited contact the secondary teacher has with each of his students. Furthermore, the number of reports which would have to be made by an average secondary teacher would run into the hundreds, whereas the average elementary teacher would report for only a few dozen.

FAILURE SEEN AS A DISGRACE

It appears, therefore, that as long as the school is part of a society that is highly competitive, we shall have a grading system of some sort. There is probably little that individual teachers can do about eliminating grades as potential hazard to emotional health. However, teachers *can* be aware that students have emotional reactions to the grades they receive. It is all very well for adults to say glibly that a child who cannot do his arithmetic must be informed of that fact —we would all agree that learning about one's shortcomings is a part of growing up. Yet, what we actually say to a child is, "You have *failed* in arithmetic." Failure is not only a fact; in a competitive culture it implies an attitude of rejection. It is almost a psychological impossibility to say to someone in our society: "You have failed in what we have set out for you to do, but this does not make any difference in our relationship. We like you just as much, and expect to go on liking you even though you continue to fail." If we do say something like this to students (and some of us do), the chances are we are not being sincere. The student and the teacher both know, down inside, that failure *does* make a difference. The student knows that he has disappointed the teacher, and the teacher has the greatest difficulty in keeping himself from being the slightest bit resentful about his disappointment. We cannot help but feel this way because we have been schooled throughout our whole lifetime to be scornful of failure and to be approving of success. And this attitude will persist, even though we are aware that the student was not personally responsible for this failure. Indeed, if it should happen that we were the ones who were partly responsible, we might, being human, become even more resentful. We might, as the psychologists say, project some of our guilt on the student who, through his failure, reminded us of our inadequacies.

Because we know that we have this tendency to overvalue the successful student and to undervalue the failing student, we should, as professional people, handle situations that involve evaluation and grading with more consideration and objectivity than would otherwise be the case. We ought to consider the effects of grades on the feelings of students and be aware of how our own biases enter into the assigning of grades. And, when we talk with a student who has been disturbed by the grades he has received, we should be able to accept some of the responsibility for his hurt—some, but not all, because both the student and the whole system of grading are also responsible—and we should administer such psychological first aid as is appropriate. If we can show children that we accept them in spite of the grades we give them, we can sometimes help them to a greater awareness and a more realistic acceptance of their inadequacies, as well as the realities of the grading system.

TESTS AND EXAMINATIONS

Tests and examinations also produce tensions and anxieties. The basis for these feelings is fear of failure—the same fear which is the central problem in the anxieties aroused by school marks and grades. However, tests produce an even more acute form of anxiety because the individual has the feeling of being "on trial," and the outcome is in doubt. Even students whose names regularly appear on the honor roll are victims of "test nerves" or "examination jitters."

Josephine McElroy has made virtually a "straight A" all through high school, but you would never know it to see her during final examination week. She is usually a pleasant, friendly girl, but during this week there is a panicky, intense quality to her behavior. Her voice quavers, and her hands tremble. She eats very little, because she cannot bear to have anything on her stomach. She is up every night till two and three o'clock, outlining, memorizing, and underlining, in what appears to be a desperate attempt to stave off failure. She tells her family and friends that this time she will fail—all the other times have been happy accidents. This time the teachers will find out that she has been bluffing all along. She continues to be jittery all through the examination period and afterward, until the time she gets her grades. And when she gets the usual A's, she feels that her teachers have been more than generous.

Few students are as panicky as Josephine is or go to the same lengths in preparing themselves for tests. However, it is a fact that a great majority of students are made more or less anxious by examinations. Somehow, teachers often overlook this fact and apparently ignore the psychological aspects of the testing situation. When writing on this subject on a previous occasion, the present writer expressed himself as follows:

> Many a teacher uses examinations as instruments of retaliation against students. Such a teacher looks on examinations as his chance to revenge himself on the students who slept through his lectures, were chronically bored and uninterested, took up his time with meaningless and stupid questions, or were merely lazy and incompetent. For him, the examination is a day of reckoning, his opportunity to punish the delinquents whose refusal to learn so often gave him a sense of futility and frustration.
>
> It may be pedagogy of the worst kind to use tests as means of punishing students, yet it is a technique which the profession tacitly condones. After all, we say, if students have refused to learn, they *should* be punished.
>
> Tests also evoke anxiety on the part of students because the material which they cover is often useless, inconsequential, trivial, and irrelevant. The use of trivia in an examination is often defended on the grounds that superior students know more trivia than inferior students. Although there is some validity to this defense, it overlooks the fact that there is very little evidence that there is a high correlation between the ability to memorize trivia and the ability to apply and relate knowledge to the problems of life.
>
> But there is an even greater danger which results when examinations are based on trivia. The student comes to feel that trivia are more important than either the broader aspects of school learning or the ability to apply it to real problems. He says to himself, in effect: "If the instructor feels that only trivia

are important, I'll learn trivia." He comes to this conclusion because we have taught him, in effect, that passing tests is more important than the learning and the application of knowledge. Indeed, we have led him into an even greater and more dangerous fallacy—that education is itself the learning of trivia.

The emphasis on trivia raises the anxieties of students because it arouses frustration and resentment. The student is unable to see the practical or educational value of spending his time learning trivia, and he suspects that he has been committed to a period of sterile and futile time-serving. He would like to spend his time more profitably, yet he must force himself to conform and submit. Since his resentment interferes with grade-getting, he must suppress or repress it. Even though he has put it out of his mind, it continues to be a source of tension and anxiety. The result of this anxiety is to compromise the effectiveness of examinations. Every instructor has had the experience of coming to recognize the unusual capabilities of a student through the media of class discussion, casual conversation, or the completion of daily assignments, only to have the student in question score low on tests. Many such students are the victims of anxiety. They find themselves unable to remember material they can recall easily under other circumstances, they misread questions, and they are unable to express themselves adequately. In other words, their thinking processes are rendered less efficient because of the presence of an overabundance of anxiety.

Reliability is also compromised by the fact that students who take examinations under stress of anxiety are more likely to cheat. Students who are normally honest will, under the threat of failure, indulge in practices which would be avoided in another context. The guilt and anxiety they feel as a result of cheating is less than that which they would feel as a result of failing, because failure would incur the disapproval of instructor and parents and would expose them to the smug superiority of their classmates.

When education is conducted on a really efficient basis, tests are used as opportunities to promote learning and intellectual growth. However, most examinations cannot be employed as learning situations because students are so concerned with coping with anxiety and avoided failure, that they are unable to undertake the reorganization of knowledge which is basic to the kind of learning which should take place during an examination.

Furthermore, education, like other forms of human relations, is essentially a process of communication which, in order to be effective, must be a two-way process. Yet we tend to look upon education as a kind of one-way communication—from instructor to the student. As matters stand in most classes and most schools, it is not easy for students to communicate with teachers. We have acted as though two-way communication were not very important, perhaps not even desirable, for we do little to facilitate such communication and much to make it more difficult. The examination is one device which can be used by the student to communicate with the instructor—it is his opportunity to tell the instructor what he has learned. But its effectiveness as a means of communication and learning is reduced or even destroyed when the examination becomes an instrument of punishment, fraught with anxiety, and concerned with trivialities, rather than with the vital material of education.

Finally, it would seem that a good case in favor of improving the testing situation could be made on a humanitarian basis alone. Many educators and laymen are concerned about the large numbers of students who drop out of school. Students often leave because to them school is a place of humiliation and frustration and because they feel that teachers lack understanding of their problems. Much of this feeling is focused on examinations because it is here that the misery of failure and the inability of teachers to understand and to sympathize with students come to a head.[2]

INTELLIGENCE TESTS

So FAR in this discussion we have been concerned about evaluational methods that are primarily a part of

---

[2] The foregoing is a somewhat revised version of a portion of: H. C. Lindgren, "Anxiety in Examinations," *School and Society.* 76:231–32;1952. Reprinted by permission.

classroom procedure. However, there are other devices that are more related to the methods of the psychological specialist. What we have reference to here are the standardized, printed tests and questionnaires that are often used to evaluate various aspects of the curriculum, to diagnose student difficulties, and to provide data for student records. In most schools these measures are administered by teachers, and in many schools teachers also score the tests and record the results.

One of the most commonly used measures of this type is the intelligence test—frequently referred to as the "IQ test." The results of such tests can be quite useful provided we keep their limitations in mind. There is some evidence that the tests usually used in schools are biased in favor of children from upper-middle-class surroundings, which means that they are biased against children from lower-class or working-class homes [9]. Special care must therefore be taken in interpreting scores made by children in the latter categories. Another thing to keep in mind is that the psychologist's concept of intelligence is different from that held by most people. Most of us think of intelligence as something that is typical or that characterizes success in a variety of undertakings. It *is* the purpose of intelligence tests to predict success, but the successes they predict most effectively are successes in school. We would probably describe their function more accurately if we were to call them "tests of academic aptitude and ability" rather than "tests of intelligence."

Tests of academic aptitude can be useful when teachers are searching into the background of academic failure. Here is Horace Daly, whose grades are between a C and a D. His IQ of 115 is indicative of somewhat better-than-average ability to do school work. Although his IQ does not explain what his difficulties are, it does tell us that here is a boy who is "working below capacity" and who needs some special help. If we are able to give him the kind of help he needs, he should respond by doing more satisfactory school work. (If the problem is an emotional one, as it often is, giving Horace "the kind of help he needs" may be a long-term process; indeed, it may even be beyond the ability of the school.) Here is Anna Castle, whose IQ, according to her latest test, is 75. If this IQ is confirmed by an individual test like the Stanford Binet or the Wechsler Intelligence Scale for Children, it may be desirable to place her in a special class that provides a curriculum and a method of instruction more suited to her special needs. Or here is Kenneth Athos, who wants to be a mechanical engineer. His high school grades are good, particularly in mathematics. But planning to become an engineer is a grave responsibility; hence, we need all the data we can get. So we check to see what scores he has made on academic aptitude tests. Kenneth has taken three of these tests since he entered school ten years ago. They show IQ's of 118, 125, and 122, respectively. It would be more reassuring if they were, say, ten points higher, but, in view of the other positive evidence, it looks as though being a mechanical engineer is not an unreasonable goal.

Tests of academic aptitude can also be useful in demonstrating the existence of individual differences in the classroom. Parents (and even teachers) often make the mistake of assuming that learning and getting good grades is primarily a matter of will power, whereas intelligence tests help to show that there are at least some other factors involved.

THE MISUSE OF IQ'S AS "LABELS" OR "STEREOTYPES"

On the negative side, we should be aware that an IQ is a label that is frequently used to mean what people want it to mean. For example, some adults might react to Horace's IQ of 115, mentioned in the above paragraph, by saying: "Why he's just lazy—doesn't apply himself. Just see to it that he studies a good two hours every night and he'll do all right. And, just for good measure, why don't you cut off his allowance till his grades get back above the passing mark?" Such solutions might yield the desired results, or they might not, for they are not based on any real understanding of Horace's problems—they are merely the reactions of someone who is looking for an excuse to punish Horace. In Anna Castle's case, the school is going to extra pains to see that she gets an education. Many schools do the opposite. "An IQ of 75? Well there's no use trying to do anything with *her!*" It may be, of course, than Anna's true IQ is much higher. This would come out in the course of administering an individual test, like the Stanford Binet or the Wechsler Intelligence Scale for Children. But if we assume that nothing can be done with people with IQ's of 75, then we never get to the point of administering an individual test. Even if Anna's "true IQ" is 75, there are many things she can learn. She can become a useful and valuable citizen, and, as an educable individual, she is entitled to the best that the school can give.

What we are objecting to here is that IQ's frequently become labels which serve as "shortcuts for thinking." In other words, instead of using an IQ as a device to raise questions which would lead to further study and further knowledge about what we can do to *help* students, we are inclined to use it as a sort of stereotyped evaluation. If a test helps us to understand a student better, we can justify the time and expense required to administer, score, and interpret it. But if it serves as a block to understanding, then its use is questionable.

PERSONALITY TESTS AND THEIR DEFICIENCIES

THERE is another kind of test which lends itself to misinterpretation and labeling—the personality test. As long as intelligence tests are used to predict academic success, most of them are dependable and valid. But we cannot place the same confidence in personality questionnaires. One study made by Albert Ellis revealed that no personality test of the questionnaire type had sufficient validity to justify its extensive use in the classroom [10]. No one can really be certain what a score on a personality test means. For one thing, virtually all of them can easily be "faked"—that is, the person who takes the test can answer the test items in such a way that the score will come out indicative of "good adjustment" or "poor adjustment," according to his intentions. For another, high and low scores do not always mean what they seem. Let us assume that the score on a certain personality test is supposedly indicative of "good adjustment" if high and of "poor adjustment" if low. What usually happens is that a sizable number of persons who would be considered "poorly adjusted" by other standards will make high scores. This does not necessarily mean that they have tried to fake their scores. More likely it is due to the fact that their very maladjustment prevents their getting a realistic perspective of their own behavior. For example, a child who does not get along well with other children may actually think that he gets along quite well, whereupon when he comes to a test item which says, "Do other children like you?" he may answer "Yes," in all sincerity. Conversely, there are children whose adjustment is quite adequate, but who are inclined to take life very seriously. They are inclined to come out with personality test scores which are indicative of "poor adjustment." In all fairness to the test we should note that the former case is more common than the latter. Therefore, "poor" scores on personality questionnaires usually "mean more" than good scores. However, the possibility of error is so great, that we must raise serious doubts about the indiscriminate classroom use of tests of this sort.

Again, as in the case of intelligence tests, we must be wary about labeling. If personality tests are given to all students, and results are entered in their permanent records, some teachers and administrators *will* use them as "shortcuts for thinking." They will label children who have "poor" scores as "maladjusted," and other children—even some who may need special attention—they will label "well-adjusted."

THE PLACE OF PERSONALITY TESTS IN THE SCHOOL PROGRAM

Nevertheless, personality tests have a place in the school program. If they are used by psychologists, guidance workers, or teachers who have the training as well as the time to use them, and if they use them with those few students who are in need of specialized attention, they can be very helpful. Actually, the personality questionnaire is a kind of standardized interview. It should not be used as a substitute for an interview, but rather as a supplementary device to locate problem areas which may have eluded the interviewer, or to confirm certain clinical hunches which he may have developed. Used in this manner, the possibility of willful and conscious faking is much reduced because the test administrator who works with a child in a clinical setting is usually able to establish the kind of relationship that eliminates or reduces faking, at least of the "conscious" variety. When a child has confidence in the counselor or psychologist and knows that the results of the test will be used *for* him rather than *against* him, he will do his best to give an honest report of himself.

To use Charlotte Buhler's classification of levels of therapy again, we can say that the personality test is a device which should be used at the *second* level of therapy or at levels where psychotherapy is "deeper" and more difficult. Unless we are prepared to work at these levels, we should not make use of such tests. The same restrictions should apply to the use of "projective tests" of personality, like the Rorschach, Thematic Apperception Test, the Picture-Story Test, and similar instruments. Projective tests should never be used except by persons who have had intensive training under professional supervision, for they are designed for deeper levels of therapy.

Much of what we have said about personality tests is corroborated by the findings of W. J. Lodge, who reviewed 200 articles and experimental studies devoted to the use of personality questionnaires and who studied the tendencies of school children to give the "right" answers to tests of this type. As a result of his study, Lodge concluded that paper-and-pencil personality tests are not yet ready for use on a survey or school-wide basis and that

. . . personality appraisal of the school child still is and perhaps always will be a matter of teacher understanding of the child. This implies the use of observations, anecdotal records, a knowledge of the social status of the child and his parents, and the use of measuring instruments as their validity is established and confirmed by independent investigators—all against a better background of knowledge of child psychology than is possessed by many teachers at present [17].

ANECDOTAL RECORDS

THE question might well be raised at this point: What *should* a teacher use in trying to understand the emotional problems of his students?

One of the most satisfactory devices is the anecdotal record. The teacher who uses this approach proceeds by jotting down little bits of behavior as he observes them in the classroom, on the playground, or elsewhere. To be most effective, this device should not be used on more than two or three children over a period of several months. If such observations are done carefully and objectively over an extended period of time, it is often possible to see trends and patterns which otherwise escape one's attention. For example, the teacher might notice that Dan's disruptive behavior breaks out at the *end* of a study period, never at the beginning. This may tell the teacher something about the causes of Dan's behavior and perhaps give him a clue as to what he might do about it in the future. Or he may come to realize that Pamela's eagerness to answer questions even though she seldom knows the answer is somehow related to the girl's attempt to be particularly friendly with the teacher during recesses.

Writing anecdotal reports is not easy. It takes a great deal of objectivity to note facts and avoid making judgments. A number of years ago, the American Council on Education sponsored a project that was reported later in a book entitled *Helping Teachers to Understand Children* [11]. The committee that worked on this project noted that teachers tended to have three kinds of habits which interfered with their objectivity when writing an anecdote. In the first place, the teacher nearly always recorded how he felt about the child in question:

> Ned is one of the most likeable children in the class. He is pleasant and can be appealed to.
>
> Chester can be sweet and good but often shows temper and bad disposition [12].

Actually, examples like these tell us more about the teacher and his values than they do about the child in question, for the teacher is telling us how *he* reacted, not how the child behaved.

The second habit that influenced the writing of anecdotes was the tendency to think of children's behavior as being dominated by a single trait or pattern. For example:

> Woodward has told me any number of tales. . . . I do not know why he does not tell the truth, but he doesn't. . . . He is not aboveboard with most that he does. . . .
>
> Jack . . . seems content to sit and dream. . . . All through the grades he has had the same traits. . . . He does not want to be bothered and resents having to do the ordinary work expected of the group. . . . He grumbles . . . is just plain stubborn [13].

The third habit noted by the committee was the tendency to offer an immediate explanation of the observed behavior without gathering sufficient data. For instance:

Chester . . . often shows temper and bad disposition. I think it may be due to feeling neglected or that he does not measure up to standards which the majority meet satisfactorily.

Jack never accomplishes anything because he does not persist long enough. . . . When I call on him for an answer to a question, I get nothing even after I have stayed with him to prepare the lesson. He knows the answer but is just plain stubborn and will not talk [14].

However, with practice under the supervision of the committee, teachers were able to write anecdotes which were not only more objective, but which also revealed important information.

Olga (age 13) came in today upset. She said, "We are having to move this week. The company officials say that we'll have to give up the house we are in since the house we live in is a house used for the assistant superintendent of the factory. Of course, as long as daddy was living and was one of them we were supposed to live there, but now we can't."

Sam (age 12) showed a decided preference for Dora today. Asked to help her committee put up curtains. Said that "girls hardly know how to put up curtain fixtures straight like they should be." Painted a picture with Dora. Told me that he probably would learn to paint a little better if he could paint with an artist like Dora. I wasn't so sure. He especially enjoyed our poetry appreciation period. Asked for "Sea Fever," "Moon Folly," and "Overheard in a Salt Marsh." When James asked for "Hiding," he said, "Oh boy, stop asking for those baby poems [15]."

However, the chief value of objectively written anecdotes cannot be fully appreciated unless one sees them in the context of a series accumulated over a period of time. Then each of them is a line or a bit of shading in a psychological portrait of a child. A series of anecdotes reveals trends and consistent patterns of behavior, it gives clues to self-concepts and self-ideals, and it may even give hints as to some of the ways in which problem behavior or learning difficulties should be handled. As Helen Bieker says,

> One of the primary values of a good anecdotal record is that it helps the teacher see the child as a developing, many-sided individual. It helps her to see the relatedness of any one bit of behavior to other types of behavior. It helps her to see an incident in its total context, to give her a truer and more objective perspective of the child [16].

Anecdotal records are useful learning devices or projects when developed in connection with teachers' in-service study groups. They also provide valuable material for case conferences. Other devices which are helpful in understanding the emotional problems of children are the sociometric techniques we discussed in Chapter 10.

STANDARDIZED ACHIEVEMENT TESTS

THERE is a third type of test whose scores often find their way into student personnel records—the printed standardized achievement test. These tests usually give results in terms of grade placement on various subject-matter areas. By comparing such reports with the actual grade placement of the child, it is possible to determine whether he is advanced or retarded for his grade. Again, this is a kind of measure which can be used to aid or to becloud our understanding of children. The results of such tests should be interpreted with appropriate reservations. Even the best of such tests measure only a small portion of the curriculum. For example, they do not measure the attainment of such important objectives as "good citizenship," "the ability to work cooperatively with other children," or "an understanding of the workings of our city government." Nor do they always measure what they seem to measure. Some children who score low on arithmetic tests can actually use arithmetic skills fairly effectively in a real life situation. This means that the scores made by any given child should be interpreted in the light of the other data the teacher has been able to gather about him. And it also means that a standardized achievement test by itself is never a fair basis for evaluating the work of a student or a teacher.

On the other hand, standardized achievement tests can be very useful for teachers who want to have some other basis than their own "home-made" tests for evaluating the work of students. Standardized tests are often very helpful in diagnosing particular weaknesses in skill subjects. Or perhaps a teacher feels that his class is particularly strong in reading, but poor in arithmetic, and wants to check this hunch against some standard or norm. If such tests are used in this manner, no complaint can be lodged against them. But if they are used to "label" students, or if a teacher comes to feel that he is a failure because of the scores made by his class on a standardized test, then we say that the tests are being misused.

TEACHER EVALUATION

THE TEACHER RATES HIMSELF

Our discussion of evaluation and diagnosis thus far has been focused on students. Most teachers realize that when they evaluate the progress of a student, they are, to a very large degree, evaluating themselves. When a student fails, it means that the teacher has failed, also. Perhaps both teacher and student failed for reasons beyond their control. On the other hand, perhaps one or the other could have prevented the failure. Perhaps the teacher could have created a classroom atmosphere which would have encouraged the student to try harder and succeed. Inasmuch as the responsibility for success and failure is a shared one, the teacher who lim-

its his evaluation to the grading of students is overlooking
an opportunity to learn some valuable and useful information about other important aspects of the classroom scene.
In short, we might raise the question: How well does the
teacher succeed?

We get a certain amount of data from our own observations. We try a different approach to the teaching of arithmetic and discover that students are more confused by it
than they were by the former method. So we drop the newer
approach. Or we are aware that a certain part of the curriculum always causes some difficulty in our classes. So we
work with it and worry with it until it functions more
smoothly. Or we overhear a student say something about a
nervous habit we have which distracts the class, and we
resolve to stop it or at least keep it under better control. And,
what is most important, we develop, over a period of months
and years, a general idea of our over-all effectiveness as
teachers. We have no precise data from which to draw these
conclusions; we depend largely on estimates—on the "feel"
of the situation.

STUDENT APPRAISAL OF TEACHERS

Yet it would appear that we would have an even better idea
of our adequacy as teachers if we could draw data from another quarter—the impressions our students have of us. It is
one thing to say: "My students like me," and to base this on
one's personal evaluation of the situation. It is quite another
thing to say, "My students like me," and to base this on
personal evaluation *plus* statements students have made on
anonymous questionnaires. What we are proposing here is
that the teacher should, from time to time, ask students to
rate his effectiveness. This could be done regularly at the
end of each semester, or it might be done at the conclusion
of curriculum units in which a new approach or a different
technique was employed.

There are a number of arguments that are raised for and

against the use of pupil ratings of teachers. Remmers and Gage list six pairs of arguments for and against their use:

1. *Against:* Pupils cannot distinguish good teaching from bad teaching; they are incompetent to judge either the methods or the results. *For:* Remmers and Gage reply that even if this argument is true (which they doubt), it is important to find out what attitudes pupils have toward the teacher, because such attitudes *do* exist and, furthermore, they exert such a powerful influence on the effectiveness of instruction. If attitudes are unfavorable, then it is unlikely that the teaching is very effective. "You can lead a horse to water, but you cannot make him drink."

2. *Against:* Asking pupils to rate the teacher is to imply that the purpose of teaching is to please children, that whatever teaching pleases them is the best kind of teaching, and that all teaching should be adjusted with these ends in mind. *For:* The authors reply: "This argument may be answered on the grounds that the best educational process *is* in essence democratic, and the use of pupil opinion makes possible a wholesome kind of cooperative effort to improve the learning situation [18]."

3. *Against:* Pupils are inclined to make off-hand or snap judgments and are therefore unreliable. *For:* The authors reply that their evidence shows that the ratings of students are equal in reliability to that of most standardized achievement tests.

4. *Against:* Some teachers are afraid that the ratings of pupils might be biased by such factors as the amount of work required, their interest in the subject, the difficulty of the subject, the reputation of the teacher, general attitude toward school, and a lack of seriousness. *For:* Remmers and Gage reply by saying that their research has shown that these objections are groundless. For example, there is little correlation between grades received by individual pupils and the ratings they give teachers.

5. *Against:* Another objection is that pupil ratings tend to disturb the morale of the teaching staff and lead to hostility, anxiety, discouragement, and to attempts to cater to pupil

opinion. *For:* The authors suggest, in reply, that teachers should be permitted to keep their ratings confidential.

6. *Against:* Some argue that pupil ratings disrupt the morale of the pupils in that they may come to feel that they are judges of the worth of teachers, curricula, and school activities. *For:* However, the evidence so far is that pupil morale is improved, rather than worsened, by opportunities to rate teachers [19].

From the standpoint of mental health in the classroom, it would appear that pupil rating of teachers would help to accomplish several of the objectives we have discussed in this text. It imparts a democratic flavor to the activities of the classroom, because it gives the teacher an opportunity to share some of the direction of the learning experience with children. Asking children to rate one's teaching is a tacit way of saying: "I have confidence in your ability to rate me objectively. Your opinions are valuable to me. I *do* think that my teaching can be improved, and I am asking you to help me improve it. The fact that I give you grades at the end of the term means to me that I accept your right to give grades to me. In this way, we both find out how we are doing."

The use of pupil ratings probably will never become a regular part of school practice as long as power and authority are such important factors in the educational scene. The more that teachers and administrators feel insecure and depend upon power for their effectiveness, the less they are likely to use this means of evaluation. This is not a device which teachers should be required to use. Teachers cannot be forced to be democratic any more than they can be forced to have better mental health. Rather, this is a device which teachers who are trying to develop a more democratic atmosphere in their classrooms—that is, an atmosphere more conducive to mental health—should be permitted and encouraged to use. It seems likely that if they *do* use it, it can be effective in helping them to improve their teaching. Research studies by Ward, Remmers, and Schmalzried [20] and by the present author [21, 22] demonstrate some of the ways in which pupil ratings can be used to improve teaching.

EVALUATION OF THE SCHOOL'S MENTAL-HEALTH PROGRAM

ONE of the special problems that teachers and administrators face is that of evaluating the extent to which the school is meeting the mental-health needs of children. Perhaps it is better to say that this is a problem that we *should* face because as teachers and administrators we appear to be more concerned with the evaluation of the academic aspects of the curriculum than with its mental-health aspects. This is partly because academic learning lends itself to measurement much more easily than does growth and maturity in mental health, partly because we are not, as a profession, as aware as we should be of the importance of mental-health goals and objectives in education, and partly because of the emphasis that academic learning has traditionally received.

Yet, assuming that we are now willing to face the need for evaluating mental-health phases of the school program, how do we go about it? How can we determine whether boys and girls are becoming more mature, emotionally and socially speaking? How do we know what effects we are having on their mental health?

The first step we must take if we plan to do such evaluation is to determine what kinds of behavior we can recognize as emotionally mature for various age levels of children —that is, what can and should we reasonably expect in the way of behavior of children in our school? We should examine these kinds of behavior carefully in the light of community patterns of behavior and social background, in terms of individual as well as group behavior. Then we should determine what areas of behavior are likely to be modified, changed, encouraged, or guided by the school. Our next step is to examine our school program to find out what we *are* doing or *should* be doing to bring about the desired forms of behavior. Following this step, or, rather, concurrently with it, we look for evidence, both positive and negative, that indicates the extent to which our objectives are being met. Finally, we use the data gathered in our evaluative study as bases for reworking and revising our curricula, methods, and school programs. We may even decide that some of our goals and objectives need modifying.

Gathering evidence is a crucial part of an evaluative program, but it is no more important than the other steps. Unless we know what we are looking for, unless we have some frame of reference which will lend meaning to the information we gather, much of our work as evaluators is wasted. However, assuming that we have done a reasonably good job of planning up to the point of actually gathering data, what techniques shall we use?

Probably standardized personality questionnaires are not of much help to us here—partly because these tests, as already noted, have a low validity and partly because they are most useful as aids to understanding the problems of individual children. Sometimes a test like the Mooney Problem Check List, which gives children an opportunity to indicate the problems that are troubling them, can be useful to the extent that it will show where the major areas of difficulty are among the students at various age levels [23]. This kind of information can be helpful in planning curricula. Perhaps administering the Check List to children at the beginning and at the end of a school year will reveal gross changes in the kinds of problems experienced by children, and will thus indicate, indirectly, whether there have been any changes that might be attributed to the school program. However, such data must be handled and interpreted with much care because of the possibility of misinterpretation. For example, the "disappearance" of a problem may have nothing to do with the school program, but may be the result of children's passing into a new stage of development. Or it may be that the bettering or worsening of a problem may be the result of changes taking place within the community or the nation rather than within the school.

Sociometric devices can be useful tools in gathering data related to mental health, both of individuals and of groups. A sociometric pattern in a class that consists of small, closely knit groups, with few intergroup choices and many "isolates" or rejected persons, is not as indicative of good mental health as is a pattern characterized by "chains" of friendship and few isolates. Therefore, a teacher who is attempting to build a cohesive group in his classroom can use sociometric tests at intervals as a way of determining the extent of his success. The sociometric chart will also show the progress made by the shy, retiring child or the hostile, aggressive child who is rejected and who later changes his behavior and becomes a part of the group.

Teachers sometimes use attitude questionnaires—either of the standardized or teacher-made variety—to measure students' attitudes toward various aspects of life. These are useful particularly in gathering some special kinds of information. The information they provide must be interpreted very carefully. Sometimes students are cynical or apathetic and check attitudes they actually do not possess. More often, they check responses indicating attitudes that they are *supposed* to develop as a result of the course, attitudes that they may even *believe* they possess, even though objective observation fails to confirm this belief. For example, students may think they believe in fair play and may mark attitude questionnaires so as to indicate their feeling in this regard. At the same time, the same students may play a dishonest brand of football or may belong to high school fraternities that are banned by law because of their undemocratic exclusiveness. Such inconsistencies and gaps between self-concept and actual behavior are of course not limited to students.

Another approach is to ask students to rate a teacher or a course or a total school program—anonymously, of course. Since students are not thereby asked to rate themselves, their responses are likely to be more objective than when they are asked to rate their own attitudes. However, even when they are asked to evaluate the education they are receiving, students may feel led to indicate answers that they feel are expected of them rather than those that are indicative of their real feelings. The present author has described an approach that attempts to get at the more subconscious evaluations of students [22]. In spite of this possible source of bias, it is the feeling of this writer that teachers can learn a great deal from the anonymous evaluations of students. Some things students say will be hard to accept, but if the teacher can accept it and use this kind of criticism, it will be of great help in developing an emotionally healthy atmosphere in his classes.

The real test of a school's mental-health goals is likely to be found in the student's actual behavior. Since it is impossible to observe all the students' behavior at all times, either in school or out, we must content ourselves with observing small samples of behavior. We may sample behavior by making anecdotal studies of the behavior of a few students, or we may do so by informal, subjective observations of the classroom scene and the organization and policies of the school. The latter approach is one that is employed in a list of suggested criteria drawn up by the National Council of Independent Schools for appraising mental health in a school. Some of the questions the Council raises are as follows: [3]

1. What kind of respect is accorded the learning that comes by way of activities? For instance:

Fine Arts	Music	Industrial Arts
Rhythms & Dancing	Dramatics	Physical Education

---

[3] The complete list of the Council's criteria may be found in the Appendix of this book under the heading: *Some Inquiries Helpful in Appraising Mental Health in a School.*

A. Are they fully respected?
B. Are they reserved for those with special talent? Is there any taint of exploitation of the young people involved? Is there too much "perfection" seeking?
C. How much time is assigned to them in the school program? At what time of the day?
D. Does the school plant reveal the results of the shop and the studio?

2. Is there a pooling of insights by the adults who deal with each child to the point of a shared approach?
3. Do the children have a sense of belonging, each one to something in which he is a responsible participant?
4. Is the teacher-pupil relationship sentimental, exclusively academic and disciplinary, or is it essentially a positive, contributing friendship?
5. Is there sufficient leeway allowed both within the classroom and without for pupils to fumble and make mistakes [24]?

All teachers evaluate their work through some sort of more or less subjective appraisals, based partly on feelings they develop regarding what goes on in the classroom and partly on their awareness of what goes on within themselves. Although these estimates lack scientific accuracy and are open to bias, they should not be ignored. Very often the teacher who lives and works with a class can present a clearer and more perceptive picture of the mental-health picture of his classroom than could be gained from a dozen tests. The better his insight and understanding, and the more he has learned about human behavior and motivation, the better able he is to make a report that is clinically valid. However, this "clinical evaluation," like other subjective forms of appraisal, should be supported, where possible, by measures that are more objective. In other words, a clinical picture of the mental health in a given classroom gains validity if it is substantiated by sociometric records, anecdotal data, student evaluations of classroom experiences, and similar material.

THE TEACHER AS AN EVALUATOR

AN IMPORTANT part of being a good teacher is being a good evaluator. This implies the ability to appraise the behavior and work of children in a variety of ways and settings, as well as a willingness to use a number of devices and approaches to gather data which may be used as a means of evaluation. The teacher who is a good evaluator needs to be both empathic and objective. He needs to be aware of the moods, feelings, and problems which children face in the classroom and in the world outside, and he needs to see these needs, feelings, and problems in their true proportions and in relationship to each other. Being a good evaluator also implies a readiness to evaluate oneself and to permit oneself to be evaluated by others. It is a demanding role, one that requires integrity, balance, and a sense of inner security.

Being a good evaluator does not mean giving a lot of tests. It may, in fact, lead to a reduction in the amount of tests given. The fact-finding committees who participated in the Midcentury White House Conference on Children and Youth raised the question of whether we do not tend to overstress the use of tests and measurements in our schools. They felt that the pupil of today is

> likely to feel himself under constant scrutiny, which to him may seem more unrelenting and critical than enlightening and helpful. Even when, as is ever more usual, he participates in the appraisal, he asks himself how he is doing, so to say, more frequently and persistently than is perhaps healthy. In addition, his teacher may sometimes come to feel more threatened than guided, with inevitable repercussions for his pupils. This all may be particularly bad for the child who comes from a home where parents are preoccupied with the significance of every move [25].

In his role as an evaluator the teacher needs to maintain a flexible approach to standards. He will not expect Jose to read as swiftly and easily as Virginia. This is partly because Jose comes from a bilingual background, partly because he does not think that being able to read is very important, and partly because he has many problems at home. Howard has the highest IQ in the class. He enjoys school work; so the teacher will expect him to do something extra when his regular assignments are completed. If he does not keep a little extra pressure on him to do this, he is likely to get into some form of harmless, but disruptive, mischief.

In short, he develops standards that are appropriate for children at various levels of competence and emotional adjustment and in various situations. Flexibility does not mean that he gives up standards altogether or abandons them in the spirit of mistaken tenderness because children sometimes complain. After a while, he learns to distinguish the legitimate complaints (yes, even the *silent* complaints) of those who are taxed beyond their ability, from the groans and gripes that students often utter as bids for sympathy or as part of a normal pattern of resistance to hard work. Learning *is* hard work. It often involves changing old, familiar points of view and ways of doing things for new and untried concepts and skills. It is perfectly natural for students to resist somewhat and to state a preference for the older, less efficient ways. The pleasant part of learning usually comes *after* the learning has taken place, when one finds out how much better a new method works or how satisfying and ego-building it is to learn something that the children do not know in the next lower grade. But the process of *arriving* at this learning is often painful or wearisome, both for students and for teachers. It is no wonder that the immature part of children (and adults, too) causes them to want reassurance that they do not have to learn this new skill or concept after all. And so students ask teachers to go easier, to lower standards, to be less demanding.

Again, as we have said, an experienced and effective teacher will know when standards can be modified, but he will also know that children need to be told what the standards are and what progress they are making if the school is to help them to grow intellectually, socially, and emotionally.

REFERENCES

1. D. Starch, *Educational Psychology,* rev. ed. New York: Macmillan, 1927. Pp. 519–24.
2. F. J. Kelly, *Teacher's Marks, Their Variability and Standardization.* Contributions to Education, No. 66. New York: Teachers College, Columbia University, 1914.
3. H. O. Rugg, "Teachers' Marks and Marking Systems," *Educational Administration and Supervision.* 1:117–42;1915.
4. H. D. Rinsland, *Constructing Tests and Grading.* New York: Prentice-Hall, 1937. Pp. 2–11.
5. T. F. Lentz, "Sex Differences in School Marks with Achievement Test Scores Constant," *School and Society.* 29:65–68;1929.
6. R. O. Billett, *Provisions for Individual Differences, Marking, and Promotion.* Bulletin No. 17. Washington: U. S. Office of Education, 1932. Pp. 424–61.
7. H. R. Douglass and N. E. Olson, "The Relations of High-School Marks to Sex in Four Minnesota Senior High Schools," *School Review.* 45:283–88;1937.
8. R. A. Norsted, "To Mark or Not to Mark?" *Journal of Education.* 121:81–84;1938.
9. K. Eells, *et al., Intelligence and Cultural Differences.* Chicago: University of Chicago Press, 1951.
10. A. Ellis, "The Validity of Personality Questionnaires," *Psychological Bulletin.* 43:385–440;1946.
11. D. A. Prescott, *et al., Helping Teachers to Understand Children.* Washington: American Council on Education, 1945.
12. *Ibid.* P. 30.
13. *Ibid.* Pp. 30–31.
14. *Ibid.* P. 31.
15. *Ibid.* Pp. 38–39. This and preceding examples reprinted by permission.
16. H. Bieker, "Using Anecdotal Records to Know the Child," in Association for Supervision and Curriculum Development, *Fostering Mental Health in Our Schools.* Washington: National Education Association, 1950. P. 192. Reprinted by permission.

17. W. J. Lodge, "What About the Use of Personality Questionnaires?" *California Journal of Educational Research.* 1:219–22; 1950.
18. H. H. Remmers and N. L. Gage, *Educational Measurements and Evaluation.* New York: Harper, 1943. P. 470.
19. *Ibid.* Pp. 470–71.
20. W. D. Ward, H. H. Remmers, and N. T. Schmalzried, "The Training of Teacher-Personality by Means of Student-Ratings," *School and Society.* 53:189–92;1941.
21. H. C. Lindgren, "Improvement of a Psychology Course through the Use of Student Evaluations," *California Journal of Educational Research.* 3:207–11, 273;1952.
22. H. C. Lindgren, "The Incomplete Sentences Test as a Means of Course Evaluation," *Educational and Psychological Measurement.* 12:217–25;1952.
23. R. L. Mooney, *Problem Check List.* Columbus: Ohio State University Press, 1947. Three forms: junior high, high school, and college.
24. National Council of Independent Schools, *Some Inquiries Helpful in Appraising Mental Health in a School.* Boston: National Council of Independent Schools, 1952. Reprinted by permission.
25. Midcentury White House Conference in Children and Youth, *A Healthy Personality for Every Child.* Raleigh: Health Publications Institute, 1951. P. 113. Reprinted by permission.

SUGGESTED READINGS

L. E. Cole and W. F. Bruce, *Educational Psychology.* Yonkers-on-Hudson: World Book, 1950. Chapter 18, "Appraising Development and Learning."

L. J. Cronbach, *Essentials of Psychological Testing.* New York: Harper, 1949.

J. G. Darley, *Testing and Counseling in the High-School Guidance Program.* Chicago: Science Research, 1945.

W. T. Donahue *et al.,* eds., *The Measurement of Student Adjustment and Achievement.* Ann Arbor: University of Michigan Press, 1949.

J. Drugman and J. W. Wrightstone, *A Guide to the Use of Anecdotal Records.* Brooklyn: Bureau of References, Research, and Statistics, Board of Education to the City of New York, 1949.

F. S. Freeman, *Theory and Practice of Psychological Testing.* New York: Holt, 1950.

C. P. Froehlich and A. L. Benson, *Guidance Testing*. Chicago: Science Research, 1948.

A. I. Gates *et al.*, *Educational Psychology*, 3rd edition. New York: Macmillan, 1948. See chapters on the practical uses of intelligence and aptitude tests, appraising progress, and appraising the school program through the study of pupils as persons.

A. M. Jordan, *Measurement in Education*. New York: McGraw-Hill, 1953.

H. C. Lindgren, *Psychology of Personal and Social Adjustment*. New York: American Book, 1953. Chapter 15 deals with various aspects of intelligence.

E. F. Lindquist, ed., *Educational Measurement*. Washington: American Council on Education, 1951. Part 1, "The Functions of Measurement in Education."

H. W. Magnuson *et al.*, *Evaluating Pupil Progress*. Sacramento: Bureau of Educational Research, California State Department of Education, 1952.

V. Sims, "Evaluating Progress toward the Satisfaction of Needs," in N. B. Henry, ed., *Fifty-Second Yearbook of the NSSE*. Part I. Chicago: National Society for the Study of Education, 1953.

C. E. Skinner, ed., *Educational Psychology*, 3rd edition. New York: Prentice-Hall, 1951. Part 4, "Measurement and Evaluation."

E. R. Smith, R. W. Tyler, *et al.*, *Appraising and Recording Student Progress*. New York: Harper, 1942. The development of tests to measure such aims and objectives as "social sensitivity," "appreciation," and "personal and social adjustment."

A. D. Woodruff, *The Psychology of Teaching*, 3rd edition. New York: Longmans, Green, 1951. Chapters 25 and 26 deal with evaluation.

See also items 9, 11, 16, and 18 listed in the References for this chapter.

19

THE TEACHER: PROBLEMS OF ADJUSTMENT

TEACHERS SHOULD BE CONCERNED ABOUT THEIR OWN MENTAL HEALTH

IT IS probably both trite and unnecessary to say that the chief concern of the teacher should be for the welfare of the children who come under his supervision. It is not so obvious that a teacher must also be concerned for his own welfare as well, if he is going to continue to function as an effective teacher. The most effective teachers are those who are able to maintain a fairly even balance between these two concerns—they are considerate of the mental health of their pupils, but they are careful of their own as well. Rudolf Dreikurs touches on this dual aspect of our responsibilities when he suggests that the best approach to children is characterized by kindness and firmness—kindness, because of one's respect for the child as an individual, and firmness, because of one's respect for oneself [1]. An effective teacher, therefore, will be one who will take on an extra heavy burden when the need arises, but who will not chronically overburden himself to the detriment of his mental and physical health. A teacher who is under continual emotional strain cannot help but produce an adverse effect on the children he supervises.

The stresses and strains of the classroom, like so many of the other emotional factors in life, frequently escape our immediate notice. Because of this, teachers often find that they are becoming short-tempered or depressed or overfatigued without being consciously aware of the pressures which affect their everyday existence. It is our purpose, in this first portion of this chapter, to review some of the sources of pressure and tension with which all or most teachers must cope with as they perform the functions of their profession.

SOURCES OF TENSION AND ANXIETY

The teacher is one of the most "exposed" persons, psychologically speaking, in the professional world today. He works under the direct or indirect scrutiny of twenty-five, thirty, forty, or more children, of principals, supervisors, and superintendents, of parents, of the school board, of the teaching profession itself, and of the community at large. All these individuals and groups feel that they have, or ought to have, something to say about the way in which he does his job; they all have thoughts and feelings about what kind of person he should be. Add to this the personal scrutiny of the teacher himself, for he is often his own severest critic.

In some of the earlier chapters of the book, when we were discussing the formation of the personality of the child, we laid great stress on the fact that anxiety is produced by interpersonal relations. Merely to associate with other people is to develop some anxieties, both of the normal and the neurotic variety. Much of the pressure that the teacher perceives in his daily work stems from his relations with his class. Some of this is produced by the expectations that each has for the other—the class has certain expectations of the teacher, and the teacher has certain expectations of the class. Students wonder whether they can live up to the teacher's expectations; the teacher wonders whether he can live up to the expectations of the class, as well as the expectations of those who employ him, not to mention his own expectations for himself. The anxiety that arises from expectations can be a normal sort of anxiety; it creates a tension or desire to do one's best, to try to meet the expectations. Or it can be a neurotic sort of anxiety, particularly if the expectations are unrealistic or exaggerated.

To be completely realistic, however, the teacher cannot completely measure up to all the expectations that he has for himself and that others have for him. For one thing, most of his expectations are end goals or hopes. It may be his aim or hope to turn out thirty-five fourth graders equally competent in the processes of long division. But he knows that there are many factors and forces which will prevent his realizing this objective. Yet he keeps this goal in mind as he works with the children on their arithmetic throughout the year. For the most part, he behaves *as if* this goal were going to be achieved. To be sure, he makes an adjustment here and there. He really does not expect the Wellman twins to learn long division—they are two years retarded in mathematical skills. And there are two or three others who never seem able to take arithmetic seriously. But he keeps a moderate amount of pressure on even these children, indicating that he expects them to try to do the work, and that he will help them if they need him.

When the end of the year comes, he administers a diagnostic test and finds that twenty-two of the thirty-four children have a very good grasp of long division, seven have what might be called a "marginal" understanding, and five show no ability at all. Has he failed? Well, it depends on his concept of failure. If he were one kind of a teacher, he might take a very severe point of view toward himself for having fallen so short of his goal. If he were another kind of a teacher, he might feel satisfied at having done as well as he had under the circumstances.

ATTITUDE TOWARD FAILURE

Indeed, it is quite likely that the teacher's attitude toward failure will be the most central factor in his ability to adjust to his role as a teacher, to derive satisfaction and pleasure from his profession, and to avoid the more or less neurotic solutions which provide temporary relief from anxiety and hurt feelings. Because teaching is the psychologically exposed profession that it is, there is much opportunity for failure. We have mentioned the possibility of failure through not living up to one's expectations. We have noted the fact that there are hosts of others who have expectations for the teacher. The "failure potential" of these expectations is high. For one thing, people do not agree regarding their expectations. In one community, the employers' group may expect the teacher to spend most of his time drilling children in the so-called basic skills; the parents may expect the teacher to provide the discipline that they themselves are unwilling or unable to administer; the superintendent and the school board may be concerned about the social adjustment of the children; and the principal may be most interested in seeing that the prescribed curriculum is followed rather closely. No matter what the teacher does, he is sure to fail to meet all these standards equally well. Each of these expectations may contain some elements that are unrealistic when it comes to dealing with the problems of motivating children in a classroom setting. Thus it requires much fortitude, stamina, and integrity for the teacher to go about his business of teaching "the best he knows how," in the face of all these expectations. It is indeed fortunate that most teachers are able to develop these qualities to a high degree—fortunate from the standpoint of their own mental health as well as that of their pupils.

Newer teachers are probably at a greater disadvantage and are more vulnerable when it comes to these anxieties and pressures. More experienced teachers know better where they stand with themselves and with others. For example, an experienced teacher who knows that he is doing a satisfactory and competent job of teaching is less likely to be disturbed by the anxious concern of parents or employers about certain aspects of the curriculum in his school. His firmness and balance when discussing the subject with lay people demonstrates that he regards himself as a competent professional person who knows what he is talking about. He can sympathize with their concern because he has felt some of it himself. But he has dealt with the problem more directly than they have and has a more realistic grasp of the total educational situation. His security has deep roots: it stems from the sound relationship he has developed with the children in his classes, from the successes he has had in helping children to learn, and from his ability to be realistic about the failures and frustrations which are inevitable in teaching. Indeed, his ability to accept these failures and to learn from them is a major source of strength.

But let no one think that this kind of inner strength is easy to come by. As we have noted elsewhere in this text, the very competitiveness of our culture leads us to place too much stress on failure—we are too prone to interpret ambiguous results as failures and to become anxious and fretful when we do not have maximum success. This is one of the reasons why teachers, particularly new teachers, need to be such careful evaluators. The conscientious teacher who is continually gathering data and information relating to the effects of his teaching on the learning of children is not only in a position to use this material in improving his teaching, but he is also in a better position than anyone else to know the extent to which he is meeting his expectations for himself. The more he knows about the success and the failure of his methods and the more he knows about how they are received by students, the firmer the base for his attitudes and concepts regarding himself. The teacher who does a thorough job of evaluation knows more about himself as a teacher and as a person; he has a firmer basis for self-understanding and can face the world with more secure footing, psychologically speaking.

THE LACK OF STATUS AND APPRECIATION

One of the factors that sometimes annoys or depresses teachers, particularly in small towns and closely knit communities, is the general reluctance of the townspeople to accept the teacher as a person, aside from his professional role. This isolation is more likely to be experienced by unmarried women teachers. One teacher expressed it by saying:

> When I first came to "X" City, I felt like a social wallflower. True, everyone was "nice" to me and all that, but I never got asked to people's homes—I never was accepted into any of the groups in the town. But after I married, things changed almost immediately. Now I am active in several social groups, and we are asked out all the time. In fact, I have difficulty, sometimes, in keeping my social life from interfering with my school work.

Part of the social isolation that unmarried women teachers feel comes as the result of the failure of our culture to accept professional women on an equal basis. True, their status is higher than it used to be, but society still has difficulty in determining "where they fit in." The married teacher we quoted above no longer has this difficulty because she derives status from her husband, which is the way we tend to assign status to women in our culture.

The study by Jenkins and Lippitt to which we referred previously in this text reports some of this feeling of social isolation. Teachers reported that they would like to be accepted by parents of their students more on the basis of equal participation in the community and less in terms of their professional roles. They also wanted students to look upon them as friends. Interestingly, neither parents nor students were very much aware of the need and the desire of teachers to establish relations on a more friendly basis [2].

Needless to say, being socially isolated makes it somewhat more difficult for teachers to cope with the stresses and strains and emotional problems that inevitably arise from teaching. We shall have more to say, later in this chapter, on the positive side of the teacher's status.

In any kind of social-service occupation, in any occupation where professional workers try to help others, there are bound to be failures, frustrations, and disappointments. If the general mental health of the teacher is good, and if the emotional pressures of his job are not too great, he can anticipate and accept most of these unfortunate circumstances. But if, on the other hand, these desirable conditions do not obtain, he may develop occasional or even chronic feelings of not being appreciated by students, parents, or even the community as a whole. And it is quite likely that teachers, taken as a professional group, are *not* appreciated by society as much as they should be. This attitude, in turn, may be related to the lay public's lack of information as to the role of the teacher, the importance of education, the difficulties inherent in the task of educating the young, and the vast amount of professional training and experience it takes to make a good teacher. Although there are some lay groups that are sufficiently interested in education to want to do something to help teachers feel more appreciated, it is quite probable that the major effort must come from teachers themselves.

On the one hand, there is a need for an increasingly effective, many-phased program of public relations, which is another way of saying that teachers need to improve their communication with the general public. On the other hand, there is also a need for teachers to take therapeutic measures to help themselves when psychological and emotional pressures become severe and the feeling of not being appreciated becomes both acute and chronic. In other words, teachers should be permitted and encouraged to use psychological or psychiatric consultation when they need help with emotional problems growing out of their professional or personal life. More and more professional workers in all fields, including teaching, are finding that either brief or extended psychotherapy is helping them to be happier and more effective in their work. Although a generation ago it was considered a sign of mental weakness to seek out help of this sort, today there is a growing awareness that the teacher who refers himself for psychotherapy shows integrity, courage, and the willingness to grow and improve. Perhaps the time will come when school departments or teachers' organizations will make psychological consultation available on a free or minimum-fee basis for any member who desires it. Such a service should do much to improve the mental health of teachers and the emotional climate of the classroom. It does not make good sense for a teacher who is troubled by a problem of emotional health to continue to work below his best level of effectiveness and to inject his personal unhappiness into the lives of the children he supervises. When we come to recognize more fully the relationship between the mental health of teachers and the mental health of their students, the way should be cleared to provide some of these necessary services.

Some school departments are beginning to meet some of these needs in a very tentative way by organizing discussion groups of teachers. While the members of such groups seldom delve into problems of a distinctly personal nature, the opportunity to get together with other teachers and discuss the problems of the classroom often helps them to eliminate or reduce some of the tensions that build up during the teaching day. The psychologists of some school departments spend much of their time talking to teachers (at the latter's request) about the problems occurring in the classroom. Again, the personal problems of teachers are not likely to be discussed at such times, but this kind of experience often helps teachers to "feel better" and more reassured about their relationships with children. And one should not, of course, overlook the fact that a similar function may also be served by supervisors who are understanding and unusually perceptive.

PSYCHOLOGICAL DEMANDS MADE
BY OVERCROWDED CLASSES

Heavy demands made upon teachers rank high among the mental-health hazards in the profession. For example, one study of such hazards reported that "teaching load too heavy" and "overcrowded classrooms" were the two factors most often mentioned [3]. Such demands absorb much of the physical and nervous energy of the teacher. On the other hand, the studies that have been made on the effect of class size on learning appear to show that the size of a class has little effect on the knowledge and skill of children as measured by standardized tests [4].[1] However, there are two other factors which are generally omitted by such studies. One is the growth in emotional and social maturity that is implicit in the more basic goals and objectives of the school, and the other is the wear and tear on the mental health of the teacher. One is tempted to say that responsibility increases geometrically rather than arithmetically when classes are enlarged. That is, the responsibilities which weigh upon the shoulders of the teacher are considerably more than doubled when the class size is doubled. The interpersonal relationships in a class of forty are infinitely more complex than in a class of twenty, and the problem of building a

---

[1] Such studies are often disconcerting to teachers' committees and other groups that are looking for objective data to support campaigns for reduction in class size because the findings run counter to the supposition that teaching is automatically more effective when classes are smaller. However, a factor which is frequently overlooked is that one of the advantages of the smaller class is the opportunity to use better teaching methods—methods which capture the imagination and enthusiasm of individual students. We should not be surprised if a study showed no difference in results between large and small classes, if a lecture-and-quiz method were used in both cases. If, on the other hand, the methods used were that of the group discussion or the project or the panel discussion, it is quite possible that there would be more significant differences between large and small groups.

cohesive group becomes far more difficult. It would seem, too, that goals like "social maturity," which involve learning to cooperate, are harder to achieve in large classes.

Probably many school boards and even a few administrators condone increases in class size as a way of getting more work out of teachers. This policy may even be effective up to a point in a few cases, particularly in the case of those teachers who work better with heavy loads than with lighter ones. But let us assume that a teacher is already spending some fifty hours a week or more on school work (this is quite usual). Adding more students to his class will very likely lead to his providing a different and less valuable kind of service for his pupils. He will spend more of his time on paper work—making reports, reading and grading papers—and less of his time in personal contact with children. Those children who need individual help would receive less of his time and attention because he would have less to give. Perhaps he might increase the number of hours he devotes to school work, but this would not be in the best interests of his own mental health. If he is a conscientious teacher, he would probably say that he was already doing less for the children in his class than he would like. Thus, increasing the size of his class will also have the effect of aggravating his feeling of failure, inadequacy, and anxiety.

THE CONFLICT BETWEEN POWER AND LOVE

Still another source of anxiety may be found in the conflict in roles that is inherent in much of what the teacher does. In its most basic sense, this is the conflict between power and love—if by love we include such things as understanding and acceptance. One form of this conflict may be seen in the dilemma faced by Miss Penn, when she discovered that Helen had copied her answers in the spelling test from Jonathan, who had been sitting next to her.

Miss Penn felt that she knew why Helen had done this because she had been watching her during the past few weeks. Helen had joined the class only a month before and so far had not been accepted into any of the cliques. She was a plain little girl, more poorly dressed than the other girls in the room. Miss Penn wondered whether that had anything to do with the fact that she hadn't been accepted. Of course, Helen had a very shy manner and tended to hang back in classroom discussions and in playground games. The only one in the room that Helen felt at all close to was Miss Penn. Knowing that the child had no one else to talk to, Miss Penn had not discouraged attempts to be friendly, although she felt that being too friendly with the teacher might not help Helen's relations with the other children. Helen was retarded on the average of one grade in most of her work. This accentuated the differences between her and the other children in the class because most of them were a half year to a year and a half advanced. Miss Penn felt sorry for Helen when she made valiant efforts to keep up with the rest of the class; she knew that one of the things that Helen was trying to do was to please her—Miss Penn. She wanted desperately to do what the teacher expected, to please the one she loved.

And so it seemed to Miss Penn that Helen's cheating was a sort of desperate effort to produce a perfect paper, to get at least one A. She was not sure that this was the case, of course —one can never be sure about such things—but it seemed to be a reasonable hypothesis. As far as she knew, Helen had never cheated before. She always seemed scrupulously honest.

Miss Penn thought about her many-sided dilemma. On the one hand, she was tempted to ignore the matter and give Helen the A—the girl needed reassurance so badly. Yet she knew that this would not be wise. She knew that she would have to talk to Helen about the matter, and she would try to use her most sympathetic and understanding manner. But there was another difficulty. Mr. Cohan, the principal, had told the teachers only yesterday that he was concerned about the amount of cheating that was going on in the school and that for the next week he wanted every child caught cheating sent to his office. Mr. Cohan was a well-meaning man, but he could be very gruff at times. Miss Penn wondered whether she dared ignore his order. She was sure that Helen would not be helped by a visit to the principal's office. As a matter of fact, it would really "finish" her, as far as the other girls of the class were concerned. Miss Penn sighed. Sometimes she wished that her fifth-grade girls weren't so moralistic. . . .

The dilemma faced by Miss Penn is essentially one of trying to decide whether justice or mercy should prevail. In essence, Miss Penn has to decide whether she is an authority figure, a functioning member of the organization of the school, or someone who is free to consider the interests of this particular child. In resolving her dilemma, she must also consider about the effects of her actions on the rest of the class. Perhaps they are aware that Helen has cheated and are watching to see how the teacher handles the matter. No matter what she decides to do, she runs the risk of offending someone.

A similar dilemma is involved in the assignment of grades. Should grades be assigned in terms of their effect on children? Or should they merely reflect the level of competence the child has reached?

According to the marks Grace received on her tests, she knows more about geography than any child in the class, but she has not worked nearly up to capacity. On the other hand, Sylvia has tried so hard. She did all her assignments with meticulous care and her cooperation on the group projects was an inspiration to the whole class. Perhaps the very low grades she got on tests were more influenced by her reading difficulties than they were by her lack of knowledge of geography. It seems a shame to discourage her. . . .

To a greater or lesser degree, all teachers have to resolve similar dilemmas as they switch their roles from that of the kindly, understanding leader of children to that of the school functionary who has to see that the rules are obeyed. Sometimes this change in roles is dictated by situations or forces beyond the immediate control of the teacher, as was the case in Miss Penn's dilemma, and sometimes this occurs because teachers find that they are unable to control or motivate their classes without the use of power. Very often, of course, teachers do not give other methods a chance and employ power methods because they feel, for real or fancied reasons, that they cannot depend on children's ability to motivate themselves.

THE LEARNING OF ROLES AS A DEFENSE AGAINST ANXIETY

WHENEVER there is a conflict in roles, whenever the teacher has trouble in making up his mind "who he is," anxiety is almost certain to develop. The teacher who is new to the profession has more trouble with this problem than does the experienced teacher, although the latter is by no means immune. The inexperienced teacher has not yet discovered what roles he should play in coping with the problems of teaching. Actually, much of the teacher's adjustment to the profession involves learning to play roles which are comfortable and appropriate. The new teacher comes into the profession with certain ideas of the kind of role he would like to play; he has had some experience in playing teacherlike roles in other settings. (One study of college students entering teacher training showed that 35 percent of them had taught in church schools, 12 percent had substituted for or helped teachers in school, and 9 percent had taught in the Armed Services [5].) Much of the time in his first few years of teaching is spent in trying out ideas, enacting previously learned roles, and depending on hunches to determine their effectiveness. As the teacher begins to find the roles that are effective and comfortable, many of his problems disappear and his anxieties diminish, for when he faces the various situations which are a part of the job of being a teacher, he knows what to do, he knows what to expect of himself, and he knows what to expect of his class. Much of the anxiety of being a new teacher stems from not knowing what will happen next and not knowing what to do about it. By learning to play certain professional roles, some of the uncertainty and unpredictability is removed from the teaching situation. Thus, the learning of a professional role (or roles) helps teachers to reduce or minimize much of the anxiety which is inherent in teaching.

ROLES CAN HAVE A NEGATIVE EFFECT

Of course, roles can also serve a negative function: sometimes teachers come to depend on the sequences of events and activities which are a part of their roles and they are reluctant to try new methods and procedures. Essentially, they are afraid that if they do not follow their tried and true, albeit somewhat inefficient, routines, they will again be exposed to the anxiety which caused them to develop the routines in the first place. This is one of the reasons why it is difficult to get even competent teachers to participate in classroom reform, even though it may improve their own emotional health as well as that of their pupils. This is why wise administrators often find it best not to force or require teachers to change their methods, but instead give them opportunities to initiate changes voluntarily and at their own pace. Occasionally, a principal or a superintendent will attempt to reform the entire school by instituting procedures, methods, or administrative changes that apparently would do much to improve the efficiency as well as the mental hygiene of the school. Yet because the proposed changes are such a marked departure from current practice and because the teaching staff has had no opportunity to participate in or even comment on the proposed change, teachers become anxious, upset, and insecure.

One of the reasons why it seems desirable to go slow in the face of resistance, is that anxious, unhappy teachers make for anxious and unhappy students. In Chapter 13 we discussed the ways in which authority figures influenced morale by influencing the group climate. When teachers are disturbed, they are likely to develop autocratic or laissez-faire climates. This is why administrators must proceed so cautiously when changes are contemplated, why they must sometimes postpone changes to more propitious times. Sometimes, of course, the change is so essential that it must be carried out in spite of tensions and hurt feelings, in which case the best remedy is to provide ways of permitting people to express their anxieties and discuss them freely. However, the important point is that aggravating the anxieties of teachers impairs their effectiveness and results, in the final analysis, in an increase in the anxieties of the children they supervise.

THE EFFECTS OF EMOTIONAL STRAIN
ON TEACHERS

WE MAY well wonder, in the light of the fact that anxieties are so much a part of teaching, whether teachers suffer any ill effects from the stresses and strains to which they are subjected. According to one study, they are at least no *more* likely to develop serious mental disease (psychosis) than any other group in the general population [6]. However, a survey of patients referred to the Mayo Clinic in Rochester, Minnesota, reveals that teachers are somewhat more likely to be affected by diseases and ailments which are associated with neurotic trends (emotional maladjustments) than are persons in other occupational groups [7]. After making a survey of several school systems, Norman Fenton reported that 22.5 per cent of the 241 teachers employed therein could be classified as "maladjusted." The same proportion of maladjustment also applied to the 54 administrators of these schools [8]. Naturally, there are insufficient data in these studies to serve as a basis for making generalizations about the entire teaching profession, but they do confirm what many observers already suspect, namely, that the stresses and strains of the teaching profession do not often lead to complete mental breakdown, although they may aggravate certain emotional disabilities.

EVERYDAY STRESSES AND STRAINS

A graphic description of some of the stresses and strains that teachers experience in their work is provided by the daily log of one of a group of teachers who were asked by Alice V. Keliher to record the incidents in one day that seemed significant for their own mental health.

> Each morning finds me enthusiastic, and I sail into school ready for work. Unfortunately, this pleasant frame of mind cannot always last through the day.
>
> Today, I signed the time book, took my keys and the notices in my box, and went upstairs. When I reached my room, I straightened my desk and looked my plan over, so that I could guide the children as they planned the day's work. Then I began to go through my mail. It contained a note telling me to prepare a Pan American Day program for the assembly. The scheduled date is April 13. The children had already planned a variety show, using all the class talent. I knew that they would be as disappointed as I was, and I tried to figure out how to tell them about the change.
>
> As I walked to the rear of the room, I noticed one of my plants lying on the floor, the pot broken to pieces. A class that had used my room for movies the previous day, last hour, must have thrown it down. I gathered up the debris, and then noticed that one of the new dark shades (that I had waited six months for) was ripped. . . .
>
> Then the bell rang and I went out on hall duty. It is not a difficult duty, but I would rather be in the room when my children come in because that is the time for confidences and quiet talks.
>
> Soon we began to plan the day's work. We read the logs of the previous day, chose the best one, and discussed the news. During the arithmetic period, a boy came dashing in. He needed the film strip machine at once. A junior-high class was scheduled for it and he had forgotten. My monitors gave him

the machine. At the end of the hour, it had not been returned. It was needed for a third-grade class. I sent the monitors out to locate the machine and to take it down to the teacher who wished to use it.

A few minutes later we were interrupted again. The machine just wouldn't work. I asked my student teacher to take over, and I went down to see if I could locate the trouble. I couldn't see anything wrong, so I decided to change the bulb. Before doing so, however, I tried it in my own room. It lit. Just then I noticed the custodian passing my door. He agreed to see what the trouble was. It seems there was a short in the wall plug and he said he would have it fixed after school hours. I promised the disappointed children that they would see the fairy tale the next day, and hurried back to my classroom, hoping it would be the last interruption for the day.

I set up the Victrola and was about to play the Peer Gynt Suite when—CRASH! Joe had backed into the table and thrown the film strip machine to the floor. The look of consternation on his face was something to behold. I told him not to worry because I was sure it could be fixed, and that it was an accident. I knew that he was not careless.

As I picked up the pieces, I knew that I couldn't possibly fix the machine, so I had it carried down to the office to be picked up by the repair service. Believe it or not, we finally settled down to work.

After lunch the afternoon progressed pretty well. There was just one interruption. A teacher brought back a moving-picture machine with a broken film in it. She left no doubt in my mind as to who she thought was to blame for the film breaking. She was not made happier by my decision not to mend the break then and there.

At two o'clock we went to the yard for games. When the weather permits, we go to a nearby park to play. It was raining today, so we had to stay in the school yard. The noise and confusion in a small yard when three classes use it at the same time is something you have to experience to understand.

After dismissal, I phoned the repair service and asked them to call for the machine. Then I spliced the broken film and rewound it, hung up my keys, signed the time book, and left.

As I walked to the bus, X's mother met me. X was very upset. Could I stop for coffee and explain a few things? Some children had been told that they were eligible for the special rapid seventh-year class next term. X had not made the grade because of her math. She knew all along that it was her weak subject, and so did her mother—but still they were both unhappy. I'm still not sure who was the more upset. I answered her questions to the best of my ability and then she walked me to the bus, boarded it with me, and rode downtown, talking about the problem all the way.

My street finally appeared and I hurried off the bus. My living room looked positively beautiful to me. It was quiet and I settled down with my book. I just won't think about it any more today [9].

After analyzing similar logs and anecdotal material provided by fifty teachers, Keliher came to the following conclusions:

1. There are too many "surprises" in the daily lives of the teacher—unexpected requests to take over other teachers' classes and duties, calls to special meetings, emergency demands for help, and so forth. The element of surprise is serious because it calls teachers away from the important job of concentrating on children's needs. Keliher feels that much of this could be avoided by making teachers a part of the planning group in the school, whereby many things that ordinarily come as surprises would be anticipated and thus be included in the teachers' plans.

2. A similar problem is that of interruptions. "Monitors" from the principal's office show up at all hours—to pick up attendance slips, to get milk money, to bring notices from the office, and so forth. Emergency interruptions of course cannot be avoided, but interruptions that are trivial in nature should be handled in other ways and at some other time. The real difficulty, says Keliher, is that teachers may come eventually to feel that working with children is of secondary importance to the meeting of minor administrative requirements.

3. Another problem is the list of assorted "duties" that teach-

ers are required to perform: yard duty, hall duty, stair duty, lunchroom duty, after-school-detention duty, and so forth. Much of this is required because enrollments of two or three thousand children create safety and traffic-management problems. Keliher feels that this means we should think seriously about construction of schools for two or three *hundred* students, although she is aware that there are "large schools with an amazing warmth and a homelike quality that have grown out of sympathetic and understanding leadership coupled with democratic participation in planning by teachers and parents [10]."

4. The fourth problem is paper work—attendance reports, forms, statistical reports, and so forth.

On the positive side, Keliher notes that her teachers did not rate the behavior of children as a really important difficulty. Her teachers were concerned with the problem of understanding and guiding child behavior and with working out better relationships with parents and the agencies that help parents and children. This interest served as a positive and integrating force as far as the mental health of this group of teachers was concerned. She ends her analysis by saying, in part:

. . . . I must warn you that the harassment of teachers is more prevalent than you think. The best of teachers cannot be free to create wholesome living if the total life of the school is unwholesome. . . .

. . . . As we grow in our recognition of the place of central importance the teacher holds, let us evaluate our impulse indiscriminately to say, "Let the teacher do it. Let the teacher attend to the absences. Let the teacher do the referring to the medical office. Let the teacher find the symptoms of emotional disorders."

I, too, want the teacher to do these things. These are key stones of the teaching job. But—let us be sure we have free the teacher to put first things first. . . . "There is so much be done—so much to be done for our children [11]."

TEACHING AS A WAY OF MEETING "BASIC NEEDS"

THE first section of this chapter has been concerned, for the most part, with the more or less disintegrative aspects of teaching—those factors and forces which make it difficult for the teacher to use his profession as a means of meeting his basic needs for self-expression, security and stability, love, status, and to be of help to others. If these were the only factors that operated, very few persons, indeed, would ever enter the profession of teaching. The fact is, of course, that teaching is numerically the largest of the professions. What attracts many, if not most, of these people is that teaching offers unique advantages and opportunities to meet basic needs and to attain lasting satisfactions.

Teaching is what might be called a "social-service occupation." The importance of this factor in attracting persons to the occupation is revealed by a study done by E. F. Hartford at the University of Kentucky, who asked some 200 undergraduates in teacher-education courses why they had elected teaching. Prominent among the reasons they gave were: "interest in and liking for children," "teaching is an opportunity to help others," and "I enjoy working with people [12]." The desire to help others is an expression of the need to be creative, a need which calls for a high level of emotional maturity. Adults who are emotionally immature tend to be wrapped up in themselves and are thus less able to be concerned about becoming involved in the problems of others. Therefore, teaching offers a way to grow emotionally. The effective teacher cannot help but grow because successful classroom teaching means becoming involved in a process that is bound to have its effect on both teacher and group. To paraphrase Jerome D. Frank (whose original statement about parents applies to teachers as well), "teaching a child not something a teacher *does* to a child but is a process of eraction *between* teacher and child [13]." It is this guiding, helping, and *becoming involved* in the process of growth that gives teaching a tremendous integrative force as far as mental health of the teacher is concerned.

A second integrative force in teaching is the opportunity to work with other adults toward common goals. Much of the satisfaction to be gained from teaching comes from the association with other people who are also concerned with promoting the welfare of children. To be united with them in common cause can be heartening, reassuring, and rewarding. To be sure, collaborating with others produces problems which try one's emotional maturity to the utmost at times, but overcoming the obstacles and resolving the frustrations which operate to hinder this mutual undertaking help to weld the teaching profession more tightly together.

Part of the satisfaction that a teacher may derive from working with others comes from the social aspects of such collaboration. Through working on committees with other teachers and members of the community, the teacher participates in the friendly give and take that is part of the life of groups which are working together for common goals. Some of the friendships made in these settings continue outside the framework of group activities.

Another source of satisfaction is that of producing or creating something through group action. A teacher cannot revise the curriculum or promote legislation for better schools all by himself, but by participating in a group he can have the feeling of doing something to bring about the improvement that he feels is needed. Without such opportunities, teachers are likely to feel frustrated, discouraged, and cynical; therefore, they owe it to themselves to take advantage of such group activities both within and without the school setting. Sometimes it is necessary to develop such groups in schools and communities where they have not previously existed. It is usually desirable to organize them as ways of meeting expressed needs. For example, when staff members in faculty meeting express doubts about the current grading system, this may be a time to form a committee to study the problem and perhaps make recommendations. Or when there is much concern expressed in P. T. A. meetings about juvenile delinquency in the community, it may be possible to form a study group composed of both parents and teachers to look into the problem.

Summer school also offers opportunities for rewarding group experiences. One of the many workshops or work conferences that are offered each summer is described by Stephen Corey and Paul M. Halverson. This particular work conference ran three weeks and was attended by forty-two teachers and administrators. Its pattern, which is very typical, consisted of daily general sessions of the total group; small groups of from six to twelve persons meeting for an hour and a half each day throughout the conference; afternoon clinics, held from time to time and involving varying numbers of delegates; and individual and team conferences with staff members on special problems. Corey and Halverson made a rather detailed study of the interpersonal relations developed during the conference and asked each delegate to evaluate the conference and his experiences. They found a rather substantial relationship between the number of persons with whom each delegate had become acquainted and the delegate's rating of the conference success. They interpreted their findings to mean that

> the conference members' conception of a successful conference was one which . . . provides them numerous opportunities for meeting and becoming well acquainted with new people, exchanging ideas and experiences with them, and enjoying their company [14].

This combination of practical and social gains is typical of the more satisfying types of group experience in the teaching profession.

Another kind of group experience is described by Leo Berman, who conducted combined seminar-and-group-psychotherapy sessions with nine teachers in the Boston area under the sponsorship of the Massachusetts Society for Mental Hygiene. The purpose of the Society in sponsoring this project was to extend the psychological understanding of educators as regards their students, their colleagues, and themselves. The experiment ran twelve sessions, at the end of which all participants felt a desire to meet further with the primary purpose of learning more about themselves [15]. The success of this experiment raises the possibility of developing similar groups in other communities.

A somewhat different, although nonetheless valuable, approach to developing group experiences for teachers is described by Shirley Leonard. Under the sponsorship of the New York City Welfare Council, a Workshop Committee on Schools and Social Agencies was formed from representatives of various welfare agencies to present two fifteen-session courses a year for public school personnel. Since 1942, when the course was first presented, it has served over seven hundred teachers.

The first two or three sessions of the course are concerned with the objectives and ideals that are common to teachers, social workers, and parents and discussion of the ways in which adults can help children to grow up to be mentally healthy and effective adults. The next ten sessions are held in various settings—a family agency, a children's court, a settlement house, a clinic, a housing project, and so forth. Informal panel discussions are used here. At three different times in the course free-for-all discussions are scheduled to deal with the questions stimulated by previous meetings.

One of the chief values of the course is that teachers and social workers both get to know each other better. As Leonard reports,

It would be hard to say which group learns most from our sessions together—the teacher or the social worker. Those of us who are in the latter group have learned that we sometimes talk too much, and with too many *clichés;* that teachers think we can tell more about what causes a child's behavior than what the teacher can do in class to correct it; that we sometimes "pick the brains" of a child's teacher and are never seen again. They wish more face-to-face contacts, and give-and-take conversation. A most frequent recommendation from the class is that principals and supervisors also take such a course [16].

THE STATUS OF TEACHERS

A THIRD source of integration is the growing feeling that teaching is important work. In the survey at the University of Kentucky, already noted, this was the most commonly mentioned reason for entering the profession of teaching. Another reason, mentioned by one fourth of the students was "teaching offers favored status and respect." This statement may come as a surprise to some teachers, who assume that the teacher's status is a low one. However, it is a factor that appears in three different studies. In 1946 Maethel E. Deeg and Donald G. Paterson asked 475 students at the University of Minnesota to rank twenty-five occupations in order of their social standing. The median ranks assigned ranged from 1 for "physician" to 25 for "ditch digger." The rank assigned to "elementary school teacher" was 8, well above the middle, and into the top third of the list. The job of "superintendent of schools" was assigned a rank of 4 [17]. These last two ratings were similar to those obtained by G. S. Counts, who did a similar study in 1925 [18]. Teachers' college students view the occupation in a much similar light, as is revealed by a similar study conducted by Maryon K. Welch with 500 students, freshmen through graduates, at Indiana State Teachers College. Ranks obtained by Welch were "superintendent of schools," 4; "high school teacher," 6; and "elementary school teacher," 8 [19].

Although no studies have been done on changes in the attitudes of lay people in recent years toward the status of teachers, it is possible that such a study would reveal a favorable trend. Indeed, there is some "clinical" evidence that favors such a finding. For one thing, teachers have, in many communities, been able to secure salaries which are far more adequate than those paid before World War II. In the city of San Francisco, for example, the annual pay of teachers at present ranges from $3,620 for teachers with minimum preparation to $7,125 for teachers with two years of graduate work and thirteen years in the school system. This compares with the current average wage of some $4,300 received by workers in the business and industrial establishments in the San Francisco Bay Area. Although it is true that the high assessed tax evaluation per capita in San Francisco permits the payment of teachers' salaries at this level, it is also true that these salaries are the result of the ability of teachers to win status for themselves as professional people worthy of receiving such pay. In a number of states organized teachers have been able to promote great improvements in the educational system—new buildings, improved facilities, reorganization of school districts, increases in salary, expansion of individualized services for children, and so forth. Although such improvements have not taken place in all states and communities, and teachers' groups are still relatively ineffective as forces in the making of governmental policy regarding education on the national level, the respect of the general public for the teaching profession is growing as a result of these local successes. Indeed, some of the attention which investigating groups of legislators are giving to the teaching profession at the present moment of writing is a negative way of recognizing the importance of teaching and of teachers.

Another bit of evidence of a more positive sort is the increase in numbers of men entering the teaching profession. Before World War II it was unusual to find a man teaching in many elementary schools. Although men are still in the minority today, their presence in the elementary schools, as well as the over-all increase in their numbers and proportion, is an indication of the higher status enjoyed by teaching. Perhaps this, too, may appear to be a sort of left-handed recognition. However, one of the inescapable facts of our male-dominated culture is that professions composed entirely of women tend to have lower status than professions that are largely male. Thus, the increase in proportion of men entering the profession may be partly the result of a more enlightened viewpoint regarding the place and importance of teaching on the part of the general public.

Further evidence of this sort is provided by the tendencies of communities to allow the teacher more individual freedom. Some communities still frown on a woman teacher's smoking or drinking or even dressing stylishly and using make-up. But the trend is very definitely to permit the teacher the same individual liberties enjoyed by other persons in the community, as long as he does nothing that interferes with or compromises his role as a leader and guider of youth. The bans against marriage of women teachers that were so prevalent in the 1930's are a thing of the past in most communities. Indeed, many schools are discovering that a married teacher with children can make a distinct and unique contribution to the welfare of her pupils. How much of this new-found freedom is due to the greater equality that women are winning in our society, or how much is due to the higher proportion of men entering the profession, or how much is due to the shortage of teachers, or how much is due to the individual and organized efforts of the members of the profession to win status, freedom, and acceptance, is hard to determine. Probably all of these factors operate to make teaching a more enjoyable, rewarding, and generally worthwhile profession than it was a decade or so ago.

THE MENTAL HEALTH OF TEACHERS

THE problems of education today—crowded schools, inadequate standards of pay, the struggle for greater acceptance and status for teachers, our tendency to overload teachers with petty, administrative details—do constitute hazards for the mental health of teachers, and we need to move aggressively and positively toward their solution. Our very working together as members of a profession that is providing a vitally needed social service will in itself provide some of the strength we need to withstand the disintegrative and abrasive effects of these difficulties. But the greatest source of strength and emotional health that the teacher has is his belief that *he has something to give,* and that the lives of some children will be better because he has given that "something." If he can keep this basic truth in mind, this will be his deepest source of satisfaction in his profession. It will also be his best defense against discouragement and despair, and against his fears that children will not like him and that he may fail. Teachers who become cynical about their roles are teachers who have forgotten that they have something to give. Teachers who are anxiously concerned about themselves find it hard to give anything of themselves. The process of finding out how to share oneself with children and with one's fellow workers is, in essence, the process of becoming an effective teacher.

REFERENCES

1. R. Dreikurs, *Character Education and Spiritual Values in an Anxious Age.* Boston: Beacon, 1952. P. 8.
2. D. H. Jenkins and Ronald Lippitt, *Interpersonal Perceptions of Teachers, Students, and Parents.* Washington: National Education Association, 1951.
3. W. P. Kvaraceus, "Mental Health Hazards Facing Teachers," *Phi Delta Kappan.* 32:349;1951.
4. H. J. Otto and F. von Borgersrode, "Class Size," in W. S. Monroe, ed., *Encyclopedia of Educational Research,* rev. ed. New York: Macmillan, 1950. Pp. 212–16.
5. D. A. Orton, "Why Do They Want to Teach?" *Phi Delta Kappan.* 30:343;1949.
6. J. L. Malloch, *A Study of State Hospital Commitments of Teachers in Comparison with Other Occupations.* Unpublished Master's Thesis, Stanford University, 1941.

7. H. L. Smith and N. C. Hightower, Jr., "Incidence of Functional Disease (Neurosis) among Patients of Various Occupations," *Occupational Medicine*. 5:182–185;1948.

8. N. Fenton, *Mental Hygiene in School Practice*. Stanford: Stanford University Press, 1943. P. 289.

9. A. V. Keliher, "A Day in the Life of the Teacher," *Mental Hygiene*. 34:455–64;1950. Reprinted by permission.

10. *Ibid*. P. 461.

11. *Ibid*. P. 464. Reprinted by permission.

12. E. F. Hartford, "Why Two Hundred Chose Teaching," *Phi Delta Kappan*. 30:126;1948.

13. J. D. Frank, "How Do Parents Learn?" *Child Study*. 30(3):14–19, 50–51;1953.

14. S. M. Corey and P. M. Halverson, "Some Inter-Personal Relations in a Curriculum Work-Conference," *Teachers College Record*. 52:98–106;1950.

15. L. Berman, "Mental Hygiene for Educators: Report on an Experiment Using a Combined Seminar and Group Psychotherapy Approach." Unpublished and undated paper.

16. S. Leonard, "Teachers and School Social Workers Learn from Each Other," *Understanding the Child*. 19:14–16, 32;1950. Published by the National Association for Mental Health, 1790 Broadway, New York, N. Y. Reprinted by permission.

17. M. E. Deeg and D. G. Paterson, "Changes in Social Status of Occupations," *Occupations*. 25:205–07;1947.

18. G. S. Counts, "Social Status of Occupations," *School Review*. 33:16–17;1925.

19. M. K. Welch, "The Ranking of Occupations on the Basis of Social Status," *Occupations*. 37:237–41;1949.

SUGGESTED READINGS

H. W. Bernard, *Mental Hygiene for Classroom Teachers*. New York: McGraw-Hill, 1952. Part 4, "The Teacher's Mental Health."

L. E. Cole and W. F. Bruce, *Educational Psychology*. Yonkers-on-Hudson: World Book, 1950. Chapter 16, "The Teacher's Task and the Barriers," and Chapter 19, "The Teacher as a Mature Person."

N. Fenton, *Mental Hygiene in School Practice*. Stanford: Stanford University Press, 1943. Part 4, "Mental Hygiene and the Teacher."

A. I. Gates *et al.*, *Educational Psychology*, 3d ed. New York: Macmillan, 1948. Chapter 22, "The Mental Health of the Teacher."

J. Grambs and W. J. Iverson, *Modern Methods in Secondary Education*. New York: Sloane, 1952. Section 6, "On the Job."

Helping Teachers to Understand Children. Washington: American Council on Education, 1945. Chapter 12 discusses the organization of a teachers' study group.

H. J. Otto, *Principles of Elementary Education*. New York: Rinehart, 1949. Chapters 14 and 15 deal with the teacher's administrative role and the teacher as a person, citizen, and professional worker.

C. Pratt, *I Learn from Children*. New York: Simon and Schuster, 1948.

F. Redl and W. W. Wattenberg, *Mental Hygiene in Teaching*. New York: Harcourt, Brace, 1951. Chapter 16, "Teachers' Problems." A very perceptive and sympathetic analysis of the psychological aspects of the professional and personal life of a teacher.

SUGGESTED FILMS

Assignment Tomorrow. How teachers can work together cooperatively for the welfare of children. National Education Association.

Teachers' Crisis. The threat of low salaries, heavy teaching loads, and poor teaching conditions. Available through McGraw-Hill.

Appendix 1

PLEDGE TO CHILDREN [1]

TO YOU, our children, who hold within you our most cherished hopes, we, the members of the Midcentury White House Conference on Children and Youth, relying on your full response, make this pledge:

From your earliest infancy we give you our love, so that you may grow with trust in yourself and in others.

We will recognize your worth as a person and we will help you to strengthen your sense of belonging.

We will respect your right to be yourself and at the same time help you to understand the rights of others, so that you may experience cooperative living.

We will help you to develop initiative and imagination, so that you may have the opportunity freely to create.

We will encourage your curiosity and your pride in workmanship, so that you may have the satisfaction that comes from achievement.

We will provide the conditions for wholesome play that will add to your learning, to your social experience, and to your happiness.

We will illustrate by precept and example the value of integrity and the importance of moral courage.

We will encourage you always to seek the truth.

We will provide you with all opportunities possible to develop your own faith in God.

---

[1] From *Proceedings of the Midcentury White House Conference on Children and Youth.* Raleigh, N. C.: Health Publications Institute, 1951. Reprinted by permission.

We will open the way for you to enjoy the arts and to use them for deepening your understanding of life.

We will work to rid ourselves of prejudice and discrimination, so that together we may achieve a truly democratic society.

We will work to lift the standard of living and to improve our economic practices, so that you may have the material basis for a full life.

We will provide you with rewarding educational opportunities, so that you may develop your talents and contribute to a better world.

We will protect you against exploitation and undue hazards and help you grow in health and strength.

We will work to conserve and improve family life and, as needed, to provide foster care according to your inherent rights.

We will intensify our search for new knowledge in order to guide you more effectively as you develop your potentialities.

As you grow from child to youth to adult, establishing a family life of your own and accepting larger social responsibilities, we will work with you to improve conditions for all children and youth.

Aware that these promises to you cannot be fully met in a world at war, we ask you to join us in a firm dedication to the building of a world society based on freedom, justice and mutual respect.

SO MAY YOU grow in joy, in faith in God and in man, and in those qualities of vision and of the spirit that will sustain us all and give us new hope for the future.

Appendix **2**

PLATFORM adopted by THE MIDCENTURY WHITE HOUSE CONFERENCE ON CHILDREN AND YOUTH [1]

BELIEVING in the primacy of spiritual values, democratic practices, and the dignity and worth of every human being, and recognizing that these are essential to individual happiness and responsible citizenship, we have come together to inquire

—How the necessary mental, emotional, and spiritual qualities may be developed in children, and
—How the physical, economic, and social conditions favorable to such development may be assured

And having found that children require, for their fullest development,

—Regard for their individual worth and sensitive respect for their feelings, from all who touch their lives
—Loving care and guidance from mothers and fathers, who have a sense of the privilege and responsibility which parenthood involves, and who have confidence in their own capacity to rear a child
—A secure home that is free from want and dread of want, and provides all family members with a satisfying physical, aesthetic, social, and spiritual environment
—A community whose citizens are dedicated to establishing the values and practices that make life meaningful

[1] From *Proceedings of the Midcentury White House Conference on Children and Youth*. Raleigh, N. C.: Health Publications Institute, 1951. Reprinted by permission.

and abundant for children of all colors, creeds and customs, and to cooperating in an endeavor to express these values and practices in daily living
—Full access to health, educational, recreational, social, and religious services and programs, directed toward the well-being of all they serve
—Concern on the part of all citizens for all children
—Devotion to the pursuit of knowledge and the wide application of that which is known

IF THEY ARE TO GROW IN

—Trust in themselves and others
—Independence and initiative coupled with a true sense of being related to others
—Satisfaction in bringing individual and shared tasks to completion
—A sense of personal destiny and of the responsible roles they will eventually play as parents, workers, citizens
—The capacity for the love that underlies the family and that ideally comes to embrace all mankind
—Creativity that brings into being new life, new relationships, new values, and new things of beauty and usefulness, and cherishes them for their worth
—Integrity that sees each life as personally meaningful within the period of history in which it is lived, and in relation to enduring values

WE THEREFORE RECOMMEND . . .

1. That research on child development and adjustment be expanded and that such research include longitudinal studies in relations and factors that affect behavior and adjustment, so that a continuing understanding of infants, children, and youth and a sound basis for practice will be provided; that public and private agencies give support to extending research pertaining to healthy personality with attention to the synthesis, interpretation and dissemination of the findings.
2. That greater emphasis be placed by the various professions on utilizing methods and seeking new means for bringing the

parents into thinking and planning with and for their children.

3. That education for parenthood be made available to all through educational, health, recreation, religious and welfare agencies maintaining professional standards and staffed by properly qualified individuals.

4. That specialists and agencies take every opportunity to foster and increase parents' feelings of satisfaction and self-confidence in their ability for child rearing; that material concerning the growth and development of children be made as reassuring and nontechnical as possible, and that false standards of perfection not be held up.

5. That elementary, secondary, college and community education include such appropriate experiences and studies of childhood and family life as will help young people to achieve the maturity essential to the role of parenthood.

6. That there be further study of the underlying causes of broken homes and the increase in divorce.

7. That children be provided with opportunities that are wide in range and challenging in nature, emphasizing exploration, participation, and social experience in an environment that is rich and stimulating; and that expectations of achievement be in harmony with each child's ability and growth.

8. That all professions dealing with children be given, as an integral part of their preparation, a common core of experiences dealing with fundamental concepts of human behavior, including the need to consider the total person as well as any specific disorder; the interrelationship of physical, mental, social, religious, and cultural forces; the importance of interpersonal relationships; the role of self-understanding; and emphasis on the positive recognition and production of healthy personalities and the treatment of variations; and that lay people be oriented through formal or informal education to an understanding of the importance of the foregoing concepts.

9. That steps be taken at national, state, and local levels to improve the facilities and increase the output of professional schools preparing persons for services to children.

10. That more energetic efforts be made by both public and private organizations for support of selective recruitment and

training of professional workers and for an extensive program of scholarships.

11. That professional workers be trained in such a way that they will understand and respect other professional skills and contributors so that they may work together to further community growth. Some of the ways this might be achieved are:

A. In all levels of undergraduate education, students should receive a broad preparation in the knowledge of human growth, behavior, and motivation which ought to be common knowledge for all students. This would also serve as a background for professional education.

B. In schools preparing for professional work, there should be included in the curriculum through both the classroom and field experience opportunities for cooperative work on problems common to all professional interests, including study of human growth and change and in family counseling.

C. The practicing professional worker should further his training by seeking, utilizing and promoting opportunities to relate to and participate with other professional and citizen groups in resolving problems of the individual and the community.

D. Orientation programs should be planned for all professional persons and inter-professional groups in the community.

12. That ways and means be found for the formal and informal inservice education of professional people and that information on promising practices be widely disseminated.

13. That an inquiring attitude be maintained toward all services, with appropriate provisions at all levels for continuous scientific study of needs, objectives, alternative methods, and effectiveness of programs. . . .

Appendix **3**

CONSENSUS of the MIDCENTURY WHITE HOUSE CONFERENCE ON CHILDREN AND YOUTH [1]

RECOGNIZING that this is a time of crisis, posing the very issue of survival, and desiring to summarize the aspirations embodied in the recommendations and to declare the spirit in which the recommendations will be interpreted and followed, the Conference adopted the following statements as representing a consensus of the group and an expression of its unity of purpose:

1. The full development of the whole child is the basic philosophy and ultimate aim of all recommendations.

2. All services, programs, and facilities for children and young people should be provided without discrimination as to race, creed, color or national origin.

3. Continuing emphasis on research and its application is essential.

4. Qualified personnel is needed in sufficient number to staff services and programs for children and youth.

5. Youth should be included as full participants in all appropriate community acitivities.

6. Effective partnership between voluntary and governmental agencies is needed in the furtherance of this program.

7. Effective team work by the professions is essential to the development of the healthy personality.

8. Full participation of all citizens is necessary in providing and sustaining all programs and services recommended by this Conference.

---

[1] Copyright 1951, Health Publications Institute, Inc., Raleigh, N. C.: reprinted by permission.

Appendix **4**

CHILD HEALTH DAY, 1953 by the

PRESIDENT OF THE UNITED STATES OF AMERICA

a Proclamation[1]

WHEREAS the Congress, by a joint resolution of May 18, 1928 (45 Stat. 617), authorized and requested the President of the United States to issue annually a proclamation setting apart May 1 as Child Health Day; and

WHEREAS the health and wholesome development of our children are matters of the deepest concern to all Americans; and

WHEREAS the stresses and strains of our times create many problems bearing on the spiritual and emotional health of our children and are reflected notably in juvenile delinquency; and

WHEREAS we have made tremendous advances in overcoming the most severe physical hazards of childhood, and are now striving to make equally significant progress in understanding the nature of emotional health, in order that our children may grow into mature, responsible citizens of a democracy:

NOW, THEREFORE, I, DWIGHT D. EISENHOWER, President of the United States of America, do hereby designate the first day of May, 1953, as Child Health Day; and I urge all parents and young people, and all other individuals, as well as agencies and organizations interested in the well-being of children, to increase their understanding of the emotional, social, and spiritual growth of children, so as to apply this understanding in their day-to-day relations with the rising generation.

---

[1] *The Child.* 17:138;1953.

IN WITNESS WHEREOF, I have hereunto set my hand and caused the Seal of the United States of America to be affixed.

DONE at the city of Washington this twentieth day of February in the year of our Lord nineteen hundred and fifty-three, and of the Independence of the United States of America the one hundred and seventy-seventh.

[Signed]　　*Dwight D. Eisenhower*

Appendix **5**

SOME INQUIRIES HELPFUL IN APPRAISING MENTAL HEALTH IN A SCHOOL[1]

INTRODUCTORY

This leaflet is not a standardized test nor is it a comprehensive survey instrument. It simply assembles a series of "loaded" questions, each with the aim of discovering to the user the "mental hygiene" point of view and the existence in use of that point of view in his school.

A faculty meeting devoted to an answering of these Inquiries can, with its collateral discussion, be a searching experience for any group of teachers. There is evidence that for such a meeting each teacher should have a copy of the Inquiries before him. Then the questions can be considered one by one with discussion lingering upon those which are most provocative. Used this way the questions should help teachers to get beneath the surface of behavior and to come to grips with the problems which all teachers face in their daily work with children.

The National Council would be interested in having some report of any faculty use of the Inquiries. This report can be as formal or as informal as suits each school and might well include criticism and revision of the questions themselves. Any reports so received will have the studied attention of the preparing committee.

---

[1] Copyright, 1952, National Council of Independent Schools, Boston, Mass.; reprinted by permission.

The questions were first assembled by a small committee. Later they were tried out in several schools for criticism and suggestion. With the help of these experiences and with the additional help of comments from specialists in the field, the Inquiries have been revised into their present form. The desire common to all is to forward the better use in schools of what is known about the nature of children and their growth.

September, 1952

> *Committee on Educational Practices*
> *National Council of Independent Schools*
> 79 Milk Street
> Boston 9, Massachusetts

APPRAISAL QUESTIONS
PROGRAM:

1. What kind of respect is accorded the learning that comes by way of activities?
   For instance:

Fine Arts	Music	Industrial Arts
Rhythms & Dancing	Dramatics	Physical Education

   A. Are they fully respected?
   B. Are they reserved for those with special talent? Is there any taint of exploitation of the young people involved? Is there too much "perfection seeking"?
   C. How much time is assigned to them in the school program? At what time of the day?
   D. Does the school plant reveal the results of the shop and the studio?

2. How important in the school life are such activities as

Student Councils and Committees	Discussion Groups
	Community Work or "Work Time" Clubs
Student Religious Activities	

3. The chance to express oneself creatively—whether in the arts or in other activities—enables young people to rid themselves of stresses and strains, to grapple with problems, and to express strong feelings in a way that is acceptable and health-giving. Is this understood and is this understanding used to advantage?

4. Are these activities related to the academic work and to each other or are they carried on in compartments? In other words, to what are these activities relevant?
5. Is the mastery of the tools of learning so treated that these tools become elements of security in a child's life?
6. In the various studies is meaning an objective—for example, the applicability to current issues outside the school? Does such work help the student to understand and face his changing world?

GUIDANCE:

1. Is there an adviser to whom each child can turn, or who, on proper occasion, would turn to his advisee?
2. Is such an adviser a counselor who sits less as judge and disciplinary agent and more as the person to whom the boy or girl can talk?
3. Is there a pooling of insights by the adults who deal with each child to the point of a shared approach?
4. Are environmental factors studied and interpreted?
5. Is the testing system used as one kind of evidence rather than as a categorizer of children, a measure of teaching, or an end in itself?
6. Is there true regard for all kinds of gifts and degrees of success —for the achievements of those limited in academic, creative or athletic ability as well as those gifted in these ways?
7. Is the marking and report system a teacher's or parent's weapon, or is it a medium of learning and teaching and guidance?
8. Is there capable guidance of staff members in the understanding of young people?
9. What is the relationship between the school and available psychologists and psychiatrists?

ATMOSPHERE:

1. Do the children have a sense of belonging, each one to something in which he is a responsible participant?
2. Does the school belong to the students in the sense that they know its activities would not go on unless individuals and groups played their parts?

3. Is there a good understanding of the relative part to be played at different ages and stages by student initiative and teacher direction?
4. Do teachers learn as they teach—and do they know that teaching is a learning process for them?
5. Is there such genuineness in all relationships that both acceptance and constructive criticism of others and of oneself are possible and natural?

APPROACHES:

1. Children only learn deeply and fully that which they are ready to accept. Is the invitation to, and the expectation from, a child based, therefore, on a knowledge of his readiness and his ability?
2. Does the routine which cares for behavior of individuals within the classroom or within the school take into account that behavior is much more than contribution or infraction; that behavior is evidence of what a pupil is inside and where he is, emotionally and on the ladder of growth and learning?
3. Is the teacher-pupil relationship sentimental, exclusively academic and disciplinary, or is it essentially a positive, contributing friendship?
4. Is sarcasm distinguished from constructive criticism and firmness and honesty?
5. Are teachers in the habit of examining their own motivation, and is dislike of a child examined as a luxury which teachers should not afford?

GENERAL:

1. Listen to the noises in a school. There are differences, and these differences are more in quality than in volume.
2. Is sufficient leeway allowed both within the classroom and without for pupils to fumble and make mistakes? The permitted area for mistakes might include room for those trials and errors which, on reflection, promote the student's knowledge of himself.
3. Are there goals and standards definite enough to provide for pupils a good degree of security?
4. Does the school unfold a life sufficiently vital to contain, for

the pupil, a vision of full and satisfying years ahead, a life which affords ample scope for his next years *as he sees them?*

5. Is there contemplation of the needs of both boys and girls and of the meaning of the sexes to each other?

6. Is there a common understanding through actual school experience of such phases of life as: independence, freedom, interdependence, responsibility, discipline, structure, and self discipline?

7. Does the school aid and encourage parents to grow as parents? Is there a natural, honest, and constructive cooperation between home and school?

8. Is the recognition of spiritual values a significant force in the life of the school?

INDEX

(The page numbers within parentheses refer to the reference citations in the text.)